The Collected Courses of the Academy of European Law

VOLUME XXIV/1
The Frontiers of Human Rights

Extraterritoriality and its Challenges

The Collected Courses of the Academy of European Law
Edited by Professor Loïc Azoulai,
Professor Nehal Bhuta, and Professor Marise Cremona
Assistant Editor: Anny Bremner

Each year the Academy of European Law in Florence, Italy, invites a group of outstanding lecturers to teach at its summer courses on Human Rights law and European Union law.

A 'general course' is given in each of the two fields by a distinguished scholar or practitioner, who examines the field as a whole through a particular thematic, conceptual, or philosophical lens, or looks at a theme in the context of the overall body of law. In addition, a series of 'specialized courses' brings together a group of highly qualified scholars to explore and analyse a specific theme in relation to Human Rights law and EU law.

The Academy's mission, to produce scholarly analyses which are at the cutting edge of the two fields, is achieved through publication of this series, the Collected Courses of the Academy of European Law.

The Frontiers of Human Rights

Extraterritoriality and its Challenges

Edited by
NEHAL BHUTA

OXFORD
UNIVERSITY PRESS

OXFORD
UNIVERSITY PRESS

Great Clarendon Street, Oxford OX2 6DP,
United Kingdom

Oxford University Press is a department of the University of Oxford. It furthers the University's objective of excellence in research, scholarship, and education by publishing worldwide. Oxford is a registered trade mark of Oxford University Press in the UK and in certain other countries.

First Edition published in 2016

Published in the United States of America by Oxford University Press
198 Madison Avenue, New York, NY 10016, United States of America

British Library Cataloguing in Publication Data
Data available

Library of Congress Control Number: 2015950644

ISBN 978–0–19–876927–9

Contents

Table of Cases

UNITED KINGDOM

EUROPEAN CASES

General Court

Court of Justice of the European Union

European Court of Human Rights

INTERNATIONAL CASES

African Commission on Human and Peoples' Rights

Arbitral Awards

Belgium

Germany

Netherlands

Permanent Court of International Justice

United Nations Human Rights Committee

World Trade Organization

Table of Legislation

EUROPEAN LEGISLATION

European Directives

European Decisions

NATIONAL LEGISLATION

United Kingdom

INTERNATIONAL INSTRUMENTS

Notes on Contributors

Nehal Bhuta is Professor of Public International Law at the European University Institute and Co-director of the Academy of European Law. He has research interests in political, social and legal theory, the history of the state and the history of international law.

Aeyal Gross is a member of the Faculty of Law at Tel Aviv University. He is also a Visiting Reader at the School of Oriental and African Studies (SOAS) at the University of London. In addition, he serves on the board of the Association for Civil Rights in Israel and is the legal commentator for the Israeli daily *Haaretz*. Dr Gross holds an LL.B from Tel Aviv University and an S.J.D. from Harvard Law School. He teaches and publishes in the areas of international and constitutional law, international humanitarian law, human rights and law and sexuality. He has published many articles and books, including *The Right to Health at the Public/Private Divide: A Global Comparative Study* (edited with Colleen Flood, 2014) and *The Writing on the Wall: Rethinking the International Law of Occupation* (forthcoming 2016).

Marko Milanovic is Associate Professor at the University of Nottingham School of Law. He obtained his first degree in law from the University of Belgrade Faculty of Law, his LL.M from the University of Michigan Law School, and his Ph.D in international law from the University of Cambridge. He is Vice-President and member of the Executive Board of the European Society of International Law, an Associate of the Belgrade Centre for Human Rights, and co-editor of *EJIL: Talk!*, the blog of the *European Journal of International Law*, as well as being a member of *EJIL*'s Editorial Board.

Cesare Pitea is Assistant Professor of International Law at the University of Parma. He obtained his LL.M in public international law from the University of London (SOAS) in 2001 and his Ph.D in international law from the University of Milan in 2004. He qualified as Associate Professor of International and European Law in 2014. He was a lawyer at the Registry of the European Court of Human Rights from 2009–2011 and legal adviser to the delegation of the Italian Ministry of Environmental Affairs to the United Nations Economic Commission for Europe (UNECE) from 2004–2009. He has published on different topics of public international law, especially in the field of human rights protection and environmental law.

Tullio Treves was Professor of Public and Private International Law at the Law Faculty of the University of Milano from 1980–2014. He was also a Judge of the International Tribunal for the Law of the Sea from 1996–2011. Within the Tribunal, he was the President of the Seabed Disputes Chamber. He has acted as arbitrator or counsel in several cases before international courts and tribunals, including the International Court of Justice. Between 1984 and 1992, Judge Treves was a Legal Adviser to the Permanent Mission of Italy at the United Nations in New York. He is a Member of the Curatorium of The Hague Academy of International Law, the *Institut de droit international*, the Law of the Sea Institute and the American, French and Italian Societies of International Law. In addition to delivering scholarly lectures at universities around the world, Judge Treves is the author of numerous books and articles in various fields of public and private international law, especially on the law of the sea, dispute settlement and environmental law.

Jorge E. Viñuales is the Harold Samuel Professor of Law and Environmental Policy at the University of Cambridge and Director of the Cambridge Centre for Environment, Energy and Natural Resource Governance (C-EENRG). He has published extensively in his specific research areas and in public international law at large and has broad experience as a practitioner. He has advised governments, international organizations and private companies and has worked in many inter-state, investor–state and commercial disputes.

Ralph Wilde is a member of the Faculty of Laws at University College London, University of London. His current research focuses on the extraterritorial application of international human rights law. His book *International Territorial Administration: How Trusteeship and the Civilizing Mission Never Went Away* (2008) was awarded the Certificate of Merit (book prize) of the American Society of International Law in 2009. He is a member of the Executive Board of the European Society of International Law, having previously served on the Executive Council of the American Society of International Law. At the International Law Association (ILA), he was Co-Rapporteur of the Human Rights Committee, one of the UK representatives on the international Executive Council, Rapporteur of the Study Group on UN Reform, and Joint Honorary Secretary of the British Branch.

The Frontiers of Extraterritoriality—Human Rights Law as Global Law

*Nehal Bhuta**

1. Human Rights and Sovereignty

The extraterritorial application of human rights treaties gives rise to fundamental theoretical questions about the nature of international human rights as a legal order.

Originally an obscure problem of interpretation—resolved *in abstracto* by terse denial[1] or a hand-waving reliance on the presumed universalism of the protection inherent in the concept of human right[2]—the issue garnered little or no attention for the first four decades of our human rights era. Apart from an incomplete debate during the early phases of the drafting of the International Covenant on Civil and Political Rights (ICCPR),[3] and a small number of cases arising from the conduct of Southern Cone dictatorships in their persecution of political adversaries,[4] neither

* I thank Rebecca Schmidt for extensive research assistance and a great deal of help in the preparation of this chapter, although she is not responsible for its errors.

1 See, for example, the brief statement by the US Department of State Legal Advisor, Conrad Harper, to the 1405th meeting of the Human Rights Committee on 31 March 1995, in which he stated simply that that International Covenant on Civil and Political Rights (ICCPR) was 'presumed to apply only within a party's territory' and that the term 'jurisdiction' in Article 2 of the treaty was adopted on the 'clear understanding that such wording would limit the obligations to within a Party's territory'. UN Human Rights Committee, 53rd session, 1405th meeting, UN Doc. CCPR/C/SR 1405, 31 March 1995, 20.

2 See, for example, the short note by Theodor Meron, in which he states that 'narrow territorial interpretation of human rights treaties is anathema to the basic idea of human rights, which is to ensure that a state should respect the rights of persons over whom it exercises jurisdiction'. Meron, 'Extraterritoriality of Human Rights Treaties', 89 *American Journal of International Law (AJIL)* (1995) 78, at 82.

3 The best account of this debate is found in the research presented in the 2010 Memorandum Opinion from US Department of State Legal Advisor, Harold Koh, to Secretary of State Hilary Clinton, on 'The Geographic Scope of the International Covenant on Civil and Political Rights', 19 October 2010, at 15–23, available online at http://www.nytimes.com/interactive/2014/03/07/world/state-department-iccpr.html (last accessed 23 July 2015).

4 See, for example, Human Rights Committee, *Lopez Burgos v. Uruguay*, Comm. no. 52/1979, UN Doc. CCPR/C/13/D/52/1979, 29 July 1981, available online at http://opil.ouplaw.com/view/10.1093/law:ihrl/2796unhrc81.case.1/law-ihrl-2796unhrc81 (last accessed 23 July 2015); and, *Sophie Martins v. Uruguay*, Comm. no. 57/1979, UN Doc. CCPR/C/15/D/57/1979, 23 March 1982, available online at http://opil.ouplaw.com/view/10.1093/law:ihrl/1749unhrc82.case.1/law-ihrl-1749unhrc82?rskey=T3FFD0&result=1&prd=OPIL (last accessed 23 July 2015).

the concept of jurisdiction in human rights treaties, nor the problems of interpretation of substantive rights raised by their extraterritorial application, were subject to sustained inquiry, litigation or adjudication. Indeed, the debate during the 1950 drafting sessions of the ICCPR indicates clearly that the drafting of the Article 2 jurisdiction clause revolved not around some *anticipation* of the extraterritorial application of the Covenant, but rather was preoccupied with *delimiting the scope* of obligations to ensure rights in such hypothetical scenarios as when a state lost control of some portion of its own territory, or where its military forces supervised some form of national government under an *occupatio post bellum* (as was the case with United States forces in Germany, Austria and Japan at the time). In other words, while the 1950 drafting debate certainly did not rule out extraterritorial application, what it showed most clearly was that the *concrete type of authority and institutional relationship* presupposed by the treaties was that of a state with respect to its citizens and on its territory.

This should hardly be a revelation. Notwithstanding our contemporary inability to agree on how to understand the recent history of human rights,[5] at least one observation rings true: at their inception, human rights treaties took for granted, rather than broke from, the so-called 'Westphalian frame'. Human rights did not purport to create, but rather *presupposed*, the Arendtian right to have rights: the legal framework for the realization of human rights depended upon and was expected to act through functioning political communities organized as sovereign states.[6] Indeed, this was a cause for some bitter disappointment among a segment of

[5] Alston, 'Does the Past Matter? On the Origins of Human Rights', 126 *Harvard Law Review* (2013) 2043; S. Moyn, *The Last Utopia: Human Rights in History* (2010); C. Roberts, *The Contentious History of the International Bill of Human Rights* (2015).

[6] 'The reason why the concept of human rights was treated as a sort of step-child by nineteenth-century political thought and why no liberal or radical party in the twentieth century . . . saw fit to include them in its program seems obvious: civil rights—that is the varying rights of citizens in different countries—were supposed to embody and spell out in the form of tangible laws the eternal Rights of Man . . . All human beings were citizens of some kind of political community; if the laws of their country did not live up to the demands of the Rights of Man, they were expected to change them, by legislation in democratic countries or through revolutionary action in despotisms.'

Indeed, Arendt's most scathing contempt was reserved for those who thought the rights of man could ever be a substitute for the rights of citizens, or that international order could substitute for concrete political order at the level of the nation-state:

> [A]ll societies formed for the protection of the Rights of Man [after 1919], all attempts to arrive at a new bill of human rights were sponsored by marginal figures—by a few international jurists without political experience or professional philanthropists supported by the uncertain sentiments of professional idealists . . .
>
> . . . The Rights of Man, supposedly inalienable, proved to be unenforceable . . . whenever people appeared who were no longer citizens of any sovereign state. To this fact . . . one must add the confusion created by the many recent [post-1945] attempt to frame a new bill of human rights, which have demonstrated that no one seems able to define with any assurance what these general human rights, as distinguished from the rights of citizens, really are . . . [N]o-one seems to know which rights [the stateless] lost when they lost these human rights.
>
> . . . The first loss which the rightless suffered was the loss of their homes, and this meant the entire social texture into which they were born and in which they established for themselves a distinct place in the world.

H. Arendt, *The Origins of Totalitarianism* (1951), at 291–294.

post-1945 intellectuals and lawyers who sought in human rights a truly global legal order subject to direct international enforcement.[7]

But an equally influential post-war intellectual current insisted on a pragmatic and realistic strategy for the institutionalization of human rights, one predicated not on a radical replacement or disempowerment of the state and its sovereign authority by international authority, but rather upon a buttressing of state sovereignty moderated through effective international institutions that could rest upon—or at least invoke—their role as focal points for the development of consensual norms and concordant practices over time.[8] The concreteness of the emerging human rights order would lean heavily, if not exclusively, upon the concreteness of the state legal order.[9] An important strain of post-war realism was not so much anti-reformist, as anti-cosmopolitan, urging moderated sovereignty against more strident (and ultimately short-lived) federal visions of international organization.[10] Consistent with the criticism of inter-war legalism as utopian, the validity and efficacy of law generally and international law in particular was understood to rest upon the essential factual and institutional conditions generated by the sovereign state and its internal ordering capacity—a capacity resting on *potentia* or *gubernaculum* (power over men and things). The legal authority of the sovereign state order was not constituted 'merely through some elaborate scheme of norms', but 'expresses the essential factual conditions that underpin legal validity'.[11]

The Westphalian frame both abstracts from and performatively produces a material and ideal organization of legal and political order. This organization, as is well known, is predicated on a unity of order resting upon the external independence, internal authority and legal supremacy of the state. The unity of order presupposed by sovereignty is without doubt a juristic idea, and need not be embodied in a singular physical or institutional locus of sovereignty. As Loughlin points out:

> The modern State has invariably assumed a constitutional form in which the sovereign rights of government are allocated among a variety of institutions . . . It is often stated that

[7] See for example, Moses Moskowitz's (founder and director of the Consultative Council of Jewish Organizations, a New York-based non-government organization dedicated to promoting human rights at the United Nations in New York) 1959 complaint that the proposed Covenants on Human Rights 'leave the individual at the mercy of the state as ever', and failed to set out the 'inalienable rights of man as distinguished from the rights of citizens'. Moskowitz, 'The Covenants on Human Rights: Basic Issues of Substance', 53 *Proceedings of the American Society of International Law* (1959), at 230–234, cited in Siegelberg, 'Egon Schwelb and the Human Rights *via media*', paper presented at the Workshop on the History of International Law, Academy of European Law, European University Institute, 8–9 June 2015. On Moskovitz, see Moyn, *The Last Utopia*, *supra* note 5, at ch. 4.

[8] I refer here to the remarkable historical work undertaken by Mira Siegelberg in her forthcoming book, *The Question of Questions: The Problem of Statelessness in International History, 1921–1961*.

[9] One might well read Humphrey's own strategy this way. Roberts, *The Contentious History of the International Bill of Human Rights*, *supra* note 5, at 42. See also the explication of Egon Schwelb's method in Siegelberg, *supra* note 7.

[10] U. Greenberg, *The Weimar Century: German Emigres and the Ideological Foundations of the Cold War* (2015), at 225–227, 236. See generally, Guilhot, 'American Katechon: When Political Theology Became International Relations Theory', 17 *Constellations* (2010), at 224–253.

[11] Loughlin, 'Why Sovereignty?', in R. Rawlings, P. Leyland and A. Young (eds), *Sovereignty and the Law: Domestic, European and International Perspectives* (2013), at 42.

'the people' is sovereign, that is, that the people now acts as the ultimate authority and bearer of 'constituent power'. This is not wrong, but since the concept of 'the people' is itself one of symbolic representation, it is more accurate to say that sovereignty has no locus: it is a set of relations through which our ideas of authority are conceived.[12]

However, the set of relations that find their expression as a juridical unity in the idea of sovereignty are not of themselves purely juridical. Political ordering requires political power-and-authority (*potentia* and *potestas*), and political power-and-authority is generated not *in abstracto* through normative reasonableness (although normative languages of political thought are indispensable to the perlocutionary and illocutionary effects of political power), but always *in concreto* in a particular territory, inhabited by particular peoples organized under specific forms of rule and with specific kinds of politics and political-legal vocabularies.[13] The political–legal vocabulary of constitutional right—the archetype for the catalogue of rights found in basic human rights treaties—is a fundamental grammar for the articulation of arguments about the nature of modern government, its limits and its legitimation.[14] Constitutional rights rest upon both an institutional structure and the historical–social substance of a given political society—they presuppose (at least, after feudalism) both the sovereignty of that political society, and the institutional arrangements put in place by that society's political history, before they can be interpreted, applied and enforced. They express, in other words, a set of concrete political relationships *within and resting upon* the frame of sovereignty.[15]

2. Human Rights and Concrete Order

The determinate content of rights, and their interpretation and application, depends upon the political and legal institutions of the state; in other words, constitutional rights are predicated on the legal order of the state in all its social, historical and political particularity. This legal order is necessarily a *concrete order*, as Lindahl argues.[16] Norms, normativity and normative arguments are indispensable conditions for legal orders understood as concrete orders; but they are not sufficient conditions. A legal order is necessarily concrete in the sense that its *ordering capacity* and *appearance of orderliness* (a seeming unity of manifold norms) relies upon:

> ... beliefs and attitudes of an ethical, legal or political nature that are alive in society, and it flows from living requirements expressed in them ... The substance of the legal should thus proceed from the social 'is' ... [L]aw is interwoven, right from the outset and by its nature, with the totality of society and its history.[17]

[12] Ibid., at 48; see also M. Loughlin, *The Idea of Public Law* (2010), at ch. 5.

[13] For variations on this theme of the historicity of political legitimacy and legal legitimation, see R. Geuss, *History and Illusion in Politics* (2001).

[14] G. de Ruggiero, *The History of European Liberalism* (1959) (R. G. Collingwood, trans.).

[15] Loughlin, *The Idea of Public Law*, *supra* note 12, at ch. 12.

[16] H. Lindahl, *The Faultlines of Globalization: Legal Order and the Politics of A-Legality* (2014).

[17] E.-W. Böckenförde, *State, Society and Liberty: Essays in Political Theory and Constitutional Law* (1991) (J. A. Underwood, trans.), at 19–20.

In an analytically more elaborate manner, Lindahl argues that legal order is always a concrete order in as much as law:

> ... is never only an order of norms that is grafted a posteriori onto the world of fact, such that it transforms the latter's meaning.... [N]o legal norm is conceivable absent spatial, temporal, material, and subjective dimensions, [meaning that] law appears, from the practical perspective of those whose behaviour it regulates, as a normative unity to the extent that it differentiates and interconnects who ought to do what, where and when.[18]

On this understanding, a legal order—and law—is an emanation of (successful) authoritative collective action.[19] Law is a form of joint action by a collectivity, in which the normativity of law follows from the normality of collective life:

> To argue that an extant legal order is a default setting of authoritative collective action is to assert that this legal order is... a representation of a political order... This means that the validity a legal order demands for itself *turns on the claim that law, as posited, gives form (Gestaltung) to—that is, expresses—what is deemed to* ***already*** *bind together a manifold of individuals as participants in the common enterprise of realizing an* ***ideé directrice***.[20]

Legal normativity follows political normality, although need not be reducible to it. The unity presupposed by the imputed unity of the legal order is a political unity, also only putative and pre-reflexively taken for granted as the background against which the interpretation and application of legal norms takes place. The objectification of legal norms with a view to isolating their meaning through interpretation, takes for granted the relative stability of this pre-reflexive putative unity.[21] It is only when social and political order is disrupted, that 'is' and 'ought' fall apart, and a legal order and its claim to validity stands in contrast to the factual: '[T]he distinction between the normal and the normative only manifests when the ordinary course of joint action is disrupted.'[22]

Such 'concrete order thinking' bears upon the interpretation of norms. The determinacy that can be given to legal norm in its interpretation and application 'develop directly out of a presumed normal condition and of a presumed normal type of man'.[23] Schmitt gives the example of the codification of the concept of 'family':

> Where there is, for example, still a family, the legislator as well as the jurist who applies the law, finds himself compelled again and again to accept the *concrete-order notions* of the concrete institution of the 'family,' instead of the *abstract arrangement of a general concept.* When they speak of the 'good head of a family' of the *bonus pater familias*, the judge and the legislator thereby subject themselves to the traditional order of the concrete pattern 'family'.

[18] Lindahl, *supra* note 16, at 17.

[19] See also R. Hardin, *Liberalism, Constitutionalism and Democracy* (1999).

[20] Lindahl, 'Law as Concrete Order: Schmitt and the Problem of Collective Freedom', in D. Dyzenhaus and T. Poole (eds), *Law, Liberty and the State: Oakeshott, Hayek and Schmitt on the Rule of Law* (2015), at 55 (emphasis added).

[21] Lindahl, *supra* note 16, at 17.

[22] Lindahl, *supra* note 20, at 58.

[23] C. Schmitt, *On Three Types of Juristic Thought* (2004) (J. W. Bendersky, trans.), at 46: 'Without persistent, unavoidable, and indispensable concrete suppositions there is neither jurisprudential theory nor jurisprudential practice.'

> ... Every order, including the 'legal order,' is bound to concrete concepts of what is normal, which are not derived from general norms, but rather *norms are generated by their specific order and for their specific order.*
>
> ... Even if a norm is as inviolable as one wants to make it, it controls a situation *only so far as the situation has not become completely abnormal and so long as the normal presupposed type has not disappeared.* The normalcy of the concrete situation regulated by the norm and the concrete type presupposed by it are ... *an inherent, characteristic juristic feature of the norm's effectiveness and a normative determination of the norm itself.* A pure, situationless, and typeless norm would be a juristic absurdity.[24]

When the normal situation or concrete type of (social–political) relationship presupposed by and grounding the norm no longer obtains, the norm does not so much lose meaning per se (it is still capable of being given meaning) but rather loses a clear determination of its necessary or obvious meaning. It seems to lose it essence, and become an abstraction, one which appears adaptable to a wide variety of circumstances and purposes. It is in this sense that Schmitt concludes:

> [I]f the normality of the concrete situation presupposed by the positive norm but ignored by positivist jurisprudence collapses, then the use of every firm, calculable, and inviolable norm collapses. Then, 'the righteousness of positivity' ... also ceases. Without the system of coordination of a concrete order, juristic positivism is capable of distinguishing neither right and wrong, nor objectivity and subjective choice.[25]

Human rights treaty norms—and the customary norms derived from them—do not purport to directly substitute for the concrete legal order of the state. The legal order of human rights is not in itself a concrete order in the sense described above. This is not only because it has limited or no means of ensuring its own efficacy, but also because it does not purport to give effect to some common global institutional order or putative global political unity.[26] Rather, it rests upon, and assumes, both

[24] Ibid., at 55, 56, 57 (emphasis added). [25] Ibid., at 71.

[26] Indeed, as Arendt (following Kant) warned long ago, such a political unity may well be a terrifying thing to behold:

> The new situation, in which 'humanity' has in effect assumed the role formerly ascribed to nature or history, would mean in this context that the right to have rights, or the right of every individual to belong to humanity, should be guaranteed by humanity itself. It is by no means certain whether this is possible. For, contrary to the best intentioned humanitarian attempts to obtain new declarations of human rights from international organizations, it should be understood that this idea transcends the present sphere of international law which still operates in terms of reciprocal agreements and treaties between sovereign states; and, for the time being, a sphere that is above the nations does not exist. Furthermore, this dilemma would by no means be eliminated by the establishment of a 'world government'. Such a world government is indeed within the realm of possibility, but one may suspect that in reality it might differ considerably from the version promoted by idealistic-minded organizations. The crimes against human rights ... can always be justified by the pretext that right is equivalent to being good or useful for the whole in distinction to its parts ... For it is quite conceivable that one fine day a highly organized and mechanized humanity will conclude quite democratically ... that for humanity as a whole it would be better to liquidate certain parts thereof.

Arendt, *supra* note 6, at 298.

the efficacy and validity of the concrete legal order of the state.[27] Human rights treaty bodies exercise a very weak form of review, under which they are not authorized to resolve a conflict between a state and an individual, but simply to determine whether the human rights norm which they are authorized to interpret has been infringed within the terms of the human rights treaty establishing the human rights body's competence.

Even more robust mechanisms such as the European Court of Human Rights (ECtHR) are best understood as *constitution-enhancing* in respect of the specific political and judicial system of each member state;[28] the ECtHR's authority to review domestic legal acts depends upon the authorization of member states' demoi, and the interpellation of the Court's interpretative authority into the domestic legal–institutional order presupposes a situation of normalcy with order-specific conditions of legitimation and normativity that make possible the reception of human rights court decisions as part of *that particular* legal order.[29] The reference to the European Convention on Human Rights (ECHR) as the constitutional instrument of a European public order[30] could be interpreted as asserting that the Convention and its Court establish a concrete order at the European level, within which ECHR member states are considered integrated sub-orders, with the ECHR human rights norms—as interpreted and applied by the ECtHR—at the apex. In fact, as both Lindahl and Krisch point out, this account is belied by the practice of states and jurisprudence of the ECtHR itself. National constitutional courts do not unconditionally receive the interpretation of human rights obligations developed by the ECtHR, but have developed elaborate counter-limits doctrines in which the touchstone for the implementation of the norm is its compatibility with the legal boundaries and self-understanding of the domestic system,[31] albeit a domestic system which (through the incorporation of the European human rights treaty) has *institutionalized an openness to the ECHR legal order as part of its collective self-understanding*.[32] The exact terms of this openness, and of the self-understanding, will vary from state to state within the European legal space, but the critical point is that this does not amount to a hierarchy of norms which dissolves the distinction

[27] Philosophers appear to have recently understood this, abandoning arguments about whether human rights are a species of natural right and turning instead to arguments about what justifies the system of international *legal* human rights, taking the legal structure of that system seriously as one which works through and on the effective legal order of the state. See A. Buchanan, *The Heart of Human Rights* (2013).

[28] Bellamy, 'The Democratic Legitimacy of International Rights Conventions: Political Constitutionalism and the European Convention on Human Rights', 25 *European Journal of International Law (EJIL)* (2014) 1019.

[29] See in particular the detailed reflection in Krisch, 'The Open Architecture of European Human Rights Law', 71 *Modern Law Review* (2008) 183.

[30] See for example, ECtHR, *Al-Skeini and Others v. United Kingdom*, Appl. no. 55721/07, Judgment of 7 July 2011 (Grand Chamber), at para. 141.

[31] Krisch, *supra* note 29. For the argument that the ECtHR's legitimacy is damaged where it fails to take into account the specificity of the state's legal and political order, see Feldman, 'Sovereignties in Strasbourg', in R. Rawlings, P. Leyland and A. Young (eds), *Sovereignty and the Law: Domestic, European and International Perspectives* (2013), at 235.

[32] Lindahl, *supra* note 16, at 112–113.

between the state legal order and the European legal order. The state legal order in each case re-establishes itself as a concrete normative unity, by incorporating its relationship to the other (human rights) legal order within terms cognizable to itself. At the same time, the ECtHR, through concepts such as the margin of appreciation and reliance on 'common grounds' and 'European consensus' as a means for its interpretation of human rights norms, creates space for considerable flexibility and relativity in the ways in which human rights guaranteed by the ECHR are institutionalized within a state legal order. Indeed, one might say that through these doctrines the ECtHR leaves room for the content of human rights to hew closely to the 'normalcy of the concrete situation' within a given member state;[33] the European public order of which the ECtHR and ECHR are expressions consists of collected and common 'normal types' of institutions and political and judicial arrangements shared or expected to be shared across European member states. (This, we might also add, is the real meaning of the concept of the *espace juridique Européen.*)

The 'human' presupposed by the legal order of human rights is not principally an abstract humanity endowed with universal subjective rights against the world. Rather, the subject of human rights norms are emplaced within a concrete and bounded legal order, whether as citizen or non-citizen, and presumed to exist within the legal and political relationships that constitute that order.[34] The legal order within which the bearer of human rights is emplaced is presumed to be an efficacious and valid legal order, even counterfactually so, such as where states are held legally responsible for failures to protect the rights of persons against foreseeable risks posed by criminal violence, organized armed groups or other non-state actors on its territory—except perhaps in limited cases where the state itself is partially replaced by a non-state actor exercising state-like functions. The legal relationship—the normal type—presupposed by human rights treaties is the relationship between the constituted sovereign and subject (citizen or not). It is a relationship not of mutual hostility between belligerents or *justis hostes*, but of political friendship;[35] not civil war or public enmity, but of locatedness within a certain unity of order under which relatively pacific social, political and economic relationships are possible. In other words, as G. I. A. D. Draper observed almost 40 years ago, the concrete

[33] Notably the ECtHR's stridency and willingness to exceed the status quo in relation to certain institutional arrangements increases markedly as it moves further East. See for example, ECtHR, *Demir & Baykara v. Turkey*, Appl. no. 34503/97, Judgment of 12 November 2008.

[34] This, indeed, is the import of Arendt's paradoxical observation that

> Man, it turns out, can lose all so-called Rights of Man without losing his essential quality as man, his human dignity. *Only the loss of a polity itself expels him from humanity.* . . . The world found nothing sacred in the abstract nakedness of being human. And in the view of objective political conditions, it is hard to say how the concepts of man upon which human rights are based—could have helped to find a solution to the problem.

Arendt, *supra* note 6, at 297, 299.

[35] This notion of friendship need not imply either common citizenship or homogeneity. Rather it marks the limits of the collectivity as a status: a territorially emplaced collective, which regulates its joint action under law that has an *idée diréctrice*. Those abiding within the framework of joint action created by the legal order are at some minimum level not enemies.

situation presupposed by human rights law is the normal relationship between government and governed,

> setting limits to the intrusions by governments on those areas of human freedom thought to be essential for the proper functioning of the human being in society and his development therein. A war or 'emergency' impinges, within specified limits, upon those guarantees and freedoms in relation to the governed, i.e. 'everyone within their jurisdiction,' and not in relation to an enemy.... *Hostilities and government-governed relationships are different in kind, origin, purpose and consequences.*[36]

The idea that human rights law represents a 'law of peace' has become closely associated with polemical arguments denying the application of human rights law *in toto* to situations of armed conflict, particularly the 'war on terrorism' of the United States. The disreputable and morally shocking consequences of this denial—enforced disappearance, systematic torture and prolonged arbitrary detention of suspected enemy combatants—as well as the consistent reiteration by the International Court of Justice that human rights law continues to apply during periods of armed conflict and is not excluded by the co-extensive application of international humanitarian law, would seem to have conclusively settled the doctrinal question of whether human rights law continues to apply during armed conflict. But while he clearly held doubts about whether human rights law *should* apply during armed conflict, the formal issue of application is not only the point of Draper's observation. Rather, his observations intimate the idea that the 'normal type' of situation around which the concrete content of human rights norms is organized is that of the relationship between governor and governed, or between constituted sovereign and person-subject-to-sovereign-power, in a context of political normality; not a relationship characterized essentially by mutual existential hostility, such as obtains between two sovereigns at war, or during a state and armed groups (or between contending armed groups) in a civil war. The latter situations involve different concrete suppositions, a different normal type, grounding the normativity of legal norms:

> There is no society and government-governed relationships [between prisoners of war (POWs) and a detaining power]. *A fortiori* there is no human-rights nexus between armed combatants engaged in military operations against each other. The protection afforded to the individual war victims under the laws of war is afforded to him as an enemy individual, and not as a governed citizen.[37]

To say that human rights law is a law of peace is not necessarily to insist on its inapplicability to situations of armed conflict. Rather, it is to point out that when it is extended beyond the Westphalian frame—the presupposition of the concrete state legal order—upon which it rests, we must ask *what kind of law* it becomes and *what kind of global legal order* it intimates?

[36] Draper, 'Humanitarian Law and Human Rights', *Acta Juridica* (1979) 193, at 204.
[37] Ibid., at 204–205.

3. Fracturing the Westphalian Frame—Human Rights as Global Law

The Westphalian frame is notoriously fracturing, although we cannot easily agree on either the nosology or pathology of its afflictions. Its faultlines, zones of a-legality between overlapping and interacting legal orders,[38] are also the meridians along which the extraterritorial application of human rights runs. With the activity of governing becoming more dispersed and less centralized, and apparently more disconnected from any putative territorial and political unity, the 'normal' legal order of the state over which human rights law is overlaid seems less natural and less inevitable.[39] Benvenisti sums up this denaturalization succinctly:

> The assumption of such a fit [between the sovereign and the affected stakeholders] was regarded as the most effective way to overcome collective-action problems in the production of public goods, such as maintaining public order or ensuring food security and public health…
>
> …But in our contemporary global condominium, the 'technology' of global governance that operates through discrete sovereign entities no longer fits. What had previously been the solution to global collective action problems has now become part of the problem of global governance… Some states regularly shape the life opportunities of persons in faraway states by their daily decisions on economic development, conservation, or health regulation [to which, in my opinion, one may also add security].[40]

As the chapters collected in this volume indicate, the extraterritorial application of human rights norms is invoked in order to address a panoply of global-scale problems, from transborder environmental harm (Chapter 6), to social and economic development and global inequality (Chapter 5), to the repression of piracy in ungoverned spaces (Chapter 4), and military occupation (Chapter 2) and armed conflict in the territory of a third state (Chapter 3). In each context, the problem of 'jurisdiction' as the hinge upon which the application of the treaty obligation hangs points to a deeper problematic: how to give content to normative human rights law obligations in circumstances where the concrete presuppositions of human rights law—relations between a constituted sovereign and subject within a bounded legal and political order—do not obtain, and yet the language of human rights law is invoked to oblige or authorize state action.

The jurisprudence of human rights courts and treaty committees has resolved the question of jurisdiction in favour of a factual control test,[41] where control over (part of) a territory or person establishes the relationship necessary to bring a person

[38] Lindahl, *supra* note 16.

[39] Benvenisti, 'Sovereigns as Trustees of Humanity: On Accountability of States to Foreign Stakeholders', 107 *AJIL* (2013) 295.

[40] Ibid., at 298.

[41] Human Rights Committee, General Comment 31, Nature of the General Legal Obligation on States Parties to the Covenant, UN Doc. CCPR/C/21/Rev.1/Add.13, 26 May 2004; Committee Against Torture, General Comment 2, Implementation of Article 2 by States Parties, UN Doc. CAT/C/GC/2, 24 January 2008, at para. 7; International Court of Justice, *Legal Consequences of the Construction of a Wall in the Occupied Palestinian Territory*, Advisory Opinion, 9 July 2004, at paras 109–110.

within a state's jurisdiction, irrespective of whether this factual control arises in circumstances of armed conflict, military occupation or anti-piracy enforcement operations on the high seas or in coastal waters. What qualifies as sufficient control over territory or persons remains controversial. The jurisprudence of the ECtHR in *Al-Skeini* and *Jaloud* concludes that a state may subject an individual to its jurisdiction for the purposes of the ECHR where the state exercises forms of public power normally to be exercised by a sovereign government (such as the maintenance of security)[42] and, pursuant to the exercise of those powers, brings individuals within their authority and control[43] (by, for example, subjecting them to security operations in the course of which they are killed, or controlling checkpoints through which individuals inadvertently pass and are shot). As has been frequently observed,[44] this functional conceptualization of jurisdiction has morally salutary consequences:[45] it does not permit states to engage in conduct outside their territory which their human rights obligations would prohibit inside their territory, and thus avoids authorizing arbitrary or bizarre results such as where torture committed on national territory by state agents is held to violate a state's human rights obligations, while torture committed by the same state's agents outside national territory is not.

The nature of the control test for jurisdiction remains ambiguous in the most recent jurisprudence of the ECtHR. *Bankovic* had rejected the notion that jurisdiction could be found solely on the basis of a state agent's factual capacity to effect a rights-violation within another territory,[46] although as Milanovic points out subsequent cases undermined this proposition by holding that a state may have ECHR obligations in respect of persons killed by its armed forces in another state's territory, even where the territory was not under the state's effective control and the deceased person was not in the custody of the state's forces.[47] By the time we reach the position in *Jaloud*, however, the line between a 'cause-and-effect' approach and an 'effective control of territory or persons' approach is blurred; under the holdings in *Al-Skeini* and *Jaloud*, actual control over territory or persons is not required. Rather, jurisdiction is found where *due to the exercise of public power characteristic of sovereignty* ('normally to be exercised by a sovereign government'), a person suffers a rights-violation at the hands of state agents because—in some way—that person comes within the authority and control of those agents as they exercise 'public power'. Thus, armed forces of one state conducting a security operation across an international border in pursuit of a non-state armed group located in another state

[42] *Al-Skeini*, *supra* note 30, at para. 149.

[43] ECtHR, *Jaloud v. The Netherlands*, Appl. no. 47708/08, Judgment of 20 November 2014, at para. 152.

[44] *Lopez Burgos v. Uruguay*, *supra* note 4; Koh, *supra* note 4, at 12; M. Milanovic, *The Extraterritorial Application of Human Rights Treaties: Law, Principles and Policy* (2011), at 83, 97–98.

[45] Milanovic, *supra* note 44, at ch. 3 in general.

[46] ECtHR, *Bankovic and Others v. Belgium and Others*, Appl. no. 52207/99, Judgment of 12 December 2001, at para. 75.

[47] Milanovic, *supra* note 44, at 183–199.

would in this sense exercise a public power, characteristic of the sovereignty of the pursuing state (the public power of national self-defence). Similarly, the armed forces of a state participating in a non-international armed conflict on the territory of another state with the consent of the territorial state's government, could be understood to exercise a public power characteristic of the territorial state's sovereignty (the quintessentially sovereign power of maintaining or restoring public order and civil security against an insurgent group). An unmanned aerial vehicle operated by French military or intelligence personnel which strikes a member of an armed group that is a party to an internal armed conflict in Mali,[48] and which is authorized to use force by the recognized sovereign government of Mali in pursuit of its objectives of regaining control over its national territory, exercises a public power. Given that unmanned aerial vehicles can closely track and observe the conduct of an individual over hours and days, and lethally strike the target at any moment while that person is under observation, it seems arguable that during such surveillance a person is brought within the authority and control of the state agents controlling the drone.

It remains to be seen how the notion of a public power 'normally exercised by a sovereign state' will be developed by the ECtHR, but *ex facie* it would appear to capture a range of extraterritorial conduct by state agents that may result in temporary 'bare control' in respect of a person or place for a fleeting period of time, as well as more intensive forms of control arising out of the detention of an individual. The morphology of relationships to which human rights law is to be applied in such circumstances is evidently very different from the 'normal type' of relationship in relation to which human rights law is formulated and applied. The most recent jurisprudence concerning jurisdiction has developed in the context of armed conflicts, where the respondent state's forces are either parties to an international armed conflict *in flagrante*, are belligerent occupiers, or are parties to an internal armed conflict and mandated by the Security Council (with the consent of the territorial state) to contribute to the restoration of peace and security.

In their capacity as occupiers, particularly prolonged occupiers, a state's agents may well exercise extensive governance functions, but this does not alter the fundamental legal and political structure of the relationship between the occupier and the occupied population: it is predicated on relations of mutual hostility, and likely occurs in parallel to ongoing armed hostilities between the occupier and armed groups mixing with the civilian population. The legal institution of belligerent occupation presupposes the absence of relationships characteristic of sovereignty between the occupier and occupied populations, and endows the occupier with certain legal powers solely by virtue of its factual capacity to control a territory or population.[49] Belligerent occupation, as a special law within the law of armed conflict, authorizes the temporary assumption of governance functions by

[48] Munoz, 'France launches armed drone campaign in Mali', *The Hill*, 19 December 2013, available online at http://thehill.com/policy/defense/193707-france-launches-armed-drone-campaign-in-mali (last accessed 23 July 2015).

[49] See Bhuta, 'The Antinomies of Transformative Occupation', 16 *EJIL* (2005) 721.

the occupier while imposing on the occupier humanitarian and civil-order maintenance duties. It also specifies rights held by the occupied population by virtue of their *status* as protected persons who have fallen under the temporary control of the occupying power but who continue to be represented by the protecting power, the erstwhile effective sovereign of the territory. The law of belligerent occupation grants the occupier considerable discretion, pursuant to the exigencies of absolute military necessity and imperative reasons of security, to requisition property and labour, impede movement within the occupied territory, and detain individuals. The political relationship is not that of constituted sovereign and subject, within a putative political and legal unity, but a horizontal relationship of legally regulated enmity between two differential statuses: a power and a population (or, more generally, between a party to a conflict and a population).[50] At its most basic, the concrete relationship presupposed is that between an alien executive power and a human-subject-to-power, unmediated (as would be the case within a state legal order) by institutions that are the product of joint action by a collectivity.

To transpose the positive norms of human rights law, with their 'normal type' of man and politics, on to a quintessentially abnormal or exceptional situation such as military occupation, armed conflict or peace enforcement operations, is to augur two opposing possibilities (unless the norm is to remain a pure fiction): that either the abnormal be transformed to correspond with the presuppositions of the normal type, or that a norm predicated on the normal be made effective by relativizing it to the concrete circumstances of the abnormal.

The realization of the first possibility requires extraordinary human and material effort, transforming the conduct of hostilities into something like police action[51] and subjecting all conflict-related security and military detention to judicial review. These may be among the morally attractive consequences of such a 'righteousness of positivity'[52] through which social facts of human conduct are adapted to realize the norm, a norming of the exception.[53] But such a thoroughgoing attempt to live

[50] See Gross, Chapter 2 in this volume. As Gross elaborates, Israeli courts' application of human rights norms to a situation otherwise regulated by the law of belligerent occupation leads to a balancing of the security rights of residents of Israeli settlements that are illegal under international humanitarian law, with the property rights of Palestinian residents of the occupied territories. Thus, citizens of the occupying power and residents of the occupied territory are treated as though they were members of the same political unity under one sovereign, rather than members of opposing political entities in a relationship of legally regulated enmity. The result is that important categorical protections afforded by the laws of war to the population of the occupied territories are weakened.

[51] Blum suggests that under the influence of new kinds of contemporary conflict between state and non-state actors across borders, this trend is already taking place—in part due to the simultaneous application of human rights law and humanitarian law: Blum, 'The Individualization of War: From War to Policing in the Regulation of Armed Conflict', in A. Sarat, L. Douglas and M. Merrill Umphrey (eds), *Law and War* (2014), at 48–79.

[52] Schmitt, *supra* note 23.

[53] Through derogation clauses, human rights treaties attempt to restrain or partially regulate states of exception that may be brought about by situations that threaten the life of the nation in two ways: holding a limited number of rights as non-derogable even during emergencies, and setting a strict necessity standard for measures taken in derogation. See the review of authorities undertaken by Lord Bingham of Cornhill in *A and Others v. Secretary of State for the Home Department; X and Others v. Secretary State for the Home Department* [2004] UKHL 56, at paras 17–44.

up, for example, to the obligation to respect and ensure a 'right to review by a court of the legality of detention [which] applies to all persons deprived of their liberty'[54] under Article 9(4) of the ICCPR in circumstances of military occupation or armed conflict should also be understood as portending deeper and more intensive forms of governance by occupiers or states intervening in an armed conflict: the creation and management of a system of courts and prisons, which themselves must comply with human rights norms.[55] The difficulty is that the legality and legitimacy of such governance rests upon sources of power-and-authority essentially external to the social and political order of the territory and population which is to be governed, and where effective domination of the territory usually remains to be achieved. No valid and effective concrete order yet exists, and thus the generation of the conditions of normality demands the intensification of the factual power of control by the intervening force, whether directly as occupiers or as instrumentalities of weak local governments. The recent history of wars in Iraq and Afghanistan, and their ongoing failure to consolidate stable political and legal orders, evokes the inherent uncertainty of such undertakings, in which external actors have become ineluctably enmeshed in intractable conflicts where the very nature and source of social and political power-and-authority in a territory and among a people, are bitterly and violently contested. To proclaim that this intensified intervention is an answer to the juridical demands posed by human rights law is to risk bringing the idea of human rights into disrepute as mere alibi for continued conflict; it also risks leading us to exaggerate our belief in the potential of human rights law to enhance the effectiveness of state-building and nation-building interventions.

The second possibility is already being realized. In its Grand Chamber decision in *Al-Skeini*, the ECtHR explicitly rejected the earlier dictum in *Bankovic* that the

[54] Human Rights Committee, General Comment No. 35, Art. 9 (Liberty and security of person), UN Doc. CCPR/C/GC/35, 16 December 2014, at para. 4. Unlike under Art. 5 ECHR, security detention is not necessarily impermissible under Art. 9 of the ICCPR, and security detention 'authorized and regulated by and complying with international humanitarian law in principle is not arbitrary' (General Comment No. 35, at para. 64). Nonetheless, the General Comment also insists that the human rights law obligation under Art. 9(4) ('anyone who is deprived of his liberty by arrest or detention shall be entitled to take proceedings before a court, in order that that court may decide without delay on the lawfulness of his detention and order his release if the detention is not lawful') requires a 'court within the judiciary' or exceptionally 'a specialized tribunal' created by legislation and which must be 'either independent of the executive and legislative branches or enjoy judicial independence in deciding legal matters in proceedings that are judicial in nature' (para. 45).

[55] Naz Modirzadeh contemplates the practical consequences of such deepened interventions:

> Human rights law asks that the State with obligations to an individual takes real steps to permanent transform institutions that structurally violate rights...I do not *want* an occupying power that has invaded my State to be recognized as having a 'rights-based' relationship with my population. I do not want that State to be in a position to argue that it has to engage in certain institutional changes in order to be able to comply with its human rights obligations back home. I do not want a State that has no relationship to civil society in my country, has no long-term understanding of my population, its history, its religious values, etc., to have a hand in shaping its human rights framework simply by virtue of its choice to invade.

Modirzadeh, 'The Dark Side of Convergence: A Pro-Civilian Critique of the Extraterritorial Application of Human Rights Law in Armed Conflict', 86 *International Law Studies Series US Naval War College* (2010) 349, at 375.

rights to be secured by a state party could not be 'divided and tailored' according to the nature of the state's conduct or its degree of control over a place or person.[56] Rather, the Court observed that 'whenever the State, through its agents, exercises control and authority over an individual . . . the State is under an obligation . . . to secure to that individual the rights and freedoms . . . *that are relevant to the situation* of that individual'.[57] At the very least, the Court seems to countenance a relativity of obligation depending on the rights 'that are relevant to the situation'. Where the circumstances in which the norm is to be applied would make a strict application of its positive content impossible, the ECtHR has accepted that the norm must be adapted and what qualifies as norm-compliant conduct can be interpreted with considerable flexibility.

In *Hassan*,[58] the applicant's brother was a security detainee at Camp Bucca in Iraq between 23 April 2003 and 2 May 2003. During this period, the United Kingdom was the detaining power but not yet an occupying power, and the active hostilities phase of the armed conflict between the United States and its allies and Iraq was ongoing. The applicant's brother, who appears to have been extra-judicially executed after his release from Camp Bucca, was detained by the United Kingdom pursuant to Article 42 of the Fourth Geneva Convention, as someone whose internment was deemed absolutely necessary for the security of the detaining power. Article 42 does not require judicial review of detention, and allows preventive detention. The applicant claimed that his brother's detention was inconsistent with Article 5 ECHR, which does not *expressis verbis* authorize any kind of preventive detention and requires that a detainee be able to challenge his detention before a regularly constituted court. In this case, the legal power of a party to a conflict under the Geneva Conventions conflicted directly with its obligations under a human rights instrument.[59] The provisions of the law of armed conflict here are indeed 'discretely stylized compromise norms',[60] in which a Party's wide discretion to detain for both intelligence and security purposes is accepted during an armed conflict, and limited review entitlements are accorded to a detainee, reflecting the highly elastic nature of the purposes of detention during an armed conflict. The applicable human rights norms, by contrast, narrowly circumscribe if not eliminate altogether the state's discretion to detain for security

[56] *Al-Skeini*, *supra* note 30, at para. 137. [57] Ibid.

[58] ECtHR, *Hassan v. United Kingdom*, Appl. no. 29750/09, Judgment of 16 September 2014.

[59] The conflict is especially stark with the ECHR, but it is equally clear with Art. 9 of the ICCPR. Article 9 does not categorically exclude preventive detention as arbitrary but nonetheless requires judicial review (or its close equivalent) of detention (see General Comment quoted in note 54 above). None of the recent practice of states in respect of Art. 42 of the Fourth Geneva Convention indicates that states consider themselves legally obliged to create review mechanisms of a judicial or even quasi-judicial nature. Article 43 of the Fourth Geneva Convention requires only that detainees be allowed to petition to have their detention reconsidered by 'an appropriate court or administrative board' and such a request for reconsideration be entertained at least twice yearly. In the case of UK forces operating in Iraq in April–May 2003, this administrative review board was composed of UK military legal officers.

[60] C. Schmitt, *Theory of the Partisan* (2007), at 32.

purposes or to exploit actionable intelligence, as one would expect within the boundaries of a civil condition.[61]

Confronted with a circumstance where a state's scrupulous compliance with international humanitarian law would place it in direct conflict with positive *ex facie* norms of a human rights treaty, the ECtHR adopted an interpretive approach in which the plain meaning of Article 5 ECHR was rendered subsidiary to the Court's assessment of the context and the need to 'take into account' the provisions of international humanitarian law in the interpretation and application of Article 5. The ECtHR held:

> [T]he court considers that, even in situations of international armed conflict, the safeguards under the Convention continue to apply, albeit interpreted against the background of the provisions of international humanitarian law. By reason of the co-existence of the safeguards provided by international humanitarian law and by the Convention in time of armed conflict, the grounds of permitted deprivation of liberty set out in subparagraphs (a) to (f) of that provisions *should be accommodated, as far as possible*, with the taking of prisoners of war and the detention of civilians who pose a risk to security under the Third and Fourth Geneva Conventions. The Court is mindful of the fact that internment in peacetime does not fall within the scheme of deprivation of liberty governed by Article 5 of the Convention without the exercise of the power of derogation under Article 15.[62]

It further ruled:

> ... [In order to be deemed 'lawful' for the purposes of Article 5(1) ECHR], the detention must comply with the rules of international humanitarian law and, most importantly,... *should be in keeping with the fundamental purpose of Article 5 § 1, which is to protect the individual from arbitrariness.*
>
> ... [The procedural safeguards under Article 5 §§ 2 and 4, right to speedy review of lawfulness of detention by a court] must also *be interpreted in a manner which takes into account the context and the applicable rules of international humanitarian law.* Articles 43 and 78 of the Fourth Geneva Convention provide that internment 'shall be subject to periodical review, if possible every six months, by a competent body'. Whilst it might not be practicable, in the course of international armed conflict, for the legality of detention to be determined by an independent 'court' in the sense generally required by Article 5 § 4 in this context, the 'competent body' should provide *sufficient guarantees of impartiality and fair procedure to protect against arbitrariness.*[63]

The operative reasoning of the ECtHR here evinces two aspects. Firstly, in order to maintain the coeval application of the ECHR with international humanitarian law's rules concerning security detention and prisoners of war, the words of Article 5

[61] As Oakeshott's reading of Hobbes elucidates, the civil condition replaces the natural (horizontal) equality of individuals or sovereigns within a state of nature with the juridical equality of persons under authoritative binding law (vertical). See M. Oakeshott, *Hobbes on Civil Association* (1975). Hobbes was of course doubtful that anything approximating a civil condition could be established between sovereigns, although Hobbes's account of the potential of international law was more generous than many 'Hobbesians' would allow. See Malcolm, 'Hobbes's Theory of International Relations', in N. Malcom, *Aspects of Hobbes* (2002), at ch. 13.

[62] *Hassan v. United Kingdom*, *supra* note 58, at para. 106 (emphasis added).

[63] Ibid., at paras 105–107 (emphasis added).

ECHR become entirely subsidiary to the Court's overall assessment of the broad purpose of the Article 5 protections, which it concludes amounts (at the highest possible level of generality) to protection from arbitrary detention. The grounds for the deprivation of liberty in Article 5(1) can no longer be 'an exhaustive list of permissible grounds for deprivation of liberty which must be interpreted strictly'.[64] Rather, they represent general values to be fulfilled, and perhaps principles to be applied. These values and principles are held to be common to both human rights law and the relevant provisions of humanitarian law, and the question of whether a human rights law norm has been breached is answered through an assessment of the extent to which the humanitarian law provisions (and the state's mode of implementing its humanitarian law obligations) can be said to uphold these values and principles.

Secondly, and as a consequence of the first aspect, the specific meanings given to words such as 'court' and standards such as 'speedy review of detention' are relativized to the abnormal situation characteristic of international armed conflict. Whereas the ECtHR has previously held that Article 5(4) reviews must take place before a body with a *judicial character* and necessitate *adversarial proceedings* respecting equality of arms (implying access to legal counsel, access to the case file, and a hearing at which legal counsel are present and can make arguments),[65] an ex parte administrative review by a panel of military lawyers with no structural guarantees of independence from the detaining armed forces' chain of command, is deemed adequate in *Hassan*.

It would appear that the price of applying norms based upon the concrete presuppositions of a state legal order, to an entirely different type of concrete situation, is a thoroughgoing deformalization of the norms: exhaustive criteria become open-ended inclusive lists; rule-like strictures become principles and values, to be balanced against other, equally deformalized, values in light of the overall context of application; 'the use of every, firm, calculable, and inviolable norm collapses'.[66] The result is an ex ante indeterminacy of the content of the human rights norms, an indeterminacy which is resolved only through ex post adjudication by a court. Between the ex ante and the ex post lies a zone of uncertainty as to what is authorized and what is prohibited under the colour of human rights law. The resulting expansion of states' discretion in the interpretation of their duties under human rights law may lead them to adopt higher standards of protection, or it might well empty norms of their established content as part of what is deemed necessary to 'take into consideration' the context in which the norms are to be applied. The extraterritorial application of human rights law generates a *law of extraterritorial human rights*, one in which human rights law norms become flexible abstract principles adapted to a new and distinctive set of 'normal types' of concrete situation—transnational armed conflicts, peace enforcement operations, anti-piracy police actions using military force, anti-people smuggling operations, etc. In these situations, 'whoever happens to be able to

[64] ECtHR, *Wloch v. Poland*, Appl. no. 27785/95, Judgment of 19 October 2000, at para. 108.
[65] ECtHR, *Reinprecht v. Austria*, Appl. no. 67175/01, Judgment of 15 November 2005, at para. 31.
[66] Schmitt, *supra* note 23, at 71.

exert brute force over the civilians at a given moment . . . such that they have some sliding degree of control will have some sliding degree of human rights obligations'.[67] The rights bequeathed by a law of extraterritorial human rights, appropriately divided and tailored (although by whom and how we cannot easily know), may be a kind of 'bare right' held by humans-subject-to-power against entities exercising power upon them. But what such a 'bare right' yields for the individual and community concerned is unclear. Kennedy comments rightly that 'unbundling the exercise of sovereignty and rethinking war as a range of related public acts on a continuum from more to less violent, more to less differentiated from the governmental routines of peacetime . . . increases the range of options for military and political leaders alike'.[68] A day in court will be had by very few, and the possibilities of such 'accountability' should not be exaggerated, as Modizardeh observes in the context of Iraq:

> [R]eplacing the domestic legal system with 'the international community' or with the legal system of another country . . . does not necessarily improve the experience of law or the accountability of actors vis-a-vis the Iraqi civilian. . . . [F]ocusing energies on supporting rare 'impact litigation' connecting a handful of victims with prominent human rights lawyers in Europe or civil rights organizations in the United States . . . may improve the Dutch, British or Canadian legal order . . . but it does not necessarily increase the rights enjoyment of Iraqis.[69]

4. Conclusion

The law of extraterritorial human rights has risen to prominence in relation to legal spaces of exception: occupation, international armed conflict and our contemporary 'global civil war' against non-state armed groups. At its most mundane, it rests on the argument that the exercise of governance functions brings with it the capacity to affect human rights, and thus gives rise to human rights law obligations vis-à-vis those affected. This account of the extraterritorial application of human rights treaties insists that the distinction between sovereignty and governance functions is irrelevant to the formal applicability of human rights law. As such, the underlying theory of this argument understands sovereignty as little more than a label attached to a bundle of governance capacities, which can be parcelled out and divided between different state and non-state actors, which through their exercise give rise to human rights-claims and human rights fulfilling-duties. What ultimately unifies and coheres this fragmentary structure is the unity of law itself, a law that connects individuals-subject-to-power with the entities exercising power through the legal order of human rights law.

But what is this legal order? In this chapter, I have argued that in its inception, structure and content, the legal order of human rights is not a global legal order as much as a supra-state legal order dependent upon the concrete legal order of states. The morphology of human rights laws concepts have rested hitherto precisely on

[67] Modirzadeh, *supra* note 55, at 371.
[68] D. Kennedy, *Of War and Law* (2006), at 147.
[69] Modizardeh, *supra* note 55, at 373.

the kinds of relationships which characterize those between a constituted sovereign and subject. The extraterritorialization of human rights law should not be understood as some kind of natural fulfilment of the telos of human rights as a cosmopolitan constitutional law for all humanity. Law cannot be sovereign without a political sovereign, and no global political sovereign is yet in the making. Rather, the extraterritorialization of human rights law would appear to augur a new reality, one which will be partly juridified and consecrated by the application of human rights norms. This new global law space, which remains *in statu nascendi*, accredits every person as bearer of human rights, opposable in principle to actors that can affect those rights. But in practice, as we have seen, the bearers of such rights are citizens without effective sovereigns, or with effective governors who are not *their* sovereigns; and the rights themselves may be 'bare' rights, indeterminate entitlements of uncertain content: values and principles interpreted in myriad ways by a range of actors, and subject to a variety of exigencies in any given context. The beneficiaries of these bare rights have the consolation of having the status of 'rights-holders', but can have recourse only to the judges of Strasbourg or the expert committees of Geneva to appreciate, in the end, whether this amounts to anything at all.

The Righting of the Law of Occupation

*Aeyal Gross**

1. Introduction

Two doctrinal developments were necessary preconditions for the application of international human rights law (IHRL) in occupied territories to become part of international law. The first development was the growing recognition of the extraterritorial application of human rights—the idea that states are also bound by international human rights norms in actions they perform outside their borders[1]—and the second was the determination that IHRL may apply together with international humanitarian law (IHL).[2] The application of human rights in occupied territories is the outcome, possibly the most important, of these two developments. Given that occupation is one of the broadest manifestations of state control exercised outside sovereign borders, and one traditionally conceived as being governed by IHL rather than by IHRL, and given the length and extent of the occupying powers' control over foreign nationals, the development that I refer to as the 'righting'[3] of the law of occupation may radically transform international law on the relationships between occupier and occupied. As this chapter will show, such a transformation has been underway in recent years.

Advocates for applying IHRL in occupied territories in addition to IHL suggest that doing so would advance the welfare of the occupied people as well as a legal culture of compliance.[4] They point out that enforcement mechanisms, such as UN treaty bodies and human rights courts, that are lacking in IHL would constitute an

* I am grateful to Yehuda Goor and Peter Teishev for their excellent research assistance, to Nehal Bhuta for his helpful suggestions and to Batya Stein for her superb editing work.

[1] M. Milanovic, *Extraterritorial Application of Human Rights Treaties: Law, Principles, and Policy* (2011).

[2] Gross, 'Human Proportions: Are Human Rights the Emperor's New Clothes of the International Law of Occupation', 18 *European Journal of International Law (EJIL)* (2007) 1, at 3–4; O. Ben-Naftali (ed.), *International Humanitarian Law and International Human Rights Law* (2011).

[3] I borrow the term 'righting' from Knop, 'The "Righting" of Recognition: Recognition of States in Eastern Europe and the Soviet Union', in Y. Le Bouthillier, D. M. McRae and D. Pharand (eds), *Selected Papers in International Law: Contribution of the Canadian Council on International Law* (1999) 261.

[4] Ben-Naftali and Shany, 'Living in Denial: The Application of Human Rights in the Occupied Territories', 37 *Israel Law Review* (2004) 17, at 23.

advantage,[5] potentially filling the enforcement gap. Some argue that 'no conceptual difference' prevails between these two bodies of law, at least as they stand today. Since both are designed to promote human dignity and physical integrity and to minimize human suffering,[6] they maintain that these common goals could be advanced by this development.

This chapter, however, argues that the application of IHRL in occupied territories may in fact lead to a radical transformation in the law of occupation because of the conceptual differences that *do* exist between IHL and IHRL. The major differences are the following:

1. IHL identifies people living under occupation as 'protected persons'.[7] By contrast, IHRL places everyone on a supposedly equal and universal plane. Given the difference between occupiers and occupied, this equation is artificial.
2. Proportionality analysis assumes different meanings in the two bodies of law. In IHL, proportionality analysis focuses on the effects that an attack against a legitimate target has on surrounding civilian people and objects in order to assess whether these effects are proportional to the objectives of military necessity at stake. In IHRL, when individuals' rights are limited in the name of public interest or of the rights of other individuals, proportionality analysis is used to assess whether the effects of the limitation on a member of the public is proportional to the public interest at stake or to the rights of the other individuals.[8] Proportionality in human rights analysis is thus different from proportionality in IHL analysis. However, as I will show, their convergence could justify excessive violations of the rights of people living under occupation. Their rights can now be limited for the sake of 'public interest' as well as for the rights of others and for military necessity, both when the consequences affect individuals against whom actions are taken and when they affect surrounding people and objects. Often, the concept of public interest or the rights of others is broader than that of military necessity, expanding the possibilities for limiting the humanitarian standards applicable to protected persons beyond what is envisaged in IHL in general and in the

[5] Y. Dinstein, *The International Law of Belligerent Occupation* (2009), at 85; E. Benvenisti, *The International Law of Occupation* (2012), at 75; Lubell, 'Human Rights Obligations in Military Occupations', 94 *International Review of the Red Cross* (*IRRC*) (2012) 317, at 319.

[6] Ben-Naftali and Shany, *supra* note 4, at 101.

[7] Art. 4 of the Geneva Convention Relative to the Protection of Civilian Persons in Time of War 1949, 75 UNTS 287(Fourth Geneva Convention).

[8] On the different contexts of proportionality and their merger by the HCJ, see Gross, 'The Construction of a Wall Between The Hague and Jerusalem: The Enforcement and Limits of Humanitarian Law and the Structure of Occupation', 26 *Leiden Journal International Law* (2006) 393. On the different meanings of proportionality in IHRL and IHL see Lubell, 'Challenges in Applying Human Rights Law to Armed Conflict', 87 *IRRC* (2005) 737, at 745–746; Haßenpflug, 'Comment', 45 *German Yearbook of International Law* (2002) 78, at 80–81. Heike Krieger lists the different meaning of proportionality in the two bodies of law as one of the reasons for the problems that arise in their co-application. See Krieger, 'A Conflict of Norms: The Relationship between Humanitarian Law and Human Rights Law in the ICRC Customary Law Study', 11 *Journal of Conflict & Security Law* (2006) 265, at 280–281.

law of occupation in particular. The concept of military necessity, however, may sometimes allow restrictions of rights beyond the public interest. The result of a merger can thus provide more, rather than fewer, justifications for limiting rights.

3. As a corollary of 1 and 2, in the context of occupation, IHL is typified by *vertical balancing* between the rights of protected persons and the legitimate security considerations of the military commander.[9] By contrast, IHRL is often typified by *horizontal balancing* between the rights of different individuals and between the rights of protected persons on the one hand and citizens of the occupying power, including settlers, on the other.

It is these conceptual differences, and indeed the enforceability of human rights by different courts, tribunals and committees, that create the effect whereby the law of occupation is transformed when human rights are added to it. As this chapter will show, this transformation is not necessarily to the benefit of protected persons living under occupation. Indeed, quite often, rather the opposite is true.

Note that the development I discuss here occurred largely as a result of human rights advocacy, which sought to expand safeguards to protected persons; against the wishes of occupying countries but with the endorsement of international, regional and national courts and tribunals. The International Court of Justice (ICJ), in the Advisory Opinion on the *Legal Consequences of the Construction of a Wall in the Occupied Palestinian Territory*[10] and in its judgment in the *Case Concerning Armed Activities on the Territory of the Congo (Democratic Republic of the Congo v. Uganda)*,[11] examined the actions of occupying armies not only through the lens of IHL but also through that of IHRL. Both decisions relied on the ICJ's previous determination in its Advisory Opinion on the *Legality of the Threat or Use of Nuclear Weapons*.[12] This opinion held that the protection of the International Covenant on Civil and Political Rights (ICCPR) does not cease in times of war except by operation of Article 4 of the Covenant, whereby certain provisions may be derogated in times of national emergency.[13]

In the *Wall* opinion and the *Armed Activities* decision, the ICJ expanded this determination to human rights conventions in general, and extended the rule on the application of human rights norms in times of war to the context of belligerent occupation.

The determinations of the ICJ in the *Wall* and *Armed Activities* decisions are a significant step in what has been described as the 'convergence' of IHRL and

[9] Art. 43 of the Hague Regulations, Convention (IV) Respecting the Laws and Customs of War on Land and its Annex: Regulation concerning the Laws and Customs of War on Land 1907, (1971) UKTS 6 Cmnd 4575 (Hague Regulations).

[10] *Legal Consequences of the Construction of a Wall in the Occupied Palestinian Territory*, Advisory Opinion, 9 July 2004, ICJ Reports (2004) 136 (*Wall*).

[11] *Armed Activities on the Territory of the Congo* (*Democratic Republic of the Congo v. Uganda*), Judgment, 3 February 2006, ICJ Reports (2005) 168 (*Armed Activities*).

[12] *Legality of the Threat or Use of Nuclear Weapons*, Advisory Opinion, 8 July 1996, ICJ Reports (1996) 226 (*Nuclear Weapons*).

[13] Ibid., para. 25.

IHL.[14] Together with the establishment of the doctrine that human rights norms apply extra-territorially—beyond the recognized borders of the states that are bound by them—this convergence was the pre-condition, as noted, for the 'righting' of the law of occupation. Parallel developments are also evident in other courts and tribunals, including the European Court of Human Rights (ECtHR) as well as the Israeli Supreme Court sitting as the High Court of Justice (HCJ), which uses human rights analysis when discussing cases from the Occupied Palestinian Territory (OPT), as will be seen later.[15] In spite of controversies and critiques,[16] the current direction of international law is clearly to apply human rights norms to situations of armed conflict in general and to situations of belligerent occupation in particular. This trend is evident not only in the two cited ICJ decisions but also in the interpretation of human rights treaties, in the decisions of treaty bodies, and in the rulings of the courts—including the ECtHR[17]—in a variety of cases, notably those involving northern Cyprus[18] and Iraq.[19] This development, however, in what may turn out to be a Pyrrhic victory, may have served to undermine rather than to expand human protection and to legitimize violations of the rights of people living under occupation. As this chapter shows, while the application of IHRL may expand the rights of protected persons, it also upsets the balance of IHL, which ensures special protection to people living under occupation, and increases the justification for limiting these people's rights beyond the scope allowed by a strict IHL analysis. In turn, the rights of citizens from the occupying power are often subsumed under security considerations, leading to a security imbalance that enables broad violations of the rights of people living under occupation. Conflating the different meaning ascribed to proportionality in IHL and IHRL also contributes to this imbalance.

In Part 2 of this chapter, I discuss the ICJ's determinations regarding the application of IHRL in situations of occupation. Part 3 looks at the case-law of

[14] For a discussion of 'convergence' preceding the recent ICJ decisions, see T. Meron, *Human Rights in Internal Strife: Their International Protection* (1987), at 3–28. For an early formulation of the convergence thesis, see Meron, 'Human Rights in Time of Peace and in Time of Armed Strife: Selected Problems', in T. Buergenthal (ed.), *Contemporary Issues in International Law* (1984), at 1.

[15] For an overview, see Droege, 'Elective Affinities? Human Rights and Humanitarian Law', 90 *IRRC* (2008) 501. In the context of occupation, see Y. Arai-Takahashi, *The Law of Occupation* (2009), at 399–547.

[16] For an evaluation of the ICJ's position that supports its determination in principle but also offers critiques see Ben-Naftali and Shany, *supra* note 4, at 109–118. For an opposite view see Dennis, 'Application of Human Rights Treaties Extraterritorially in Times of Armed Conflict and Military Occupation', 99 *American Journal of International Law* (*AJIL*) (2005) 119 (Dennis 2005); Dennis, 'Non-Application of Civil and Political Rights Treaties Extraterritorially During Times of International Armed Conflict', 40 *Israel Law Review* (2007) 453 (Dennis 2007).

[17] For a discussion of recent European cases on human rights in armed conflict see Abresch, 'A Human Rights Law of Internal Armed Conflict: The European Court of Human Rights in Chechnya', 16 *EJIL* (2005) 741; Heintze, 'The European Court of Human Rights and the Implementation of Human Rights Standards During Armed Conflicts', 45 *German Yearbook of International Law* (2002) 60; Droege, *supra* note 15, at 513–517; Gioia, 'The Role of the European Court of Human Rights in Monitoring Compliance with Humanitarian Law in Armed Conflicts', in Ben-Naftali, *supra* note 2, 201.

[18] See *infra* notes 82–102 and accompanying text.

[19] See *infra* notes 103–123 and accompanying text.

the Israeli HCJ in this regard, focusing on cases relating to the OPT. Part 4 considers the relevant case-law of the ECtHR, especially in relation to Iraq and Cyprus. Part 5 considers patterns in the application of IHRL in occupation, pointing to the difference between vertical and horizontal balancing, and suggests that generally, IHRL can expand protections in occupation when regulating a vertical relationship, such as in due process cases that do not involve balancing the rights of other persons, but may narrow the protections of protected persons in cases involving horizontal relationships. Finally, Part 6 offers some concluding thoughts on the questions at stake.

2. The International Court of Justice's Determinations

In the *Wall* decision, the ICJ held that 'the protection offered by human rights conventions does not cease in case of armed conflict, save through the effect of provisions for derogation'.[20] Moreover, the ICCPR, the International Covenant on Economic, Social and Cultural Rights (ICESCR) and the Convention on the Rights of the Child (CRC) extend to individuals outside a state's territory but who are subject to that state's jurisdiction. Thus, the ICJ found that all three conventions apply in the OPT.[21]

Concerning the relationship between IHRL and IHL, the ICJ made the following determination in the *Wall* opinion, which was cited with approval in its *Armed Conflict* judgment:

> As regards the relationship between international humanitarian law and human rights law, there are thus three possible situations: some rights may be exclusively matters of international humanitarian law; others may be exclusively matters of human rights law; yet others may be matters of both these branches of international law. In order to answer the question put to it, the Court will have to take into consideration both these branches of international law, namely human rights law and, as *lex specialis*, international humanitarian law.[22]

Based on these principles, the ICJ found in the *Wall* decision that Israel's construction of the wall in the OPT violated certain provisions of the ICCPR, the ICESCR and the CRC. In the *Armed Activities* judgment, the ICJ determined that Uganda was the occupying power in the Ituri district in the Democratic Republic of the Congo (DRC) and that the Uganda People's Defence Force (UPDF), whose actions it held attributable to Uganda, violated norms enshrined in the ICCPR, the CRC and its Optional Protocol on the Involvement of Children in Armed Conflict, and the African Charter on Human and Peoples' Rights, besides IHL.[23] These

[20] *Wall*, *supra* note 10, at para. 106.

[21] Ibid., at paras 107–114.

[22] Ibid., at para. 106, cited in *Armed Activities*, *supra* note 11, at para. 216. The last sentence in the quoted passage, referring to the *lex specialis* doctrine, was omitted when quoted in *Armed Conflict*. For a discussion of problems in the application of *lex specialis* in this context see Bianchi, 'Dismantling the Wall: The ICJ's Advisory Opinion and Its Likely Impact on International Law', 47 *German Yearbook of International Law* (2004) 343, at 369–378.

[23] *Armed Activities*, *supra* note 11, at paras 217–220.

actions included torture and other forms of inhumane treatment of the civilian population, destroying villages and civilian buildings, failing to distinguish civilian from military targets, failing to protect the civilian population in its fight with other combatants, inciting ethnic conflict and involvement in the training of child soldiers.[24]

Moreover, the ICJ determined in this decision that the duty to secure respect for the applicable rules of IHRL as well as IHL was part of Uganda's duty as the occupying power in Ituri, according to Article 43 of the Hague Regulations of 1907.[25] Recall that Article 43 grants the commander the authority to 'take all the measures in his power to restore, and ensure, as far as possible, public order and safety, while respecting, unless absolutely prevented, the laws in force in the country'.

3. The Israeli High Court of Justice and Human Rights in the OPT

The Israeli HCJ is probably the court, both at the national or international level, with the largest number of occupied territories cases.[26] Its jurisprudence on the matter is thus wide and varied. Although the Israeli government's official position rejected the application of IHRL in the OPT,[27] the HCJ took a different position in some of its judgments. One of the benchmark rulings on the matter by the HCJ is *Ma'arab*.[28] In this ruling, the Court scrutinized the military order on arrests in the OPT according to both IHL and IHRL and determined that the rule allowing the Israeli army to arrest Palestinians for 12 or 18 days before they are brought before a judge violates international law. Article 9(1) of the ICCPR, which guarantees the person's right to liberty, security and freedom from arbitrary arrest or detention, and especially Article 9(3) of the same Convention, which determines that anyone arrested or detained on criminal charges shall be brought 'promptly'

[24] Ibid., para. 211.

[25] Ibid., para. 178. This decision is also significant because it involves a situation of occupation that did not share what has been called 'the unusual circumstances of Israel's prolonged occupation'. Dennis suggested that the ICJ's determination on this matter in *Wall* may be attributed to this feature of the Israeli occupation, and that it remains unclear whether the opinion could be read as generally endorsing the view that the obligations assumed by states under IHRL apply extraterritorially in situations of armed conflict and military occupation: Dennis (2005), *supra* note 16, at 122. By repeating the same determination in the *Armed Activities* Case (*supra* note 11) the ICJ clarified its position on this point and implicitly rejected Dennis' suggestion for a possible narrow reading of its determination on this matter in the *Wall* opinion (*supra* note 10).

[26] The discussion in this section draws on my article: Gross, *supra* note 2. See also A. Gross, *The Writing on the Wall: Rethinking the International Law of Occupation* (forthcoming 2016).

[27] The position of the Israeli government is discussed in detail in Ben-Naftali and Shany, *supra* note 4, at 25–40, and criticized at 40–100. Although most of the debate pertains to questions of principle about the relationship between IHL and IHRL, it also addresses the question of Israel's effective control of the OPT, or at least parts thereof, following the establishment of the Palestinian Authority.

[28] High Court of Justice (Israel) 3239/02, *Ma'arab v. The IDF Commander in Judea and Samaria*, 57(2) PD 349 (*Ma'arab*). An English translation is available online at http://elyon1.court.gov.il/files_eng/02/390/032/A04/02032390.a04.pdf (last accessed 23 July 2015).

before a judge or another officer authorized to exercise judicial power, played a central role in the HCJ's reasoning. The Court also took note of provisions in the 'Body of Principles for the Protection of All Persons under Any Form of Detention or Imprisonment', ratified by the United Nations General Assembly in 1988, as well as the interpretation adopted by the United Nations Human Rights Committee, and the interpretation of a similar provision in the European Convention on Human Rights (ECHR) adopted in the ECtHR. In addition to these sources, the HCJ cited Articles 43 and 78 of the Fourth Geneva Convention (Article 43 requires that a protected person who has been interned be entitled to have such action reconsidered as soon as possible by an appropriate court or administrative tribunal).[29] Yet, it regarded these articles as applying only to administrative arrest and not to an arrest conducted for the purpose of investigation and possible prosecution, as in this case.

Not only did the HCJ rely on the ICCPR as the main source for its *Ma'arab* ruling but it also addressed the question of its applicability in occupied territories. While it did not engage in an elaborate discussion, the Court did note that the balance between individual liberty and public security must be preserved in arrests conducted for investigation purposes both within and outside the state, and between detainees in areas under belligerent occupation and the occupying state, both in peacetime and in war. The rule in Article 9(1) of the ICCPR thus applies in all these situations.[30]

After expressing an agnostic position on the question for some years,[31] the HCJ once again explicitly cited IHRL as relevant and applicable when it examined the legality of Israel's policy of so-called 'targeted killings', aimed at individuals in the OPT held to be responsible for terrorist acts. When detailing the normative framework relevant to this question, the HCJ noted that the armed conflict between Israel and terrorist groups in the OPT is governed by the law of international armed conflict. IHL, including in this case the law of belligerent occupation, is the *lex specialis* applicable to such a situation. When IHL is 'lacking', noted the HCJ, citing the *Wall* and *Armed Conflict* decisions of the ICJ, it can be complemented by IHRL.[32] The HCJ did not elaborate on the question of when IHL would be considered 'lacking' in such a way as to warrant turning to IHRL. Throughout the case, however, in addition to its strong reliance on IHL, it did make some determinations echoing IHRL norms while citing decisions of the ECtHR, as discussed later.

Today, human rights analysis plays an important role in the HCJ's judicial review of the situation in the OPT. The HCJ may variously rely for its analysis on specific treaty provisions, especially the ICCPR, or on the military commander's

[29] Ibid., paras 19–36. [30] Ibid., para. 19. [31] Gross, *supra* note 2, at 9–13.

[32] High Court of Justice (Israel) 769/02, *The Public Committee Against Torture v. The Government of Israel* (unpublished, 14 December 2006) (*Public Committee Against Torture*), at para. 18. An English translation is available online at http://elyon1.court.gov.il/files_eng/02/690/007/a34/02007690.a34.pdf (last accessed 23 July 2015).

general obligation to respect human rights. Especially when dealing with the rights of Israelis, Israeli Basic Laws also play a role, though that role differs according to the nature of the case, which fall into three broad categories: (a) cases dealing with conflicting rights of Palestinians and Israelis; (b) cases involving Palestinians' rights to due process; and (c) other cases involving the rights of Palestinians vis-à-vis the military government, where the HCJ has invoked human rights norms.

A. Cases Dealing with Conflicting Rights of Palestinians and Israelis

This group of cases best illustrates the argument regarding the failure of human rights norms formulated in this chapter. A typical case is *Hass*,[33] where the HCJ dealt with a petition challenging the Israeli army's land seizures and the destruction of several structures in Hebron for the purpose of widening the road that Kiryat Arba's Jewish settlers use in order to access the Cave of the Patriarchs in Hebron. The military commander decided on the seizure after several soldiers were killed in a number of attacks against the settlers and against members of the security forces guarding them. After the petition was submitted and after the HCJ had asked the military commander to examine alternative options for achieving its security goals, the army revised its original plan, reducing the number of buildings to be demolished and making other changes as well.[34] Nevertheless, since the army insisted on the need to seize and destroy structures, the decision to carry out these measures remained pending before the HCJ.

Hass in many ways illustrates the legal issues at stake in the occupation. The HCJ noted that the houses that were to be destroyed by the army were 'deserted', a fact that supposedly alleviates the gravity of the violation of rights. For their part, the petitioners argued that the purported security reasons were a cover for a political motive: creating territorial continuity between Kiryat Arba and Hebron to enable an eventual expansion of Jewish settlement in the area. They also challenged the army's security arguments by pointing out that the area in question had already been declared a closed military zone and had been abandoned by its residents,[35] possibly explaining why the buildings in question had been deserted.

The petitioners' arguments rested both on applicable norms of IHL (The Hague Convention on the Law and Customs of War 1907, and the Fourth Geneva Convention Relative to the Protection of Civilian Persons in Time of War 1949) and on rights guaranteed within Israeli constitutional law.[36] The HCJ examined the issue on the basis of these sources, following its previous determination that the military commander's actions are subject not only to the rules of international law but also to Israeli public law, by which he is bound as an agent of the Israeli

[33] High Court of Justice (Israel) 10356/02, *Hass v. Commander of the IDF forces in the West Bank*, 58(3) PD 443 (*Hass*). An English translation is available online at http://elyon1.court.gov.il/files_eng/02/970/104/r15/02104970.r15.pdf (last accessed 23 July 2015).

[34] Ibid., at para. 5. [35] Ibid., at para. 3. [36] Ibid.

government.[37] It determined that the Hague Convention authorizes the military commander to act both to guarantee the legitimate security interest of the holder of the territory and to secure the needs of the local population in an area under belligerent occupation. 'The local population for this purpose', held the HCJ, 'includes the Arab and the Israeli residents as one'. The first of these needs is military and the second is civil–humanitarian. The HCJ held that in the context of civil–humanitarian needs, the military commander is in charge of maintaining the residents' rights, and especially their constitutional human rights. 'The concern for human rights is thus in the center of the humanitarian considerations that the commander must weigh, in accordance with Regulation 43 of the Hague Convention.'[38] More specifically, the HCJ cited to the rules of international law which prohibit the seizure or destruction of civilian property unless 'imperatively demanded by the necessities of war'[39] or 'rendered absolutely necessary by military operations'.[40] The HCJ noted that any violation of civilian property thus needs to balance military needs against damage to the property owner. It further noted that, in addition to the rules of international law, the Israeli law binding on the military commander requires him not to violate the property of residents in the area unless for a purpose within his authority and as required by critical necessity. Both according to international law and to Israeli public law, such authority must be exercised for a proper purpose, in reasonableness and proportionality, while carefully weighing the necessity of the purpose to be attained and the nature and dimension of the violation involved.[41]

The HCJ determined that the security arguments adduced by the military commander had not been successfully refuted by the petitioners, and proceeded to examine the balance he had struck between the exercise of the Jewish settlers' right to pray in a holy place in relative security and the private property rights of the Palestinian residents. Disregarding the question of the legality of the settlers' residence, which the HCJ said was not before it, it held that the very fact of their residence gives rise to the military commander's duty to maintain their security and their human rights, as part of the humanitarian dimension of a military force in a belligerent occupation. This includes all aspects of life, including the constitutional human rights of the area's residents, both Jews and Arabs. These rights include freedom of movement, freedom of religion and property rights. Sometimes the protection will require balancing conflicting human rights.[42] Given the strong constitutional status of freedom of movement and of the right to approach holy places, which in this case are connected as they pertain to the right of Jewish

[37] Ibid., at para. 8. [38] Ibid.

[39] Art. 23(g) of the Hague Regulations, *supra* note 9. The HCJ also cited Art. 52 of the Hague Regulations, which determines that requisition in kind and services shall not be demanded from municipalities or inhabitants except for the needs of the army of occupation.

[40] Art. 53 of the Fourth Geneva Convention, *supra* note 7. This provision deals only with destruction and not with seizure as such.

[41] *Hass*, *supra* note 33, at para. 9. [42] Ibid., at para. 14.

worshippers to reach the Cave of the Patriarchs on the Jewish Sabbath and on Jewish holidays, violating the right to private property is reasonable and proportional. This conclusion was supported by the determination that if the military commander had refrained from violating property rights he would have precluded the adoption of essential security measures for the worshippers' protection and, possibly, would also have denied their rights to pray in the Cave on the Jewish Sabbath and on Jewish holidays, i.e., their freedom of religion and movement.[43]

Although *Hass* did not rely on IHRL as such, it adduced three sources for inserting rights analysis into the question at stake: (i) a consideration of the duty to maintain human rights as part of the military commander's humanitarian duties under Article 43; (ii) a commitment on the part of the military commander as an agent of the Israeli government who is bound by Israeli public law; (iii) 'constitutional rights' proclaimed without any specific elaboration of their source, but probably as a derivative of the previous source, i.e., the application of the constitutional rights recognized in Israeli constitutional law. In any event, this decision is part of the 'righting' of the law of occupation and the blending of IHL and human rights law. Consider first that the HCJ, early in the judgment, pointed to the Hague Regulations and the Fourth Geneva Convention and noted that they prohibit, respectively, the destruction of civil property unless it is 'imperatively demanded by the necessities of war' or 'absolutely necessary for military operations'. Those are IHL norms which, in this case, include a strong, albeit not absolute, prohibition on such destruction. Without dismissing the importance of the settlers' religious rights, it is doubtful that securing their access to the Cave of the Patriarchs falls within the category of imperative military necessity.

However, the HCJ transplants[44] human rights norms onto these IHL norms, that purportedly apply in times of occupation. After implying that violating property rights is possible for the proper protection of the human rights of others *as well*, the HCJ shifts the terms of the discourse. From a balance between security and the rights of the local population, as envisaged in IHL (*vertical balancing*), the HCJ moves to a *horizontal balancing* between the rights of different individuals, whose rights, it holds, are arguably supposed to be protected by the military commander under his obligations deriving from Article 43. This form of analysis makes this an abstract rights case, stripped from the occupation context. The result of this balancing act is almost predetermined: freedom of religion and personal security, which is part of 'security' as an overarching concept, must trump the 'poor relation' in this analysis—the right to private property which, whilst the HCJ stops short of stating so explicitly, may be lower in the hierarchy of rights. Framing the damage caused to the Palestinian residents of Hebron as one of damage to private property may, in this and in many other cases, diminish the meaning of the military commander's acts and their possible effects on the residents' lives and security.

[43] Ibid., at paras 15–21.

[44] The term is borrowed from A. Watson, *Legal Transplants: An Approach to Comparative Law* (1993).

Whatever the case, this supposed balancing act is in fact an *imbalance*, since it places the burden of the settlers' security on the people living under occupation, it conceptualizes the need for balance between the rights involved as if they were the rights of equal parties, and it allocates the rights to be balanced in a way that predetermines the results.[45]

Scrutinizing the military commander's decisions in terms of reasonableness and proportionality illustrates this imbalance even further: in situations of belligerent occupation, and specifically in the context of this occupation, we may assume that the military commander will give preference to the interests of his fellow citizens. Practice has shown that the Israeli army destroys Palestinian property for the sake of the settlers' security and not vice-versa: the settlers' interests are conceived as 'security' interests, justifying the limitation of Palestinians' rights. Settlers' rights are interchangeably discussed as their human rights and as the military commander's supposedly legitimate security considerations. This framing of the question makes the answer predictable. Instead of showing suspicion toward the military commander's decisions, the HCJ legitimizes them under a doctrine that merges administrative and international law transplanted from other contexts.

Proportionality is a valuable tool because it allows us to weigh conflicting considerations through a means-ends test. It is a consideration to be used with caution, however, because it shifts the human rights discourse to an analysis consistently focused on their infringement and on the extent to which violations are still 'proportional'. The use of this administrative principle as part of a rights analysis in the context of a military occupation is particularly problematic. When used within human rights analysis to review administrative action, the principle of proportionality assumes the existence of an accountable democratic government committed to the collective good of its citizens, occasionally forced to violate the rights of the whole or part of the population in order to attain legitimate ends. The benefits to the population are then weighed against the infringement of their rights, the point being that the benefits accrue to a collective, of which the population whose rights were violated is a part. But it is questionable whether this logic can apply when the government is a military occupation promoting the collective security interests of its *own* citizens while violating the rights of the people of the territory it occupies. Even more questionable is the applicability of this principle to Israel's military occupation. The establishment of settlements that channelled land, water and rule of law resources to their own inhabitants at the expense and

[45] On the (im)balance of security see Gross, *The Writing on the Wall, supra* note 26, at ch. 5; Ben-Naftali, Gross and Michaeli, 'Illegal Occupation: Framing the Occupied Palestinian Territory', 24 *Berkeley Journal of International Law* (2005) 551, at 590–592, 603–605. In any balancing attempt, much depends on the choices made in the balancing process. As Marc Tushnet has shown, balancing is responsible for much of the indeterminacy of rights analysis, as the one making the balance can choose the necessary measure of value, the necessary consequences and the necessary level of generality, and thus deny the claim that a right has been violated. A court can also choose any of many generally protected interests and balance them as it chooses: see Tushnet, 'An Essay on Rights', 62 *Texas Law Review* (1984) 1363, at 1371–1375.

dispossession of the Palestinian residents[46] makes the use of a proportionality perspective a dubious proposition indeed.

The notion of proportionality in administrative law developed as part of the idea of a free democracy, where the state's very attempt to maximize freedom can have the opposite effect of minimizing the freedom of the citizens. In this equation, the rule of proportionality provides that one should only interfere with individual rights if and insofar as it is necessary to satisfy a compelling public interest.[47] Transplanting this notion to the context of the occupation as a tool for the horizontal balance of rights is thus improper, especially given the features of this occupation. A proper proportionality analysis in this case would have been limited to the question of whether the military commander weighed the balance between legitimate security needs within IHL and the rights of the local population, as envisaged in the relevant provisions of The Hague and Geneva Conventions. Proportionality is a limiting element only with respect to harm that is otherwise permitted. The joint application of IHL and IHRL thus mixes, as noted, the two different contexts of proportionality: that of human rights law—which normally exists in the context of an accountable democracy and assesses the effect on an individual of a government action carried out in pursuit of a general public interest; and that of humanitarian law—where proportionality analysis focuses on the collateral effect of an attack on a legitimate target in pursuit of military necessity.

The horizontal balance assumed in *Hass* is removed not only from the situation of occupation but also from the structural inequality between the two populations,[48] and is particularly blind to the illegality of the settlements. Although the HCJ holds that the question of the settlements' legality is irrelevant, this determination fails to note that the entire structure developed by the Court, whereby the military commander's duties include protection of the settlers' rights (in this case at the expense of the local residents' rights), upends the meaning of Article 43 upon which it relies. The rationale of Article 43 is that the military commander should preserve existing laws 'unless absolutely prevented', that his duty is of temporary duration, and that his role is to manage the territory in a manner that protects civil life, exercising authority as a trustee of the sovereign.[49] Article 43, then, does not confer sovereign powers on the occupant; rather, it limits the occupant's authority to the maintenance of public order and civil life.[50] A reading of Article 43 that allows limitation of the

[46] On these policies as creating a breach of trust by the military commander, see Ben-Naftali, Gross and Michaeli, *supra* note 45, at 579–592.

[47] N. Emiliou, *The Principle of Proportionality in European Law: A Comparative Study* (1996), at 40–43. Emiliou points to this rationale for proportionality which was developed in German public law. On proportionality as a tool for judicial review in constitutional democracies—a form of judicial review that relies on this principle to tell judges when the *elected representatives* of the people and their officials are acting properly and when they are not, see D.M. Beatty, *The Ultimate Rule of Law* (2004), at 159–161.

[48] On the different legal regimes that apply to the two populations, see Ben-Naftali, Gross and Michaeli, *supra* note 45, at 583–588.

[49] Under contemporary international law, and in view of the principle of self-determination, sovereignty is vested in the population under occupation. Ibid., at 554.

[50] Ibid., at 570–575.

rights of the occupied for the sake of the settlers' rights takes the law of occupation intended to prevent the military commander from changing the nature of the territory under occupation and turns it on its head. The settlements were built in violation of Article 49(6) of the Fourth Geneva Convention, which prohibits occupants from transferring part of their own civilian population into the territory under occupation.[51] The military commander was the one who formally erected the settlements and, as the HCJ held in a ruling on the Gaza withdrawal,[52] he has the authority to dismantle them. In this context, note that although the HCJ did not cite IHRL directly in this case, the right to freedom of movement as articulated in Article 12 of the ICCPR is granted to '[e]veryone lawfully within the territory of a State' and applies only 'within that territory'. This definition of the right, had it not been ignored, may have negated its applicability to the settlers in this case,[53] given the actual illegality of the settlements. Thus, even when IHRL specifically restricts the universality of the right, the HCJ chose to ignore this.

A reading of *Hass* thus shows how the HCJ's 'righting' of the case distorts IHL, which prohibits settlement activity as well as the destruction of the local residents' civilian property. IHL prohibits the transfer of civilian population from the occupying country to the territory under occupation and protects the rights of people under occupation, defined as 'protected persons' in the Geneva Convention. Transplanting a rights analysis onto this situation puts the local residents and the settlers who reside in the occupied territory illegally on a supposedly equal, and thus false, par. The HCJ's analysis in this case leaps back and forth between the two branches of the law in a way that ultimately allows a broader violation of the residents' rights than IHL would allow.

Consider now that in the *Armed Activities* judgment the ICJ held that the duty to secure respect for the applicable rules of IHRL as well as IHL was part of Uganda's duty as the occupying power in Ituri, according to Article 43 of the Hague Regulations of 1907.[54] Since IHRL must apply universally, this determination of

[51] For an elaborate discussion of the application of this prohibition to the settlements see ibid., at 581–582.

[52] High Court of Justice (Israel) 1661/05, *Regional Council Gaza Beach v. the Knesset*, 59 (2) PD 481, at paras 78–80.

[53] I am grateful to Ahmed Amara for this point. More generally, Victor Kattan has argued that Israeli settlers cannot invoke human rights law to justify their living in the OPT, based, *inter alia*, on the prohibition on settlements in IHL which is *lex specialis*. See Kattan, 'The Legality of the West Bank Wall: Israel's High Court of Justice v. the International Court of Justice', 40 *Vanderbilt Journal of Transnational Law* (2007) 1425, at 1443–1444. The question remains, however, whether the exclusion suggested by Kattan will be accepted within a human rights discourse built on universality. In any event, it appears to be limited to the right of the settlers to live in the OPT and may still be distinguished from cases pertaining to their right to life, freedom of movement and religion.

[54] See *supra* note 25 and accompanying text. For a critique of this determination, see (Dennis 2007), *supra* note 16, at 493–497. Dennis points to the gap between the ICJ's determination on this issue and the duty of an occupying force under Art. 43 to maintain the law in force. This gap may arise if the territorial sovereign of the occupied territory has not ratified an international human rights treaty prior to the occupation, or if it has not adopted necessary implementing legislation. On the other hand, Grant Harris suggests that the application of IHRL in case of occupation requires occupants to institute a system of government and create institutions that preserve human rights. Thus, according to Harris, modern occupations present the international community with the choice of calling for

the ICJ, 'righting' the law of occupation, may be read as parallel to the position taken by the HCJ in *Hass*. By determining that the military commander's duty is to guarantee the human rights of all the area's residents, the balance struck in IHL is lost.

The protection of human rights for all and the universality of human rights are noble and attractive goals. However, as *Hass* illustrates, the price of attaining them is abstraction and imbalance rather than a balance of rights and, ultimately, a possibly unwarranted consequence: the ICJ's determination serves to justify *greater* restrictions of the rights of people living under occupation.

Theodor Meron has indicated how the human rights doctrine allowed for a flexible definition of 'protected persons' in the jurisprudence of the ICTY.[55] This flexibility is indeed welcome when it allows a transcending of formal tests for the examination of substance. In an occupation context, however, neglecting the 'protected persons' rubric as the central category and instead applying human rights norms universally may mean reducing rather than strengthening the protections envisaged in IHL. The HCJ repeated the rationale of *Hass* in other cases, some not necessarily involving settlers but Israeli citizens in general.[56]

A few significant cases involve the wall built by Israel in the West Bank.[57] In *Mara'abe*[58] the HCJ held that building the wall in the OPT is legal even though its route was established for the protection of settlers living in Israeli settlements in the

observance of the law of occupation, including deference to previous institutions, or of international human rights law through nation building. In his view, the world has opted for the latter option. See Harris, 'The Era of Multilateral Occupation', 24 *Berkeley Journal of International Law* (2006) 1, at 15–20. Similarly, Hamda Zahwai suggests that the application of human rights law by occupying regimes can provide the correct framework for transformative moves by the occupying forces, which will benefit the occupied population. See Zahawi, 'Redefining the Laws of Occupation in the Wake of Operation Iraqi Freedom', 95 *California Law Review* (2007) 2295. On the role of IHRL in cases of 'transformative occupation', see Roberts, 'Transformative Military Occupation: Applying the Laws of War and Human Rights', 100 *AJIL* (2006) 580, at 589–601. On the tension between the limited role of the occupier and the application of human rights, see also Modirzadeh, 'The Dark Side of Convergence: A Pro-Civilian Critique of the Extraterritorial Application of Human Rights in Armed Conflict', 86 *U.S. Naval War College International Law Studies (Blue Book) Series* (2010) 349, at 365–367, 386–387; Lubell, *supra* note 5, at 328–329; Milanovic, *supra* note 1, at 257–259. The different positions on this issue further attest to additional conflicts emerging from the application of human rights law in the context of occupation, beyond those discussed in the text, reflecting the tension between 'preservative' and 'transformative' understandings of belligerent occupation. This issue was addressed in Judge Bonello's powerful concurrence in the ECtHR *Al-Skeini* decision discussed later: See the discussion *infra* in text at notes 157–164. See ECtHR, *Al-Skeini v. United Kingdom*, Appl. no. 55721/07, Judgment of 7 July 2011 (*Al-Skeini*). For a discussion of the issue in the context of the UK judgments in this case, see Wilde, 'Compliance with Human Rights Norms Extraterritorially: "Human Rights Imperalism"?', in L. Boisson de Chazournes and M. Kohen (eds), *International Law and the Quest for its Implementation* (2010) 319; Wilde, 'Complementing Occupation Law? Selective Judicial Treatment of the Suitablity of Human Rights Norms', 42 *Israel Law Review* (2009) 80.

55 Meron, 'The Humanization of Humanitarian Law', 94 *AJIL* (2000) 239, at 256–261.

56 Gross, *supra* note 2, at 20–26.

57 For a detailed discussion see Gross, *supra* note 8.

58 High Court of Justice (Israel) 7957/04, *Mara'abe v. The Prime Minister of Israel*, 60(2) PD 477 (2006) (*Mara'abe*). An English translation is available online at http://elyon1.court.gov.il/files_eng/04/570/079/a14/04079570.a14.pdf (last accessed 23 July 2015).

OPT. The HCJ accepted the petition based on the determination that the violation of Palestinian rights in this case was not proportional. Anchoring its answer in both international and Israeli law, the Court held that, although Israelis living in the occupied area are not 'protected persons' according to the meaning of this term in Article 4 of the Fourth Geneva Convention, the military commander is authorized to protect their lives and defend their safety. The troubling aspect of the *Mara'abe* judgment is that it is not limited to a determination that the military commander is authorized to protect the lives and security of Israeli Jews residing in the West Bank, but rather leaps from the protection of the lives of settlers to the protection of illegal settlements.[59]

The HCJ determination was based upon Article 43, which it read as requiring the military commander to secure the safety of any person present in the territory under belligerent occupation, and also upon the Israeli Basic Law: Human Dignity and Liberty, which the HCJ applied to Israeli settlers. While leaving open the question of the application of IHRL in the OPT, the HCJ held that the settlers' security should be considered by the military commander and could be a factor against which the rights of the local population should be balanced.[60] Thus, while *Mara'abe* frames the question as one of vertical rather than horizontal balancing, i.e., as a balance between the rights of the local population and security needs ascertained by the military commander, the latter are defined in a way that includes the rights of the settlers. This case, then, illustrates the merging of these two forms of analysis.

In many of the wall cases, the HCJ used the normative framework it had set up in *Mara'abe* to rule against Palestinian rights. For example, Palestinian petitioners argued in one case against the construction of a fence and a 'special security zone' around a Jewish settlement in northern Samaria. Building the fence required the seizure of Palestinian agricultural land and the uprooting of olive trees. Based on *Mara'abe*, the HCJ held that the construction of a wall in the occupied territory for the purpose of securing the life and security of Israelis living there was within the military commander's authority. Thus, held the HCJ, the military commander had to take into account security considerations, the rights of the local Palestinian population anchored in IHL, and the human rights of the Israelis living in the area anchored in Israeli law.

This triad of considerations, regularly cited by the HCJ in cases involving the wall, replaces the dual structure (rights of the local population vs security) envisaged in IHL. In this, and in several other cases, the HCJ held that the balance that had been struck was proportionate and rejected the petition. Notably, in some of the other cases, the HCJ cited the rights of the local Palestinian population recognized in international law without limiting their scope to IHL.[61]The sources

[59] See Gross, *supra* note 8. [60] See *Mara'abe, supra* note 58, at paras 25–29.

[61] High Court of Justice (Israel) 11395/05, *Mayor of Sebastia v. State of Israel* (unpublished, 30 May 2006), available in Hebrew online at http://elyon1.court.gov.il/files/05/950/113/A04/05113950.a04.pdf (last accessed 23 July 2015); High Court of Justice (Israel) 426/05, *Bido Village Council v. The Government of Israel* (unpublished, 10 September 2006), available in Hebrew online at http://elyon1.court.gov.il/files/05/260/004/A29/05004260.a29.pdf (last accessed 23 July 2015). In the latter case,

of the rights cited vary, and at times no specific sources were cited, but the structure recurs. The HCJ has repeatedly pointed to the duty of the military commander planning the route of the wall to take into account: (i) military–security considerations; (ii) the rights of Palestinian residents who are 'protected persons'; (iii) the rights of Israelis living in settlements and, as noted in some cases, the rights of Israeli citizens more generally. This balancing structure regularly leads to a rights analysis that enables restrictions of Palestinians' rights.[62]

This discussion shows that, in most cases, the HCJ has held that the balance struck was proportional, and rejected the petition in a way that allowed a restriction of the Palestinians' rights for the purpose of protecting settlers' rights. Cases like *Mara'abe*, where the restrictions on Palestinians were deemed especially extreme, represent the exception. Other than *Mara'abe*, where the effect of the wall on Palestinians was considered particularly severe, the HCJ held in favour of Palestinian petitioners in cases involving this triad of considerations only when it could be proved that the wall had been built for the purpose of settlement expansion, i.e., to protect areas planned for future settlement.

In one illustrative case the HCJ addressed a petition of residents from the Palestinian village of Dir Kadis, whose land had been taken for the planned construction of a segment of the wall built to protect the Jewish settlement of Modi'in Illit. The route of the proposed segment of the wall discussed in this case required the seizure of Palestinian agricultural lands, including private lands, worked by Dir Kadis residents. It also implied the separation of Dir Kadis from other agricultural lands, access to which would now depend on a system of gates and permits. The HCJ was petitioned not only by the Palestinian residents of Dir Kadis but also by real estate companies building in the Modi'in Illit Jewish settlement. These companies, invoking their own property rights, objected to the route and, together with the settlement, called for a return to the route as previously planned. Addressing the proportionality of the wall's route in this area, the HCJ reiterated the triad of considerations it had established in previous case-law—military–security considerations, the benefit to the local population of 'protected persons' under IHL, and the human rights of the Israeli settlers, including their rights to life, dignity, property and privacy. Notably, the list of rights articulated in the Dir Kadis case is not limited to protecting the life and security of settlers as discussed in some of the earlier wall cases. It also includes protection of their property, with the discussion, as in *Mara'abe*, slipping from the protection of the settlers and their rights to the protection of the settlements.[63]

the HCJ anchored in international law Palestinian human rights that are part of this triad, while anchoring settlers' rights in Israeli law. In some cases, however, the HCJ cited both international law and Israeli law as sources for settlers rights. See e.g. High Court of Justice (Israel) 11205/05, *Izriya Village Council v. Government of Israel* (unpublished, 23 May 2006), available in Hebrew online at http://elyon1.court.gov.il/files/05/050/112/A06/05112050.a06.pdf (last accessed 23 July 2015).

[62] See Gross, *supra* note 8.

[63] High Court of Justice (Israel) 2645/04, *Nasser v. The Prime Minister* (unpublished, 25 April 2007), available in Hebrew online at http://elyon1.court.gov.il/files/04/450/026/N54/04026450.n54.pdf (last accessed 23 July 2015).

An exception to the pattern described in this section is a case in which the HCJ accepted a Palestinian petition invoking human rights, where the violation of Palestinian rights had reached an absurd extreme: the Israeli army forbade Palestinians to work their lands in order to protect *them* from settlers' attacks.[64] The Supreme Court described this as a very serious violation of the most basic rights of Palestinians in the OPT,[65]and considered that this policy violated notions of justice.[66] It held that this policy was illegal, citing the rights to freedom of movement and property protected in both Israeli and international law.[67] This part of the HCJ decision invoked human rights law, but did not involve any clash between the Palestinians' and the settlers' rights. In the same case, however, the HCJ upheld a decision to prevent Palestinians from approaching agricultural lands when the purpose of this measure was to protect settlers living in adjoining Jewish settlements. Although the HCJ emphasized the need to minimize reliance on this policy, it still allowed the rights of Palestinians to be limited in order to protect settlers,[68] addressing the matter interchangeably as a security issue and as a question bearing on the settlers' rights. This decision points to a blurring of the human rights and security discourses, which characterizes the current international discourse: like humanitarianism, human rights arguments often overlap rather than challenge security arguments.

The problems identified in cases such as *Hass* date back to earlier determinations by the HCJ regarding the military occupier's duties toward settlers.[69] However, with the 'righting' of the law of occupation as shown, this determination has been expanded to include a duty to protect the human rights of the entire population of the occupied territory, including the settlers. The convergence also frustrates the expectation that incorporating a human rights analysis into the equation will ensure the local Palestinian population better protection. The introduction of IHRL may maintain the existing (im)balance of security, whereby the rights of settlers, conceived as security, usually trump the rights of the local population. The new framing of those conflicts in human rights terms may turn IHRL into the emperor's new clothes of the law of occupation.

B. Cases Involving Palestinians' Rights to Due Process

Contrary to the cases discussed in the previous section, IHRL norms did play a role in expanding the rights of the local population in one significant case. As mentioned, *Ma'arab* is the HCJ case regarding the OPT which relies most extensively, expressly, and directly on IHRL, with a positive determination regarding its application in the context of occupation. The HCJ found that the provisions

[64] High Court of Justice (Israel) 9593/04, *Rashad Murar, Head of the Yanun Village Council v. IDF Commander in Judea and Samaria* (unpublished, 26 June 2006) , available in Hebrew online at http://elyon1.court.gov.il/files/04/930/095/N21/04095930.n21.htm (last accessed 23 July 2015).

[65] Ibid., at para. 11.

[66] Ibid., at para. 25.

[67] Ibid., at paras 14, 24–28.

[68] Ibid., at para. 21.

[69] Gross, *supra* note 2, at 25–26.

allowing the arrest of Palestinians for 12 or 18 days prior to bringing them before a judicial authority violate international law, and especially the ICCPR.[70] This case is notable for the HCJ's rather rare intervention in decisions of the military commander but, like the cases discussed in the previous section, it continues a pattern that had existed before the 'righting' of the law of occupation: the HCJ's infrequent intervention in decisions concerning the OPT have usually been restricted to issues of procedural rights and due process.[71] Hence, although the turn to IHRL in *Ma'arab* can be viewed as a significant expansion of the sources for Palestinians' rights, it should be read within the HCJ's general willingness to intervene in matters of this kind.

Clearly, the person's liberty and the prevention of prolonged non-supervised detention are important human rights issues, but all that the HCJ required in this case was the preservation of due process, ensuring that a judicial authority decide on the matter of the arrest.[72] The mere fact of earlier judicial review might contribute to the protection of liberty but the question of whether, as required in this decision, earlier scrutiny of arrests by military judges increases individual liberty or gives due process approval to extensive arrests by the Israeli army remains open. Other cases where the HCJ turned to IHRL in a way that contributed to improved conditions in detention facilities established by the Israeli army may also be read as part of the HCJ's tendency to be more receptive to petitions of OPT Palestinians that deal with procedural matters and due process rights.[73]

The cases discussed in this section do not involve limiting the rights of Palestinians for the sake of protecting the rights of Israelis, be they settlers or others. We can then hypothesize that in such cases the 'righting' of the law of occupation may not have the detrimental effect found in cases discussed in the previous section. When evaluating the application of IHRL in a situation of occupation, this distinction concerning its possible effects should be borne in mind.

C. Other Cases Involving Palestinians' Rights vis-à-vis the Military Government

Most of the cases in which the HCJ turns to IHRL or to a more general rights analysis when dealing with the OPT were covered in the two previous categories. The HCJ, however, has occasionally invoked human rights in other contexts without specifically relying on IHRL. Although these cases are rare and drawing general conclusions from them may be problematic, they do deserve a brief

70 See *supra* notes 28–30 and accompanying text.

71 See Shamir, 'Landmark Cases and the Reproduction of Legitimacy', 24 *Law & Society Review* (1990) 781.

72 Compare with decisions in the context of home demolitions, where the HCJ was willing to intervene on the subject of giving a right to appeal to people whose homes were about to be demolished: High Court of Justice (Israel) 358/88, *ACRI v. Central Command*, 43(2) PD 529. Concerning home demolitions per se, however, the HCJ usually declined to intervene.

73 For a discussion of these cases see Gross, *supra* note 2, at 26–27.

mention in order to illustrate other forms that the 'righting' of the law of occupation may take.

The right to equality was cited, without any specific source,[74] in a case in which the HCJ mandated the Israeli Ministry of Defence to issue gas masks to Palestinians living in the OPT, after the ministry had already issued such masks to Israelis residing there before the first Iraq war.[75] Another instance of mentioning rights without a specific source is the HCJ's reliance on the right to freedom of association when it accepted a petition against regulations issued by the Israeli army on the establishment of a lawyers' association in the OPT.[76] In yet another case, the HCJ considered—and upheld—a decision to refuse the registration of a lawyer in the OPT because he had previously been convicted in a military court. The HCJ invoked the right to freedom of occupation, which it said is protected both by Israeli case-law and by the Basic Law: Freedom of Occupation. The HCJ again noted in this judgment that, although Israeli law did not apply in the OPT, the military commander's activities were reviewed according to this law.[77]

A case that stands out as unique concerns so-called 'targeted killings'.[78] As noted, the HCJ held in this case that, if IHL was found 'lacking', it could be complemented by IHRL. Even though the HCJ did not explicitly shift its discussion to IHRL, it did make some determinations that resonate with IHRL norms while citing to ECtHR decisions. After determining that OPT civilians who participate directly in hostilities might be targeted, it set four limitations on such actions: (i) possessing well-grounded information provided by the state regarding the identity and activity of the civilian allegedly taking part in the hostilities; (ii) refraining from attacks on civilians if less harmful means, such as arrest, interrogation and trial can be used; (iii) conducting a thorough and independent investigation regarding the attack; (iv) desisting from harming combatants and terrorists if the expected damage to nearby innocent civilians is disproportionate to the military advantage anticipated from harming the combatants and terrorists.[79] Marko Milanovic points out that only proportionality, the last of these limitations, is anchored in IHL. The other three draw solely on IHRL, as evident from the HCJ's citation to cases on related matters decided by the ECtHR. In this reading, then, human rights law was used to restrict the application of humanitarian norms, albeit IHL norms that allow killing in this case, thus expanding the protection of the occupied population. Milanovic suggests that the HCJ used human rights to impose these obligations because of the

[74] The announcement of rights without a textual source is not strange to the Israeli constitutional system, which until 1992 had developed without constitutional texts on human rights and, even today, includes only two partial and limited Basic Laws on human rights. Much of Israel's rights law, then, developed through case-law. See Gross, 'The Politics of Rights in Israeli Constitutional Law', 3 *Israel Studies* (1998) 80; Barak-Erez, 'From an Unwritten to a Written Constitution: The Israeli Challenge in American Perspective', 26 *Columbia Human Rights Law Review* (1995) 309.

[75] High Court of Justice (Israel) 168/91, *Miladi Morcus v. Minister of Defence*, 45(1) PD 467.

[76] High Court of Justice (Israel) 507/85, *Bahig Tamimi v. Minister of Defence*, 41(4) PD 57.

[77] High Court of Justice (Israel) 3940/92, *Ghasan Mohamed Hasin Gerar v. Military Commander for Judea and Samaria*, 47(3) PD 298, at para. 5.

[78] See *Public Committee Against Torture*, *supra* note 32.

[79] Ibid., at para. 40.

nature of the situation as one of prolonged occupation.[80] This case may thus be an exception to others discussed in this chapter, where applying IHRL expanded protection rather than restricting it. This unique decision results from the HCJ's choice to regard individuals who would otherwise be considered protected persons living under occupation as though they were involved in the armed conflict. The HCJ thereby turned the norms of international armed conflict into norms which allowed killings under certain circumstances relevant to the relationship between an occupying army and an occupied population, which is normally governed by the law of occupation and therefore precludes extra-judicial killings. The protection of human life could be expanded here through human rights law because the case is not really about occupation law, which is at the focus of the problems I identify throughout this chapter, but about the part of IHL that deals with the management of armed conflict, i.e., *jus in bello*. Indeed, given that *jus in bello* does not prohibit the taking of human life to the same extent as human rights law, human rights law may serve in this part of the law to expand rather than narrow protection. In this case, then, achieving protection through human rights law is part of a trade-off—in exchange for a general permission to lift protection from protected persons, the focus of the discussion shifts from the laws of occupation to the laws of armed conflict.

4. Human Rights and Occupation in the Case-law of the European Court of Human Rights

The previous section shows that introducing human rights analysis into OPT cases does not lead to a jurisprudence that ensures greater protection to people living under occupation but, often, legitimizes the violation of their rights, invoking the human rights of Israelis, be they settlers or Israeli citizens in general.

So far, the analysis has been limited to HCJ decisions. The application of IHRL to situations of occupation in general and to the Israeli occupation of the OPT in particular might have arguably been more effective if enforced by international courts and treaty bodies. The failures of the HCJ might have been avoided without its proclivity to defer to Israeli security forces. This is perhaps a valid point; but note that the implication of 'righting' the law of occupation for the jurisprudence of national courts is a primary concern in legal realist evaluations of this development. Usually, the decisions of local courts are enforced more directly and effectively than those of international courts and treaty bodies. The high level of compliance with the ECtHR's jurisprudence is an exception, but even the ECtHR is claimed to be

80 Milanovic, 'Lessons for Human Rights and Humanitarian Law in the War on Terror: Comparing Hamdan and the Israeli Targeted Killing Case', 89 *IRRC* (2007) 373, at 389–392. See also Milanovic, *supra* note 1, at 254–257; Arai-Takahashi, *supra* note 15, at 439–457.

least effective in situations involving systematic human rights violations,[81] such as occupation or armed conflict.

Should a distinction then be drawn between the practice of domestic and international courts? In the rest of this section, I consider ECtHR jurisprudence on these matters in the contexts of Cyprus and Iraq. In so doing, I try to draw some broader conclusions on the role of human rights when applied in situations of occupation, identifying some potential similarities between the practice of the Israeli HCJ and that of the ECtHR.

A. Cyprus

In *Lozidiou*,[82] the Court held for the Greek–Cypriot applicant, whose rights to home and property had been denied as a result of the occupation of northern Cyprus by Turkey. While referring to the need to re-house displaced Turkish–Cypriot refugees, the ECtHR noted that it had not received an explanation on how this need could justify the complete negation of the applicant's property rights.[83] The ECtHR also refrained from referring to IHL and based its decision entirely on European human rights law.[84] A broader scope of issues concerning northern Cyprus, including the recognition that the rights of Greek Cypriots living in northern Cyprus had been breached, was addressed from a human rights perspective in *Cyprus v. Turkey*.[85] Despite the ECtHR's limited influence in situations of systematic violations, turning to human rights law did help in these cases to address violations resulting from continuing occupation. These cases show how human rights law and its concomitant enforcement mechanisms in particular, which are lacking in IHL, may support the expansion of protection for people living under occupation.

The ECtHR's later case-law on Cyprus, however, reveals the same problems identified in the Israeli cases discussed earlier. In *Demopoulos*,[86] the ECtHR dealt with the exhaustion of domestic remedies, holding that the Immovable Property Commission (IPC) set up in the 'Turkish Republic of northern Cyprus' (TRNC) to adjudicate the property claims of Greek Cypriots amounted to 'domestic remedies'. Greek–Cypriot applicants who claimed that their property rights in the territory controlled by the TRNC had been violated should, therefore, turn to the IPC before petitioning the ECtHR.[87] The programme allowed for restitution in some cases, but only if the properties had not been transferred to a natural or legal person other than

[81] Gross, '"Once More Unto the Breach": The Systematic Failure of Applying the European Convention of Human Rights to Entrenched Emergencies', 23 *Yale Journal of International Law* (1998) 437.

[82] ECtHR, *Lozidiou v. Turkey*, Appl. no. 15318/89, Judgment of 18 December 1996.

[83] Ibid., at para. 64.

[84] For a discussion of the relevance and possible application of IHL to this case see Heintze, *supra* note 17, at 65–70.

[85] ECtHR, *Cyprus v. Turkey*, Appl. no. 25781/94, Judgment of 10 May 2001. See also ECtHR, *Xenides-Arestis v. Turkey*, Appl. no. 46347/99, Judgment of 22 December 2005.

[86] ECtHR, *Demopoulos and Others v. Turkey*, Appl. no. 46113/99, Admissibility Decision of 5 March 2010.

[87] Ibid., paras 18 and 127.

the state, had not been allocated for public interest reasons, and were not located in military areas or installations. Additional restrictions included a requirement that restitution should not endanger national security and public order. The Turkish government noted that a considerable number of land transactions had taken place in the northern area over the years, and the ECHR rights of third parties had to be protected. The law was designed to establish a 'fair balance' between these conflicting rights in a way that was compatible with the Annan Plan—the failed Cyprus peace plan.[88] The IPC Statute further provided that, where property restitution was not possible, compensation or an exchange with equivalent Turkish–Cypriot property in the south could be arranged, as determined by the IPC.[89]

The applicants claimed that, although restitution should be automatic barring material impossibility, the actual return of property under the IPC Statute was likely only in very limited circumstances, because of what they claimed were numerous and broadly framed exceptions.[90] The Cypriot government argued that Turkey, as an invader, could not impose its own procedures for complaints about the occupier's violation of human rights on the people whose land it occupied.[91] The IPC Statute was claimed to be null and void because it was the product of an unlawful legislature.[92]

But the ECtHR, while referring to northern Cyprus as 'under the occupation and the control of the Turkish military forces',[93] rejected these claims. On route to its decision, the ECtHR described the failed Annan peace plan[94] as providing 'for the property rights of Greek Cypriots to be balanced against the rights of those now living in the homes or using the land, some of them Turkish–Cypriot refugees from the south of the island who had lost homes of their own, but many others of them Turkish settlers'.[95] The plan was rejected by a majority of Greek Cypriots and did not pass.[96] The ECtHR also took note of the fact that 35 years had elapsed since the applicants had lost possession of their property in northern Cyprus. The Court stated that generations had passed and the local population had not remained static, with settlers from Turkey arriving in large numbers and a great deal of Greek–Cypriot property changing hands at least once.[97] The ECtHR noted that its own interpretation and application of the ECHR could not be static or blind to concrete factual circumstances.[98] Decades after the loss of possession by the then owners, the ECtHR noted, property had in many cases changed hands, and those who claimed title might never have seen or used the property. To what extent is the notion of legal title and the expectations of enjoying its full benefits actually realistic in such circumstances? Loss claims then become increasingly speculative and hypothetical, said the ECtHR, and the passage of time might empty the holding of title of any practical consequences.[99] The Court held that applicants had not lost their

[88] Ibid., para. 52. [89] Ibid., para. 53. [90] Ibid., para. 59.
[91] Ibid., para. 64. [92] Ibid., para. 65. [93] Ibid., para. 18.
[94] Kofi Annan's Comprehensive Settlement of the Cyprus Problem, described by the ECtHR in *Demopoulos and Others v. Turkey*, *supra* note 86, paras 8–16.
[95] Ibid., para. 10. [96] As discussed by the ECtHR in ibid., para. 9. [97] Ibid., para. 84.
[98] Ibid., para. 86. [99] Ibid., para. 111.

ownership, since military occupation should not be regarded as a form of adverse possession by which title can be legally transferred to the invading power. Yet, the expectation that the ECtHR should or could directly order the Turkish government to ensure that applicants obtain access to and full possession of their properties, irrespective of who is currently living there, or whether the property is in an allegedly militarily sensitive zone, or is used for vital public purposes, is unrealistic.[100] Thirty-five years after the applicants or their predecessors had left the property, the ECtHR asserted, attempting to impose an obligation to effect restitution in all cases, or even in all cases save those in which there is material impossibility, would risk being arbitrary and injudicious.[101] Addressing the argument that this would allow Turkey to benefit from its illegality, the Court held that, from the ECHR perspective, property is a material commodity that can be valued and compensated for in monetary terms. If compensation was paid in accordance with the case-law, no unfair balance could be claimed to prevail between the parties. The ECHR system deals overwhelmingly with individual applications, which concern interferences with individual property rights. These applications, held the ECtHR, cannot be used as a vehicle for the vindication of sovereign rights or of breaches of international law between contracting states.[102]

Demopoulos adopts the pattern found in Israeli cases: a human rights analysis that ignores IHL entirely, abstracts from the context of occupation and looks at the issue as one of individual rights, and specifically at property as a commodity. Had the issue been examined from an IHL perspective, the story would have clearly been different. Despite its declarations, the ECtHR did partly legitimize dispossession in this decision by allowing the settlement of citizens of the occupying country in ways that undermine the law of occupation. The illegality of this practice under IHL (specifically Article 49(6) of the Fourth Geneva Convention) was neither mentioned nor considered by the ECtHR. Other than referring to the territory as occupied and, moreover, under illegal occupation, the ECtHR never really applied the norms of occupation in the case. Quite the opposite, it balanced the claims of Greek Cypriots whose property rights were violated against the rights of Turkish settlers and thus undermined the protections of the law of occupation.

B. Iraq

Issues bearing on the application of human rights in the occupation of Iraq first emerged in domestic courts in the United Kingdom when Iraqi petitioners, suing for actions of UK occupation forces in Iraq, relied on the UK Human Rights Act 1998. These cases raised questions about the extraterritorial application of the Human Rights Act and the ECHR, which the Human Rights Act incorporates. They attest that human rights law can be used to tighten control over occupying forces in ways that could expand accountability. Even if the approach adopted by

[100] Ibid., para. 112. [101] Ibid., para. 116. [102] Ibid., para. 115.

the House of Lords allowed only limited room for such claims, ECtHR decisions significantly widened this option.

In the ECtHR's decision in *Al-Skeini*,[103] citing to the ICJ's *Wall* and *Armed Activities* decisions, the ECtHR considered its position on the application of IHRL in times of occupation.[104] It rejected the narrow interpretation of the UK House of Lords and effectively held that, in their actions in occupied territories, occupying powers are bound by the ECHR. A full discussion of the complex issues involved in the extraterritorial application of the ECHR is beyond the scope of this chapter and touches on a broader matter—the extraterritorial application of human rights treaties.[105] The *Al-Skeini* decision is significant in its holding that, while a state's jurisdictional competence under Article 1 of the ECHR is primarily territorial, some circumstances—state agent authority and control, effective control over an area and action within the ECHR's 'legal space'—give rise to extraterritorial jurisdiction.[106]

Though this holding was made in the context of a regional rather than universal human rights treaty, what matters for our purposes here is that, in implementing these principles, the ECtHR held that Iraq was under occupation at the time relevant to the events discussed in the case.[107] Moreover, it held that the United Kingdom 'exercised authority and control over individuals killed in the course of such security operations, so as to establish a jurisdictional link between the deceased and the United Kingdom for the purposes of Article 1 of the Convention'.[108] Noam Lubell points out that the ECtHR did not rely solely on the 'effective control over an area' test in this case, but included elements of the 'state agent authority' test, in a way that created what he calls a 'badly mixed cocktail'.[109] The issue in *Al-Skeini* was the need to investigate killings by the UK forces, and the ECtHR held that the issue fell under UK jurisdiction as far as the ECHR was concerned. It also stated that Article 2, which guarantees the right to life, had been violated by the lack of effective official investigation into the killings of individual Iraqi civilians as a result of the United Kingdom's use of force in Iraq.[110] *Al-Skeini*, then, is about the right to life and about the duty to carry out an effective and independent investigation into the killings.[111] Yet, although *Al-Skeini* deals with the right to life (an area where, as I will show, human rights law may indeed expand protection over IHL), it can also be read as overlapping with the Israeli cases that had dealt mostly with due process, and where human rights law had expanded protection.

In a second major case, *Al-Jedda*,[112] the ECtHR once again relied on the ICJ's determination in *Armed Activities*, which had held that it was the duty of an occupying power to secure respect for applicable human rights.[113] This decision also found that relevant Security Council resolutions, while authorizing the United Kingdom to take measures to contribute to the maintenance of security and

[103] *Al-Skeini*, *supra* note 54. [104] Ibid., paras 90–91.
[105] See, generally, Milanovic, *supra* note 1. [106] *Al-Skeini*, *supra* note 54, paras 131–138.
[107] Ibid., para. 148. [108] Ibid., para. 149. [109] Lubell, *supra* note 5, at 321.
[110] *Al-Skeini, supra note* 54, para. 163. [111] Ibid., paras 151 and 167.
[112] ECtHR, *Al-Jedda v. the United Kingdom*, Appl. no. 27021/08, Judgment of 7 July 2011.
[113] Ibid., para. 107.

stability in Iraq, did not explicitly or implicitly require the United Kingdom to place an individual considered to be a risk to the security of Iraq into indefinite detention without charge.[114] Accordingly, persons put under such detention could therefore successfully argue that their liberty rights had been violated under Article 5 of the ECHR.[115] The ECtHR held that the detention could be attributed to the United Kingdom and fell within its jurisdiction. It also held that Article 5 had been violated, given that this article does not allow preventive detention without the intention of bringing criminal charges within a reasonable time.[116] The ECtHR considered that the events had taken place after an end to the occupation in Iraq had been declared. Hence, in its examination of this issue it assumed that Security Council Resolution 1546 was meant to maintain the IHL position that had applied previously, even after authority had been transferred from the Coalition Provisional Authority (CPA) to the interim government of Iraq.[117] The Court held that Article 43 of the Hague Regulation does grant an occupier the authority to provide for public order and security, but does not place it under obligation to use internment. Rather, it places a duty on the occupier to secure respect for IHRL, as held in *Armed Activities*.[118] In its judgment, the ECtHR cited provisions in the Fourth Geneva Convention that *allow* occupiers to detain protected persons for imperative reasons of security,[119] but noted that internment should be a measure of last resort.[120] It also found that Article 5(1) of the ECHR had been violated, given that internment for security purposes is not one of the grounds for permissible detention listed in that article.[121] Article 5(1), the Court noted, does not allow preventive detention, barring intent to bring criminal charges within a reasonable time.[122]

This decision, dealing with due process, attests that applying IHRL in occupation may expand the protection of the person's liberty. Yet, it also attests to a neglect of the *lex specialis* doctrine, and arguably points to the limits of human rights law in situations of armed conflict, if applied without regard for IHL. Applying only the criminal model of detention may not fit situations of armed conflict where, in some circumstances, IHL does allow internment of civilians. The use of human rights norms to limit these internments is appropriate, and the experience of Palestinians' administrative detentions by Israel and those of Guantanamo Bay point to the inherent risks of such detentions. The question, however, is whether the ECtHR logic in *Al-Jedda* totally erases the special provisions of IHL allowing preventive detention in some circumstances. While restraining its use as a 'last resort' measure is a positive development, the ECtHR's analysis, holding that no such detention can be allowed according to Article 5(1), seems to be imposing a blanket prohibition on it.[123]

[114] Ibid., para. 109. [115] Ibid., paras 109 and 110.

[116] Ibid., para. 100. [117] Ibid., para. 107. See the discussion in Gross, *supra* note 44, ch. 2.

[118] *Al-Jedda v. the United Kingdom, supra* note 112, para. 107.

[119] Arts 43 and 78 of the Fourth Geneva Convention, cited in ibid., at para. 43.

[120] See *Al-Jedda v. the United Kingdom, supra* note 112, at para. 107.

[121] Ibid., para. 110. [122] Ibid., para. 100.

[123] For a critique see Pejic, '*Al-Jedda* Judgment: The Oversight of International Humanitarian Law', 93 *IRRC* (2011) 837. Pejic points to the way the ECtHR's reasoning may affect the legality not only of the detention of civilians under the Fourth Geneva Convention, but also that of combatants as prisoners of war (POWs) under the Third Geneva Convention. She shows that the implication of the

But in a third case, *Hassan*,[124] the ECtHR interpreted *Al-Jedda* much more narrowly. This case addressed the co-application of IHL and IHRL in a situation that the ECtHR described as one of armed conflict prior to the establishment of an occupation regime.[125] Citing the various determinations of the ICJ on the matter, the ECtHR held that both bodies of law are applicable in times of armed conflict (and not only in times of occupation),[126] but held that important differences of context and purpose prevail between arrests carried out during peacetime and arrests carried out under the Third and Fourth Geneva Conventions. The ECtHR considered that, in *Al-Jedda*, the question was whether the United Kingdom was under an obligation to the UN Security Council to place the applicant in internment and whether this *obligation* took primacy over ECtHR duties. In *Hassan* it then interpreted this ruling in a very limited way, determining that in this latter case no such obligation existed.[127] But a proper interpretation of the ECHR that takes into account other rules of international law, including IHL, would suggest that, in cases of international armed conflicts, where taking prisoners of war (under the Third Geneva Convention) and detaining civilians who pose a threat to security (under the Fourth Geneva Convention) are accepted features of IHL, Article 5 could be interpreted as permitting the exercise of such broad powers.[128] Thus, while holding that Article 5 of the ECHR can be relevant in assessing internments, given that the Convention safeguards continue to apply (even if interpreted in light of the provisions of IHL),[129] the ECtHR upheld the United Kingdom's request to 'disapply' its obligations under Article 5.[130] Given these determinations, the ECtHR held that, regardless of whether the situation in Iraq was characterized as one of occupation or as an active international armed conflict when the detention in question took place, the four Geneva Conventions apply.[131] The detention in question was thus consistent with the powers available to the United Kingdom, not 'arbitrary' under Article 5 of the ECHR[132] and not in violation of the ECHR.[133]

Although *Demopoulos* and *Al-Jedda* are significantly different—the former *undermining* IHL protections against an occupying power and the latter *strengthening* them—common to both is a human rights analysis dismissive of the relevant IHL norms (even though the Court does refer to these norms in *Al-Jedda*, but not

judgment is that states may not detain people during armed conflict without explicit Security Council authorization or a derogation from the ECHR. While I am not sure one should actually read *Al-Jedda* as Pejic suggests (as preventing detention of POWs under the Third Geneva Convention) her analysis indeed points out how human rights law in this case seems to trump IHL. For a discussion of the conflict between IHRL and IHL on the norms on preventive detention, see also Milanovic, *supra* note 1, at 252–254.

124 ECtHR, *Hassan v. United Kingdom*, Appl. no. 29750/09, Judgment of 16 September 2014.

125 Ibid., para. 75.

126 Ibid., para. 37

127 Ibid., para. 99.

128 Ibid., paras 100–104.

129 Ibid., paras 104 and 107.

130 Ibid., para. 99. The ECtHR rejected the position that state parties would have to derogate from Art. 5 under Art. 15 of the ECHR in order to detain persons under the Third and Fourth Geneva Conventions. See also paras 101–103. For a critique of this position, see the partly dissenting opinion by Judge Spano in *Hassan v. United Kingdom*, *supra* note 124, paras 16–17.

131 *Hassan v. United Kingdom*, *supra* note 124, para. 108.

132 Ibid., para. 110.

133 Ibid., para. 111.

in *Demopoulos*). In both these cases, though in diverse ways, ECHR norms as interpreted by the Court trump IHL norms, shifting the balance away from the vertical rights/security balance in IHL to a slightly different human rights analysis. In *Demopoulos*, as in the Israeli cases involving settlers, the shift is to a horizontal balancing between members of different populations in a way that *restricts* the protection of those deprived of their property rights in the occupied territory. In *Al-Jedda*, as in the Israeli due process cases, the vertical balancing remains but human rights norms actually *expand* protection.

The narrow interpretation of *Al-Jedda* in *Hassan*, however, again shifted the balance by making human rights norms subservient to IHL. In his partial dissent in *Hassan*, Judge Spano, who wished to give 'priority' to the ECtHR right, 'accused' the ECtHR majority of attempting to 'reconcile the irreconcilable' and of failing to 'reflect an accurate understanding of the scope and substance of the fundamental right to liberty under the Convention, as reflected in its purpose and its historical origins in the atrocities of the international armed conflicts of the Second World War'.[134]

5. Patterns in the Application of IHRL in Occupation: Vertical vs Horizontal Balancing

The analysis of the case-law of the Israeli HCJ and of the ECtHR has pointed to the emergence of similar patterns: when the cases involve the rights of citizens from the occupying country, applying human rights law may undermine the protection of people living under occupation. In both these contexts, the application of human rights dilutes the protections of property and land rights available in IHL. If applied strictly, IHL could accord more protection vis-à-vis the occupying powers, given that IHL is more restrictive when it comes to the violation of property rights and given its prohibition on settlements. When the cases involved due process rights, however, IHRL accorded more protection, both because the rights of the protected persons were not balanced with the rights of citizens of the occupying country and because human rights law is usually more protective of rights and more restrictive of government action when due process (and specifically detention) is involved. In *Hassan*, however, IHRL's protection was narrowed by the ECtHR's interpretation of the relationship between the two bodies of law as allowing, both in wartime and under occupation, detentions that would not normally be permitted under human rights law.

Another context where human rights law is more protective of rights than IHRL is that relating to the right to life. When dealing with targeted killings, the HCJ relied on human rights norms to place some limits on the power to kill civilians who participate directly in hostilities. Though IHRL was introduced into an IHL context in the targeted killing case, the interplay of IHL and IHRL in the context of

[134] Ibid., para. 19.

the right to life may be viewed as actually diluting prohibitions established in IHRL (as evident in the *Nuclear Weapons* Advisory Opinion). The ICJ determined there that Article 6 of the ICCPR, guaranteeing the right to life and holding that '[n]o one shall be arbitrarily deprived of his life', applied to the question before it, concerning the legality of the threat or use of nuclear weapons. This, it was held, is because the protection provided under the ICCPR does not cease in times of war, unless under the derogation mechanism provided within the ICCPR, from which the right to life is excluded.

The ICJ therefore held:

> In principle, the right not arbitrarily to be deprived of one's life applies also in hostilities. The test of what is an arbitrary deprivation of life, however, then falls to be determined by the applicable *lex specialis*, namely, the law applicable in armed conflict which is designed to regulate the conduct of hostilities. Thus whether a particular loss of life, through the use of a certain weapon in warfare, is to be considered an arbitrary deprivation of life contrary to Article 6 of the Covenant, can only be decided by reference to the law applicable in armed conflict and not deduced from the terms of the Covenant itself.[135]

The ICJ's ultimate conclusion, which was also based on a discussion of IHL, was that international law does not include a general prohibition on the threat or use of nuclear weapons. In this decision, then, which did not deal with occupation but with IHL generally, the merging of the two branches of the law did not serve to expand the protection of individuals by holding that IHL should be read in light of the principle established in Article 6 of the ICCPR, but rather the opposite: the protection of human life in Article 6 was subordinated to the rules of the law of war. The result was an erosion of IHRL protection.[136]

This approach is not the only one possible, and the HCJ's decision in the targeted killing case, as noted, may also be read as one where IHRL was used to expand the protection of human life beyond that ensured in IHL. The question of what is the subordinate set of norms is critical, and a court's choices on how, if at all, to turn to the *lex specialis* doctrine is obviously a determining factor.[137] In the

[135] *Nuclear Weapons*, *supra* note 12, para. 25.

[136] For a critique of the ICJ's position on this point see Gowlland-Debbas, 'The Right to Life and Genocide: The Court and an International Public Policy in International Law', in L. Boisson de Chazournes and P. Sands (eds), *The International Court of Justice and Nuclear Weapons* (1999) 315, at 315–337. Gowlland-Debbas argues that relegating the interpretation of the term arbitrary exclusively to humanitarian law at times of armed conflict is a setback to a tendency that sees human rights law as relevant to the laws of war (see at 330). For further discussion of the interaction of the human right to life and IHL, see Doswald-Beck, 'The Right to Life in Armed Conflict: Does International Humanitarian Law Provide All the Answers?', 88 *IRRC* (2006) 881.

[137] See Droege, 'The Interplay between International Humanitarian Law and International Human Rights Law in Situations of Armed Conflict', 40 *Israel Law Review* (2007) 310, at 337–348. According to Droege, one should aim for complementarity between the two systems and turn to *lex specialis* in cases of conflicts between norms. For a discussion of the *lex specialis* doctrine in this context, see also Krieger, *supra* note 8, at 268–276; Milanovic, *supra* note 1, at 249–252, Dinstein, *supra* note 5, at 85–88. For advocacy of using *lex specialis* on a case by case basis to decide conflicts between bodies of law, see Campanelli, 'The Law of Military Occupation Put to the Test of Human Rights Law', 90 *IRRC* (2008) 653. William Schabas contrasts the *lex specialis* approach of the ICJ with the 'belt and suspenders' approach espoused by the United Nations Human Rights Committee, which makes the

Nuclear Weapons Advisory Opinion, the ICJ subordinated the human right to life to IHL's permission to take human life in war. In this case, then, human rights law imposes a stricter prohibition by requiring absolute necessity as a condition for violating these rights, whereas IHL allows broad violations of the right to life. The implications are a function of a decision on how to co-apply the norms, and on which norms are brought to the foreground and which remain in the background. The ECtHR's *Al-Skeini* decision can also be read from this perspective: although the complaint, as noted, was limited to procedural considerations, the right invoked was the right to life guaranteed in Article 2 of the ECHR. When the ECtHR noted that 'the obligation under Article 2 to safeguard life entails that, even in difficult security conditions, all reasonable steps must be taken to ensure that an effective, independent investigation is conducted into alleged breaches of the right to life',[138] it used human rights to reinforce the right to life even in an extreme situation of hostilities. Contrast this with the question of property discussed earlier, where IHL places a stricter limit on the destruction of civilian property and requires proof of absolute military need, whereas IHRL allows the limitation of this right through balancing and proportionality with less strict restrictions.[139] This contrast may not be merely fortuitous. IHL developed in a war context and therefore assumes that mutual killings are part of the situation within which it operates. Thus, IHRL protections will be stronger with regard to the right to life.

It seems that, generally, IHRL can expand protections in occupation situations when regulating a vertical relationship, such as in the due process cases that do not involve balancing the rights of other persons, unless those rights become subservient to IHL as occurred in *Hassan*. On the other hand, IHRL can narrow the protection of persons when it is applied in horizontal relationships. This conclusion points to the difference between occupier–occupied relationships and citizen–citizen relationships. The former are part of the exceptional situation regulated by IHL, which is predicated on a concrete relationship of hostility between the authorities and the population. The latter is part of a law that is predicated on the civic solidarity between the population and the state.

Some of the problems entailed by the application of IHRL, such as that of abstracting from background conditions, may be true of rights analysis in general.

two systems additive. Schabas argues that both approaches have shortcomings and limitations and, in cases of fundamental incompatibility, they cannot be reconciled. See Schabas, 'Lex Specialis? Belt and Suspenders? The Parallel Application of Human Rights Law, and the Law of Armed Conflict, and the Conundrum of Jus ad Bellum', 40 *Israel Law Review* (2007) 592. For a critique of *lex specialis* in this context as vague and elusive, see Prud'homme, 'Lex Specialis: Oversimplfying a More Complex and Multifaceted Relationsip?', 40 *Israel Law Review* (2007) 356, at 380–383. For a discussion of the rule and its relevance, see Dinstein, *supra* note 5, at 85–88.

[138] *Al-Skeini*, *supra* note 54, para. 164. Similarly, in *Jaloud v. the Netherlands*, Appl. no. 47708/08, Judgment of 20 November 2014, the ECtHR found a violation under Art. 2 of the ECHR, given that an inquiry into the circumstances of an Iraqi citizen who had died while crossing a checkpoint in Iraq had failed to meet the standards required by Art. 2. See ibid., at paras 227–228, this being yet another case where the right to life and due process coalesce. The ECtHR did not consider in this case whether the Netherlands should be viewed as an occupying power in Iraq but noted that, in any event, the incident had taken place under Dutch jurisdiction for ECHR purposes, see paras 140–153.

[139] See *supra* notes 38–45 and the accompanying text.

In an occupation context, however, a tension prevails between the universal aspiration of human rights applying to everyone in all situations, and the fact that human rights discourse is built upon the model of a relationship between an accountable state and its citizens. Gerald Draper points out that society and government–governed relationships collapse in occupation situations, making the attempt to conflate IHL and IHRL intolerable in theory and inadequate in practice, leading to potential harm to both bodies of law.[140] But government–governed relationships exist during occupation as well, although they assume a different nature because the ruled have not given their consent and the ruler is not accountable by democratic means. Transplanting human rights to a situation of occupation may thus blur its inherently undemocratic rights-denying nature, and confer upon it the perceived legitimacy of an accountable regime. In the *Wall* opinion, for instance, when examining the actions of Israel under IHRL, the ICJ turned to the ICESCR's provisions, and stated that rights set out in the Convention should be limited only 'for the purpose of promoting the general welfare in a democratic society',[141] and noted that the restriction of rights enumerated in the Convention resulting from the construction of the wall failed to meet this condition.[142] The inadequacy of the democracy discourse here is telling: merging a democracy discourse into a non-democratic situation characterizes the 'righting' of the law of occupation.[143]

6. Conclusion: 'Human Rights Imperialism'?

The tension between the fear of legitimacy and the utopian wish to extend the entitlements of people living under occupation is at the heart of the dilemma posed by co-application. As shown in this chapter, however, transplanting IHRL to the context of occupation often fails to meet either one of these ends: it does not deliver the utopian aspirations *and* it legitimizes these failures by stamping them with the seal of a human rights analysis.

In his discussion of whether international human rights are 'part of the problem', David Kennedy notes that toting up costs and benefits is not simple, since the

[140] Draper, 'Humanitarian Law and Human Rights', *Acta Juridica* (1979) 193, at 204–206. On the question of whether the absence of a democratic system involving a relationship between 'citizens' and 'government' makes human rights law inappropriate to situations of occupation, see Roberts, 'Prolonged Military Occupation: The Israeli-Occupied Territories Since 1967', 84 *AJIL* (1990) 44, at 72.

[141] Art. 4 of the International Covenant on Economic, Social and Cultural Rights (ICESCR) 1966, 993 UNTS 3.

[142] *Wall, supra* note 10, para. 136.

[143] On the difference between human rights law, developed mostly in democratic states ruled by law as a yardstick for regular government activity, and the application of human rights analysis in the context of armed conflict, see also Krieger, *supra* note 8, at 284–286. On the relevance of the difference between the government agent–citizen relationship anticipated in IHRL on the one hand, and the soldier–enemy civilian relationship anticipated in IHL on the other, and on the difference between a legitimate national government and an occupying power, see Modirzadeh, *supra* note 54, at 362–366. Modirzadeh points out that an occupying power is not supposed to control law-making and infrastructure in ways that facilitate meaningful human rights compliance. See also the discussion in *supra* note 54, on the relation of this issue to the 'transformative occupation' debate.

'human rights' effect is hard to isolate when used alongside other languages. Whatever the assessment of the human rights vocabulary, it must be weighed against the costs and benefits of other emancipatory vocabularies.[144] These observations about international human rights in general are also relevant to my examination of the role of human rights in the context of occupation. Kennedy suggests that human rights can serve as denial, apology, legitimation, normalization and routinization of the very harms they seek to condemn,[145] and this chapter has shown that the occupation context magnifies these risks. Rights can indeed serve as legitimizing tools not only in the context discussed in this chapter but, as shown earlier, human rights within an occupation context may legitimize a situation that represents their very denial.

The study of human rights in occupation situations thus leads to an awareness that their application creates a double bind. Denying the full scope of human rights to people under occupation is another instance of the problematic linkage between rights and the nation-state, a linkage that leaves stateless people 'rightless'.[146] It also undermines the universality of rights idea at the heart of IHRL. The wish to grant the full scope of IHRL to people living under occupation may thus be seen, in Hannah Arendt's terms, as a recognition of the 'right to have rights'.[147] It can be considered an attempt to return the 'rule' (of rights) to the 'exception' (of an occupation situation), saving the people affected from abandonment.[148] The attempt at abandonment is especially apparent in the Israeli position stating that neither IHRL nor the Fourth Geneva Convention, which is the core of IHL, apply *de jure* to the Palestinian residents of the OPT.[149]

Not only have the rule and the exception changed places in the context of the Israeli occupation of the OPT, in the sense that this long-term occupation has become an indefinite situation,[150] but its 'righting' has proved that recognizing the right to have rights may not necessarily alleviate the conditions of people under occupation. This is the double bind apparent here: introducing rights into an occupation situation supposedly rescues the people under occupation from the abandonment of exception. But rights are introduced into this situation with their abstractions and indeterminacy.[151] Moreover, when an exception is no longer an exception,[152] re-introducing

[144] D. Kennedy, *The Dark Side of Virtue: Reassessing International Humanitarianism* (2004), at 5.

[145] Ibid., at 33.

[146] See H. Arendt, *The Origins of Totalitarianism* (1968), at 267–302.

[147] Ibid., at 296–298.

[148] Following Carl Schmitt's discussion of the state of exception, the contemporary discussion of exception as a relation of ban is discussed in detail in the work of Giorgio Agamben. See C. Schmitt, *Political Theology: Four Chapters on the Concept of Sovereignty* (1988); G. Agamben, *Homo Sacer: Sovereign Power and Bare Life* (1999) . On the relation of exception as a relation of abandonment, see ibid., at 28–29. See also G. Agamben, *State of Exception* (2005). Reading a situation of occupation as one of exception or ban does not mean there are no legal rules regulating the lives of people living under occupation. Indeed, there are many such rules. It does imply, however, that human rights rules meant to protect the people from the absolute power of the sovereign (or, in this case, of the occupying military) do not apply. This is the result of the rights–citizenship linkage discussed by Arendt and Agamben.

[149] On the Israeli position, see Ben-Naftali and Shany, *supra* note 4, at 100–101.

[150] Ben-Naftali, Gross and Michaeli, *supra* note 45, at 592–608.

[151] On the indeterminacy of rights, see Tushnet, *supra* note 45, at 1371–1383.

[152] Ben-Naftali, Gross and Michaeli, *supra* note 45.

rights into the occupation makes them part of the occupation structure and its regulation. Regardless of whether we accept Giorgio Agamben's broader argument about the state of exception having become the rule in our times, the convergence of IHL and IHRL may be seen as a blending, if not a reversal, of the purported exception and the rule. Indeed, the merging of IHL and IHRL into what she calls the 'new humanitarianism' is, in Ruti Teitel's words, 'the rule of law for contemporary political circumstances of heightened political disorder'.[153]

Reversing the rule–exception relationship, however, may operate as a legitimizing device that allows discussion of specific human rights violations invoking security considerations or the rights of others as if they were the exception, thus blurring a reality in which violations have become the rule.[154] In the Israeli context it is questionable how rights analysis is at all possible, given the structural inequality between Jewish settlers and Palestinians.

My position is that people living under occupation should be entitled to the full scope of rights enumerated in international law. I do not insist on the exclusivity of IHL, nor do I argue that introducing IHRL into the context of occupation will necessarily be detrimental to the rights those living under occupation. I am not staking an essentialist argument. Courts could have ruled differently on some of the cases discussed, and it could be argued that in some cases they were simply wrong and issued decisions that are bad law. This argument is particularly relevant concerning some of the HCJ's decisions where, had the Court taken the *lex specialis* doctrine seriously and given preference to restrictions embedded in IHL, it might have reached different results.[155] My analysis, however, is a legal realist one, looking at the consequences of norms rather than at their internal logic. Logically, it seems right that IHRL should also apply in an occupation context but, as Oliver Wendell Holmes teaches, the life of the law has not been logic but rather experience.[156] The purpose of my analysis is to show the risks and double bind entailed in the transplanting of a human rights analysis to a situation of belligerent occupation, pointing out that this analysis might obscure rather than challenge the violation of rights inherent in the structure of the occupation, and allow for more rather than fewer restrictions of the rights of people living under occupation.

Further questions remain about the scope of rights that an occupier can in fact guarantee. This issue was addressed in Judge Bonello's concurring opinion in the ECtHR *Al-Skeini* judgment, where he suggested that a state should be obliged to ensure the observance of all those human rights which *it is in a position to ensure*:

It is quite possible to envisage situations in which a Contracting State, in its role as an occupying power, has well within its authority the power not to commit torture or extra-judicial killings, to punish those who commit them and to compensate the victims—but at

[153] Teitel, 'Humanity's Law: Rule of Law for the New Global Politics', 35 *Cornell International Law Journal* (2002) 359, at 371.

[154] Ben-Naftali, Gross and Michaeli, *supra* note 45, at 607–608.

[155] But see the critique of this doctrine in this context as vague and elusive given, *inter alia*, the difficulty of identifying which norm is 'general' and which is 'specific'. Prud'homme, *supra* note 137.

[156] O. Wendell Holmes Jr., *The Common Law* (1881), at 1.

the same time that Contracting State does not have the extent of authority and control required to ensure to all persons the right to education or the right to free and fair elections.[157]

Some may argue for the need to develop workable modalities for the co-application of IHL and IHRL in occupation situations, given the difficulties inherent in this association. Lubell points to the limits of the 'all or nothing' approach that the ECtHR seems to have endorsed in *Al-Skeini*. Given that the occupying power has control and responsibility for the territory, practical and legal impossibilities may play a role in the limitation of its power to implement human rights obligations in the same manner that it does domestically.[158] He suggests that, although the starting assumption may presuppose the full range of obligations, the circumstances should be considered in context for each case. Territorial control, including occupation, does trigger the applicability of the full range of human rights obligations that the state is committed to uphold. The substantive elements of the obligation and the assessment of whether a violation has occurred, however, must be determined in light of the factual and legal context, including questions of logistical ability to act or restrictions on the occupying power in the occupation regime.[159] In Lubell's view, the 'mode of application' question should therefore be separated from that of 'applicability'.[160]

The courts, some may suggest, should apply the most protective norm rather than using the *lex specialis* doctrine.[161] But this again begs the question: most protective of whom? A human rights analysis that considers all persons on a universal basis does not leave room for applying the norm that is most protective of the people living under occupation.

[157] *Al-Skeini*, *supra* note 54, Concurring Opinion of Judge Bonello, para. 32.

[158] Lubell, *supra* note 5, at 322.

[159] Ibid., at 323–324. See also Vite, 'The Interrelation of the Law of Occupation and Economic, Social and Cultural Rights: The Examples of Food, Health and Property', 90 *IRRC* (2008) 629. For a discussion of the human rights duties of occupiers in the context of social economic rights, see also den Heijer and Lawson, 'Extraterritorial Human Rights and the Concept of "Jurisdiction"', in M. Langford, W. Vandenhole, M. Scheinin and W. van Genugten (eds), *Global Justice, State Duties: The Extraterritorial Scope of Economic, Social and Cultural Rights in International Law* (2012) 153, at 168–172; Langford, Coomans and Gomez Isa, 'Extraterritorial Duties in International Law', in ibid., 51, at 97–113.

[160] Lubell, *supra* note 5, at 324.

[161] For an argument of the first type, see Ben-Naftali, 'The Extraterritorial Application of Human Rights to Occupied Territories', 100 *ASIL Proceedings* (2006) 90. See also Lubell's elaboration of the problems entailed by the application of human rights law to armed conflict and his discussion of the need to address these challenges. See Lubell, *supra* note 8. See also Prud'homme's suggestion of replacing the *lex specialis* doctrine, which she finds vague and elusive, with multiple pre-determined criteria using the principle of harmonization, while admitting there will never be a 'perfect theoretical model'. Prud'homme, *supra* note 137, at 386–395. For an example concerning a specific right, see Jonathan Horowitz's discussion of the right to education in occupied territories, where he suggests 'injecting' standards of the international human right to education into the provisions on the right to education in occupation law. Horowitz, 'The Right to Education in Occupied Territories: Making More Room for Human Rights in Occupation Law', 7 *Yearbook of International Humanitarian Law* (2004) 233. For a critique of the dismissal of dilemmas on the application of human rights in situations of armed conflict as pointing to underlying problems in the debate, and for a discussion of the lack of rigor and clarity in the argument for extra-territorial application of human rights, see Modirzadeh, *supra* note 54, at 368–370, 386–387. Modirzadeh also points to problems in the application of *lex specialis* in this context (at 379–380).

Hence, although the difficulties discussed in this chapter could perhaps have been avoided or narrowed, my position is that the double-edged nature of rights[162] in general, and their transplantation to the occupation context in particular, threaten such a project with the risk of constant frustration. These concerns should be kept in mind, given the hopes placed on human rights law as part of the justification for a 'transformative occupation' that will lead to greater democracy.[163] Judge Bonello's concurrence in the ECtHR's *Al-Skeini* decision included a compelling statement critical of the United Kingdom's argument that 'exporting' the ECHR to Iraq would have amounted to 'human rights imperialism'. Instead he argues that it 'ill behoves a state that imposed its military imperialism over another sovereign State ... to resent the charge of having exported human rights imperialism to the vanquished enemy'.[164] However, as this chapter has shown, the victory of human rights in this context may be a Pyrrhic victory: the discussion pointed out how the often abstract nature of rights analysis may dilute the protections of the law of occupation. Perhaps a judicial approach more sensitive to the protective purposes of IHL and IHRL and to the *lex specialis* doctrine may ensure different results. However, given that the problems entailed are a by-product of the rights and occupation structures per se as well as of their intersection, I question the possibility of a modality able to fully elude the risks of transplanting IHRL to this context.

[162] On rights as a double-edge sword see Horwitz, 'Rights', 23 *Harvard Civil Rights–Civil Liberties Law Review* (1988) 393.

[163] See *supra* note 54, and the sources cited there.

[164] *Al Skeini*, *supra* note 54, Concurring Opinion of Judge Bonello, para. 3.

Extraterritorial Derogations from Human Rights Treaties in Armed Conflict

*Marko Milanovic**

1. Introduction

This chapter does not purport to provide a comprehensive account of the rules and the existing case-law regarding derogations from human rights treaties.[1] Rather, it examines one specific question: whether states are allowed to derogate from human rights treaties for situations which take place outside their territories, especially in armed conflict. Can the United Kingdom, for instance, derogate from the European Convention on Human Rights (ECHR) or the International Covenant on Civil and Political Rights (ICCPR) for events that take place in Afghanistan and involve its armed forces deployed there, to the extent that the ECHR and the ICCPR apply in Afghanistan?

Derogations allow states parties to depart from the full extent of their obligations in situations of emergency. But no state has ever derogated from a human rights treaty in an extraterritorial setting. The United States did not derogate from the ICCPR with respect to Iraq and Afghanistan, nor did the United Kingdom or any other European state do so under the ECHR. But the relevance of the question

* Much of the research for this chapter was done while I was visiting professor at the University of Michigan Law School in Fall 2013, and I am most grateful to the Michigan Law Library staff for their invaluable research assistance, as well as to Haleema Wahid, legal researcher at the University of Nottingham. Thanks are also due to Kjetil Mujezinovic Larsen, Jelena Pejic, Aurel Sari and Stuart Wallace for their helpful comments. The substantive content of this chapter was finalized in June 2014.

[1] For the principal works on the subject, see, e.g. A. Svensson-McCarthy, *The International Law of Human Rights and States of Exception* (1998); J. Fitzpatrick, *Human Rights in Crisis: The International System for Protecting Human Rights During States of Emergency* (1994); R. Ergec, *Les droits de l'homme à l'épreuve des circonstances exceptionnelles: étude sur l'article 15 de la Convention européenne des droits de l'homme* (1987); Higgins, 'Derogations under Human Rights Treaties', 48 *British Yearbook of International Law* (1978) 281. See also D. Harris *et al.*, *Law of the European Convention on Human Rights* (2nd edn, 2009), at 617–645; M. Nowak, *CCPR Commentary* (2nd edn, 2005), at 83 ff.

For an argument that existing approaches need to be radically reconsidered, see Sheeran, 'Reconceptualizing States of Emergency under International Human Rights Law: Theory, Legal Doctrine, and Politics', 34 *Michigan Journal of International Law* (2013) 491.

I am posing should not be in doubt. The first line of defence for most states engaged in extraterritorial adventures of one kind or another has generally been to deny that human rights treaties apply extraterritorially in the first place. That line is now faltering. Cases regarding the extraterritorial application of human rights continue to pile up, and the treaties are increasingly found to apply by courts and treaty bodies driven by the moral imperative of universality, bounded by pragmatic considerations of effectiveness.[2] And the wider the geographical scope of human rights treaties, the more relevant the question of extraterritorial derogations becomes. Such derogations might start looking increasingly appealing to states, especially those which have initially miscalculated in arguing that the treaties do not apply at all, and have avoided derogating for fear that doing so would count as an admission that the treaties do apply. Derogations have the potential of bringing both clarity and flexibility to the applicable legal framework, especially in situations of armed conflict and with regard to possible interactions between human rights and international humanitarian law (IHL).

But are extraterritorial derogations even possible in principle? In the *Al-Jedda* case before the House of Lords,[3] Lord Bingham recalled that Article 15 ECHR allows for derogations in 'time of war or other public emergency threatening the life of the nation', only to the extent strictly required by the exigencies of the situation, and considered the language of this article as follows:

> It is hard to think that these conditions could ever be met when a state had chosen to conduct an overseas peacekeeping operation, however dangerous the conditions, from which it could withdraw. The Secretary of State does not contend that the UK could exercise its power to derogate in Iraq (although he does not accept that it could not). It has not been the practice of states to derogate in such situations, and since subsequent practice in the application of a treaty may (under article 31(3)(b) of the Vienna Convention) be taken into account in interpreting the treaty it seems proper to regard article 15 as inapplicable.[4]

Lord Bingham made two points. Firstly, that the life of the nation—the life of the nation seeking to derogate from the human rights treaty—simply cannot be threatened by an overseas situation which it entered into voluntarily and from which it could withdraw at any time. He refers us to a serious interpretative problem, which I will return to later. His second point is that the absence of any extraterritorial derogations under Article 15 ECHR should be taken into account under Article 31(3)(b) of the Vienna Convention on the Law of Treaties (VCLT) and lead us to the conclusion that such derogations are impermissible. Indeed, in making this argument Lord Bingham was following the lead of the European Court of Human Rights (ECtHR) in *Bankovic*, which regarded the absence of

[2] See generally M. Milanovic, *Extraterritorial Application of Human Rights Treaties: Law, Principles, and Policy* (2011).

[3] *R (Al-Jedda) v. Secretary of State for Defence* [2007] UKHL 58, [2008] 1 AC 332 (hereinafter *Al-Jedda HL*).

[4] Ibid., para. 38.

extraterritorial derogations as evidence that the ECHR should apply extraterritorially in exceptional cases only.[5]

But this argument—very formal as it is—fails on equally formal grounds. Article 31(3)(b) VCLT does not merely refer to the subsequent practice in the application of a treaty, but to such practice 'which establishes the agreement of the parties regarding its interpretation'. Not only is there not even an inkling of any kind of agreement between states parties as to the territorial scope of the derogation clauses, but there are plenty of reasons why states may have not derogated extraterritorially, other than thinking that such derogations were categorically impermissible. They may just as easily have thought that these derogations were unnecessary, as they could obtain the same results through other means, or that doing so would cost them politically. Nor did states give any serious thought to the question of the extraterritorial application of human rights treaties generally until the mid-1990s.[6]

In other words, that states have historically not made any extraterritorial derogations does not *ipso facto* mean that they could not do so in the future, especially if the need for them arises. And it is in my view more likely than not that such a need will arise, and will become progressively more acute as the approach of courts and human rights bodies with regard to the extraterritorial application of the treaties themselves becomes more generous. If that approach becomes *very* generous, as I have argued elsewhere it should be, so that (at a minimum) states have the negative obligation to respect human rights which is territorially unbounded, and a positive obligation to secure or ensure human rights whenever they exercise de facto effective control over territory,[7] then the inability of states to derogate extraterritorially would look increasingly anomalous.

[5] ECtHR, *Bankovic and Others v. Belgium and Others*, Appl. no. 52207/99, Decision on Admissibility of 12 December 2001, para. 62:

> The Court finds State practice in the application of the Convention since its ratification to be indicative of a lack of any apprehension on the part of the Contracting States of their extra-territorial responsibility in contexts similar to the present case. Although there have been a number of military missions involving Contracting States acting extra-territorially since their ratification of the Convention (*inter alia*, in the Gulf, in Bosnia and Herzegovina and in the FRY), no State has indicated a belief that its extra-territorial actions involved an exercise of jurisdiction within the meaning of Article 1 of the Convention by making a derogation pursuant to Article 15 of the Convention. The existing derogations were lodged by Turkey and the United Kingdom in respect of certain internal conflicts (in south-east Turkey and Northern Ireland, respectively) and the Court does not find any basis upon which to accept the applicants' suggestion that Article 15 covers all 'war' and 'public emergency' situations generally, whether obtaining inside or outside the territory of the Contracting State. Indeed, Article 15 itself is to be read subject to the 'jurisdiction' limitation enumerated in Article 1 of the Convention.

[6] See also K. da Costa, *The Extraterritorial Application of Selected Human Rights Treaties* (2012), at 132–135; Roxstrom, Gibney and Einarsen, 'The NATO Bombing Case (*Bankovic et al. v. Belgium et al.*) and the Limits of Western Human Rights Protection', 23 *Boston University International Law Journal* (2005) 55, at 117–118; A. Sari, *Derogations from the European Convention on Human Rights in Deployed Operations, Written Evidence to the House of Commons Defence Committee*, 4 December 2013, available online at http://www.publications.parliament.uk/pa/cm201314/cmselect/cmdfence/writev/futureops/law10.htm (last accessed 23 July 2015), paras 17–18.

[7] See Milanovic, *supra* note 2.

As mentioned above, the permissibility of extraterritorial derogations is especially important in situations of armed conflict which involve the forces of a state but take place outside its territory. That conflict can in terms of IHL be either an international armed conflict (IAC), which is inter-state in character, or a non-international armed conflict (NIAC), which involves (at least) the forces of the state fighting a non-actor.[8] The International Court of Justice (ICJ) has famously held in its *Nuclear Weapons* and *Wall* advisory opinions that 'the protection offered by human rights conventions does not cease in case of armed conflict, save through the effect of provisions for derogation of the kind to be found in Article 4 of the International Covenant on Civil and Political Rights'.[9] The Court's holding seems to apply equally to IACs and NIACs.

If IHL and human rights treaties simultaneously regulate the same conduct, and do so in both types of armed conflict, the most difficult question is what to do in situations in which the rules of the two bodies of law themselves arguably conflict. For example, while IHL explicitly allows the status-based targeting of combatants in IACs or fighters in NIACs and of civilians taking a direct part in hostilities in both types of conflict, as well as the preventive security detention of all kinds of individuals, such as prisoners of war, human rights law generally sets more stringent standards on the use of lethal force, permitting it only as a last resort, abhors preventive detention, and mandates judicial review of any detention.[10] Any analysis of derogations must seek to explain the role they play in mediating norm conflicts between IHL and human rights, and how they fit together with other tools for avoiding or resolving such conflicts, such as the *lex specialis* principle.

In that regard, I will argue that extraterritorial derogations are not only permissible, but may even be necessary and desirable, as part of the price worth paying for the extensive and effective application of treaties outside states' boundaries. I will focus my discussion on three treaties—the ICCPR, the ECHR and the American Convention on Human Rights (ACHR).[11] Some of the other human rights treaties explicitly exclude any derogation, such as the Convention against Torture,[12] while others, such as the International Covenant on Economic, Social and Cultural Rights or the African Charter on Human and Peoples' Rights, simply do not mention

[8] The circumstances in which such conflicts can arise are varied, and can be classified under several descriptive subtypes—see further Milanovic and Hadzi-Vidanovic, 'A Taxonomy of Armed Conflict', in N. White and C. Henderson (eds), *Research Handbook on International Conflict and Security Law* (2013) 256.

[9] *Legal Consequences of the Construction of a Wall in the Occupied Palestinian Territory*, Advisory Opinion, 9 July 2004, ICJ Reports (2004) 136, para. 106. See also *Legality of the Threat or Use of Nuclear Weapons*, Advisory Opinion, 8 July 1996, ICJ Reports (1996) 226, para. 25.

[10] See further Milanovic, *supra* note 2, at 229 ff.

[11] International Covenant on Civil and Political Rights 1966, 999 UNTS 171; Convention for the Protection of Human Rights and Fundamental Freedoms 1950, 213 UNTS 221; American Convention on Human Rights 1969, 1144 UNTS 123.

[12] Convention against Torture and Other Cruel, Inhuman or Degrading Treatment or Punishment 1987, 1465 UNTS 85. Art. 2(2) provides: 'No exceptional circumstances whatsoever, whether a state of war or a threat of war, internal political instability or any other public emergency, may be invoked as a justification of torture.' Note that the CAT's provisions hence undoubtedly apply in wartime.

them.[13] I make no claim in this chapter with regard to the application during armed conflict of human rights treaties without derogation clauses. I will start by comparing the texts of the three treaties, which exhibit many similarities, but also some important differences.

2. Interpreting the ICCPR, ECHR and ACHR

A. Comparing the Texts

That the derogation clauses of the three treaties—Article 4 ICCPR, Article 15 ECHR, and Article 27 ACHR—are in many respects similar should come as no surprise. They address the same problem, the drafting of the ICCPR and the ECHR mostly overlapped in time, and those drafting the ACHR were able to draw inspiration from the older drafting materials and experiences of the two other treaties. They share the same basic structure. The first paragraph of each of the articles sets up the general power to derogate, and the substantive conditions for the exercise thereof. The second paragraph then specifies that some rights are non-derogable even in the gravest of emergencies. The third paragraph then crafts procedural rules regarding the international supervision of any derogation.

The first paragraphs of each clause are the most important and the most complex, so let us now compare them. Article 4(1) ICCPR provides that:

> In time of public emergency which threatens the life of the nation and the existence of which is officially proclaimed, the States Parties to the present Covenant may take measures derogating from their obligations under the present Covenant to the extent strictly required by the exigencies of the situation, provided that such measures are not inconsistent with their other obligations under international law and do not involve discrimination solely on the ground of race, colour, sex, language, religion or social origin.

Article 15(1) ECHR stipulates that:

> In time of war or other public emergency threatening the life of the nation any High Contracting Party may take measures derogating from its obligations under this Convention to the extent strictly required by the exigencies of the situation, provided that such measures are not inconsistent with its other obligations under international law.

Finally, Article 27(1) ACHR provides that:

> In time of war, public danger, or other emergency that threatens the independence or security of a State Party, it may take measures derogating from its obligations under the present Convention to the extent and for the period of time strictly required by the exigencies of the situation, provided that such measures are not inconsistent with its other obligations under international law and do not involve discrimination on the ground of race, color, sex, language, religion, or social origin.

[13] See generally Ouguergouz, 'L'absence de clause de dérogation dans certains traités relatifs aux droits de l'homme: les réponses du droit international général', 98 *Revue générale de droit international public* (1994) 289.

We can observe several interesting points of comparison. Firstly, when it comes to defining a situation that enables a derogation, the ECHR and the ACHR explicitly mention 'war', whereas the ICCPR does not.

Secondly, the ICCPR and the ECHR both require a public emergency that threatens, or is threatening, 'the life of the nation', whereas the ACHR requires 'public danger, or other emergency that threatens the independence or security' of the state. At least on the face of it, the ACHR's reference to 'security' seems more permissive than the ICCPR's and the ECHR's threat to the 'life of the nation'. The draft by the Inter-American Commission on Human Rights which ultimately became Article 27 was in fact originally based on the texts of the ECHR and the ICCPR; the 'life of the nation' wording was later dropped for unclear reasons, but apparently without the intention of allowing for more expansive recourse to derogations.[14]

Thirdly, only the ICCPR expressly requires that the existence of the public emergency be 'officially proclaimed'.

Fourthly, all three treaties demand that the derogating measures should not be inconsistent with the state's other obligations under international law. The most obvious body of such obligations in times of armed conflict would be IHL, which would set a floor below which human rights law could not be derogated from.[15] Indeed, the insertion of this language into the ICCPR was first proposed by the United States precisely in order to take into account the law of armed conflict.[16]

Fifthly, the ICCPR and the ACHR also explicitly require the derogating measures to not be discriminatory on the specified grounds, whereas the ECHR does not.

Finally, under all three treaties the derogating measures must be 'strictly required by the exigencies of the situation', while the ACHR also adds that the measures must be taken 'to the extent and for the period of time' that they are strictly required, with this temporal element only being implicit in the other treaties.

[14] See generally Norris and Desio Reiton, 'The Suspension of Guarantees: A Comparative Analysis of the American Convention on Human Rights and the Constitutions of the States Parties', 30 *American University Law Review* (1981) 189, at 191–193.

[15] See, e.g. Human Rights Committee, General Comment 29, UN Doc. CCPR/C/21/Rev.1/Add.11 (2001), at paras 3 and 9. See also Buergenthal, 'To Respect and to Ensure: State Obligations and Permissible Derogations', in L. Henkin (ed.), *The International Bill of Rights* (1981) 72, at 82; Moir, 'Law and the Inter-American Human Rights System', 25 *Human Rights Quarterly* (2003)182, at 184; Nowak, *supra* note 1, at 99; Ergec, *supra* note 1, at 215, 223–230.

[16] See Commission of Human Rights, 6th Session, Summary Record of the 195th Meeting, UN Doc. E/CN.4/SR.195, 29 May 1950, at 10, para. 45:

> There were fortunately a great many conventions governing the conduct of States in time of war. They included, in particular, the four conventions recently drawn up at Geneva. The United States delegations considered that the Commission [on Human Rights] should take full advantage of those conventions which had been carefully worked out by big international conferences and it accordingly proposed that the text of article 4, paragraph 2, should be replaced by the following: "No derogation may be made by any State under this provision which is inconsistent with international law or with international agreements to which such State is a party.

The wording was later added to paragraph 1, while the list of non-derogable rights in paragraph 2, which the amendment initially intended to replace, remained.

The textual differences are not insignificant, and for our purposes the most notable is the omission of 'war' from the ICCPR, and the fact that the ACHR does not require a threat to the 'life of the nation'. When it comes to the list of non-derogable rights in the second paragraphs of the derogation clauses, the most obvious difference is that the ECHR's list is the narrowest, the ACHR's the broadest, and the ICCPR's somewhere in between. Thus, the ECHR considers as non-derogable the right to life (but only conditionally), the prohibition against torture and cruel, inhuman and degrading treatment or punishment, the prohibition of slavery, and the prohibition of retrospective punishment without law. The ICCPR adds to this list the prohibition of imprisonment merely because of failure to fulfil a contractual obligation, the right to recognition as a person before the law, and the freedom of thought, conscience and religion. The ACHR finally adds the rights of the family, the right to a name, rights of the child, the right to nationality, and the right to participate in government, as well as the judicial guarantees essential for the protection of such rights. The ACHR's additions were apparently the product of entirely ad hoc drafting within a working group during a 15-minute recess of what was probably no more than an hour-long discussion of draft Article 27.[17]

But the most important difference for our purposes is that while it *generally* prohibits derogations from its Article 2 on the right to life, the ECHR *does* allow them 'in respect of deaths resulting from lawful acts of war'. It is the only treaty to do so. And in doing so it creates a clear window through which IHL can enter, as IHL would presumably be the benchmark for testing whether any acts of war were lawful. But despite this opportunity in Article 15(2) ECHR, no state has ever derogated from Article 2, either for purely internal or for IACs, and this part of Article 15(2) has never been interpreted by the ECtHR.

We will come to derogations and IHL later in the chapter, but it must be noted here that the ECHR's permissibility of derogations from the right to life with respect to lawful acts of war is coupled with a significant difference between how the right to life is formulated in Article 2 and how it is set out in the ICCPR and the ACHR. Article 6(1) ICCPR and Article 4(1) ACHR both provide that '[n]o one shall be arbitrarily deprived of his life'. Article 2(1) ECHR, on the other hand, says that '[n]o one shall be deprived of his life *intentionally* save in the execution of a sentence of a court following his conviction of a crime for which this penalty is provided by law' (emphasis added). Article 2(2) ECHR then provides a further exception to the prohibition of *intentional* killing:

> Deprivation of life shall not be regarded as inflicted in contravention of this Article when it results from the use of force which is no more than absolutely necessary:
> (a) in defence of any person from unlawful violence;
> (b) in order to effect a lawful arrest or to prevent the escape of a person lawfully detained;
> (c) in action lawfully taken for the purpose of quelling a riot or insurrection.

[17] See Minutes of the 14th Session of Committee I, 17 November 1969, in T. Buergenthal and R. Norris (eds), *Human Rights: The Inter-American System, Part 2: The Legislative History of the American Convention on Human Rights* (1982), at 131, 136–137.

An intentional killing of a person by a state would thus be lawful only if it was *absolutely necessary* for achieving one of the three specified aims, which are a *numerus clausus*. This is a significantly stricter standard than that of arbitrariness in the ICCPR and the ACHR,[18] and indeed the ECHR's drafters wanted to avoid the ambiguity and the possibility of abuse that an arbitrariness standard would bring. On the other hand, this explains why they made Article 2 derogable in times of war, since status-based targeting could not on its face fit any of the Article 2(2) exceptions, whereas the arbitrariness standard in the other treaties leaves ample room for harmonious interpretation in accordance with the relevant rules of IHL.

We can observe the same difference in drafting technique with respect to the liberty of person. While Article 9(1) ICCPR prohibits 'arbitrary arrest or detention' and Article 7(3) ACHR prohibits 'arbitrary arrest or imprisonment', Article 5(1) ECHR again sets out a closed list of six grounds for detention, which exclude the possibility of preventive security detention,[19] but the right is derogable in the ECHR as well as in the other treaties. All three, however, require judicial control of detention in very similar terms.[20]

Finally, the third paragraphs of the derogation clauses require derogating states to inform the other states parties, through the UN Secretary-General (Article 4(3) ICCPR) or the Secretary General of the Organization of American States (Article 27(3) ACHR), or the Secretary General of the Council of Europe (Article 5(3) ECHR), of the provisions from which the derogation is made, the reasons for the derogation, and the termination of the derogation. This is an essentially procedural requirement of international supervision.

Bearing in mind the texts of the three treaties we can now proceed to look at several specific interpretative problems that will be addressed in turn: firstly, whether we should assign any importance to the absence of an explicit reference to 'war' in Article 4(1) ICCPR, and, secondly, how we should interpret that reference in the other two treaties; thirdly, whether derogations require a formal public act or can take effect automatically; and, finally, the meaning of the 'life of the nation' standard in the ICCPR and the ECHR, and specifically whether it precludes extraterritorial derogations.

B. No 'War' in the ICCPR

The explicit reference to 'war' in Article 15 ECHR and Article 27 ACHR is the best possible evidence that the treaties' drafters intended them to apply in times of

[18] Note that despite the textual differences the Human Rights Committee and the Inter-American Court have interpreted the arbitrariness standard in the right to life context as strictly as the ECHR's absolute necessity standard, at least in peacetime conditions.

[19] See ECtHR, *Al-Jedda v. United Kingdom*, Appl. no. 27021/08, Judgment of 7 July 2011, para. 100: 'It has long been established that the list of grounds of permissible detention in Article 5 § 1 does not include internment or preventive detention where there is no intention to bring criminal charges within a reasonable time.'

[20] See Art. 9(4) ICCPR, Art. 5(4) ECHR, Art. 7(6) ACHR.

armed conflict.[21] But should we *a contrario* construe the absence of an explicit reference to 'war' in Article 4 ICCPR as evidence that the drafters of that treaty did *not* intend armed conflict to fall under the umbrella concept of a public emergency threatening the life of the nation?

Such an inference would be entirely unwarranted. The drafting history of the Covenant is replete with references to war as the paradigmatic example of a public emergency justifying a derogation, and indeed the initial drafts of Article 4 expressly mentioned war, much like the ECHR and the ACHR.[22] The explicit reference to war was dropped from the final text of Article 4 not because the drafters believed that the ICCPR was completely inapplicable to wartime situations, or because they thought that wartime situations do not justify derogations.[23] Rather, '[w]hile it was recognized that one of the most important public emergencies was the outbreak of war, it was felt that the covenant should not envisage, even by implication, the possibility of war, as the United Nations was established with the object of preventing war'.[24]

During the drafting of the derogation clause,[25] the United Kingdom, which had initially proposed the inclusion of 'war' in the clause, also proposed wording that would allow derogations from the right to life 'in respect of deaths resulting from lawful acts of war',[26] the same wording we find today in Article 15(2) ECHR, also on the basis of the UK proposal.[27] To just get a flavour of the debates, this was objected to by the Soviet delegate on the grounds that such an expansive reference to the possibility of war 'would seem sheer mockery to the peoples of the world'.[28] The UK delegate, for her part, 'protested against the suggestion that she favoured

[21] See also Art. 72 of Protocol Additional to the Geneva Conventions of 12 August 1949, and relating to the Protection of Victims of International Armed Conflicts (Protocol I), 8 June 1977, which refers to 'other applicable rules of international law relating to the protection of fundamental human rights during international armed conflict', as well as the second preambular paragraph of Protocol Additional to the Geneva Conventions of 12 August 1949, and relating to the Protection of Victims of Non-International Armed Conflicts (Protocol II), 8 June 1977, referring to 'international instruments relating to human rights [that] offer a basic protection to the human person'.

[22] See generally M. Bossuyt, *Guide to the 'Travaux Préparatoires' of the International Covenant on Civil and Political Rights* (1987) at 81–87.

[23] See also Buergenthal, *supra* note 15, at 79; Higgins, *supra* note 1, at 286–287; Y. Dinstein, *The International Law of Belligerent Occupation* (2009), at 72.

[24] Bossuyt, *supra* note 22, at 86.

[25] For a detailed account see Svensson-McCarthy, *supra* note 1, at 199 ff.

[26] See Commission of Human Rights, 5th Session, Summary Record of the 195th Meeting, UN Doc. E/CN.4/SR 126, 17 June 1949, at 5.

[27] See Nowak, *supra* note 1, 88–89. Generally on the UK government's involvement and the motivations of its various officials in the drafting of the ICCPR and the ECHR, and of their derogation clauses in particular, as well as on the first cases involving the United Kingdom's resort to derogations in its then still extant colonial empire, see B. Simpson, *Human Rights and the End of Empire* (2004), especially at 874 ff.

[28] UN Doc. E/CN.4/SR 126, *supra* note 26, at 6. At the same meeting, the Soviet delegate was not however opposed to the inclusion of the reference to war as such in Art. 4(1), but proposed that the words 'directed against the interests of the people' should be inserted after the words 'In time of war or other public emergency'. That was a most important limitation clause, designed to limit derogations from human rights to cases where the interests of the people were at stake. Thus it would be made clear that that was the 'exclusive purpose of the limitation, which must only be put into effect as a measure of defence against aggression and other acts of war directed against the interests of the people'. Ibid.

war. It was because she hated and loathed war that she desired safeguards for human rights in the event of its occurrence.'[29] During much of the drafting this diplomatic rigmarole continued, with some states arguing that the inclusion of war in the derogation clause was useful, and other claiming that doing so would undermine the UN's basic mission to outlaw the recourse to war, or would be potentially problematic for some other reason. Yet, even so, most states expressly agreed that wars may very well happen in the future and that a derogation clause would substantively cover such situations, regardless of the language used.[30]

A few states doubted the wisdom of having a derogation clause altogether. This was, for instance, the view of the United States, whose opposition to a derogation clause stemmed in part from the view that the limitation clauses in the various specific articles of the Covenant 'made adequate allowance for cases of war or public emergency'.[31] The Philippines, on the other hand, 'considered it useless to envisage the possibility of war in the Covenant, for if a war were to break out, conventions on the rules of war would take precedence over all other international instruments'.[32] The United States later added that 'it was unfortunately necessary to take the threat of war or other serious situations into account and that was the reason for the provisions of article 4'.[33]

The reference to war was removed from Article 4 ICCPR at the Commission's session of 16 May 1950, when a French proposal, which allowed derogation in a 'state of emergency officially proclaimed by the authorities or in the case of public disaster',[34] replaced the original UK-proposed text.[35] The stated purpose of the French amendment was 'to prevent states from derogating arbitrarily from their obligations under the covenant when such an action was not warranted by events'.[36] Again, France at no point argued that wartime situations would be excluded. The

[29] Ibid., at 9.

[30] Thus, the French delegate for his part noted that the concept of an emergency justifying a derogation should not be *limited* to war. Ibid., at 8. The Indian delegate noted that the reference to a public emergency might enable the word 'war' to be avoided, while the Chinese delegate thought that war should not be mentioned because 'to mention war as a condition permitting derogation of certain human rights would involve recognition of the concept of rules of war, which he deemed questionable, at the very least'. Ibid., at 8–9. Australia argued that the 'Commission [on Human Rights] should be practical and reasonable enough to see that the Covenant must provide for the possibility of a war'. Commission of Human Rights, 5th Session, Summary Record of the 127th Meeting, UN Doc. E/CN.4/SR.127, 17 June 1949, at 4. The Guatemalan delegate expressed similar views (ibid.), as did Egypt (ibid., at 6). France then objected to the inclusion of the word 'war', but again without arguing that the concept of an emergency should exclude situations of war. Ibid., at 8. At later stages of the drafting, Yugoslavia proposed that the word 'defensive' should be inserted before the word 'war', see UN Doc. E/CN.4/SR.195, *supra* note 16, at 9.

[31] See UN Doc. E/CN.4/SR.127, *supra* note 30, at 3. [32] Ibid., at 5.

[33] See UN Doc. E/CN.4/SR.195, *supra* note 16, at 10. See also the views of the delegate of Chile, ibid., at 13, para. 63 (proposing the deletion of Art. 4 because it was open to abuse, while other provisions of the Covenant 'sufficiently covered all cases which might arise in time of war').

[34] See Commission of Human Rights, 6th Session, Provisional Agenda, UN Doc. E/CN.4/356, 22 March 1950, at 19.

[35] See UN Doc. E/CN.4/SR.195, *supra* note 16, at 18, para. 97. The French amendment was adopted by six votes to three, with four abstentions.

[36] Ibid., at 16, para. 82.

British proposal to allow for derogations from the right to life in respect of deaths arising from lawful acts of war was then narrowly defeated, with the French delegate arguing that the amendment was necessary since such acts would not violate the right to life, which clearly covered cases of self-defence.[37]

Two years later, the drafting of the Covenant was nearing its end within the Commission. After the adoption of the ECHR,[38] the United Kingdom tried to reverse the changes brought about by the French amendment. It again tried to include a reference to war in the first paragraph and to the possibility to derogate from the right to life in war in the second paragraph of the derogation clause.[39] Both of these points were met with significant opposition and the United Kingdom withdrew its amendment. However, the United Kingdom was successful in aligning the text of Article 4(1) ICCPR with that of Article 15(1) ECHR, so that it now referred to public emergencies threatening the life of the nation, with the addition of the official proclamation requirement from the French amendment. The reason again given by states for opposing the reinsertion of the reference to war into the derogation clause was not that they thought that the clause would not apply to wartime situations, but that they wanted to avoid the implication that a UN treaty would endorse continued resort to war in international relations.[40]

In sum, the drafting history of the ICCPR is (on this matter at least) perfectly clear; the Article 4 derogation clause was meant to apply to situations of war, however these were defined.[41] The absence of an express reference to war cannot be

[37] Ibid., at 21, paras 128–130. The UK amendment failed as there were four votes in favour, four against and five abstentions.

[38] The *travaux* of the ECHR are generally even less helpful that those of the ICCPR, as the various interpretative difficulties regarding Art. 15 were never really discussed systematically, or at least such discussions were not recorded. For brief overviews of the drafting, see Secretariat of the European Commission, Preparatory Work on Article 15 ECHR, 22 May 1956, available online at http://www.echr.coe.int/LibraryDocs/Travaux/ECHRTravaux-ART15-DH%2856%294-EN1675477.pdf (last accessed 23 July 2015); St. J. Macdonald, 'Derogations under Article 15 of the European Convention on Human Rights', 36 *Columbia Journal of Transnational Law* (1997) 225, at 225–233.

[39] See UN Doc. E/CN.4/L.139.

[40] For instance, the delegate of Chile stated that 'it would be inappropriate in an international covenant to include a reference to war. Moreover, from a strictly legal point of view such a reference was unnecessary because public emergency would be deemed to cover a time of war'. Commission of Human Rights, 8th Session, Summary Record of the 313th Meeting, UN Doc. E/CN.4/SR.330, 1 July 1952, at 4. Uruguay believed that a reference to 'war' would be acceptable only if it was specified that the war was recognized only in self-defence or was otherwise compliant with the UN Charter. Ibid., at 5. The United States representative similarly considered that 'the reference to war in paragraph 1 was unnecessary in view of the inclusion of the words "public emergency" and added that in an international covenant it would be regrettable to include any allusion to war'. Ibid., at 5. The Soviet Union was now opposed in principle to any reference to war, but argued that the concept of a public emergency was broad enough. Ibid, at 6–7. The French representative insisted on the official proclamation requirement, and felt that the existing wording of the clause 'would cover war and added that from the legal and psychological point of view a direct reference to war was undesirable'. Ibid., at 7. The Belgian delegate claimed that in the case of war the covenant would be at least suspended between belligerents (and was the only delegate to say so). Ibid., at 7. The Egyptian representative agreed that an explicit reference to war was undesirable. Ibid., at 8.

[41] See also Svensson-McCarthy, *supra* note 1, at 214; Nowak, *supra* note 1, at 89–90; McGoldrick, 'The Interface between Public Emergency Powers and International Law', 2 *International Journal of Constitutional Law* (2004) 380, at 393.

taken as suggesting that the ICCPR cannot apply in wartime, or that it is somehow completely displaced by the law of war. But, having said so, what are we to make of the references to 'war' in the ECHR and the ACHR? And specifically, what are we to make of the possibility to derogate from the right to life under the ECHR, which is, as we have seen, unique to that treaty?

C. 'War' in the ECHR, the ACHR and the Modern Law of Armed Conflict

A major problem with the references to 'war' in the ECHR and the ACHR is that the legal concept of war has fallen into disuse in modern international law. Starting from the adoption of the UN Charter and the 1949 Geneva Conventions, international law has drawn a (relatively) firm distinction between the *jus ad bellum* and the *jus in bello*,[42] and replaced 'war' in both settings with different concepts. In the *ad bellum* arena we now employ concepts such as a use of force or an armed attack.[43] In the *jus in bello*, the Geneva Conventions introduced two new thresholds for their own application: IAC in Common Article 2, and NIAC in Common Article 3 of the Conventions. In a gradual process which entailed the evolution of custom as well as the adoption of new treaties such as the 1977 Additional Protocols to the Conventions, the IAC and NIAC concepts became thresholds for the application of the whole of the law of armed conflict, or IHL, not merely the Conventions themselves.[44] The main reason for discarding 'war' was that it was a concept that was considered to be too subjective, rigid and technical—many wars in the material sense were historically fought but did not qualify as war in the technical, formal legal sense, thus depriving those affected by them of legal protection. 'War' also produced consequences across the board in the legal relations between the belligerents, moving them from the law of peace into the law of war and abrogating or suspending all peacetime treaties between them. IAC and NIAC were thus devised as—or rather grew to become—thresholds which are as objective and factual as possible, and produce consequences mainly at the level of the law of armed conflict.

Hence, when we look at the references to 'war' in the ECHR and the ACHR, as well as at the introduction and the removal of the concept from the text of the ICCPR, we must appreciate that the general framework of war and peace was very much in flux at the time the treaties were drafted. It is true that the 1949 Geneva Conventions were adopted before the human rights treaties, but their IAC and NIAC thresholds had not yet penetrated the whole of the law of war, as it was then

[42] For a strong defense of the separation between the *jus ad bellum* and the *jus in bello*, and the concomitant principle of equal application of the *jus in bello* to all parties to a conflict, see Sloane, 'The Cost of Conflation: Preserving the Dualism of *Jus ad Bellum* and *Jus in Bello* in the Contemporary Law of War', 34 *Yale Journal of International Law* (2009) 47.

[43] See further Kritsiotis, 'Topographies of Force', in M. Schmitt and J. Pejic (eds), *International Law and Armed Conflict: Exploring the Faultlines: Essays in Honour of Yoram Dinstein* (2007) 29.

[44] See further Milanovic and Hadzi-Vidanovic, *supra* note 8, at 258–269, and the sources cited therein.

understood. The drafters were, inevitably, partly influenced by the classical position, which rigidly distinguished between war and peace, while the new one was yet to solidify. Examinations of the text and the drafting history are thus inevitably somewhat anachronistic.

Bearing this in mind, there are three possible ways in which the word 'war' in the ECHR and the ACHR can be interpreted:

(1) As a reference to the technical legal concept of 'war' as it existed in classical international law;[45]
(2) As a reference to the modern concept of IAC, which is like 'war' inter-state in nature but is objective and factual, and was indeed meant as a replacement for 'war',[46] with perhaps the addition of belligerent occupation as a subspecies of IAC;
(3) As a reference to any type of armed conflict regulated by contemporary IHL, thus including both IAC and NIAC, as well as occupation and possibly any third type of armed conflict if it ever evolves through custom or is created by treaty.

When a treaty refers to a legal concept without defining it, and the meaning of that concept evolves over time, we normally have recourse to the general rules of treaty interpretation to establish whether the concept as set out in the treaty should be allowed to evolve or should be applied as it stood at the time the treaty was adopted.[47] But the general rules on treaty interpretation do not exclude any of these three options, nor is the drafting history of the treaties of any help at all in determining whether the reference to 'war' was meant to evolve with the current state of the law of armed conflict, or not.

The choice between these three options is hence really up to the interpreter, and will depend on a policy assessment of the consequences each option would produce. The consequence of option (1) would be that derogations could hardly ever be applied on the grounds of war alone, since war in the formal, classical sense is exceptionally rare today. Option (2) would have the benefit of clarity due to the factual nature of the IAC threshold and alignment with contemporary IHL, but it would exclude the vast majority of contemporary conflicts, which are NIACs. Option (3) would hence allow for the most expansive recourse to derogations.

This choice is only of limited relevance in interpreting the reference to 'war' in Article 15(1) ECHR and Article 27(1) ACHR, since even if we opt for the most restrictive interpretation of 'war', IACs and NIACs could still comfortably qualify as some 'other public emergency threatening the life of the nation' or a 'public

[45] See, e.g. Fitzpatrick, *supra* note 1, at 57–58.

[46] See, e.g. Norris and Desio Reiton, *supra* note 14, at 195 (arguing that the definition was meant to cover the classical concept of (inter-state) war which would exclude civil conflicts, but that it 'does not necessarily exclude the more modern concept of an international armed conflict'). See also Ergec, *supra* note 1, at 123 ff.

[47] See, e.g. Institut de Droit International, Resolution on the Intertemporal Problem in Public International Law, 11 August 1975, para. 4.

danger, or other emergency that threatens the independence or security of a State Party,' respectively. But the choice between the three alternatives is *absolutely crucial* for interpreting Article 15(2) ECHR, which allows derogations from the right to life 'in respect of deaths resulting from lawful acts of war'. Thus, while option (2) would allow for status-based targeting in IACs under the relevant rules of IHL, without option (3) status-based targeting in NIACs would (at least on the face of it) be more problematic, since in the absence of a derogation the applicable standard would be Article 2(2) ECHR, which requires the use of force to be 'no more than absolutely necessary' for the three aims it set out, one of which is 'quelling a riot or insurrection'.[48]

Note that because of the absence of any reference to 'war' in Article 4(1) ICCPR, a derogation from the ICCPR would need to satisfy the 'public emergency which threatens the life of the nation' test.[49] Depending on how strictly we interpret the 'life of the nation' standard, one may very well argue that not all armed conflicts would necessarily satisfy that test,[50] for instance in the case of a NIAC which is very localized or an IAC that is limited in the duration and intensity of hostilities,[51] as, for example, with the relatively bloodless occupation of Crimea by Russia in February and March 2014. Similarly, satisfying an IHL qualification exercise and the 'war' criterion in Article 15(1) ECHR or Article 27(1) ACHR, might not dispense with the need to establish that the 'war' is sufficiently serious to justify a derogation.[52] In other words, the issue would be whether war is merely listed as an example of a public emergency threatening the life of the nation/public danger, or other emergency that threatens the independence or security of a state party, or is an independent justification for a derogation in its own right.

D. 'Life of the Nation'

Recall how in *Al-Jedda* Lord Bingham expressed doubts that an extraterritorial situation, in which a state had put itself voluntarily and from which it could withdraw, could ever satisfy the 'life of the nation' test in Article 15 ECHR.[53] Lord Bingham's doubts were later echoed in two cases before the UK Supreme Court dealing with the ECHR rights of British soldiers deployed in Iraq vis-à-vis the United Kingdom, both confusingly called Smith. In the first case, Lord Philips briefly noted that the United Kingdom did not derogate with regard to the events in Iraq, and that 'troops were deployed abroad in circumstances falling short of

[48] See also N. Melzer, *Targeted Killing in International Law* (2008), at 122.

[49] See General Comment No. 29 States of Emergency (Art. 4), *supra* note 15, para. 3: 'The Covenant requires that even during an armed conflict measures derogating from the Covenant are allowed only if and to the extent that the situation constitutes a threat to the life of the nation.' See also Nowak, *supra* note 1, at 90.

[50] See, e.g. Svensson-McCarthy, *supra* note 1, at 214.

[51] See Moir, *supra* note 15, at 183.

[52] See, e.g. Norris and Desio Reiton, *supra* note 14, at 194 (arguing that this is the correct position under both the ECHR and the ACHR).

[53] See *supra* note 4 and accompanying text.

those permitting derogation under article 15'.[54] In the second case, Lord Hope, joined by three other justices, remarked that:

> [T]he phrase 'threatening the life of the nation' suggests that the power to derogate under this article is available only in an exceptional situation of crisis or emergency which affects the whole population and constitutes a threat to the organised life of the community of which the state is composed: *Lawless v Ireland (No. 3)* (1961) 1 EHRR 15, para 28. . . . [discusses Lord Bingham's views in *Al-Jedda*] I do not think therefore that it would be right to assume that concern about the practical consequences in situations such as those with which we are dealing in this case can be answered by exercising the power to derogate. The circumstances in which that power can properly be exercised are far removed from those where operations are undertaken overseas with a view to eliminating or controlling threats to the nation's security. The jurisprudence of the Strasbourg court shows that there are other ways in which such concerns may be met.[55]

The concerns Lord Hope referred to were the potentially excessive rigidity of Article 2 ECHR positive obligations if they are applied to military deployments overseas, which is why one of the interveners invoked the possibility of derogations as a means of introducing needed flexibility. Lord Hope rightly observed that such concerns could be accommodated even without derogations, since the due diligence positive obligations are inherently flexible and also leave ample room for the state's margin of appreciation.[56]

However, the same cannot be said of the negative obligation under Article 2 to refrain from intentionally taking human life unless it is absolutely necessary to do so, and it is there that the full impact of a derogation 'in respect of deaths result from lawful acts of war' might be felt, both with regard to the targeting itself and to permitting a degree of collateral damage in accordance with an IHL proportionality analysis. The ECtHR's case-law has been much less flexible when it comes to the actual killing of individuals by a state, rather than the state's obligation to protect individuals from harm or investigate deaths.[57]

Lord Hope's holding that circumstances in which derogations would be appropriate 'are *far removed* from those where operations are undertaken overseas with a view to eliminating or controlling threats to the nation's security' is at best an overstatement. It is true that there are plenty of authorities, like the ECtHR's judgment in *Lawless*, that at first glance seem to set a threshold for derogation very high: 'the natural and customary meaning of the words "other public emergency threatening the life of the nation" is sufficiently clear . . . they refer to an exceptional situation of crisis or emergency which affects the whole population and constitutes

[54] *R (Smith) v. Secretary of State for Defence* [2010] UKSC 29, para. 57.

[55] *R (Smith and others) v. The Ministry of Defence* [2013] UKSC 41, paras 59–60.

[56] Ibid., para. 61

[57] But see ECtHR, *Finogenov and Others v. Russia*, Appl. nos. 18299/03 and 27311/03, Judgment of 20 December 2011, dealing with the hostage-taking in the Dubrovka theatre in Moscow, in which the Court found that the use of an anaesthetic gas in the theatre by Russian authorities, which also led to the deaths of a number of hostages, did not in itself amount to a violation of Art. 2 ECHR. In effect, the Court allowed for the possibility of collateral damage under human rights law.

a threat to the organised life of the community of which the State is composed'.[58] But let us also look at the facts on which the ECtHR found the life of the nation to have been threatened: 'in the first place, the existence in the territory of the Republic of Ireland of a secret army engaged in unconstitutional activities and using violence to attain its purposes; secondly, the fact that this army was also operating outside the territory of the State, thus seriously jeopardizing the relations of the Republic of Ireland with its neighbour; and thirdly, the steady and alarming increase in terrorist activities from the autumn of 1956 and throughout the first half of 1957'.[59] The terrorist activities took place both in Northern Ireland, i.e. the United Kingdom, and within the Republic of Ireland itself, and involved a number of armed attacks, mostly with explosives, against property and infrastructure. The most serious attack was an IRA ambush against a police patrol, during which one policeman was ambushed and one injured.[60]

This, then, was a threat to the life of the nation that was found sufficient for a derogation in *Lawless*. It was on any reasonable appraisal quite real, but far from *existential*. The same goes for IRA activities within the United Kingdom, which were also found to justify a derogation.[61] The Human Rights Committee has also been reluctant to directly challenge arguable state determinations of the existence of a public emergency, merely *urging*, for example, the United Kingdom in 1995 to keep the issue under review and consider the *appropriateness* of withdrawing the derogation in respect of Northern Ireland due to the diminution of violence there.[62] Similarly, both the House of Lords and the ECtHR accepted the UK government's view that an emergency threatening the life of the nation existed for the United Kingdom after Al-Qaeda's 9/11 attacks, even though no attack had at the time taken place on British soil.[63] The Court explicitly said that it was prepared to look at a broad range of factors in establishing whether an emergency exists, and that the emergency need not be so severe as to imperil the state's institutions and the existence of a civil community.[64] The Court has also been ready to accept an emergency which was *localized* to a part of a state's territory only; in other words, it did not directly affect the whole of its population, or the 'nation' as such.[65]

It must be said that the vast majority of very genuine emergencies in which courts or human rights bodies accepted that a derogation was justified pale in

[58] ECtHR, *Lawless v. Ireland (No. 3)*, Appl. no. 332/57, Judgment of 1 July 1961, section on 'The Law', para. 28.

[59] Ibid.

[60] Ibid., section on 'The Facts', para. 14, and section on 'The Law', para. 29.

[61] ECtHR, *Ireland v. United Kingdom*, Appl. no. 5310/71, Judgment of 18 January 1978, para. 205.

[62] See Concluding Observations of the Human Rights Committee on the United Kingdom, UN Doc. CCPR/C/79/Add.55, 27 July 1995, para. 23.

[63] See ECtHR, *A and others v. United Kingdom*, Appl. no. 3455/05, Judgment of 19 February 2009 (Grand Chamber), paras 177–181.

[64] Ibid., para. 179.

[65] See, e.g. ECtHR, *Aksoy v. Turkey*, Appl. no. 21987/93, Judgment of 18 December 1996, paras 70 and 84 (emergency existed in South-East Turkey, but incommunicado detention without recourse to judicial review was not strictly required by the exigencies of the situation); *Ireland v. United Kingdom, supra* note 61, paras 205, 212 (emergency in Northern Ireland).

comparison to the horrors of Iraq (both during and after the formal end of occupation) and the brutality of the insurgency there. So why should a derogation not have been permitted? Even if we took the *Lawless* test at face value, all we would need to do to enable its application to UK activities in Iraq would be to adjust the very last part of the sentence: 'an exceptional situation of crisis or emergency which affects the whole population and constitutes a threat to the organised life of the community *in which the Convention is applied*'. In *Serdar Mohammed* Mr Justice Leggatt endorsed a similar approach:

Now that the Convention has been interpreted, however, as having such extraterritorial effect, it seems to me that Article 15 must be interpreted in a way which reflects this. It cannot be right to interpret jurisdiction under Article 1 as encompassing the exercise of power and control by a state on the territory of another state, as the European Court did in the Al-Skeini case, unless at the same time Article 15 is interpreted in a way which is consonant with that position and permits derogation to the extent that it is strictly required by the exigencies of the situation. [...] Article 15, like other provisions of the Convention, can and it seems to me must be 'tailored' to such extraterritorial jurisdiction. This can readily be achieved without any undue violence to the language of Article 15 by interpreting the phrase 'war or other public emergency threatening the life of the nation' as including, in the context of an international peacekeeping operation, a war or other emergency threatening the life of the nation on whose territory the relevant acts take place.[66]

In other words, if we accept that the human rights treaty can apply outside a state's own territory, and not just in very limited circumstances, then the mere fact of extraterritoriality does not seem to be an adequate reason to categorically ban recourse to derogations.[67]

One potential solution for the extraterritoriality problem is for the state acting outside its territory to be able to rely on any derogation by the territorial state. But to my eyes this approach would not be sound either conceptually or practically. At the conceptual level, it is the state whose obligations are at issue that needs to derogate if it wishes to diminish the scope of its own obligations. And that state and the territorial state may not even be bound by the same treaty—for instance, although the United Kingdom is a party to both the ECHR and the ICCPR, Afghanistan and Iraq are parties to the ICCPR but not to the ECHR, and it is precisely with regard to the ECHR's more rigid standards on the deprivation of life and liberty that a derogation might be needed. At a purely practical level, I fail to see why an intervening state should be at the mercy of the territorial state's choice as to whether to derogate. Note that even though Iraq had ratified the ICCPR as early as in 1971, and Afghanistan had acceded to it in 1983, neither of these states ever

66 *Serdar Mohammed v. Ministry of Defence* [2014] EWHC 1369 (QB), paras 155–156.

67 See also Sassòli, 'The Role of Human Rights and International Humanitarian Law in New Types of Armed Conflicts', in O. Ben-Naftali (ed.), *International Humanitarian Law and International Human Rights Law* (2011) 34, at 66: '[O]ne cannot simultaneously hold a state accountable because it has a certain level of control abroad and deny it the possibility to derogate because there is no emergency on that state's own territory. An emergency on an occupied territory or a territory where the state has a certain limited control must be sufficient; ... '. K. Mujezinovic Larsen, *The Human Rights Treaty Obligations of Peacekeepers* (2012), at 308–309; Sari, *supra* note 6, para. 16.

derogated despite all the unfortunate events they went through, tragedies of such magnitude and scale that they surpass most other situations in which other states had derogated.[68] This is not to say that that any derogation by the territorial state would be completely irrelevant—they could serve as evidence that a genuine emergency existed as a matter of fact, and as to what measures were strictly required by the exigencies of the situation.

Lord Bingham also pointed out in *Al-Jedda* that Article 15 ECHR should be inapplicable because the state voluntarily embarked on an overseas military operation, from which it could withdraw. But this argument also fails to persuade.[69] After all, Ireland and the United Kingdom could also have given in to the IRA's demands and thus had averted or mitigated the public emergency. And so could any other state that derogated due to an internal problem.

In sum, if we accept that the 'life of the nation' test does not require a truly existential threat to a state, and that it can be applied even to localized emergencies within the state,[70] then I do not see why it could also not be applied to localized emergencies outside the state, if the human rights treaties themselves apply.[71] And while it did not directly address the issue in *Al-Jedda*, the ECtHR did note the UK failure to derogate, thus implying that it did not think that extraterritorial derogations would be categorically impermissible.[72]

Of course, derogation measures would still need to be strictly required by the exigencies of the situation. If we again take the United Kingdom and Iraq as an example, such measures would be justifiable only to the extent that they related to Iraq. In other words, that a real emergency existed in the parts of Iraq in which British troops were deployed, which could for instance have justified the preventive security detention of an insurgent detained in UK military operations, does not mean that the same measures could have been used in the United Kingdom itself where no such emergency existed.

Perhaps there is some other reason to categorically prohibit extraterritorial derogations, but such a prohibition does not formally flow from the text or the

[68] Status of ratifications and notifications of derogation available online at the UN Treaty Collection website at https://treaties.un.org/Pages/ViewDetails.aspx?src=TREATY&mtdsg_no=IV-4&chapter=4&lang=en (last accessed 23 July 2015).

[69] I set aside for the moment the issue of the intervention's legality under other rules of international law, to which I will turn later in this chapter—see Section 4 *infra*.

[70] See, e.g. Buergenthal, *supra* note 15, at 80; Macdonald, *supra* note 38, at 239–241; El Zeidy, 'The ECHR and States of Emergency: Article 15—A Domestic Power of Derogation from Human Rights Obligations', 4 *San Diego International Law Journal* (2003) 277, at 284–285; Mujezinovic Larsen, *supra* note 67, at 310.

[71] See Dinstein, *supra* note 23, at 73 (arguing that the rationale for localized emergencies 'applies even more vigorously to occupied territories (as completely separate entities) than to parts of the territory of a Belligerent Party'). See also Ergec, *supra* note 1, at 129 (arguing that 'l'Etat occupant doit par conséquent répondre, sur le terrain de l'article 15, de toute mesure dérogatoire qu'il serait amené à imposer dans le territoire occupé' [The occupying state shall therefore be responsible, under Article 15, for any derogation measure which it will bring about in the occupied territory]).

[72] *Al-Jedda v. United Kingdom*, *supra* note 19, para. 100. See also ECtHR, *Georgia v. Russia (II)*, Appl. no. 38263/08, Decision of 13 December 2011, para. 73 (noting that neither Georgia *nor Russia* made a derogation in the context of their 2008 conflict, which entirely took place on Georgian territory).

treaties, their travaux or subsequent practice.[73] The only plausible policy argument in that regard is that the state acting extraterritorially has no business—or has no *right*—to determine that an emergency exists in a territory over which it exercises no sovereign authority, or to take derogating measures. That argument partly turns on the issue of the *legality* of the extraterritorial state's intervention under other rules of international law, to which I will turn in Section 4. As I will explain, that question—whether, for example, the United Kingdom had any right to resort to derogations because it had *unlawfully* invaded Iraq in 2003—poses a serious dilemma. However that question is answered, one possible way of taking the peculiar nature of extraterritorial derogations into account would be to review the decision to derogate and the measures implemented by the state somewhat less deferentially than when a state derogates in its own territory.

E. Automaticity and Proclamation

I do not wish to examine at length the various issues that may arise regarding the derogation procedure. These include, for instance, whether notifications of derogation need to be communicated immediately or whether the derogating state is permitted a grace period, or indeed what might be the consequences of a failure to notify, namely whether it results in the nullity of the derogation or is a mere procedural defect that may be taken into account in assessing whether a genuine emergency existed.[74] For present purposes, it suffices to say that derogations cannot be automatic, in the sense that a human rights treaty is derogated from whenever a particular emergency arises as a matter of fact, including situations of IAC and NIAC. Nor can derogations simply be effected by resort to measures that would otherwise violate the treaty, such as security detention. Rather, derogations always remain the choice of the relevant state and that choice must be made formally by some public act, regardless of any notification of derogation to the other states parties. Thus, for instance, while in one of the Cyprus/Turkey inter-state cases the European Commission did not want to take a position on what sanctions should follow from Turkey's failure to notify any derogation with respect to northern Cyprus, it held that:

> Art. 15 requires some formal and public act of derogation, such as a declaration of martial law or state of emergency, and that, where no such act has been proclaimed by the High Contracting Party concerned, although it was not in the circumstances prevented from

[73] And, as we have seen, the more permissive text of Art. 27(1) ACHR does not seem to pose any problem for extraterritorial derogation.

[74] For example, while Art. 4(3) ICCPR requires derogating states to 'immediately' inform the other states parties of the derogation and the reasons therefor, Art. 15 ECHR does not use the same language, and the ECtHR in *Lawless*, *supra* note 58, para. 47, did not consider a derogation communicated by Ireland 12 days after the derogation measures took effect to have been made with undue delay. See further Higgins, *supra* note 1, at 290–296; Harris *et al.*, *supra* note 1, at 640–641. One could certainly imagine situations of dire emergency which can disrupt the normal functioning of a government, e.g. a surprise attack on its capital, that would justify delays in notifying derogations. Cf. Roxstrom *et al.*, *supra* note 6, at 119–120.

doing so, Art. 15 cannot apply.... The Commission, by twelve votes against three votes, concludes as regards the present case that it cannot, in the absence of some formal and public act of derogation by Turkey, apply Art. 15 of the Convention to measures taken by Turkey with regard to persons or property in the north of Cyprus.[75]

Notably, the Commission implicitly accepted the possibility of extraterritorial derogation, in other words that Turkey could have potentially derogated due to war or public emergency in Cyprus. Dissenting from the Commission's finding that a formal act of derogation was required, two of its members considered that the concurrent applicability of IHL in effect created an automatic derogation: '[M]easures which are in themselves contrary to a provision of the European Convention but which are taken legitimately under the international law applicable to an armed conflict, are to be considered as legitimate measures of derogation from the obligations flowing from the Convention.'[76]

The automaticity approach is, in my view, seriously flawed in the derogation context. Note that the applicability of IHL in both IAC and NIAC is automatic, in the sense that the application of IHL is triggered as soon as a certain objective factual threshold is reached, regardless of whether the relevant parties recognize the existence of an armed conflict. But the same is not true of derogation measures under human rights treaties, which remain the choice of the state, subject to certain conditions. Any automaticity would remove the voluntary nature of the act of derogation and elide the distinction between violations of a human rights treaty and measures derogating from it. If the Article 15(2) ECHR reference to deaths resulting from lawful acts of war operated automatically, by mere fact of killing in wartime without any formal act of derogation, it would have been included in the list of exceptions in Article 2(2) ECHR rather than in the provision on derogation.[77] Automaticity would be especially difficult to square with those situations, particularly NIACs, in which the relevant states deny the existence of an armed conflict, as with the United Kingdom in Northern Ireland or Russia in Chechnya, but an armed conflict did exist as a matter of fact, as was undoubtedly the case in Chechnya. In other words, IHL did automatically apply to the NIAC in Chechnya, regardless of what the Russian government said on the matter—thus, for example, a direct attack on Chechen civilians would have constituted a war crime. But the ECHR was not automatically derogated from in the sense of Article 15 merely because a NIAC objectively existed.[78] Formality is a key safeguard for the interests of the people

[75] *Cyprus v. Turkey*, Appl. nos. 6780/74 and 6950/75, Commission Report of 10 July 1976, at paras 527–528.

[76] Ibid., Dissenting Opinion of Mr. G. Sperduti, Joined by Mr. S. Trechsel, para. 7. See also Ergec, *supra* note 1, at 305.

[77] See also E. Wicks, *The Right to Life and Conflicting Interests* (2010), at 82.

[78] Cf. ECtHR, *Isayeva v. Russia*, Appl. no. 57950/00, Judgment of 24 February 2005, at para. 191 (noting that 'No martial law and no state of emergency has been declared in Chechnya, and no derogation has been made under Article 15 of the Convention (see § 133). The operation in question therefore has to be judged against a normal legal background.'); *Georgia v. Russia (II)*, *supra* note 72, para. 73 (noting that neither Georgia *nor Russia* made a derogation in the context of their 2008 conflict); *McVeigh and Others v. United Kingdom*, Appl. nos. 8022/77, 8025/77 and 8027/77, Commission Report of 18 March 1981, at 44, paras 155–156 (noting that while it had derogated

living in the area and other individuals affected, as well as for the other states parties, and it entails the state taking public political responsibility for its decision.[79] One could also wonder what automaticity would entail when the ECHR encountered areas of international law other than IHL.[80] Recall also that Article 4(1) ICCPR requires the existence of public emergencies to be officially proclaimed, and that since all ECHR states parties are also parties to the ICCPR such proclamation is necessary in order for the derogation not to be inconsistent with the states' other obligations under international law.[81]

This is not to say that IHL would be irrelevant in the absence of a derogation. Even if IHL can prevail over inconsistent provisions of human rights treaties in times of armed conflict, this would be due to some higher-order principle such as *lex specialis* or due to the policy choice of the interpreter, not due to the effect of the derogation clauses. An automatic derogation is no derogation at all.

F. Plausibility of Several Different Interpretations

I hope to have shown in the preceding discussion that the text of Article 4(1) ICCPR and Article 15(1) ECHR, specifically the reference to the 'life of the nation,' does not present a categorical bar to extraterritorial derogations.[82] Article 27(1) ACHR uses a different standard in any event. The question of extraterritorial derogation was not discussed during the drafting of the three treaties, and the purpose of the 'life of the nation' standard was to qualify the gravity and nature of the public emergency, not its geographical scope. The existing case-law on the 'life of the nation' standard has interpreted that standard relatively flexibly, and does not of itself stand in the way of extraterritorial derogations.

In sum, the derogation clauses are open to several reasonable interpretations. If states or courts do decide against extraterritorial derogations this should be not on the account of the (supposedly clear) text alone.[83] This interpretative choice cannot be made solely by formal means, but on the basis of whether one believes, or not,

with respect to the situation in Northern Ireland the UK government did not seek to invoke Art. 15 ECHR with respect to arrests and detention of individuals in mainland Great Britain, and that accordingly Art. 15 was inapplicable).

[79] See also Nowak, *supra* note 1, at 92: '[O]fficial proclamation is a *conditio sine qua non* . . . it is to prevent *de facto* derogations, as well as subsequent attempts to justify human rights violations that have already been committed.'

[80] See also Harris *et al.*, *supra* note 1, at 640.

[81] Cf. ECtHR, *Brannigan and McBride v. United Kingdom*, Appl. nos. 14553/89 and 14554/89, Judgment of 25 May 1993, at para. 73.

[82] See also Krieger, 'After *Al-Jedda*: Detention, Derogation, and an Enduring Dilemma', 50 *Military Law and the Law of War Review* (2011) 419, at 436: 'Although the wording of Article 15 para. I ECHR refers to the life of the nation seeking to derogate, it is not so strictly formulated that it could not allow for a more dynamic interpretation, so to include unstable foreign territories where the Member State in question would operate'; Wilde, 'The Extraterritorial Application of International Human Rights Law on Civil and Political Rights', in S. Sheeran and N. Rodley (eds), *Routledge Handbook of International Human Rights Law* (2014) 635, at 654–655.

[83] See Sari, *supra* note 6, para. 19: '[T]he term "nation" in Article 15 should be construed as extending to any third States in which the armed forces of the contracting parties operate. While some have suggested that such a reading would constitute an exercise in "dynamic" treaty interpretation, it

that extraterritorial derogations would be normatively desirable.[84] In the context of armed conflict in particular, the desirability or the need for derogations is directly tied to how we conceptualize the relationship between human rights and IHL and the scope of the *lex specialis* principle. Historically, the great concern on the part of human rights bodies and scholars alike with respect to derogations was the possibility of their abuse as enablers of *domestic* repression.[85] Today those concerns are no less relevant, but the issue of the relationship with IHL is relatively new and may call for a more expansive recourse to derogations. But let us first see what the options are.

3. The Link to IHL

Both the text and the *travaux* of the major human rights treaties support the proposition that they will continue applying during 'war' or armed conflict and as, we have seen, this is also the view of the ICJ and human rights bodies. But that is all that the text tells us, and the drafting history is equally of little help. If the question is what the treaties' drafters really *intended* with regard to their relationship with IHL, the simple answer is that we have no idea, assuming that the drafters did actually intend *something*.

For example, the ICCPR's *travaux* tell us virtually nothing about how the treaty would apply to concrete problems in military operations. We have one isolated statement by the Philippine delegate, as already quoted, to the effect that 'conventions on the rules of war would take precedence over all other international instruments',[86] which is clearly rooted in the classical, hard distinction between the law of war and the law of peace. But other delegations expressed neither agreement nor disagreement with this statement, even though the general tenor of their discussion assumed the continued applicability of the ICCPR in wartime. No delegation during the entire drafting process ever mentioned the much-vaunted *lex specialis* principle. At another session, and again echoing the classical position, the Belgian delegate briefly said that the ICCPR would at the very least be suspended between belligerents in wartime.[87] But two years earlier that very same Belgian representative questioned the inclusion of the prohibition of torture and other forms

may amount to nothing more than a contextual reading of the text in line with the general rule of interpretation laid down in Article 31(2) of the Vienna Convention on the Law of Treaties.'

[84] See also Mujezinovic Larsen, *supra* note 67, at 313 (arguing that 'resort to [extraterritorial] derogations in UN-mandated peace operations would be a clear advantage. It would create a coherent and transparent legal framework for the assessment of human rights obligations in such operations, it would allow troop contributing states to avoid obligations that it would be unrealistic to comply with, and it would in fact lead to an increased level of human rights protection in the area of deployment, since the scope of application of the ECHR would shift from "nothing" to "some"').

[85] This is, for instance, what inspired projects such as the Siracusa Principles on the Limitation and Derogation Provisions in the International Covenant on Civil and Political Rights, UN Doc. E/CN.4/1985/4, Annex (1985) and the International Law Association's Paris Minimum Standards of Human Rights Norms in a State of Emergency, 79 *American Journal of International Law* (1985) 1072.

[86] UN Doc. E/CN.4/SR.127, *supra* note 30, at 5.

[87] UN Doc. E/CN.4/SR.330, *supra* note 40, at 7.

of ill-treatment in the list of non-derogable rights since, he said, during the First World War prisoners of war were mistreated by one of the belligerents and it was only through the use of reprisals that the belligerent was induced to mitigate those practices.[88] In other words, the same delegate who thought that the Covenant would be suspended in wartime also thought that the Covenant's blanket prohibition of ill-treatment would impede belligerent reprisals against prisoners of war (and that this would be a bad thing!), a situation obviously relevant only in wartime.[89]

So let us forget the drafting history—we are, otherwise, only liable to be confused. The *travaux* of the ICCPR do show us that the drafters intended the ICCPR to continue applying in wartime, and that the Article 4 derogation clause would govern such situations. But that is the sum total of their usefulness. Forget also for the moment the fact that in the vast majority of situations human rights and IHL complement each other well and their rules go in the same basic direction. Rather, let us consider two problems where the regime-specific rules do not go in the same direction—killing and detention. These are the hardest cases, in which the danger of a norm conflict is the most acute. I have explained elsewhere that states are perfectly capable of assuming contradictory obligations, and that we should not assume that the diffuse and decentralized international law-making processes will necessarily always lead to a unified, coherent system.[90] Coherence is not an inevitability, and there may be norm conflicts which are both unavoidable and unresolvable.

But, even so, let as assume that through the adoption of human rights states could not have intended to completely outlaw status-based targeting or preventive security detention in armed conflict. At the very least, states must have in some circumstances retained the liberty to kill combatants merely on the grounds that they are combatants, without inquiring into whether they pose an imminent threat to another person or could be neutralized in some other way, or to detain prisoners of war until the cessation of active hostilities merely because they otherwise might rejoin the enemy. Yet, on the other hand, the text and the logic of human rights treaties can run against this outcome,[91] and we need to establish how we can avoid the position that the same conduct would *inevitably* be lawful under IHL, but unlawful under international human rights law (IHRL). Clearly, this will be an explicitly result-oriented analysis, in the sense that one particular outcome would be regarded as absurd, and any interpretative chain that led to that outcome would be suspect.

[88] UN Doc. E/CN.4/SR.195, *supra* note 16, at 22, para. 132.

[89] Incidentally, both the Convention Relative to the Treatment of Prisoners of War 1929 (Art. 2(3)) and the Convention (III) Relative to the Treatment of Prisoners of War 1949 (Art. 13(3)) expressly prohibit reprisals against prisoners of war.

[90] See Milanovic, *supra* note 2, at 229 ff.

[91] See, e.g. Krieger, *supra* note 82, at 423: 'When comparing both regimes, it follows that security detention under international humanitarian law could hardly meet the standards of Article 5 ECHR since it is not related to a specific offence. There is no prospect that detainees are promptly brought before a judge and the sufficient preciseness of the laws of war is at least doubtful.'

To appreciate the full complexity of the problem and the possible solutions, let us thus consider killing and preventive detention—both presumptively lawful under IHL but potentially unlawful under IHRL—in four factual scenarios, progressing from the easiest to the most difficult:

(A) Killing and detention in a NIAC on the state's territory—for example, Russia targeting or detaining the members of rebel armed group during the conflict in Chechnya;

(B) Killing and detention in an IAC on the state's territory—for example, if Georgian soldiers fired at or detained a Russian soldier on Georgian territory during the 2008 conflict;

(C) Killing and detention in an IAC outside the state's territory—for example, looking at the Georgian conflict from the Russian perspective, or if UK or US soldiers killed or detained Iraqi combatants during the 2003 invasion of Iraq;

(D) Killing and detention in a NIAC outside the state's territory—for example, if US or UK troops killed or detained a Taliban insurgent in Afghanistan in say 2010.

Again, assume that in all of these scenarios the conduct in question is lawful under IHL, but is potentially unlawful under IHRL. For instance, the persons killed were undoubtedly combatants (in IACs) or fighting members of an armed opposition group (in NIACs), with all IHL rules on targeting complied with, but they were killed while they were sleeping in their barracks (for example, by an air strike) and posed no immediate threat to anyone else, and perhaps could even have been captured.[92] Similarly, with regard to detention, the persons in question were lawfully detained under IHL for the duration of the hostilities to prevent them rejoining the enemy, but they were charged with no crime and were provided with no judicial review of their detention. So what are our options for dealing with this apparent norm conflict?

Option 1: deny that the human rights treaties apply. The easiest way of avoiding the conflict, superficially at least, is to deny that human rights treaties even apply to the four scenarios. Some states, such as the United States and the United Kingdom, chose this option as their first (and sometimes only) line of defence. There are two basic ways of making this argument. The first is to reject the extraterritorial application of human rights treaties. But while that would dispose of scenarios C and D, it would leave scenarios A and B unaffected. The second is to claim that IHL completely displaces or excludes human rights treaties—this argument is sometimes made by reference to *lex specialis*, and I will call this approach *lex specialis* as total displacement.[93]

[92] The mainstream IHL position would be that it would be perfectly lawful to make sleeping combatants the object of attack. For a more limited approach to IHL targeting rules combined with the unnecessary suffering principle, see Goodman, 'The Power to Kill or Capture Enemy Combatants', 24 *European Journal of International Law* (2013) 819.

[93] See also *Serdar Mohammed v. Ministry of Defence*, *supra* note 66, paras 273 ff.

Both variants of the first option are becoming increasingly unsustainable. In particular, the opponents of extraterritorial application have not been able to offer a convincing normative explanation as to why human rights should stop at the border,[94] and the case-law is certainly trending towards a more expansive approach to extraterritoriality. States thus have to argue this point in increasingly narrowing terms, for example, that even though the treaties would apply in an occupied territory, they would not apply to air strikes in an area not under the state's effective control.[95] But again, this approach is likely to fail in the long term. I have argued, for instance, that at a minimum the negative obligations of state (for example, the obligation not to deprive people of their lives or liberty without sufficient justification) should apply without any territorial limitation.[96] But even on a more modest approach the treaties will at the very least apply to operations in an occupied territory or territory under some other form of de facto control, per the spatial model of jurisdiction as effective control over areas.[97] They will also apply to the detention of individuals under the personal model of jurisdiction as authority and control over persons.[98] Whether they would also apply to killing under the personal model of jurisdiction in the absence of territorial control is thus to an extent beside the point for the purpose of this chapter (but they would). Hence, for the purpose of further discussion I will assume that human rights treaties do apply to all four scenarios, and that this avoidance option is unavailable.

[94] Consider, in that regard, the leak of internal memoranda written by Harold Koh, then the US State Department Legal Adviser, arguing for the US government to drop its opposition to the extraterritorial application of human rights treaties. See Savage, 'U.S. Seems Unlikely to Accept That Rights Treaty Applies to Its Actions Abroad', *The New York Times*, 6 March 2014, available online at http://www.nytimes.com/2014/03/07/world/us-seems-unlikely-to-accept-that-rights-treaty-applies-to-its-actions-abroad.html?_r=0 (last accessed 23 July 2015); Memorandum Opinion on the Geographic Scope of the International Covenant on Civil and Political Rights, U.S. Department of State, Office of the Legal Adviser, 19 October 2010, available online at http://justsecurity.org/wp-content/uploads/2014/03/state-department-iccpr-memo.pdf (last accessed 23 July 2015); Memorandum Opinion on the Geographic Scope of Application of the Convention Against Torture and Its Application in Situations of Armed Conflict, U.S. Department of State, Office of the Legal Adviser, 21 January 2013, available online at http://justsecurity.org/wp-content/uploads/2014/03/state-department-cat-memo.pdf (last accessed 23 July 2015); Milanovic, 'Harold Koh's Legal Opinions on the US Position on the Extraterritorial Application of Human Rights Treaties', *Just Security*, 7 March 2014, available online at https://www.justsecurity.org/8010/harold-kohs-legal-opinions-position-extraterritorial-application-human-rights-treaties (last accessed 23 July 2015).

[95] For example, the UK government has argued that the ECtHR's *Al-Skeini* judgment is confined only to the facts of Iraq, and that the ECHR would not apply to UK forces in Afghanistan—see Communication from the United Kingdom concerning the case of *Al-Skeini* against United Kingdom to the Committee of Ministers, DH–DD(2012)438, 2 May 2012, available online at https://wcd.coe.int/com.instranet.InstraServlet?command=com.instranet.CmdBlobGet&InstranetImage=2082643&SecMode=1&DocId=1885434&Usage=2 (last accessed 23 July 2015) ('The UK considers that the *Al-Skeini* judgment is set in the factual circumstances of UK's past operations in Iraq and that it has no implications for its current operations elsewhere, including in Afghanistan').

[96] See Milanovic, *supra* note 2.

[97] See ECtHR, *Loizidou v. Turkey*, Appl. no. 15318/89, Judgment (preliminary objections) of 23 February 1995, para. 62.

[98] See HRC, *Sergio Euben Lopez Burgos v. Uruguay*, Comm. no. R.12/52, UN Doc. Supp. No. 40 (A/36/40), 6 June 1979, at 176 (1981), paras 12.2–12.3; IACHR, *Coard et al. v. United States*, Case no. 10.951, Report No. 109/99, 29 September 1999, para. 37; ECtHR, *Al-Skeini v. United Kingdom*, Appl. no. 55721/07, Judgment of 7 July 2011, paras 133–137.

As for the total displacement variant of *lex specialis*,[99] it is even less plausible. It stems from the rigid classical divide between the law of war and the law of peace (which would most certainly have no relevance to NIACs, a concept post-dating that rigid divide), has no support in any formal source of modern international law, is contradicted by the text of the derogation clauses themselves, and has been rejected as such by the ICJ and virtually all other authorities.

Option 2: interpret human rights treaties in light of IHL. The second option would be to interpret the substantive standards of IHRL while taking into account the relevant rules of IHL. Thus, in assessing whether a killing is 'arbitrary' in the sense of Article 6(1) ICCPR, we would rely on the rules of IHL on targeting, precautions in attack, prohibited weapons, etc. This is in fact precisely what the ICJ did in its *Nuclear Weapons* Advisory Opinion.[100] We can call this approach *lex specialis* as an aid to interpretation or a rule of norm conflict avoidance. This weak version of *lex specialis* is in my view unobjectionable,[101] but it is also one of limited utility. Firstly, it assumes that the test of arbitrariness will *necessarily* always be confined only to the rules of IHL. In other words, that the ICCPR or the ACHR could not impose any *further* conditions for a non-arbitrary deprivation of life or liberty if IHL applied, regardless of the particular circumstances.[102] Secondly, we should recall at this time the important textual differences between the ICCPR and the ACHR, on the one hand, and the ECHR on the other, in particular the fact that unlike the other two treaties the ECHR does not employ open standards such as arbitrariness when it comes to deprivations of life and liberty. Articles 2 and 5 ECHR use closed lists of permissible grounds which would exclude targeting on the basis of status alone or preventive security detention, and no amount of interpretation in light of IHL could change that. Put differently, if *lex specialis* was only an interpretative tool it could not help solve any of the four scenarios under the ECHR, even if it could do

[99] For an articulation of this approach, see, e.g. Response of the US to the request for Precautionary Measures on behalf of the detainees in Guantanamo Bay, Cuba, (2002) 41 ILM 1015, available online at http://www.derechos.org/nizkor/excep/usresp1.html (last accessed 23 July 2015): '[I]nternational human rights law is not applicable to the conduct of hostilities or the capture and detention of enemy combatants, which are governed by the more specific laws of armed conflict . . . It is humanitarian law, and not human rights law, that governs the capture and detention of enemy combatants in armed conflict. To the extent the ICJ's decision in the *Nuclear Weapons Case* implies otherwise, the United States reserves its judgment.' See also the ECtHR's summary of Russia's arguments in *Georgia v. Russia (II)*, *supra* note 72, para. 69: '[T]he Convention did not apply to a situation of international armed conflict where a State Party's forces were engaged in national defence, including in respect of any required operations abroad. In such circumstances the conduct of the State Party's forces was governed exclusively by international humanitarian law.'

[100] *Nuclear Weapons*, *supra* note 9, para. 25: 'In principle, the right not arbitrarily to be deprived of one's life applies also in hostilities. The test of what is an arbitrary deprivation of life, however, then falls to be determined by the applicable *lex specialis*, namely, the law applicable in armed conflict which is designed to regulate the conduct of hostilities. Thus whether a particular loss of life, through the use of a certain weapon in warfare, is to be considered an arbitrary deprivation of life contrary to Article 6 of the Covenant, can only be decided by reference to the law applicable in armed conflict and not deduced from the terms of the Covenant itself.'

[101] See, e.g. Milanovic, *supra* note 2, at 249 ff, and the sources cited therein; Moir, *supra* note 15, at 192–193, 207 and 212.

[102] Consider, for example, the possibility of capturing the soldiers sleeping in the barracks if this operation would pose little or no risk to the forces of the adversary.

so under the ICCPR and the ACHR, nor could it for that matter remove the explicit requirements of judicial review of detention in all three treaties.

Option 3: Option 2 plus derogation. The third approach would complement the second option with derogations, whether the situation is territorial or extraterritorial. Thus, while the right to life is non-derogable in the ICCPR and the ACHR even in times of war or armed conflict, it is derogable in the ECHR. Hence, a state that wished to liberate itself from the constraints of Article 2 ECHR and rely on IHL as much as possible would need to derogate from that article.[103] One issue, as we have seen, is whether the reference to 'lawful acts of war' in Article 15(2) ECHR would encompass both IAC and NIAC. If that reference is limited to IACs only, killing in NIACs would need to comply with stricter standards as no possibility of derogation would be available. Similarly, an ECHR state party that wanted to have recourse to preventive detention would need to derogate from Article 5, and states would need to derogate from all of the treaties if they wanted to suspend or significantly delay judicial review of detention. In all of these situations, states would need to show that the derogation measures were strictly required by the exigencies of the situation.

Option 4: lex specialis as partial displacement. The fourth option would conceive of *lex specialis* not merely as a guide to interpretation, but as a rule of norm conflict resolution. In case of a genuine conflict between rules of IHL and IHRL, for instance with respect to killing or detention, conflict that could not be avoided through interpretation alone (because, for example, the text of Article 2 ECHR could not be stretched enough to accommodate the IHL approach to targeting, and/or because extraterritorial derogations would be unavailable), then the more 'special' IHL rule would displace or prevail over the inconsistent IHRL rule.[104] Regardless of the highly problematic construction of a hierarchical relationship between the general and the special, one issue with this approach is that it is unclear, even among its adherents, whether it would apply in the same way to IACs and to NIACs. Recall that at the moment of the creation of NIAC as a legal concept, Common Article 3 of the Geneva Convention was the sum total of all international law applying to NIACs. There were originally, in other words, no 'special' rules of the IHL of NIACs, say on targeting, that could override IHRL. While the customary law of NIACs has developed largely by analogy to IACs, it has done so relatively recently, and significant differences between the two types of armed conflict remain. It is thus perfectly possible to argue that *lex specialis* as partial displacement option is available for IACs only, in which IHL confers positive entitlements to the belligerent states.

But the bigger problem with this approach is that there is simply no support in any formal source of international law for the proposition that *lex specialis* is a rule of norm conflict resolution capable of overriding the clear text of conflicting treaty merely on grounds of 'specialness,' however exactly defined. Neither the VCLT nor any other treaty even mention *lex specialis*. As we have seen, it has been used by the ICJ in the *Nuclear Weapons* opinion only as an aid to interpretation, to fill in the

103 See Sari, *supra* note 6, paras 11–14.

104 See, e.g. Sassòli, *supra* note 67, at 71–73; Roxstrom *et al.*, *supra* note 6, at 120–121.

arbitrariness standard in Article 6 ICCPR, which created a window through with IHL could enter. The ICJ never ruled that IHL as *lex specialis* could punch a hole through the wall where no such window existed. And indeed applying this option to Article 2 ECHR would render the availability of derogations with respect to deaths resulting from lawful acts of war under Article 15(2) ECHR entirely superfluous. If *lex specialis* was so powerful as to create unwritten exceptions from Article 2, what purpose would have been served by the derogation clause?

Option 5: interpretation as amendment. This final option would essentially lead to the same outcomes as option 4, but without relying on the formal device of *lex specialis* as a (supposed) tool of norm conflict resolution. The appeal of *lex specialis* lies precisely in the fact that it lends the appearance of objectivity, of some kind of mathematical or logical inquiry into what is special and what is general, and thus hides patently political judgments behind the veneer of a catchy Latin phrase. But a court (or some other authoritative interpreter) may decide to dispense with the obfuscation and openly choose to 'read down' a categorical text so that it includes some unwritten exceptions in order to avoid results that the court considers unreasonable or impracticable. In essence, the text would be amended through interpretation. This is, in fact, precisely what the advocates of *lex specialis* as displacement want to achieve. The difference is in that this operation would have to be conducted openly, as a series of value or policy choices that it is,[105] which of course raises legitimacy concerns as to whether courts or other interpreters are entitled to make such choices and on what basis.

These are then the five options we have for dealing with our hard cases. Note that we do not necessarily need to choose one option for dealing with all four scenarios, but that they enable us to understand the linkages between otherwise conceptually distinct questions and to better appreciate the consequences of choosing one option over another. We can see that there is a direct connection between the availability of (extraterritorial) derogations and the effects of the *lex specialis* principle. A strong version of *lex specialis* as total or partial displacement makes derogations unnecessary in situations of armed conflict. A weak version of *lex specialis* as a mere interpretative tool will require derogations in order to enable status-based targeting, or preventive detention, or to suspend judicial review of such detention.[106] And this would not depend on (extra)territoriality. The choice between weaker or stronger *lex specialis* would apply equally to scenarios B and C, and A and D. If, in other words, we think a derogation is necessary to allow for status-based targeting under Article 2 ECHR when the hostilities take place within the state party's

[105] For an example of this pragmatic approach, see the *Amicus Curiae* Brief submitted by F. Hampson and N. Lubell in *Hassan v. United Kingdom*, Appl. no. 29750/09, available online at https://www.essex.ac.uk/hrc/documents/practice/amicus-curae.pdf (last accessed 23 July 2015).

[106] Assuming that human rights bodies would permit derogations from judicial review of detention, which they are unlikely to do despite the fact that the right is not expressly specified as non-derogable in the treaties—see General Comment No. 29, *supra* note 15, para. 16; IACtHR, *Habeas Corpus in Emergency Situations*, Advisory Opinion, 30 January 1987, decision available online online at http://www.corteidh.or.cr/docs/opiniones/seriea_08_ing.pdf (last accessed 23 July 2015).

territory, and that *lex specialis* is of no help to us there, then that same reasoning would extend to hostilities outside the state's territory.

The real difficulty for the proponents of a strong version of *lex specialis* is whether the displacement of human rights standards, inconsistent with IHL, would operate in both IACs and NIACs.[107] Consider, for example, the United Kingdom's position with respect to the situation in Northern Ireland. While many observers believed that the situation at least at some points in time legally qualified as a NIAC, the UK government categorically refused to acknowledge this. But it still sought to have recourse to internment, and in order to do that it derogated from Article 5 ECHR, which would otherwise have prohibited preventive detention—a derogation found to be lawful by the ECtHR.[108] Now, if the United Kingdom had acknowledged the existence of a NIAC in Northern Ireland, would that have dispensed with the need to derogate from Article 5, as a strong *lex specialis* would have precluded the wrongfulness of any resort to internment that would comply with IHL? Or would a derogation be necessary in in the undisputed presence of a NIAC? The Northern Ireland situation finds a parallel in Chechnya, with the caveat that, unlike the United Kingdom, Russia never derogated with respect to events in Chechnya itself.

The ECtHR will inevitably have to choose between the options presented above in at least some of the cases currently pending before it,[109] for instance in the second inter-state case brought by Georgia against Russia, in *Hassan v. United Kingdom*,[110] or in the inter-state case brought by Ukraine against Russia. To take the last case as an example, there is little doubt that an IAC existed between Ukraine and Russia at some point in March 2014, even in the absence of intense armed hostilities.[111] The control established by Russia over Crimea can also be described as a belligerent occupation,[112] and one that is likely to last for a very long time. Both IHL and the ECHR will hence apply to Russia's conduct in Crimea. Russia thus seized by force Ukrainian military bases in Crimea, capturing and detaining some of the Ukrainian personnel.[113] Captured Ukrainian soldiers would qualify as

[107] See, e.g. Sassòli, *supra* note 67, at 81–82 and 88–90; Hampson, 'The Relationship between International Humanitarian Law and Human Rights Law from the Perspective of a Human Rights Treaty Body', 90 *International Review of the Red Cross* (2008) 549, at 563–566.

[108] See *Ireland v. United Kingdom, supra* note 61.

[109] As of 1 June 2014.

[110] Appl. no. 29750/09. See further Milanovic, 'Hassan v. United Kingdom, IHL and IHRL, and Other News in (Extra-)Territoriality and Shared Responsibility', *EJIL: Talk!*, 18 December 2013, available online at http://www.ejiltalk.org/hassan-v-united-kingdom-ihl-and-ihrl-and-other-news-in-extra-territoriality-and-shared-responsibility (last accessed 23 July 2015).

[111] See Blank, 'The Continuing Importance of a Low Threshold for LOAC Application in International Armed Conflict', *Just Security*, 19 March 2014, at https://www.justsecurity.org/8348/guest-post-continuing-importance-threshold-loac-application-international-armed-conflict (last accessed 23 July 2015).

[112] Note that under Common Art. 2 of the 1949 Geneva Conventions, the Conventions 'apply to all cases of partial or total occupation of the territory of a High Contracting Party, *even if the said occupation meets with no armed resistance*' (emphasis added).

[113] See, e.g. 'Russian Troops "Overrun Crimea's Feodosia Naval Base"', *BBC News*, 24 March 2014, available online at http://www.bbc.co.uk/news/world-europe-26710884 (last accessed 23 July 2015).

prisoners of war under IHL, and could be held under IHL until the cessation of active hostilities. But what about the ECHR? A strong version of *lex specialis* would remove the categorical prohibition on preventive detention in Article 5, whereas a weak one could not, absent a derogation—the detention would be lawful under IHL, but unlawful under the ECHR. Indeed, this was precisely the finding of the European Commission with regard to Turkey's internment of Cypriot combatants and civilians, which it found could not be justified under Article 5 without a derogation.[114]

Those advocating for a strong version of *lex specialis* rely precisely on the fact that by and large states do not derogate to enable status-based targeting and security detention in situations of armed conflict, but as I have explained above this failure is not necessarily the result of any agreement among states about the proper scope of the *lex specialis* principle. And extending the strong version of that principle to NIACs in particular—today much more widespread than IACs—would remove the key safeguards that the derogation process offers. Note in that regard that those who advocate for strong *lex specialis* in NIACs logically must do so both for NIACs which are purely internal and those that are cross-border in nature. In other words, if one thinks that even though a NIAC existed in Northern Ireland the United Kingdom still had to derogate from Article 5 ECHR in order to resort to preventive security detention, then one must also accept that the United Kingdom had to derogate to authorize such detention in say post-2001 Afghanistan. *Lex specialis* might vary in strength depending on the type of armed conflict (IAC or NIAC), but it cannot vary depending on whether a human rights treaty is applied intra- or extraterritorially.

My own view is that *lex specialis* exists only in its weak variant, as an aid to interpretation,[115] and that even with respect to the arbitrariness standards in the ICCPR and the ACHR the principle will not inevitably mean that IHL-compliant conduct will necessarily also comply with human rights law. Arbitrariness might bring something new to the table. Consequently, derogations—be they internal or extraterritorial—would be a key tool, albeit not an infallible one, in avoiding conflicts between IHL and IHRL, providing not only flexibility for states when they need it the most, but also important substantive and procedural safeguards.

If states refuse to derogate out of political calculation (as they are free to do),[116] then they must also suffer the consequences of their choice and the application of more stringent human rights scrutiny. In so doing, states expose themselves to the

[114] *Cyprus v. Turkey*, *supra* note 75, paras 309–312. Hampson considered such a result to be absurd—see Hampson, *supra* note 107, at 565. But there is nothing absurd about states being able to assume more stringent obligations than what IHL allows, especially if they fail to use the derogation mechanism that they themselves have put into place. The outcome would be absurd only if it could not be avoided through derogations, in which case the only option would be resort to a stronger variant of *lex specialis*.

[115] See Milanovic, *supra* note 2, at 249–260. See also Prud'homme, 'Lex Specialis: Oversimplifying a More Complex and Multifaceted Relationship?', 40 *Israel Law Review* (2007) 356.

[116] See Dinstein, *supra* note 23, at 74 (arguing that that the fact that a derogation can be validly made does not mean that the state will indeed make it, as this is a matter of its own discretion and judgment).

risk that the same conduct may be lawful under IHL, but not lawful under IHRL. I do not think there is anything unnatural, anomalous or unreasonable about such a result. After all it is international law orthodoxy to say that the same conduct can be lawful under the *jus in bello* but unlawful under the *jus ad bellum*, and vice versa. The same logic applies to the relationship between IHL and IHRL, since states can freely assume contradictory commitments, and have only themselves to blame if they do not use the tools that the treaties foresee for avoiding such norm conflicts.

4. The Link to Sovereignty and the *Jus ad Bellum*

The final relationship that I want to examine is precisely that between extraterritorial derogations and legitimacy of government and/or possible violations of the *jus ad bellum*. One possible objection to extraterritorial derogations is that because they involve the diminishment of human rights, it is only the legitimate government of a territory which can undertake them. At the very least, an intervening state that violates the UN Charter and other rules of the *jus ad bellum* should not be permitted to invoke derogations—an aggressor has no right to liberalize the rules on the use of force or on the deprivation of liberty just because this would suit its interests. Thus, for example, Russia would have no right to derogate with regard to the situation in Crimea even if it wanted to, nor could the UK government have derogated for the situation in Iraq which it had invaded unlawfully.

Support for this view can be found in the text of the derogation clauses themselves, when they provide that derogation measures must not be inconsistent with the state's other obligations under international law. Similarly, the object and purpose of human rights treaties is inseparable from the Charter regime and its mission to preserve international peace and security.[117] Finally, there are several points in the drafting history during which some state delegations argued—without opposition—that references to 'war' should be understood as requiring compliance with the Charter regime, for example, as to a purely *defensive* war.[118]

But this objection could be met with several counter-arguments. Firstly, derogations only concern the relationship between the derogating state and the individuals concerned, not the territorial government which may or may not be temporarily or permanently displaced, in whole or in part. The extent of the United Kingdom's obligations under the ECHR towards the people of Iraq should depend only on an objective assessment of the exigencies of the situation. Secondly, the derogation clauses only require the derogation measures, not the wider context in which they

[117] For arguments along those lines, see, e.g. Wilde, *supra* note 82, at 652–656; El Zeidy, *supra* note 70, at 291–292; Da Costa, *supra* note 6, at 135–136; Roxstrom *et al.*, *supra* note 6, at 118–119; Schabas, '*Lex Specialis*? Belt and Suspenders? The Parallel Operation of Human Rights Law and the Law of Armed Conflict, and the Conundrum of *Jus ad Bellum*', 40 *Israel Law Review* (2007) 592; Bennoune, 'Toward a Human Rights Approach to Armed Conflict: Iraq 2003', 11 *U.C. Davis Journal of International Law and Policy* (2004) 171, 213–216.

[118] See *supra* notes 30 and 40.

are implemented, such as to the initial decision to use force against another state, to be consistent with the state's other obligations under international law. Thirdly, because *jus ad bellum* issues can be both politically and legally complex and controversial, insulating human rights from the *jus ad bellum* can help preserve the integrity of human rights and the institutional competence of human rights bodies.[119] This is precisely why, for example, the European Commission did its best to avoid considering *jus ad bellum* legality of the Turkish invasion of Cyprus in its consideration of Article 15,[120] and why the ECtHR in *Loizidou* found that the ECHR would apply extraterritorially whenever a state exercises effective control of an area, whether that control was obtained *lawfully* or *unlawfully* under the *jus ad bellum*, i.e. regardless of whether Turkey had the right to invade Cyprus.[121] That same principle can be extended to derogations, which would depend on a purely factual relationship between the governor and the governed.

In other words, just like we can separate the *jus in bello* from the *jus ad bellum*, so can we separate human rights from the *jus ad bellum*. Whether we should do this or not is—yet again—a choice. Integrating IHRL with the *jus ad bellum* would send a symbolic message about the importance of the convergence between the ideals of peace and human rights. It may provide a disincentive to states against breaching the Charter, if they would also be subject to human rights scrutiny in doing so, but it could also render derogations ineffective and lead to a spiral of non-compliance. For example, whatever the United Kingdom did in Iraq after invading it unlawfully would be tainted by the initial illegality and breach of the Charter, and would be hard or impossible to justify under the ECHR—at least until a new Iraqi government emerged that validly consented to the presence of British troops on its territory, or such presence obtained the explicit approval of the Security Council. Similarly, Russia's aggression on Ukraine would render any killing or detention of a Ukrainian soldier by Russian forces unlawful under the ECHR, and so on.

Alternatively, we could treat IHRL just as we treat IHL, and insulate both from *jus ad bellum* considerations as far as possible. The domain of human rights proper would be the treatment of individuals qua individuals by the state, not subject to the inter-state concerns of the *jus ad bellum*, which are better dealt with through the substantive rules and institutions established for that purpose. In any event, both options can be legitimately argued for.

[119] See Macdonald, *supra* note 38, at 247: 'This [*jus ad bellum* legality], I believe, is not a question for the Strasbourg Court. The issue is intrinsically political and too far removed from the main task with which the Convention is concerned'; Harris, *supra* note 1, at 638: 'Such matters are for the UN Security Council and the consideration of them by the Strasbourg authorities would raise enormously complicated problems of fact-finding and intricate legal questions'; Ergec, *supra* note 1, at 129–134.

[120] For example, in one of the inter-state cases the Cypriot government did argue that derogations were not permissible in aggressive wars—see *Cyprus v. Turkey*, *supra* note 75, para. 512, an argument that the Commission avoided as it found that Turkey had not resorted to derogation in the first place.

[121] *Loizidou*, *supra* note 97, para. 62: 'Bearing in mind the object and purpose of the Convention, the responsibility of a Contracting Party may also arise when as a consequence of military action—whether lawful or unlawful—it exercises effective control of an area outside its national territory. The obligation to secure, in such an area, the rights and freedoms set out in the Convention, derives from the fact of such control whether it be exercised directly, through its armed forces, or through a subordinate local administration.'

5. Conclusion

The problem of extraterritorial derogations presents us with a series of choices, choices which cannot be made merely on formal grounds. The question really is whether we want extraterritorial derogations, and for what purpose. In answering that question we must strive to balance universality and effectiveness, and find a solution which is fair, practicable, predictable and legally sound. Allowing for a more expansive use of derogations in an extraterritorial setting could promote these goals, especially if derogations as resorted to by states with strong domestic courts and democratic institutions,[122] but it could also lead to an increase in the abuse of derogations, both internally and externally. At the same time, the differences between the ICCPR and the ACHR on the one hand, and the ECHR on the other, allow us to better appreciate the distinctions between weaker and stronger variants of *lex specialis*. In doing so, the choice becomes clearer: opting for a weaker variant of *lex specialis*, or a stronger one that would apply only to IACs, will of necessity require recourse to extraterritorial derogations in we want to enable ECHR states parties to engage in status-based targeting and administrative detention in cross-border NIACs.[123] Conversely, a stronger version of *lex specialis*—with all its faults and the uncertainties it brings—would make extraterritorial derogations less necessary.

At present, human rights courts and treaty bodies have yet to adopt a clear approach on these sets of issues and choose between the options that are available to them. Until relatively recently there was little need to do so. When, for example, during the first Gulf War the UK government preventively detained 35 Iraqis studying at British universities as prisoners of war, on the basis of their real or supposed ties with the Iraqi military, and did so without derogating from the ECHR, nobody thought of challenging the Article 5 compliance of that detention before the ECtHR.[124] But that has changed. Bearing in mind not only the cases

[122] See Hafner-Burton, Helfer and Fariss, 'Emergency and Escape: Explaining Derogations from Human Rights Treaties', 65 *International Organization* (2011) 673 (arguing that it is precisely such states that will most frequently resort to derogations, since they possess 'compliance constituencies' that can hold governments to account for repressing individual rights, whereas authoritarian states will violate individual rights with or without derogations).

[123] Other options, such as security detention clearly and expressly authorized by the Security Council, which could potentially prevail over human rights treaties by virtue of Art. 103 of the Charter, are not only fraught with their own conceptual problems but are unlikely to provide a systematic solution, since they depend on the agreement of the Council members to pass such an unambiguous resolution.

[124] On this episode see especially Risius, 'Prisoners of War in the United Kingdom', in P. Rowe (ed.), *The Gulf War 1990–91 in International and English Law* (1993) 255. The author wisely declined to discuss the impact, if any, of the ECHR and the ICCPR on the internment of these individuals. The United Kingdom also detained a number of Iraqi civilians, but it did not do so on the basis of the internment provisions of the Fourth Geneva Convention, but rather did so under immigration law, pending their deportation from the United Kingdom. Such detention could be accommodated under Art. 5(1)(f) ECHR, and would accordingly not pose the derogation/relationship with IHL problem. See further Walsh, 'Detention and Deportation of Foreign Nationals in the United Kingdom during the Gulf Conflict', in ibid., 268; 'Middle East Watch condemns Great Britain for holding 35 Iraqi

that are currently pending, but the inevitability of other cases that will follow, the time for making that choice is now. This is especially true of the ECtHR, whose longstanding (if understandable) evasiveness with regard to explaining the relationship between IHL and the ECHR soon must come to an end.[125]

residents as prisoners of war and detaining dozens of Arabs for deportation', *Human Rights Watch Newsletter*, 10 February 1991, available online at http://www.hrw.org/reports/pdfs/u/uk/uk912.pdf (last accessed 23 July 2015); Roberts, 'The Laws of War in the 1990–91 Gulf Conflict', 18 *International Security* (1993) 134, at 153–154.

[125] In that regard, the ECtHR's presumption of compatibility in *Al-Jedda, supra* note 19, para. 102 is squarely directed at the interpretation of Security Council resolutions in the context of Art. 103 of the Charter, and should not be taken as any kind of general statement regarding the ECHR's relationship with IHL—but see Pejic, 'The European Court of Human Rights' *Al-Jedda* Judgment: The Oversight of International Humanitarian Law', 93 *International Review of the Red Cross* (2011) 837. If the Court wanted to, it could still find that IHL rules on internment trump Art. 5 ECHR by virtue of a strong *lex specialis* without having to depart from *Al-Jedda* (although I think it should not do so).

Piracy, International Law and Human Rights

*Tullio Treves and Cesare Pitea**

1. The Changing International Legal Framework for Combating Piracy

A. The Revival of Piracy and the Applicable Rules of International Law

During the last decade pirate activity off the coast of Somalia has raised attention to a phenomenon whose interest previous to this seemed merely historical.[1] Other areas around the world have also recently witnessed significant pirate activity, like in Southeast Asia and the Gulf of Guinea. Nonetheless, it is the pirate activity off the coast of Somalia that has raised particular attention and alarm, resulting in the emergence of frequent resolutions of the United Nations Security Council, acting under Chapter VII of the Charter, and a massive naval presence of about 20 different states in the area.[2] In addition to this it is worth noting that while the

* Section 1 and Section 2, sub-sections F–H and J were written by Tullio Treves and Section 2, sub-sections A–E and I were written by Cesare Pitea.

[1] The present section draws from, and updates, the following essays: Treves, 'Piracy, Law of the Sea and Use of Force: Developments off the Coast of Somalia', 20 *European Journal of International Law* (2009) 399–414; T. Treves, 'Piracy and the International Law of the Sea', in D. Guilfoyle (ed.), *Modern Piracy* (2013) 117–146; Treves, 'The Fight Against Piracy and the Law of the Sea', 22 *Italian Yearbook of International Law* (2012) 23.

[2] Interesting legal and factual elements are discussed in the report of the International Expert Group on Piracy off the Somali Coast, *Piracy off the Somali Coast, Workshop Commissioned by the Special Representative of the Secretary-General of the UN in Somalia Ambassador Ahmedou Ould-Abdallah,* Nairobi, 10–21 November 2008, available online at http://www.imcsnet.org/imcs/docs/somalia_piracy_intl_experts_report_consolidated.pdf (last accessed 23 July 2015); as well in the UN Secretary-General's Reports, see Report of the Secretary-General pursuant to Security Council Resolution 1846 (2008), UN Doc. S/2009/146, 16 March 2009; Report of the Secretary-General pursuant to Security Council Resolution 1846 (2008), UN Doc. S/2009/590, 13 November 2009; Report of the Secretary-General on Possible Options to Further the Aim of Prosecuting and Imprisoning Persons Responsible for Acts of Piracy and Armed Robbery at Sea off the Coast of Somalia, UN Doc. S/2010/394, 26 July 2010; Report of the Secretary General Pursuant to Security Council Resolution 1897, UN Doc. S/2010/556, 27 October 2010; Letter Dated 24 January 2011 from the Secretary-General to the President of the Security Council, UN Doc. S/2011/30, 25 January 2011 (hereinafter Lang Report); Report of the Secretary-General on the Modalities for the Establishment of Specialized Somali Anti-Piracy Courts, UN Doc. S/2011/360, 15 June 2011; Report of the Secretary-General on the Protection of Somali Natural Resources and Waters, UN Doc. S/2011/661, 25 October 2011; Report of the Secretary-General pursuant to Security Council Resolution 1950 (2010), UN Doc. S/2011/662, 25 October 2011. An

Security Council adopted a resolution on piracy in relation to the Gulf of Guinea in 2011,[3] it made no reference to Chapter VII of the Charter.

It is generally recognized that the international law rules as set out in the United Nations Convention on the Law of the Sea (UNCLOS) are the appropriate legal framework to examine questions concerning piracy. From the first one adopted in 2008[4] to the latest of 12 November 2014,[5] all Security Council resolutions on piracy off the coast of Somalia reaffirm that 'international law as reflected in the United Nations Convention on the Law of the Sea ("The Convention") sets out the legal framework applicable to activities in the ocean, including countering piracy and armed robbery at sea'. Adopted in 2011, the resolution on piracy in the Gulf of Guinea when referring to UNCLOS emphasizes 'in particular its articles 100, 101 and 105'.[6] The reason for this specification, which was not repeated in the 2012, 2013 and 2014 resolutions on piracy off the coast of Somalia, is not clear. In any case the three articles quoted in the 2011 resolution, which deal with the duty to cooperate in the repression of piracy, the definition of piracy and the seizure of a pirate ship respectively, are those that describe the essential features of piracy and set down the international law rules.

accurate short general survey of international law concerning piracy is in Shearer, 'Piracy', in R. Wolfrum (ed.), *The Max Planck Encyclopedia of Public International Law* (2010), available online at http://opil.ouplaw.com/home/ORIL (last accessed 23 July 2015), while an older, but penetrating analysis is in M. Giuliano, *I diritti e gli obblighi degli Stati, I, L'ambiente dell'attività degli Stati* (1956), at 393–401. Recent developments are examined in Vœlckel, 'La piraterie entre Charte et Convention: à propos de la résolution 1816 du Conseil de Sécurité', 12 *Annuaire du Droit de la Mer* (2007) 479; Kontorovich, 'International Legal Responses to Piracy off the Coast of Somalia', 13(2) *ASIL Insights* (2009); Guilfoyle, 'Piracy off Somalia: UN Security Council Resolution 1816 and IMO Regional Counter-Piracy Efforts', 57 *International and Comparative Law Quarterly* (2008) 690; Tancredi, 'Di pirati e Stati "falliti": il Consiglio di Sicurezza autorizza il ricorso alla forza nelle acque territoriali della Somalia', 91 *Rivista di Diritto Internazionale* (2008) 937; Kraska, 'Developing Piracy Policy for the National Strategy for Maritime Security and the International Maritime Organization', in M. H. Nordquist *et al.* (eds), *Legal Challenges in Maritime Security* (2008) 331; Menefee, 'An Overview of Piracy in the First Decade of the 21st Century', in ibid., 441; and Skaridov, 'Hostis Humani Generis', in ibid., 479; D. Guilfoyle, *Shipping Interdiction and the Law of the Sea* (2009), at 26–74; *Piracy off Somalia: The Challenges for International Law*, Panel with remarks by D. Guilfoyle, A. P. Rubin, M. Halberstam, J. A. Roach, K. Shepherd, R. Beckman, 103 *American Society of International Law, Proceedings of the 103rd Annual Meeting* (2009) 89; Roach, 'Countering Piracy in Somalia: International Law and International Institutions', 104 *American Journal of International Law* (2011) 397; F. Graziani, *Il contrasto alla pirateria marittima nel diritto internazionale* (2011); Munari, 'La "nuova" pirateria e il diritto internazionale: spunti per una ricerca', 92 *Rivista di Diritto Internazionale* (2009) 325; Tuerk, 'The Resurgence of Piracy: A Phenomenon of Modern Times', 17 *University of Miami International and Comparative Law Review* (2009) 1, at 5; R. Geiss and A. Petrig, *Piracy and Armed Robbery at Sea, The Legal Framework for Counter-Piracy Operations in Somalia and the Gulf of Aden* (2011); Dinstein, 'Piracy *Jure Gentium*', in H. P. Hestermeyer *et al.* (eds), *Coexistence, Cooperation and Solidarity, Liber Amicorum Rüdiger Wolfrum* (2012) 1125; Golitsyn, 'Maritime Security (Case of Piracy)', in ibid., 1157; and Neuhold, 'The Return of Piracy: Problems, Parallels, Paradoxes' in ibid., 1239; R. C. Beckman and J. A. Roach, *Piracy and International Maritime Crimes in ASEAN, Prospects for Cooperation* (2012); D. Guilfoyle (ed.), *Modern Piracy* (2013); Kateka, 'Piracy and Armed Robbery', in *International Law of the Sea, Essays in Memory of Anatoly L. Kolodkin* (2014) 301; Annoni, 'International Action against Piracy and Armed Robbery at Sea Off the Coast of Somalia', 23 *Italian Yearbook of International Law* (2013) 175.

[3] SC Res. 2018, 31 October 2011.

[4] SC Res. 1814, 15 May 2008, 4th preambular para.

[5] SC Res. 2184, 12 November 2014, 7th preambular para.

[6] SC Res. 2018, *supra* note 3, 6th preambular para.

The definition of piracy according to Article 101 of UNCLOS requires the presence of two ships (the pirate ship and the victim ship) and that the act of piracy—described as an act of violence or depredation committed for private ends—must be conducted on the high seas. The rule of Article 105 of UNCLOS permits every state to seize a pirate ship on the high seas and to arrest the persons and seize the property on board. It also states that 'the courts of the State which carried out the seizure may decide upon the penalties to be imposed'. This article creates an exception to the principle of the freedom of the high seas, according to which a vessel cannot be interfered with by a foreign state on the high seas, and removes any doubt as to whether domestic laws establishing universal jurisdiction over piracy conform with international law.

The rule set out in Article 105 is permissive because it contains the verb 'may'. According to the rule, states do not contravene international law if they define the jurisdiction of their courts, as existing independent of any connection with the pirates' criminal activity, and the missions of their naval vessels, as including seizure of pirate ships wherever they may be, provided that this does not take place in another state's territorial sea.

Only Article 100 of UNCLOS contains a positive obligation, namely that: 'All States shall co-operate to the fullest possible extent in the repression of piracy on the high seas or in any other place outside the jurisdiction of any State.'

B. The Security Council and Piracy off the Coast of Somalia

The Security Council has linked the activities of pirates off the coast of Somalia with the notion of a threat to international peace and security. Since Resolution 733, the Security Council has routinely invoked Chapter VII with regards to the situation in Somalia,[7] and has stated that this situation constitutes or continues to constitute 'a threat to international peace and security'.[8] Since its first Resolution on piracy off the coast of Somalia, which was adopted in 2008, the Security Council has consistently 'determine[d]' that such piracy 'exacerbate[s] the situation in Somalia which continues to constitute a threat to international peace and security in the region'.[9] A declaration made on 16 December 2008 by the Chinese Minister of Foreign Affairs at the Security Council meeting, which was held at the level of Foreign Ministers and approved Resolution 1851, clearly reflects this approach: 'The long-term delay in the settlement of the Somali issue is posing a serious threat to international peace and security, while the rampant piracy off the Somali coast has worsened the security situation in Somalia.'[10] The link is made indirectly, avoiding the criticism that the Council often incurs when applying the notion of

[7] SC Res. 733, 23 January 1992, para. 5.

[8] SC Res. 1814, *supra* note 4, penultimate preambular para. The determination has been repeated in most resolutions of the Security Council on piracy off the Somali coast, most recently SC Res. 2184, *supra* note 5, penultimate preambular para.

[9] SC Res. 1816, 2 June 2008, last preambular para., and thereafter in all the Council's resolutions on piracy off the Somali coast.

[10] Security Council, 63rd Year, 6046th Meeting, UN Doc. S/PV.6046, 16 December 2008, at 5.

threat to international peace and security to matters previously not considered to be covered by this notion. Nevertheless, it meets the objective that action against piracy off the Somali coast is to be undertaken within the framework of Chapter VII of the UN Charter.

Since 2008 and up to the end of 2014, the Security Council, acting under Chapter VII of the UN Charter in all cases, had adopted 13 resolutions on piracy off the coast of Somalia.[11] These subsequent resolutions repeat the main points made in the previous ones. They have, however, become richer and more nuanced as the Security Council becomes progressively aware of the increasingly sophisticated practice of pirates and of states and international organizations engaging in counter-piracy operations. The reports of the Secretary General have helped to collect and present such practices.

These resolutions, while using the term 'piracy', do not define it. References to the provisions of UNCLOS and statements referring to how these provisions set 'out the legal framework applicable to combating piracy and armed robbery at sea' and 'provide guiding principles for cooperation to the fullest possible extent in the repression of piracy' indicate that the starting point is the definition in the Convention. These resolutions, however, always mention piracy in conjunction with 'armed robbery'. Armed robbery is also not defined in these resolutions. It is a term routinely used within the framework of the International Maritime Organization (IMO). It may be understood to include all acts of violence whose purposes are identical or similar to those of piracy but are not covered by the conventional definition of it, in particular because they may be perpetrated without using a ship against the target ship.[12] More importantly, in IMO parlance 'armed robbery' refers only to activities in waters under the jurisdiction of a state, so that it does not include acts committed on the high seas without the presence of two ships. By using the expression 'piracy and armed robbery against vessels in the territorial waters of Somalia and the high seas off the coast of Somalia'[13] the Security Council resolutions are meant to overcome such conventional limitations. As in most of the

[11] The relevant Security Council resolutions are: SC Res. 1816, *supra* note 9; SC Res. 1838, 7 October 2008; SC Res. 1846, 2 December 2008; SC Res. 1851, 16 December 2008; SC Res. 1897, 3 November 2009; SC Res. 1918, 27 April 2010; SC Res. 1950, 23 November 2010; SC Res. 1976, 11 April 2011; SC Res. 2015, 24 October 2011; SC Res. 2020, 22 November 2011; SC Res. 2077, 21 November 2012; SC Res. 2125, 18 November 2013; and SC Res. 2184, *supra* note 5.

[12] International Maritime Organization, Resolution A.922(22), Code of Practice for the Investigation of the Crimes of Piracy and Armed Robbery against Ships, 22 January 2002, Art. 2.2: '"Armed robbery against ships" means any unlawful act of violence or detention or any act of depredation, or threat thereof, other than an act of "piracy" directed against a ship or against persons or property on board such a ship within a State's jurisdiction over such offences'; the definition is almost literally repeated in the Regional Cooperation Agreement on Combating Piracy and Armed Robbery against Ships in Asia (adopted 11 November 2004, entered into force 4 September 2006), (2005) 44 ILM 829, Art. 1(2); and in the Code of Conduct Concerning the Repression of Piracy and Armed Robbery Against Ships in the Western Indian Ocean and the Gulf of Aden, adopted in Djibouti (adopted 29 January 2009), IMO Doc. C 102/14, 3 April 2009, Art. 1(2), available online at http://www.imo.org/OurWork/Security/PIU/Documents/DCoC%20English.pdf (last accessed 23 July 2015). See Section 1.E *infra*.

[13] SC Res. 1816, *supra* note 9, penultimate preambular para.; SC Res. 1846, *supra* note 11, penultimate preambular para.; recently SC Res. 2020, *supra* note 11, penultimate preambular para.

Somali cases, in which two or more ships are involved, reference to 'armed robbery' would not appear to be strictly dictated by the needs of existing practice but rather inspired by the aim of including all acts connected with piracy, such as preparatory acts, and future possible acts involving one ship only.

The key element in the resolutions is set down in paragraph 7 of Resolution 1816. It deals with the limitation of the definition of piracy to acts perpetrated on the high seas. Such limitation, under customary rules, prevents states other than Somalia from dealing with acts of piracy as they take place in practice. For instance, acts of piracy sometimes take place wholly within the Somali territorial sea. More frequently, an attack on the high seas is followed by the retreat of either the pirate skiff or the pirated ship into the territorial and internal waters of Somalia.

The key element, expressed in paragraph 7 of Resolution 1816, consists in granting certain states authorization to:

(a) enter the territorial waters of Somalia for the purpose of repressing acts of piracy and armed robbery at sea, in a manner consistent with such action permitted on the high seas with respect to piracy under relevant international law; and

(b) use, within the territorial waters of Somalia, in a manner consistent with action permitted on the high seas with respect to piracy under relevant international law, all necessary means to repress acts of piracy and armed robbery.

The basic effect of these provisions is to make the rules of international law dealing with piracy on the high seas applicable to territorial waters, *inter alia*, permitting pursuit from the high seas into these waters, and clarifies that states acting under these rules within the territorial waters of Somalia may use 'all necessary means'.

Furthermore, following an episode in which French troops pursued pirates onto the Somali mainland,[14] Resolution 1851 of 16 December 2008 included an additional authorization to conduct 'all necessary measures that are appropriate in Somalia for the purpose of suppressing acts of piracy and armed robbery at sea' (paragraph 6, emphasis added). The expression 'in Somalia' clearly alludes to action undertaken on the mainland.[15]

[14] This is the operation conducted on 11 April 2008 in Somali territory that succeeded in capturing six of the pirates, and in recovering part of the ransom collected in an act of piracy against the passengers of the French cruise ship *Le Ponant*, freed at sea by French forces. See facts and comments in *Sentinelle* No. 145 (20 April 2008), available online at http://www.sentinelle-droit-international.fr/bulletins/a2008/20080420_bull_145/sentinelle_145.htm#securitemer1 (last accessed 23 July 2015). On 20 April 2008, the Somali Prime Minister Nur Hassan Hussein, stated in the international media: 'The French forces arrested six Somali pirates and took them to France to face justice. We encourage such steps by the French. The Somali government asks the international community to take action against piracy' (ibid.). The uncertainty as to the real meaning and scope of such a statement brought France to propose the draft of what became SC Res. 1851, *supra* note 11. This episode gave rise to the case of ECtHR, *Ali Samatar and others v. France*, Appl. nos. 17110/10 and 17301/10, Judgment of 4 December 2014 (at the time of writing the judgment is only available in French), which will be considered in Section 2 *infra*.

[15] See the Interventions by the British Minister for Foreign Affairs and by the US Secretary of State upon Approval of Resolution 1851, in UN Doc. S/PV.6046, *supra* note 10, at 4 and 9.

C. Do the Security Council's Resolutions Have an Impact on Customary Law

A very interesting question raised by the Security Council resolutions concerning piracy off the coast of Somalia is whether the rules introduced by these resolutions have had an impact on general international law as codified in UNCLOS.

As is well known, there are two main differences. Firstly, under the resolutions of the Security Council, the rights that all states enjoy in repressing piracy on the high seas extend to Somalia's territorial waters. Secondly, the resolutions extend the expanded UNCLOS regime to include 'armed robbery', which is constantly mentioned together with piracy.

The resolutions explicitly state that they apply 'only with respect to the situation in Somalia and shall not affect the rights or obligations or responsibilities of Member States under international law, including any rights or obligations under the [UNCLOS] with respect to any other situation'. They underscore in particular that they 'shall not be considered as establishing customary international law'.[16] These observations, together with statements made in the debates of the Security Council, make clear that when adopting the resolutions the members of the Security Council had no intention to contribute to a practice that has the effect of changing existing customary law.

Notwithstanding this approach, it seems worth considering whether the implementation of the resolutions in practice has brought about some changes to the general law of piracy. When examining this question it seems useful to distinguish between changes to customary rules codified in UNCLOS and interpretations or clarifications of the existing rules, which can be inferred from the resolutions as elements illuminating *opinio juris*.

In light of the explicit and repeated remarks to the contrary in the resolutions discussed above, it can be ruled out that the customary (and UNCLOS) rule limiting repression of piracy to the high seas has been changed by extending it to the territorial sea. One could imagine that authorizations of the kind contained in the resolutions addressing the situation in Somalia, if repeated in different contexts could pave the way for such extension. However, in the first case of piracy after Somalia, namely piracy in the Gulf of Guinea, the Security Council reiterated that UNCLOS is 'the legal framework applicable to countering piracy and armed robbery at sea', without authorizing states to act in the territorial sea.[17]

D. The Impact of Instability in Somalia on the Extension to the Territorial Sea of the International Law Rules for the Repression of Piracy

When the Security Council adopted its first resolution in 2008, the extension of the rights set down in Article 105 of UNCLOS to the territorial sea was strictly linked to

[16] See for instance SC Res. 2077, *supra* note 11, para. 13.
[17] SC Res. 2018, *supra* note 3.

the lack of effective government in Somalia. The Security Council underlined 'the crisis situation in Somalia, and the lack of capacity of the Transitional Federal Government (TFG) to interdict pirates or patrol and secure either the international sea lanes off the coast of Somalia or Somalia's territorial waters'.[18] This preambular paragraph was repeated in subsequent resolutions adopted by the Security Council until 2011.[19] In 2012, however, Resolution 2077 omitted this paragraph and only left a paragraph, already contained in previous resolutions, recognizing the 'ongoing instability' in Somalia and 'stressing the need for a comprehensive response by the international community to repress piracy and armed robbery at sea and tackle its underlying causes'.[20]

This change reflects the fact that at the time Resolution 2077 was adopted the situation in Somalia had started to change. After the adoption of the 'road map' on 11 September 2011,[21] 'new Somali authorities' were established. They replaced the TFG for the purpose of the authorizations set out in the anti-piracy resolutions of the Security Council.[22] While Resolution 2077, which was followed in 2013 by Resolution 2125,[23] repeats the authorization for 'cooperating States' to operate in the Somali territorial sea, this is the first resolution to underline 'the primary responsibility of Somali authorities in the fight against piracy and armed robbery off the coast of Somalia'.[24] It also calls '*upon* the Somali authorities to interdict, and upon interdiction to investigate and prosecute pirates and to patrol the territorial waters off the coast of Somalia to suppress acts of piracy and armed robbery at sea'.[25] For the first time the Security Council refers to the right and duty of the Somali authorities to exercise the powers that coastal states normally exercise in the territorial sea.

This admittedly prudent evolution of the Security Council's attitude seems to confirm the reason for limiting the scope of the international law rules concerning piracy to the high seas as codified in UNCLOS, which is due to the fact that the coastal state enjoys the exclusive exercise of police powers in the territorial sea (including, but not limited to, those with respect to piracy). International law presupposes that the coastal state effectively exercises these powers and does not accept that other states participate uninvited in such an exercise. When effective governmental authority over the coastal state is lacking, such an assumption becomes moot. According to the Security Council, in these cases other states may

[18] SC Res. 1816, *supra* note 9, 7th preambular paragraph, repeated in all resolutions up to SC Res. 2020, *supra* note 11, 4th preambular para.

[19] SC Res. 1851, *supra* note 11, 5th preambular para.; SC Res. 1897, *supra* note 11, 5th preambular para.; SC Res. 1950, *supra* note 11, 7th preambular para.; SC Res. 2020, *supra* note 11, 8th preambular para.

[20] SC Res. 2077, *supra* note 11, 4th preambular para.; SC Res. 2125, *supra* note 11, 5th preambular para. This language is retained in SC Res. 2184, *supra* note 5, para. 2.

[21] Report of the Secretary-General on Somalia, UN Doc. S/2011/759, 9 December 2011, Annex.

[22] SC Res. 2067, 18 September 2012, para. 14, and also SC Res. 2184, *supra* note 5.

[23] SC Res. 2077, *supra* note 11, 4th preambular para. and para. 12. Also SC Res. 2125, *supra* note 11, para. 12.

[24] SC Res. 2077, *supra* note 11, paras 4 and 12. Also SC Res. 2184, *supra* note 5, para. 4.

[25] SC Res. 2077, *supra* note 11, para. 6 (italics in original). Also SC Res. 2125, *supra* note 11, para. 6.

expand their police powers and exercise the powers set out in Article 105 in all waters, including those nominally belonging to the territorial sea but adjacent to a territory on which there is no effective exercise of governmental authority.

It can be clearly argued that the extension of police powers to include Somalia's territorial sea under Article 105 of UNCLOS is based on a Chapter VII decision of the Security Council and on the authorization of the TFG, which was subsequently replaced by the 'new Somali authorities'. It can be observed that either of these two bases is sufficient to justify such an extension.[26] Nevertheless, there is a fictional nature attached to the TFG and possibly (hopefully not for long) to the 'new Somali authorities'. The question is whether police activity by interested governments would be considered illegal in a situation similar to that of Somalia, where there is intense piracy activity in waters near the coast of a territory with no effective government. It could be argued that legality is a natural consequence because sovereignty over the territorial sea depends on sovereignty on the land attached to the coast. Therefore, without such sovereignty there would be no territorial sea and the high seas or a high seas-like regime would extend to include the coast.

This does not imply a change in the customary law of the sea or contradict the provisions of UNCLOS. It is a clarification in relation to the meaning of existing rules to the effect that when these refer to powers of all states to suppress piracy 'in the high seas', they mean in all parts of the sea in which there is no effective exercise of sovereignty by a coastal state. The same conclusion may be reached by referring to a specific sentence in Article 105 of UNCLOS, which confers the right on all states to seize a pirate ship '[o]n the high seas *or in any other place outside the jurisdiction of any State*' (emphasis added). While this extension to other places outside the jurisdiction of any state has normally been seen as referring to activity in unoccupied islands or territories and unclaimed parts of Antarctica,[27] it may equally apply to waters adjacent to a territory, where there is no effective exercise of sovereignty.

In light of the above, it may be argued that the Security Council's resolutions do not contribute to changing the international law of the sea with regard to this point under consideration and that repression of piracy in the waters adjacent to the Somali coast would be licit even in the absence of such resolutions. In the hypothetical situation where there is a lack of effective power on a coastal territory, this conclusion would be correct. Political reality, however, means that the Security Council considers it necessary to provide a double legal basis—that of the TFG's, and now the new Somali authorities' authorization and that of decisions under Chapter VII of the UN Charter—for the repression of piracy by all states in the 'territorial sea of Somalia'.

[26] As remarked in Treves, 'Piracy, Law of the Sea . . .', *supra* note 1, at 406–408; Treves, 'Piracy and the International Law of the Sea', *supra* note 1, at 129–131.

[27] See ILC, 'International Law Commission's Commentary to the Draft Articles on the Law of the Sea', *Yearbook of the International Law Commission* (1956), Vol. 2, part 2, at 283, under Art. 39, para. 4; E. D. Brown, *The International Law of the Sea*, Vol. I (1994), at 302; Y. Tanaka, *The International Law of the Sea* (2012), at 357.

The situation in Somalia is extremely peculiar. Most states accept the fiction that there is an effective government in Somalia and consider that, through the Security Council resolutions like those on piracy, they contribute to transforming this fiction into reality. In other words, through the resolutions and the role given by the Security Council to the TFG, which was replaced by the 'new Somali authorities', they endeavour to contribute to the effectiveness of these authorities. Other states do not share this policy but accept that repression of piracy in the waters immediately adjacent to the Somali coast ought to be conducted under Chapter VII of the UN Charter.

E. The Notion of 'Armed Robbery': An Addition to General International Law?

In several provisions, the Security Council resolutions mention 'armed robbery' together with piracy. This term is not defined in the resolutions and, unlike the term 'piracy', it is not defined in UNCLOS either. Armed robbery is defined in the IMO resolutions adopting specific Codes of Conduct and in the Regional Cooperation Agreement on Combating Piracy and Armed Robbery Against Ships in Asia of 11 November 2004. While the definitions adopted in these instruments do not perfectly coincide, they all include acts of violence or depredation directed against a ship or persons or property on board such a ship. They diverge, however, when indicating where such acts must be committed. According to the 2001 Code of Practice for the Investigation of Crimes of Piracy and Armed Robbery against Ships,[28] they must be committed 'within a State's jurisdiction over such offences'.[29] According to the Regional Cooperation Agreement of 2004, they must be committed 'in a place within a State's jurisdiction over such offences'.[30] Under the Djibouti Code of Conduct Concerning the Repression of Piracy and Armed Robbery against Ships in the Western Indian Ocean and in the Gulf of Aden of 29 January 2009, they must be committed 'within a State's internal waters, archipelagic waters and territorial sea'.[31] Two of these three definitions, with the exception of the definition in the 2004 Regional Cooperation Agreement, specify that the acts of violence or detention covered in the notion of armed robbery are 'other than . . . act[s] of piracy'.

These definitions differ from that of piracy because they do not require the presence of two ships. They clearly include acts committed in the territorial sea, and do not include acts committed on the high seas. It is not specified whether they

[28] Code of Practice for the Investigation of Crimes of Piracy and Armed Robbery against Ships 2001, (2005) 44 ILM 829.

[29] Ibid., Art. 1(2). Art. 1(1) defines 'piracy', repeating the UNCLOS definition.

[30] Art. 1(2) of the Regional Cooperation Agreement on Combating Piracy and Armed Robbery Against Ships in Asia 2004, 2398 UNTS 199. Art. 1(1) defines 'piracy' repeating the UNCLOS definition. International Maritime Organization, Code of Practice for the Investigation of the Crimes of Piracy and Armed Robbery against Ships, A 22/Res.922, 29 November 2001 in lieu of 'a place under the jurisdiction' speaks of 'within a State's jurisdiction'.

[31] International Maritime Organization, Council, 102nd Session, Agenda item 14, Protection of Vital Shipping Lanes, Doc. C-102/14, 3 April 2009, Art. I.2(a).

include acts committed in the exclusive economic zone. These acts, however, remain covered by the notion of piracy, with its two ship requirement because, as already mentioned, for the purposes of the UNCLOS rules on piracy, the rules concerning activities on the high seas also apply to the exclusive economic zone.

In light of the foregoing, consider a situation on the high seas off the coast of Somalia, in which a group of hijackers posing as passengers or as crew members take possession of a vessel and request ransom for its release. Would all states be entitled to seize the vessel and to arrest the persons involved?

If any one of the three definitions of armed robbery just examined were to be followed, this situation would not be included and the rule of Article 105 of UNCLOS would not apply. However, as already mentioned, the IMO definitions are not referred to in the Security Council's resolutions. Can the reference to armed robbery in the resolutions be read as including all acts of violence and depredation against a ship not included in the notion of piracy even on the high seas? This interpretation would in practice extend the rules regarding repression that are applicable under the Security Council's resolutions to all acts of violence and depredation against a ship committed for private ends off the coast of Somalia with or without the involvement of a ship different from the victim ship. The purpose of the resolutions is to provide a 'comprehensive response' to piracy,[32] and the fact that the resolutions sometimes use 'piracy and armed robbery' and sometimes only 'piracy', without giving a clear reason for distinguishing between the two, brings us to the following conclusion. In light of the text and the purpose of the resolutions, in those resolutions, 'piracy' and 'piracy and armed robbery' have the same meaning; namely, all acts of violence and depredation against a ship committed for private ends in whatever maritime zone, from the territorial sea to the high seas, and involve one ship, or more.[33] Under the resolutions, it would therefore seem possible to argue that vessels of all states (if 'cooperating' with Somalia) are entitled to seize a vessel hijacked on the high seas (as well as on the territorial sea) by persons present on board without the involvement of another vessel.

A further and different question is whether the current notion of piracy under general international law no longer requires the prerequisite of the presence of two ships. A negative answer seems necessary in light of the specific provisions cited in the resolutions above, indicating that they should not be considered as establishing customary international law. Still, a margin of doubt remains. As these provisions are in paragraphs referring to the authorization of cooperating states to act in Somalia's territorial sea with the same rights as on the high seas, they do not refer to the broadening of the notion of piracy to include armed robbery. Even if this observation is considered decisive, international practice has not yet given rise to the scenario where a hijacked vessel is seized on the high seas by a ship flying a flag

[32] Recently, SC Res. 2125, *supra* note 11, para. 3.

[33] Geiss and Petrig, *supra* note 2, at 72–75, after reviewing the ambiguities of the notion of armed robbery at sea, accept the very restrictive conclusion that in the Security Council resolutions piracy should be understood according to the definition in Art. 101 of UNCLOS, while armed robbery 'should be intended as encompassing acts of violence against a ship, committed in the territorial sea'.

different from its own. While it cannot be ruled out that in such situations acquiescence by the flag state of the hijacked vessel could occur, it would seem more likely that a form of authorization would be granted by it to the seizing state.

F. Prosecution by Non-Seizing States: Security Council's Resolutions and the Interpretation of the Second Sentence Article 105 of UNCLOS

Another clarification of the meaning of general rules on piracy codified in UNCLOS concerns the interpretation of the second sentence of Article 105. This provision states that '[t]he courts of the States that carried out the seizure may decide upon the penalties to be imposed...' and 'the action to be taken with regards to the ships, aircraft and property'. It may be argued that while the first sentence of Article 105 permits 'every State' to seize a pirate ship, arrest the persons and seize the property on board, only the courts of the seizing state may institute legal proceedings according to a possible reading of Article 105. This view has been asserted in the legal literature. The opposite view also finds support, however.[34]

The practice often followed in the repression of piracy off the coast of Somalia is to transfer pirates captured by vessels of states located far removed from Somalia to authorities of nearby states (like Kenya for instance) for the purpose of prosecution, but this contradicts the first interpretation. These states have even entered into agreements for such purpose with the states exercising policing activity in the seas off the coast of Somalia.[35] The Security Council commends these states for their efforts to prosecute suspected pirates, without specifying whether these states actually seized the pirates.[36]

This attitude of the Security Council and of the states exercising policing activity and capturing pirates off the coast of Somalia, as well as of the states to which captured pirates are transferred, would seem to reflect a particular interpretation of the second sentence of Article 105. According to this interpretation, while the seizing state would not be violating international law in instituting proceedings against captured pirates, even in the absence of a connection to the pirates other than their presence in its territory, this jurisdiction would not be exclusive. Other states in which the pirates happen to be present, in particular because they have been transferred to them by the capturing state, would not contravene international law if, on the basis of their domestic criminal substantive and procedural law, they instituted proceedings against the pirates. This interpretation seems to be consistent with the reading of universal jurisdiction already proposed with regards to the first sentence of Article 105.

Again, the Security Council resolutions and the related practice, while not giving rise to a new rule of customary law, may be considered to be relevant factors in favour of one of two possible interpretations of a provision of UNCLOS, in this

[34] For a review of the different views held in legal literature, Geiss and Petrig, *supra* note 2, at 143–151.

[35] See Treves, 'Piracy and the International Law of the Sea', *supra* note 1, at 137–139.

[36] SC Res. 2077, *supra* note 11, 18th preambular para.; SC Res. 2125 (2013), 23th preambular para.

case the second sentence of Article 105, and of a corresponding determination of the contents of the customary rule reflected in that provision.

G. The Security Council Resolutions and the Meaning of Cooperation Under Article 100 of UNCLOS

As mentioned above, one of the basic international law rules concerning piracy is the duty of all states to 'cooperate to the fullest possible extent in the repression of piracy on the high seas or in any other place outside the jurisdiction of any state', as stated in Article 100 of UNCLOS, which is the first of the articles on piracy in the Convention. As also stated, this is the only rule which is not of a permissive character because it establishes a positive obligation. Yet this is an obligation 'to cooperate', and it is not preceded or followed by an obligation of all states to repress piracy. Its content does not prescribe precise conduct but establishes an obligation of due diligence, consisting in deploying best efforts in establishing forms of cooperation and conducting them. This provision legitimizes cooperation in the fight against piracy. A state cannot lightly refuse to cooperate in the fight against piracy, whether it concerns a specific incident, a particular region or is general.

Does this mean that, as has been argued, 'a State may not lightly decline to intervene against acts of piracy'?[37] In other words, is the duty to cooperate as set out in Article 100 of UNCLOS a duty not to lightly refrain from participating in cooperative activities for the repression of piracy, or is it to be interpreted as expressing a broader duty, perhaps reflecting an unwritten obligation with such content, to fight piracy?

Again, the Security Council resolutions on piracy are helpful for answering this question. These resolutions, *inter alia*, call on states to take part in the fight against piracy and armed robbery off the coast of Somalia. In addition to this, they call on all states to cooperate in determining jurisdiction and in the investigation and prosecution of all persons responsible for acts of piracy and armed robbery, and to criminalize piracy under their domestic law. In 'calling upon' states to take the measures indicated above, the resolutions build on the obligation to cooperate in Article 100. Stressing their urgency and importance, they indicate the measures that states are encouraged to take in order to comply with their obligation to cooperate. In most cases, they refer to the specific situation off the coasts of Somalia but, sometimes, they make reference to criminalizing piracy under domestic law in very general terms. They do not, however, go beyond this 'calling upon'. They do not set down 'decisions' that would be binding under Chapter VII of the UN Charter.

An example concerns the basis of jurisdiction of domestic courts. The resolutions have not seized the opportunity to bind states to grant their judges universal jurisdiction or specific bases of jurisdiction with regards to acts of piracy. They presuppose that domestic courts already have an adequate basis of jurisdiction for

[37] Wolfrum, 'The Obligation to Cooperate in the Fight Against Piracy, Legal Considerations', in *Essays in Commemoration of the Seventieth Anniversary of Professor Yanai Shunji, Hogaku Shimpo*, 116 *Chuo Law Review* (2009) 81, at 95.

fulfilling their duty to cooperate in repressing piracy under Article 100 of UNCLOS. This emerges in the report commissioned by the UN Secretary General to the former French Minister, Professor Jack Lang. In Lang's view: 'There is no lack of legal bases allowing States to exercise universal jurisdiction. General international law provides for multiple forms of jurisdiction without establishing priority rules.(...) Those bases enable a large number of States to fulfil their duty to cooperate in the repression of piracy to the fullest possible extent in accordance with article 100 of the Convention'.[38] In actual fact, the Security Council directs its 'calling upon' to cooperate in determining jurisdiction to all states, but 'in particular flag, port and coastal States, States of the nationality of victims and perpetrators of piracy and armed robbery, and other States with relevant jurisdiction under international law and national legislation'.[39]

2. The Capture, Detention, Transfer and Prosecution of Pirates: Between Human Rights and Expediency Concerns

A. Human Rights and Counter-Piracy Operations

Counter-piracy operations raise several concerns about human rights.[40] In a European context, a focus on issues of responsibility under the European Convention on Human Rights (ECHR) seems warranted, the latter instrument being unique in providing victims with access to an international judicial remedy. It is worth taking a look at the jurisprudence under the ECHR to litigate human rights arising out of counter-piracy operations. For instance, the European Court of Human Rights (ECtHR) delivered two judgments concerning piracy in Somalia on 4 December 2014.[41] Both cases involved acts of piracy off the coast of Somalia, which were followed by enforcement operations by French military personnel on the mainland with the consent of the Somali TFG[42] or in the Somali territorial sea pursuant to the authorization of the Security Council.[43] This resulted in the suspects being arrested, held in custody and transferred to France, and then prosecuted. While the cases actually focus on questions of deprivation of liberty only, they show the potential of the European system to provide an international forum for litigating human rights issues arising out of counter-piracy operations.

[38] UN Doc. S/2011/30, *supra* note 2, para. 48.

[39] SC Res. 2125, *supra* note 11, para. 16. The same formulation is in other SC resolutions starting with SC Res. 1816, *supra* note 9, para. 9.

[40] See generally, Guilfoyle, 'Counter-piracy Law Enforcement and Human Rights', 59 *International and Comparative Law Quarterly* (2010) 141, at 152–169, Geiss and Petrig, *supra* note 2, at 101–135, and Piedimonte Bodini, 'Fighting Maritime Piracy under the European Convention on Human Rights', 22 *European Journal of International Law* (2011) 829.

[41] *Ali Samatar*, *supra* note 14, and ECtHR, *Hassan and Others v. France*, Appl. nos. 46695/10 and 54588/10, Judgment of 4 December 2014. At the time of writing both judgments are not final and are available only in French.

[42] *Ali Samatar*, *supra* note 14, paras 5–14.

[43] *Hassan v. France*, *supra* note 41, paras 5–9. France was among the cooperating States named by the Somali TFG on 2 September 2008.

In the context of extraterritorial enforcement action carried out pursuant to a Security Council authorization and often within the framework of multinational military operations under the aegis of regional international organizations—such as NATO[44] or the European Union (EU)[45]—the protection offered by the European human rights regime rests on two assumptions that need to be verified on a case-by-case basis: firstly, that the ECHR applies in this specific context and, secondly, that the relevant conduct is attributable to the contracting state to which the participating military and naval forces belong.[46]

These complex questions of state responsibility, which touch upon both the constituent elements of the international wrongful act,[47] must be considered before turning to the substantive human rights issues.

B. The Applicability of Human Rights Treaties to Counter-Piracy Activities

The rights guaranteed by the ECHR are to be secured by contracting parties to 'everyone within their jurisdiction'.[48] This provision sets a threshold criterion for the spatial applicability of the ECHR,[49] but has been applied inconsistently by the ECtHR, with the well-known *Banković* decision of 2001 being the catalyst of a restrictive view on extraterritorial application.[50] After this decision, the ECtHR

[44] NATO has deployed three consecutive operations for the purpose of combating piracy off the coast of Somalia, namely 'Operation Allied Provider' (October-December 2008), 'Operation Allied Protector' (March–June 2009) and 'Operation Ocean Shield' (August 2009–ongoing), see Geiss and Petrig, *supra* note 2, at 22–24.

[45] The European Union has established the European Naval Force Operation *Atalanta* in 2008 (Council Joint Action 2008/851/CFSP of 10 November 2008, OJ 2008 L 301/33). Initially established for one year, the operation has been extended *via* subsequent amendments of the Joint Action until 12 December 2016, see Council Decision 2014/827/CFSP of 21 November 2014, OJ 2014 L 335/19, Art. 1(d)). On Operation *Atalanta*, see De Guttry, 'Fighting Piracy and Armed Robbery in the XXI Century: Some Legal Issues Surrounding the EU Military Operation Atalanta', 5 *Studi sull'Integrazione Europea* (2010) 325.

[46] Further issues of multiple responsibilities, which do not involve attribution issues, will not be discussed. For an overview, see Nollkaemper and Jacobs, 'Shared Responsibility in International Law: A Conceptual Framework', 34 *Michigan Journal of International Law* (2013) 359, and other research papers of the project SHARES, available online at http://www.sharesproject.nl (last accessed 23 July 2015).

[47] This useful clarification of the relationship between 'state jurisdiction' and 'attribution' under Art. 1 ECHR is pointed out by Lawson, 'Life After Bankovic: On the Extraterritorial Application of the European Convention on Human Rights', in F. Coomans and M. T. Kamminga (eds), *Extraterritorial Application of Human Rights Treaties* (2004) 83, at 86.

[48] Art. 1 ECHR. For a more elaborate analysis and further references see Milanovic, Chapter 3 in this volume.

[49] See ECtHR, *Al-Skeini v. United Kingdom*, Appl. no. 55721/07, Judgment of 7 July 2011, para. 130.

[50] ECtHR, *Banković and Others v. Belgium and Others*, Appl. no. 52207/99, Decision on Admissibility of 12 December 2001. Scholars have criticized the ECtHR for both the conceptual underpinnings of its interpretive approach and the lack of consistency in its jurisprudence. However, attempts have been made at reconstructing a coherent and unitary notion of 'state jurisdiction' across human rights treaties, see P. De Sena, *La nozione di giurisdizione statale nei trattati sui diritti dell'uomo* (2002), and M. Milanovic, *Extraterritorial Application of Human Rights Treaties: Law, Principles, and Policy* (2011).

confirmed the basic doctrine according to which the term 'jurisdiction' must be interpreted as it is understood in public international law.[51] However, since then, starting with the Grand Chamber judgment in the *Al-Skeini* case, some of the most controversial aspects of *Banković* have been overruled. It is now accepted that the ECHR may apply beyond its so-called '*espace juridique*',[52] and that the Convention obligations can be 'divided and tailored' when applied extraterritorially.[53] In fact, while jurisdiction based on '*de facto* effective control over an area' (spatial model) places the duty on the controlling states to guarantee the full range of conventional obligations,[54] under the 'authority and control over a person' test (personal model), the controlling state only has those obligations that are relevant to the positions of the person(s) concerned.[55]

The personal model, which is gaining increased importance, is not limited to cases of detention and custody of a person, but extends to temporary control over premises and facilities, where a person is confined or found.[56] It may also cover the space under the purview of a coercive action by a contracting state's agents, within which a person may accidentally find him or herself.[57] This situation may now be labelled as falling under a '(*de facto*) control over a person', which amounts to the first limb of the personal model. At the same time, the ECtHR accords growing importance to the fact that the impugned conduct of the contracting state either constitutes the exercise of a lawful extraterritorial competence under international law or occurs under a normative framework in which the contracting state has assumed the responsibility of guaranteeing public security in an area outside its territory.[58] These cases seem to fall within the second limb of the personal model, namely that of 'authority (or *de jure* control) over a person'.

The complex nature of counter-piracy operations adds to the inherent uncertainty in forecasting objections that are based on lack of state jurisdiction.[59] *Medvedyev v. France* clearly indicates that they would fail if related to conduct taking place *after* a suspect has been taken into custody. The case was brought by crew members of the *Winner*, a merchant ship flying the Cambodian flag. Following the authorization of the flag state, the ship had been intercepted and boarded in the high seas by a French warship under suspicion of being involved in smuggling narcotic drugs, and the crew was arrested. The Grand Chamber noted that France had 'exercised full and exclusive control over the Winner and its crew, at least de facto, from the time of its interception'.[60] In the 'piracy cases', France—relying on *Medvedyev*—did not dispute that it had jurisdiction over the applicants since the time of their apprehension and the ECtHR took note with approval of this

[51] *Banković*, *supra* note 50, para. 59. [52] *Al-Skeini*, *supra* note 49, para. 142.
[53] *Banković*, *supra* note 50, para. 75. [54] *Al-Skeini*, *supra* note 49, para. 138.
[55] Ibid., para. 137. [56] Ibid., para. 136. [57] Ibid., paras 149–150.
[58] Ibid., paras 134–135. [59] Geiss and Petrig, *supra* note 2, at 103.
[60] ECtHR, *Medvedyev and Others v. France*, Appl. no. 3394/03, Judgment of 29 March 2010, para. 67.

position, regardless of whether the facts took place on the territorial sea or on the mainland.[61]

Less straightforward is whether the relevant human rights obligations apply at any time *before* a state gains actual control over the ship involved in piracy and/or the persons on board. During this phase, possibly involving the use of force,[62] crucial human rights issues may arise.[63]

It has been argued that the cooperating states may exercise effective control over Somali territorial waters and adjacent high sea zones through extensive patrolling.[64] Yet, recourse to the spatial model fails to take into account that foreign military presence in areas under Somali jurisdiction is functionally limited to combating piracy, pursuant to the resolutions of the Security Council. This functional restriction is inconsistent with the blanket application of the ECHR flowing from effective control over the area. Consequently, a different and sounder ground for asserting state jurisdiction must be sought.

Before doing so, it should be recalled that the various models of jurisdiction do not operate in separate boxes. In a given situation, jurisdiction may be grounded on a plurality of criteria and the criteria themselves may partially overlap, as exemplified by the *Hirsi Jamaa and others v. Italy* case.[65] Not only was Italy's jurisdiction found on the (alternative) basis of the de facto control over the persons and of the flag state principle,[66] but also the latter criterion itself may be seen as a form of a lawful extraterritorial exercise of jurisdiction or as a corollary of the territorial principle,[67] therefore not as a case of extraterritorial jurisdiction strictly speaking.[68]

[61] *Hassan v. France*, *supra* note 41, para. 39, and *Ali Samatar*, *supra* note 14, para. 31. Indeed, on the basis of *Medvedyev*, jurisdiction is engaged from the gaining of control over the vessel, but this was not relevant to the complaints formulated in the piracy cases. Among many authorities relating to jurisdiction on detained persons on foreign territory see: ECtHR, *Öcalan v. Turkey*, Appl. no. 46221/99, Judgment of 12 May 2005, para. 91; ECtHR, *Al-Saadoon and Mufdhi v. the United Kingdom*, Appl. no. 61498/08, Decision on Admissibility of 30 June 2009, paras 86–89. In ECtHR, *Hassan v. United Kingdom*, Appl. no. 29750/09, Judgment of 16 September 2014, paras 75–80, a person held in custody abroad by a contracting party has been deemed to fall within that party's jurisdiction, even in the absence of *de facto* effective control over, or authority to maintain security in, the area where custody took place.

[62] Treves, 'Piracy, Law of the Sea . . . ', *supra* note 1, at 412–414.

[63] The references in Security Council resolutions to consistency with 'applicable human rights' as a limit to powers conferred to states, such as in SC Res. 1851, *supra* note 11, para. 6, do not provide an argument in this respect. The very wording of the statement seems to exclude that the resolution itself intends to extend the spatial reach of any human rights treaty, but see ECtHR, *Jaloud v. The Netherlands*, Appl. no. 47708/08, Judgment of 20 November 2014, para. 144 (a similar statement contained in resolution 1483 on Iraq was mentioned, and possibly taken into account, in the reasoning that lead to the conclusion that the Netherlands had jurisdiction).

[64] Geiss and Petrig, *supra* note 2, at 106–108. See also, Piedimonte Bodini, *supra* note 40, at 844, who argues that even the mere presence of a single warship might be considered as exercising effective control over the zone within its fire range.

[65] ECtHR, *Hirsi Jamaa and Others v. Italy*, Appl. no. 27765/09, Judgment of 23 February 2012.

[66] The ECtHR took note of the fact that Italy exercised control over rescued migrants but grounded its finding on state jurisdiction solely on the basis that the applicants were transferred on board Italian military ships, thus being subject to Italian *de jure* authority under the customary rule of flag state jurisdiction, ibid., paras 74, 77, 78 and 81.

[67] *SS Lotus (France v. Turkey)*, 1927 PCIJ Series A, No. 10, at 25.

[68] This hypothesis is discussed and rejected, by Geiss and Petrig, *supra* note 2, at 105.

From this perspective, several factors point to the conclusion that the ECHR is also applicable in counter-piracy enforcement operations.

Firstly, in *Medvedyev* the ECtHR found that France had jurisdiction 'from the time of interception'. Although 'interception' does not have a precise meaning in international law,[69] the term—and consequently the principle stated by the ECtHR—can include the use of coercion aimed at gaining physical control over the targeted vessel.[70] In this case, jurisdiction of the state would be established as '*de facto* control over a person', under the personal jurisdiction model.

Secondly, the exercise of jurisdiction under a permissive rule of international law entails, as a matter of principle,[71] the applicability of the ECHR. The ECtHR stated:

> the exercise of extraterritorial jurisdiction by a Contracting State when, through the consent, invitation or acquiescence of the Government of that territory, it exercises all or some of the public powers normally to be exercised by that Government (...). Thus, where, in accordance with custom, treaty or other agreement, authorities of the Contracting State carry out executive or judicial functions on the territory of another State, the Contracting State may be responsible for breaches of the Convention thereby incurred, as long as the acts in question are attributable to it rather than to the territorial State.[72]

With regards to powers at sea, the ECtHR has referred in principle to flag state jurisdiction as a typical case of extraterritorial jurisdiction,[73] and has explicitly applied it in *Hirsi*.[74] Overall, the view may be taken that 'jurisdiction provided

[69] Art. 101 UNCLOS refers to the obviously much narrower idea of the 'right of visit'. See, generally, E. Papastavridis, *The Interception of Vessels in the High Seas. Contemporary Challenges to the Legal Order of the Oceans* (2013) and references at the following footnote.

[70] Scholars tend to give this broad meaning to the term, see Papastavridis, *supra* note 69, at 61 (under customary law, the term encompasses 'any physical interference with vessels on the high seas'); Ronzitti, 'Coastal State Jurisdiction over Refugees and Migrants at Sea', in N. Ando *et al.* (eds), *Liber Amicorum Judge Shigeru Oda* (2002) 1271, at 1278 (it includes 'the mere harassment by navigational means and warning shots aimed at diverting the ship from its route'); Geiss and Petrig, *supra* note 2, at 106, describe it as 'the phase during which an alleged pirate ship is pursued, stopped and ultimately boarded'.

[71] For a critical view, see Milanovic, *supra* note 50, at 21 ff.

[72] *Al-Skeini*, *supra* note 49, para. 135. See also, *Jaloud*, *supra* note 63, para. 141 ('For the purposes of establishing jurisdiction under the Convention, the Court takes account of the particular factual context and relevant rules of international law'). Moreover, this approach is backed by the assertion by the ICJ that international human rights instruments are applicable 'in respect of acts done by a State in the exercise of its jurisdiction outside its own territory', *Legal Consequences of the Construction of a Wall in the Occupied Palestinian Territory,* Advisory Opinion, 9 July 2004, ICJ Reports (2004) 136, at 178–181, paras 107–113. It is, however, singular that this expression was instrumental to the finding that human rights treaties concluded by the occupying power apply to territories under military occupation, a situation that can hardly be reconciled with the exercise of 'jurisdiction' in a narrow sense, see Milanovic, *supra* note 50, at 28.

[73] *Banković*, *supra* note 50, para. 75.

[74] In previous cases the ECtHR had only assumed that the ECHR applied to the conduct of contracting states which were consistent with the international law of the sea, see ECtHR, *Xhavara and Others v. Italy and Albania*, Appl. no. 39473/98, Decision of 11 January 2001 (sinking of an Albanian ship in Albanian territorial waters after it was boarded by an Italian military vessel authorized to do so under an agreement between the two states); *Dieman and Others v. Norway*, Appl. no. 33678/96, Decision on Admissibility of 4 May 2000 (enforcement activities relating to the exploitation of living resources in the exclusive economic zone).

for in the law of the sea has generally been accepted [by the ECtHR] as a valid basis for the applicability of human rights treaties'.[75]

Therefore, any counter-piracy enforcement operation carried out by a contracting party in accordance with custom (i.e. in the high seas) or with the consent of the territorial/coastal state[76] would constitute an exercise of jurisdiction. In the Somali situation, a state acting in conformity with and under the authority of, a Security Council resolution exercises public powers outside its territory in accordance with rules of international law, as modified by the resolutions,[77] and therefore exercises 'jurisdiction' for the purposes of Article 1 of the ECHR under the 'authority (or de *jure* control) over' limb of the personal model.[78]

Finally, the authority granted to cooperating states, as provided for by paragraph 6 of Resolution 1851, may also be considered as bringing enforcement action carried out on the Somali territory within the scope of the ECHR, albeit only functionally, within the limits of their mission and for the purpose of asserting *authority and control over suspected pirates*.[79]

To conclude, the authorization given by the Security Council to cooperating states to use all the necessary means for the purpose of suppressing acts of piracy and armed robbery at sea brings persons affected by their enforcement action within their authority, and therefore their jurisdiction.

This approach, which is based on a normative, and not a factual, criterion, has a drawback: the ECHR would place limits on states lawfully exercising a competence under international law and, at the same time, would leave their unlawful action uncontrolled. However, in cases of extraterritorial unlawful action, establishing the applicability of the ECHR on this basis does not necessarily exclude the possibility that a finding of jurisdiction may be reached if the exercise of de facto control over persons, and the surrounding premises or small areas, is positively

[75] Papanicolopulu, 'International Judges and the Protection of Human Rights at Sea', in N. Boschiero *et al.* (eds), *The Development of International Law by International Courts and Tribunals. Essays in Honor of Tullio Treves* (2013) 535, at 540.

[76] See, for example, the *note verbale* of the Somali TFG to the French authorities in *Ali Samatar*, *supra* note 14, para. 9. The legal basis of the enforcement action did not play any role in the reasoning, since neither France contested that it had jurisdiction, nor the applicants challenged the legality of their detention. See also, *Xhavara*, *supra* note 74, in which the point relating to jurisdiction was not explicitly addressed.

[77] The same conclusion would hold if the legal basis for exercising jurisdiction is identified in the authorization by the relevant Somali governmental authorities. For a discussion of this possibility see Treves, 'Piracy, Law of the Sea . . . ', *supra* note 1, at 406–407 ff.

[78] For the opposite view, see Geiss and Petrig, *supra* note 2, at 116.

[79] See, *mutatis mutandis*, *Jaloud*, *supra* note 63, where the Grand Chamber found that the responsibility of the Netherlands in relation to the fatal shooting of an Iraqi national by Dutch troops at a checkpoint in south-east Iraq could be engaged on a similar basis. Indeed, the Netherlands, not an occupying power nor a State exercising effective control over the area concerned, was acting under SC Res. 1483, 22 May 2003, retained full command over its own force, had exclusive competence in formulating military policies for its own troops, including the rules of engagement, and had assumed responsibility for providing security in the interested area (ibid., paras 144, 146, 147 and 149). It thus 'exercised its "jurisdiction" within the limits of its SFIR mission and for the purpose of asserting *authority and control* over persons passing through the checkpoint' (ibid., para. 152, emphasis added).

demonstrated.[80] Yet, this line of reasoning would be in direct contrast with what is left of *Banković*,[81] and is far from being established as an accepted criterion by the ECtHR.

C. The Attribution of Conduct by Armed Forces Involved in Multinational Authorized Counter-Piracy Operations

The reasoning developed in the previous paragraph presupposes that the impugned conduct is attributable to a state that is a party to the ECHR. If the conduct was attributable to one of the organizations involved in counter-piracy efforts, rather than to the state of the military personnel, a gap in protection would ensue.[82] While the organization would enjoy immunity before domestic courts,[83] the international judicial mechanism established by the ECHR would be unavailable.

The fundamental criterion for attributing conduct to a subject of international law is institutional: states and international organizations must be held responsible for the internationally wrongful conduct of those persons and entities possessing the quality of an organ or agent in accordance with that state's or organization's own internal laws.[84] The problem arises when a state organ is placed at the disposal of an organization.[85] According to the ILC Commentary, if a state's organ is fully seconded to the organization, its conducts are attributed to the latter under Article 6 Draft Articles on the Responsibility of International Organizations (ARIO). The rationale being that in this situation the organic link with the sending state is temporarily, and fictionally, severed.[86] When this does not occur, only conduct that is under the effective control of the organization, at which disposal the organ is

[80] ECtHR, *Issa and Others v. Turkey*, Appl. no. 31821/96, Judgment of 16 November 2004; *Pad and Others v. Turkey*, Appl. no. 60167/00, Decision on Admissibility of 28 June 2007; *Isaak v. Turkey*, Appl. no. 44587/98, Judgment of 24 June 2008.

[81] See Milanovic, '*Al-Skeini* and *Al-Jedda* in Strasbourg', 23 *European Journal of International Law* (2012) 121, at 124.

[82] Sari, 'Jurisdiction and International Responsibility in Peace Support Operations: The *Behrami* and *Saramati* Cases', 8 *Human Rights Law Review* (2008) 151, 167–168 (underscoring that this would allow states to escape from their own human rights constraints).

[83] ECtHR, *Stichting Mothers of Srebrenica and Others v. the Netherlands*, Appl. no. 65542/12, Decision on Admissibility of 11 June 2013.

[84] See Draft Articles on the Responsibility of States for Internationally Wrongful Acts, with Commentaries (hereinafter ARSIWA and ARISWA Commentary), Art. 4, in Report of the International Law Commission, 53rd Session (2001), UN Doc. A/56/10 (2001), 31; and Draft Articles on the Responsibility of International Organisations, with Commentaries (hereinafter ARIO and ARIO Commentary), Art., in Report of the International Law Commission, 63rd Session (2011), UN Doc. A/66/10 (2011), 52.

[85] If the receiving subject is a State, the conduct is attributed to the latter when 'the organ is acting in the exercise of elements of the governmental authority of the State at whose disposal it is placed' (Art. 6 ARISWA). The commentary makes very clear that 'Article 6 deals with the limited and precise situation in which an organ of a State is effectively put at the disposal of another State so that the organ may temporarily act for its benefit and under its authority. In such a case, the organ, originally that of one State, acts exclusively for the purposes of and on behalf of another State and its conduct is attributed to the latter State alone', ARISWA Commentary, *supra* note 84, at 44.

[86] Art. 6 ARIO, *supra* note 84, and ARIO Commentary, *supra* note 84.

put, are attributable to the latter, under Article 7 ARIO.[87] Several questions remain under this approach: what is the meaning of 'effective control' in this context? Does attribution to the sending state also depend on 'effective control'? Is multiple attribution possible under Article 7 ARIO? If yes, when?

Before addressing these questions, it is necessary to settle whether conduct in the course of counter-piracy operations pursuant to the Security Council authorization can be attributed to the UN. In the controversial *Behrami* and *Saramati* decision,[88] the ECtHR found that the conduct of the contingents in the NATO-led Kosovo Force (KFOR) took place under the UN's 'ultimate authority and control' and was therefore exclusively attributed to the UN.[89] This precedent has been read as suggesting that this would always be the case with respect to any action taken under Security Council Chapter VII authorization.[90] However, the opposite conclusion is clearly stated by the ILC,[91] which is supported by two arguments. Firstly, it can be disputed that the national armed forces are ever 'placed at the disposal' of the UN, an organization lacking any operational responsibility for military action.[92] Even if, allegedly under the delegation of powers theory, one considers that national contingents are indeed placed at the disposal of the UN, the limited ex post monitoring powers of the Security Council can hardly amount to 'effective control'.[93] In the same vein, the ECtHR, starting with the *Al-Jedda* judgment, has departed from *Behrami* and *Saramati* [94] and has routinely held contracting states responsible for violations related to their military presence in Iraq under the authority of Resolution 1511 from 2003.[95] Moreover, France did not raise this point in *Hassan and others v. France*, and the ECtHR did not examine the matter on its own motion. This confirms that states involved in counter-piracy operations

[87] ARIO Commentary, *supra* note 84, at 87.

[88] *Behrami v. France* and *Saramati v. France, Germany and Norway*, Appl. nos. 71412/01 and 78166/01, Decision on Admissibility of 2 February 2007.

[89] Ibid., para. 141. The ECtHR opined that the KFOR exercised, by delegation of authority through a lawful Chapter VII authorization, powers of the UN (ibid.). The underlying rationale can be traced to the desire not to interfere with the delicate task of the UN Security Council under Chapter VII of the Charter (ibid., para. 149).

[90] See *R (Al-Jedda) v. Secretary of State for Defence* [2007] UKHL 58, Opinion of Lord Rodger of Earlsferry (dissenting on this point), see the case note by Orakhelashvili, 'UK House of Lords Judgment on Relationship between UN Security Council Resolution Authorizing Detention in Iraq and European Convention on Human Rights', 102 *American Journal of International Law* (2008) 337, at 339–340.

[91] ARIO Commentary, *supra* note 84, at 83.

[92] The commentary to Art. 6 ARISWA, *supra* note 84, which sheds light on Art. 7 ARIO, *supra* note 84, explains that an organ to be 'placed at the disposal of' the receiving state requires that it acts 'in conjunction with the machinery of that State and under its exclusive direction and control, rather than on instructions from the sending State' (ARISWA Commentary, *supra* note 84, at 44).

[93] Palchetti, 'The Allocation of Responsibility for Internationally Wrongful Acts Committed in the Course of Multinational Operations', 95 *International Review of the Red Cross* (2013) 727, at 736–738.

[94] In *Al-Jedda*, *supra* note 90, 'effective control' was used alongside 'ultimate authority and control' to conclude that the UN was short of both in the decision to detain the applicant (ibid., para. 84). The ECtHR has not openly rejected its own precedents. Instead, it unconvincingly tried to distinguish *Al-Jedda* from *Behrami* and *Saramati* on factual grounds, see Messineo, 'Things Could Only Get Better: Al-Jedda Beyond Behrami', 50 *Military Law and the Law of War Review* (2011) 321, at 333–336.

[95] *Al-Saadoon and Mufdhi*, *supra* note 61; *Hassan v. the United Kingdom*, *supra* note 41.

pursuant to the authorization of the Security Council cannot solely rely on arguments based on attribution to the UN as a shield against allegations of human rights violations before the ECtHR.

A closer examination of the meaning and scope of Article 7 of ARIO is necessary in order to allocate responsibility in the context of counter-piracy operations led by regional organizations, such as the EUNAVFOR Operation *Atalanta*.[96] Admittedly, the EU exercises a significant degree of normative and operational control over contingents deployed under the EU's mission, but cooperating states retain rights and obligations at least in terms of day-to-day management of the operation.[97] National contingents do not qualify as *de jure* organs or agents of the EU,[98] but they are integrated into the machinery of the organization through the chain of command leading to the Council of the EU, without the organic link with the sending state being severed.

It is possible to argue that because national contingents are not characterized as EU organs, Article 7 of ARIO is irrelevant.[99] However, this reading seems overly restrictive. Article 7 of ARIO—and its 'effective control' test—is considered to apply to situations such as the Operation *Atalanta* in order to ensure accountability of the receiving organization.[100] According to the ILC, 'effective control' is a criterion 'based [...] on the factual control that is exercised over the specific conduct'.[101] In this context it does not necessarily require instructions or direction over each specific conduct.[102] Moreover, it is possible to envisage that controversy

[96] For a discussion of similar issues arising in the context of NATO operations, see Guilfoyle, *supra* note 40, at 151.

[97] See, *a contrario*, Joint Action 2008/851/CFSP, *supra* note 45, Art. 10, para. 4.

[98] See, *mutatis mutandis*, Case T-271/10 R, *H v. Council and Commission,* Order of the President of the General Court [2010] ECR II-00154 (ECLI:EU:T:2010:315), paras 19–20, and Spagnolo, 'Il trasferimento di presunti pirati nell'ambito dell'operazione Atalanta: gli accordi tra l'Unione europea e i Paesi terzi', 7 *Studi sull'Integrazione Europea* (2012) 669, at 685–686. See also Sari and Wessel, 'International Responsibility for EU Military Operations: Finding the EU's Place in Global Accountability Regime', in B. Van Vooren, S. Blockmans and J. Wouters (eds), *The EU's Role in Global Governance. The Legal Dimension* (2013) 126, at 134–137 (concluding that national forces do not constitute *de jure* organs of the EU military but arguing that they should be considered as de facto organs).

[99] '[Art. 7 ARIO, *supra* note 84] does not concern the issue whether a certain conduct is attributable *at all* to a State or an international organization, but rather to which entity—the contributing State or organization *or* the receiving organization—conduct has to be attributed' (ARIO Commentary, *supra* note 84, at 88, emphasis added). This suggests that unless attribution to the organization is possible under the general rule, i.e., on the basis of an institutional link, Art. 7 ARIO does not possess an autonomous role. Nevertheless, responsibility of the international organization could be engaged, notably for directing and controlling the wrongful act of a member state, if the restrictive conditions set forth in Art. 15 ARIO are met, without attributing the conduct of the directed state.

[100] In this context, it is accepted that the general rules on the responsibility of international organizations apply to the EU, at least as far as action taken within the former 'second pillar'. For a discussion, see Sari and Wessel, *supra* note 98, at 127–130.

[101] ARIO Commentary, *supra* note 84, at 87 (emphasis added). See Palchetti, *supra* note 93, at 732 ff.

[102] See, generally, Palchetti, *supra* note 93. See also *The Netherlands (Ministry of Defence and Ministry of Foreign Affairs) v. Nuhanović*, Judgment (Supreme Court, 6 September 2013), ECLI/NL/HR/2013/BZ9225, *ILDC* 2061 (NL 2013), 12/03324, para. 3.11.3.

would arise in a situation when a certain course of action is taken on the field, presumably upon orders of the commander of the unit involved.[103] One can think of a case in which an action aimed at defending a vessel from a pirate attack or at intercepting and boarding a pirate skiff involves a grossly disproportionate use of force resulting in the sinking of the skiff and the death of the suspected pirates. In this hypothetical scenario, in which applicable rules of engagement would also be breached, it is hard to consider that the conduct is the effect of a specific order or direction from either the EU or the national chain of command.

Different positions emerge on how to allocate attribution in similar situations. One argument is that the organic link established with the receiving organization creates a rebuttable presumption of attribution to the latter,[104] but its proposed application to the Operation *Atalanta* is based on the questionable assumption that the contingents are viewed as de facto organs of the EU.[105] A similar presumption has also been based on arrangements relating to the transfer of powers from the troop-contributing state to the organization, since 'the delimitation of the respective powers agreed upon by the two parties provides an indication as to which entity, in principle, has control over the troops in relation to a given conduct'.[106] While this case-by-case normative analysis may apply to *ultra vires* acts also,[107] a recent domestic decision has employed the latter approach to reach opposite conclusions, namely that those *ultra vires* acts are always attributable to the sending state.[108] This conclusion can be reached also by arguing that the conduct is to be attributed to the organization only when the latter 'is best positioned to act effectively and within the law to prevent the abuse in question'.[109] Against this background, a conclusion on whether a given conduct in the context of the Operation *Atalanta*

[103] Dannenbaum, 'Translating the Standard of Effective Control into a System of Effective Accountability: How Liability Should Be Apportioned for Violations of Human Rights by Member State Troop Contingents Serving as United Nations Peacekeepers', 51 *Harvard International Law Journal* (2010) 113, at 156.

[104] This position is maintained by the UN with regards to peacekeepers, see Letter of 3 February 2004 by the United Nations Legal Counsel to the Director of the Codification Division, UN Doc. A/CN.4/545, 25 June 2004, Section II.G, and find support in the case-law of the ECtHR, see *Behrami* and *Saramati*, *supra* note 88, para. 143. The same reasoning was followed, but rejected on subsequent appeals, in *Hasan Nuhanović v. Netherlands* (Ministry of Defence and Ministry of Foreign Affairs), Judgment (District Court, 10 September 2008), No. LJN: BF0181, Case no. 265615, *ILDC* 1092 (NL 2008), para. 4.8, available at http://zoeken.rechtspraak.nl (last visited 23 July 2015). In literature, see Condorelli, 'Le statut des forces de l'ONU et le droit international humanitaire', 78 *Rivista di Diritto Internazionale* (1995) 881–906.

[105] Sari and Wessel, *supra* note 98, at 137–140.

[106] Palchetti, *supra* note 93, at 734. See also Sari and Wessel, *supra* note 98, at 133.

[107] Palchetti, *supra* note 93, at 735–736.

[108] This is based on the consideration that the state has responsibility for the selection, training and preparation of the troops and retains disciplinary jurisdiction, *Stichting Mothers of Srebrenica et al v. Netherlands*, Judgment (District Court, 16 July 2014), paras 4.57–4.58, available online at http://uitspraken.rechtspraak.nl (last accessed 23 July 2015).

[109] Dannenbaum, *supra* note 103, at 157–159. This approach is shared in *Hasan Nuhanović v. the Netherlands,* Judgment (The Hague Court of Appeal, 5 July 2011), LJN:BR5388, *ILDC* 1742 (NL 2011), para. 5.9. Note, however, that the Court of Appeal examines the ability to prevent the conduct as a matter of fact and not as a mere normative power, see Nollkaemper, 'Dual Attribution. Liability of the Netherlands for Conduct of Dutchbat in Srebrenica', 9 *Journal of International Criminal Justice* (2011) 1143, at 1152.

can be attributed to the EU requires not only a choice between different theoretical approaches, but also a detailed case-specific assessment of the facts. For the purposes of the present argument, it is enough to conclude that a specific conduct of national forces deployed in the framework of Operation *Atalanta* may result in attribution to the EU when the latter exercises 'effective control'.

Whether attribution to the contributing state is, alternatively or cumulatively, possible, depends in the first place on the weight given to the continuing organic link between the troops and their sending state. It has been suggested that an organ's conduct is always imputable to the sending state regardless of the considerations about factual control,[110] or unless it is positively demonstrated that effective control lies on the receiving organization.[111] This approach may result in double attribution becoming the rule, rather than the exception.[112]

The approach of the ILC is different and its conformity with general international law has been disputed.[113] Article 7 of ARIO is conceived as a provision aimed at identifying the 'entity—the contributing State or organization or the receiving organization—[to which] conduct has to be attributed'.[114] Despite the wording of Article 7 of ARIO, 'effective control' would thus work as a discerning criterion,[115] with reference to both the sending state and the receiving organization.[116] Double attribution is not ruled out, but would be exceptional.[117]

[110] Condorelli, *supra* note 104, and Condorelli, 'De la responsabilité internationale de l'ONU et/ou de l'état d'envoi lors d'actions de Forces de Maintien de la Paix: l'écheveau de l'attribution (double?) devant le juge néerlandais', *Questions of International Law, Zoom-in 1* (2014) 3, available online at http://www.qil-qdi.org/wp-content/uploads/2014/05/DUAL-ATTRIBUTION_Condorelli_FINAL.pdf (last accessed 23 July 2015). Reliance on the organic criterion was central in *Attorney Gen. v. Nissan*, [1970] AC 179 (H.L. 1969). Some support for this approach may be found in *Jaloud*, *supra* note 63, para. 155.

[111] d'Argent, 'State Organs Placed at the Disposal of the UN, Effective Control, Wrongful Abstention and Dual Attribution of Conduct', *Questions of International Law, Zoom-in 1* (2014) 17, at 25–27, available online at http://www.qil-qdi.org/wp-content/uploads/2014/05/DUAL-ATTRIBUTION_DArgent_FINAL.pdf (last accessed 23 July 2015).

[112] Condorelli, 'De la responsabilité internationale…', *supra* note 110 (arguing that once an organic or agency link is established and maintained with both the lending state and the receiving organization, dual attribution would ensue by default). See also, Messineo, 'Attribution of Conduct', 32 *SHARES Research Paper* (2014), available online at www.sharesproject.nl (last accessed 12 February 2015), at 27–34 (arguing, on the basis of the drafting history of Art. 7 ARIO (*supra* note 84) and contrary to the ARISWA Commentary (*supra* note 84) that attribution to the UN would be exclusive only when 'true transfers of organs has occurred').

[113] Larsen, 'Attribution of Conduct in Peace Operations: The "Ultimate Authority and Control" Test', 19 *European Journal of International Law* (2008) 509, at 518 (noting that practice relied on by the ILC refers exclusively to UN peace-keeping operations); Condorelli, 'De la responsabilité internationale…', *supra* note 110, at 11 ('l'introduction du critère du "contrôle effectif" (…) représente une "proposition" de la CDI: une nouveauté, en somme').

[114] ARIO Commentary, *supra* note 84, at 88, emphasis added.

[115] For an inquiry regarding the origins and rationale for this approach, see Nollkaemper and Jacobs, *supra* note 46, at 385 ff.

[116] See, critically, d'Argent, *supra* note 111, but see Spagnolo, 'The "Reciprocal" Approach in Art. 7 ARIO: A Reply to Pierre d'Argent', *Questions of International Law, Zoom-in 1* (2014) 33, available online at http://www.qil-qdi.org/the-reciprocal-approach-in-article-7-ario-a-reply-to-pierre-dargent/ (last accessed 23 July 2015).

[117] ARIO Commentary, *supra* note 84, at 81.

Domestic courts have applied the 'effective control' test to attribute the conduct of troops to their sending states, but have taken diverging views as far as double attribution is concerned. While older cases support the understanding of the ILC,[118] more recently dual attribution has been openly admitted,[119] allegedly when the factual assessment reveals that both subjects had effective control over the conduct.

With specific regard to piracy off the coast of Somalia, in the *MV Courier case*, Germany argued that the transferral of a suspect pirate arrested on the high seas by a German frigate acting within Operation *Atalanta* was not attributable to itself, but to the EU.[120] The Administrative Court of Cologne and, on appeal, the Supreme Administrative Court of North Rhine-Westphalia, held that, notwithstanding the integration of the German frigate within the structure of EUNAVFOR, the conduct was attributable to Germany since the order to proceed with the transfer had plainly come from German authorities. While both courts discussed the issue against the background of the *Behrami* and *Saramati* cases, rather than the ILC codification, they seem to have applied the effective control criterion.

In conclusion, one may be disappointed by the fact that a crucial issue of state responsibility, such as attribution in the context of multinational military operations abroad, is not clearly regulated. Recalling Anzilotti's remarks on the intrinsic legal nature of the attribution operation,[121] a paradox becomes evident: the generic and purely factual criterion of 'effective control', which requires a case-by-case assessment, has turned into the crucial legal standard for deciding issues of attribution. One cannot but observe that reliance on the established, simple and foreseeable principle that a state and an organization are always responsible in principle for the conduct of their organs, even in the context of complex military operations, would have beneficial effects in terms of legal certainty and access to remedies by potential victims. From this perspective, one may also wonder why dual attribution, which would increase accountability of both states and international organizations, still strives to be accepted in state practice and among scholars.

However, practice shows that, in the context of the global fight against piracy, the attribution to a state of a given conduct taken by its military personnel is always arguable, opening the way to litigation at the domestic and international level.

[118] *Mukeshimana-Ngulinzira and others v. Belgium and others*, Judgment (Tribunal of First Instance of Brussels, 8 December 2010), RG No. 04/4807/A, 07/15547/A, ILDC 1604 (BE 2010), para. 38 (the decision by the commander of the Belgian force of the United Nations Assistance Mission for Rwanda (UNAMIR) to abandon a de facto refugee camp at Kigali in April 1994 was 'une décision prise sous l'égide de la Belgique et non de l'UNAMIR').

[119] *Nuhanović*, Appeals Judgment, *supra* note 109, para. 5.3 and Supreme Court Judgment, *supra* note 102, para. 3.11.2. See also, *Al-Jedda*, *supra* note 90, para. 80.

[120] Verwaltungsgericht Köln, *Re 'MV Courier'*, K 4280/09, Judgment of 11 November 2011. The judgment was upheld on appeal; see Oberverwaltungsgericht Münster, *Re'MV Courier'*, A 2948/11, Judgment of 18 September 2014.

[121] D. Anzilotti, *Teoria generale della responsabilità dello stato nel diritto internazionale* (1902), reprinted in D. Anzilotti, *Scritti di diritto internazionale pubblico*, Vol. II, Part 1 (1956) 1, at 121–148, quoted by Messineo, *supra* note 112, at 8.

D. The Right to Life at Sea: The Interplay Between Human Rights and the Law of the Sea

Having established that counter-piracy coercive action may be attributed to states and having argued the obligations of states under the ECHR may apply, it is now possible to turn to substantive human rights issues.

Seizing a pirate ship under the power granted to all states by UNCLOS implies the possibility of the use of force. This is even clearer under the above resolutions of the Security Council, which mention the use of 'all necessary means for repressing acts of piracy and armed robbery'. It is well known that in the parlance of the Security Council 'all necessary means' means 'use of force'. The EU Council Joint Action makes this explicit in defining the mandate of Operation *Atalanta* when it says that 'all necessary measures, including use of force' shall be taken. Although in practice self-defence against an armed attack, or the threat thereof, seems to be a guiding principle of states whose navies are engaged in fighting pirates off the coast of Somalia and neighbouring states, force has also been used independently of self-defence, for instance in order to set hostages free.

Enforcement action may be limited by the duty to respect human rights, in particular by the obligation to protect life, under Article 2 of the ECHR.[122] While the use of force in order to prevent unlawful violence or to effect a lawful arrest is obviously allowed, it is constrained by a requirement of strict necessity.[123] Moreover, positive obligations arise in both preventing and repressing possible abuses. Several aspects of anti-piracy enforcement action, which have resulted in the death of suspects or other persons, or in a serious danger to their life, may come under the scrutiny of the ECtHR. This ranges from the appropriateness of the legal framework governing the use of force, and in particular rules of engagement,[124] to the actual planning and conduct of a specific enforcement action,[125] and the successive activity of investigation and criminal repression if issues concerning the right to life arise.[126]

As much as humanitarian law is relevant for assessing claims of violation of the right to life in the course of an armed conflict, it is argued that applying the rules on human rights to enforcement action at sea also requires considering the rules of the law of the sea.[127] In particular, in an assessment of whether the requirement of due diligence in protecting the right to life has been respected, reference should be made to respecting the limits of such use of force in the exercise of police action

122 See, generally, D. Harris *et al.*, *Harris, O'Boyle, and Warbrick: Law of the European Convention on Human Rights* (3rd edn, 2014), at 203 ff.

123 ECtHR, *McCann and Others v. The United Kingdom*, Appl. no. 18984/91, Judgment of 27 September 1995, para. 109.

124 See, *mutatis mutandis*, ECtHR, *Makaratzis v. Greece*, Appl. no. 50385/99, Judgment of 20 December 2004, para. 60 ff.; and ECtHR, *Nachova and Others v. Bulgaria*, Appl. nos. 43577/98 and 43579/98, Judgment of 6 July 2005, paras 99–100.

125 *McCann*, *supra* note 123, para. 202 ff.

126 *McCann*, *supra* note 123, para. 161, See, *mutatis mutandis*, *Makaratzis v. Greece*, *supra* note 124 para. 60 ff.; and *Nachova and Others v. Bulgaria*, *supra* note 124, paras 99–100.

127 See, generally, Treves, 'Human Rights and the Law of the Sea', 28 *Berkeley Journal of International Law* (2010) 1–14.

authorized by international law. In fact, judicial practice in this field confirms that a standard of strict necessity applies. Repeating and developing points made in the *S.S. I'm Alone* arbitration award and in the report of the Commission of Enquiry on the *Red Crusader* case, the International Tribunal for the Law of the Sea in its *M/V Saiga No. 2* judgment stated that 'international law . . . requires that the use of force must be avoided as far as possible and, where force is unavoidable, it must not go beyond what is reasonable and necessary in the circumstances. Considerations of humanity must apply in the law of the sea, as they do in other areas of international law.'[128] In the same vein, the UN Fish Stocks Agreement states that '[t]he degree of force used [after the boarding] shall not exceed that reasonably required in the circumstances'.[129] As to the measures taken prior to resorting to force against a vessel, the *M/V Saiga No. 2* judgment further recalls the practice concerning visual and auditory signals to stop, firing shots across the bows, and a variety of other measures, is normally followed.[130]

In addition to this, and in keeping with the due diligence nature of positive obligations, the assessment of whether incidents have been effectively investigated allows for some flexibility when 'difficult security conditions' prevail.[131] Therefore, the special conditions of policing at sea in the context of the fight against piracy should be taken into consideration.

E. The Human Rights Guarantees Against Arbitrary Detention of Suspect Pirates

Actual human rights litigation concerning piracy before the domestic courts of European states and the ECtHR has focused on issues relating to the detention at sea of apprehended suspects. In fact, the direction was paved by cases relating to the capture and detention of criminals at sea, although not pirates, who were later brought to trial in remote courts of the state of the arresting vessel, in particular in *Rigopoulos*,[132] *Medvedyev* and, more recently, *Vassis*.[133] It is against these precedents that the ECtHR has examined the complaints by the applicants in the *Hassan v. France* and *Ali Samatar* cases.

The first complaint raised by the applicants in *Hassan v. France* relates to the lawfulness of their detention. Article 5(1) of the ECHR states that '[n]o one shall be deprived of his liberty save . . . in accordance with a procedure prescribed by law'.

128 ITLOS, *M/V Saiga (No. 2) (St. Vincent and the Grenadines v. Guinea)* (1 July 1999), (1999) *ITLOS Reports* 10, para. 155. See also *Guayana v. Suriname*, Arbitral Award of 17 September 2007, (2008) 47 ILM 166.

129 Agreement for the Implementation of the Provisions of the United Nations Convention on the Law of the Sea of 10 December 1982 Relating to the Conservation and Management of Straddling Fish Stocks and Highly Migratory Fish Stocks, A/CONF.164/37, 8 September 1995, Art. 22(1)(f).

130 *M/V Saiga (No. 2)*, *supra* note 128, para. 156.

131 See, *mutatis mutandis*, *Al-Skeini*, *supra* note 49, para. 164, and *Jaloud*, *supra* note 63, para. 226.

132 ECtHR, *Rigopoulos v. Spain*, Appl. no. 37388/97, Decision on Admissibility of 12 January 1999.

133 ECtHR, *Vassis and Others v. France*, Appl. no. 62736/09, Judgement of 27 June 2013.

The Court in *Medvedyev* reiterated this as being the provision aimed at protecting the individual against arbitrariness and possible abuses, stating:

> [i]t is therefore essential that the conditions for deprivation of liberty under domestic *and/or international* law be clearly defined and that the law itself be foreseeable in its application, so that it meets the standard of 'lawfulness' set by the Convention, a standard which requires that all law be sufficiently precise to avoid all risk of arbitrariness and to allow the citizen—if need be, with appropriate advice—to foresee, to a degree that is reasonable in the circumstances of the case, the consequences which a given action may entail . . . [134]

Therefore, the lawfulness test under Article 5 of the ECHR is comprised of two limbs: firstly, whether a legal basis exists and, secondly, whether it has the qualities of clarity and foreseeability necessary to prevent arbitrariness.

The passage above shows that international law may in principle provide a basis for a lawful detention. In *Medvedyev*, given that UNCLOS was not applicable[135] the ECtHR did not rule out the possibility that an ad hoc international agreement incorporating the consent of the flag state could satisfy the first limb of the test.[136] However, it strongly denied that it could satisfy the conditions required by Article 5 of the ECHR. The content of the diplomatic note, which established the legal basis, was scrutinized and the lack of clarity on whether and to what extent it covered the fate of the crew was emphasized.[137] More radically, the ECtHR held that, failing international customary law to provide a clear permissive rule on inspection and boarding of vessels to combat the illicit traffic of narcotic drugs on the high seas[138] and in the absence of the establishment of either a stable treaty-based cooperation[139] or a long-standing cooperative practice by the states involved,[140] an ad hoc agreement could not satisfy the requirement of foreseeability embodied in Article 5 of the ECHR.

Given the Court's reasoning, the possibility of a similar decision seemed highly unlikely in the case of piracy, particularly in light of the broad powers recognized by general international law and the Security Council resolutions.[141] This view was only partially confirmed by the ECtHR, when faced with the issue in *Hassan v. France*. As to the first limb of the lawfulness test under Article 5 of the ECHR, the ECtHR was satisfied that France was acting under the authority of Resolution

134 *Medvedyev*, *supra* note 61, para. 80 (emphasis added).

135 Not only was Cambodia, the flag state, not a party to UNCLOS, but Arts 108 and 110 thereof, as interpreted by the ECtHR, do not provide a legal basis for inspecting and boarding ships flying a third state's flag on the high seas, see ibid., paras 83–89.

136 Ibid., paras 95–97.

137 Guilfoyle, *supra* note 40, at 160, comments: 'A general public international law lawyer might well be puzzled that this result could follow from an ostensibly plenary grant of authority.'

138 *Medvedyev*, *supra* note 61, paras 85 and 93.

139 Cambodia was not a party to the United Nations Convention against Illicit Traffic in Narcotic Drugs and Psychotropic Substances 1988, 1582 UNTS 95.

140 *Medvedyev*, *supra* note 61, para. 100.

141 According to Piedimonte Bodini, *supra* note 40, at 829, the *obiter dictum* set out in para. 85 of the *Medvedyev* judgment 'seems to imply that the anti-piracy provisions contained in the Convention [i.e. UNCLOS] would pass the "sufficient legal basis" test under article 5(1) when it comes to intercepting pirate vessels and detaining their crews'.

1816.[142] As to the second limb, it held that detention of suspected pirates for the purpose of their prosecution by cooperating states was foreseeable, given that the terms of the resolution were clear and that the authorization was intended to extend the scope of the rules on piracy codified in UNCLOS.[143] However, the ECtHR found that the requirements of clarity were not satisfied, since:

> le droit [français] applicable à l'époque des faits à la situation des personnes arrêtées par les forces françaises à raison d'actes de piraterie commis en haute mer ne comportait aucune règle définissant les conditions de la privation de liberté susceptible de leur être ensuite imposée dans le but de les conduire devant l'autorité judiciaire compétente.[144]

This decision was to a large extent based on the shortcomings of French legislation, already highlighted and officially recognized by a circular letter of the French Ministry of Justice, which were confirmed by its subsequent amendment.[145] Within this framework, it may be concluded that, in order to constitute a proper legal basis for detention, customary law on piracy, and its extension through resolutions of the Security Council, must be detailed by a further normative activity at the domestic level in order to respect the strict demands of legality embodied in Article 5 of the ECHR.[146]

The second complaint raised in the piracy cases before the ECtHR was whether the significant lapse of time, almost 10 days and 7 days respectively,[147] between the initial deprivation of liberty and the presentation of the applicants to a judicial authority complied with Article 5(3) of the ECHR.[148] According to this provision—which embodies the fundamental principle of *habeas corpus*[149]—arrested or detained persons must, *inter alia*, 'be brought promptly before a judge or other officer authorized by law to exercise judicial power'. The ECtHR confirmed that enforcement action at sea may take place in conditions falling within those 'wholly exceptional circumstances' that may justify a delay longer than the four days limit that is generally set by the case-law.[150] In the past, the ECtHR had

[142] *Hassan v. France*, *supra* note 41, paras 63–64.

[143] Ibid., paras 65 and 68.

[144] 'The [French] law applicable at the material time to the situation of persons arrested by French forces on accusation of piracy on the high seas did not lay down the conditions for subsequently depriving them of liberty in order to bring them before the competent judicial authority', ibid., para. 69.

[145] Ibid., para. 70.

[146] Compare, however, with *MV Courier* (Verwaltungsgericht Köln), *supra* note 120, paras 31–37, in which Arts 105, 106 and 110 UNCLOS were deemed to be a sufficient legal basis for detention for the purposes of Art. 5(1) ECHR. See, critically, Petrig, 'Arrest, Detention and Transfer of Piracy Suspects: A Critical Appraisal of the German *Courier* Case Decision', in G. Andreone *et al.* (eds), *Insecurity at Sea: Piracy and Other Risks to Navigation* (2013) 153, at 155–161.

[147] See *Hassan v. France*, *supra* note 41, para. 88 and *Ali Samatar*, *supra* note 14, para. 44.

[148] On the characteristics of a 'judge' for the purposes of Art. 5(3) ECHR, see *Medvedyev*, *supra* note 61, paras 123–125.

[149] In the words of the ECtHR, 'the importance of the promptness or speediness of the requisite judicial controls under article 5 §§ 3 and 4' ranks among the most fundamental guarantees against arbitrary deprivation of liberty, and '[s]uch automatic expedited judicial scrutiny provides an important measure of protection against arbitrary behaviour, incommunicado detention and ill-treatment', see *Medvedyev*, *supra* note 61, paras 117–118.

[150] See *Hassan v. France*, *supra* note 41, para. 94, and *Ali Samatar*, *supra* note 14, para. 50.

accepted as 'prompt' judicial control taking place up to 16 days after the arrest in the high seas that was far away from the state's territory.[151] In the piracy cases the ECtHR has confirmed the generous standard of review in this regard. At the same time, however, it has specified that this situation imposes a stricter obligation of promptness on the authorities once the suspects actually reach the territory of the arresting state. It found that placing the suspects in *garde à vue* for an additional 48 hours after their arrival in France—taking into account that supervision of the police detention by the public prosecutor did not satisfy the standard of Article 5(3)[152]—was not justified and constituted a breach of the ECHR.[153]

Overall, the case-law of the ECtHR shows that, while the peculiarities of the fight against piracy are taken into account when interpreting Article 5 of the ECHR, this is generally made without prejudice to the fundamental guarantees of the individual.

F. What to Do with Captured Pirates and Armed Robbers? The Reluctance to Prosecute the 'Seizing' Ship's Flag States

As mentioned already, international law recognizes universal jurisdiction in the courts of the seizing state. This jurisdiction, applicable under Article 105 of UNCLOS for seizures and arrests of pirates on the high sea, also applies to seizures and arrests in the territorial sea of Somalia under the Security Council resolutions cited above.

The seizing states—for example, the states fighting pirates and armed robbers in the waters off Somalia and responsible for their arrest—are, however, reluctant to exercise such broad powers by prosecuting and submitting the arrested pirates and armed robbers to criminal proceedings in their courts.[154] They have several concerns which include: the expense involved; the legal complexities, especially in relation to evidence, for example,[155] which are inherent in criminal proceedings held in remote places where the alleged crime was committed; the human rights

[151] See *Rigopoulus*, *supra* note 132, and *Medvedyev*, *supra* note 6, paras 127–134. Equally the Administrative Court of Cologne found a delay of seven days compatible with Art. 5 ECHR, see *MV Courier* (Verwaltungsgericht Köln), *supra* note 120, paras 39–48. Conversely, the Rotterdam District Court in the *Cygnus Case (Somali Pirates)*, 145 ILR 491, stressed that the time of 40 days elapsed before captured pirates were brought to justice constituted a breach of Art. 5 of the ECHR, although no consequences followed in the criminal proceedings before the Dutch Court.

[152] ECtHR, *Moulin v. France*, Appl. no. 37104/06, Judgment of 23 November 2010, paras 55–59.

[153] See *Hassan v. France*, *supra* note 41, paras 100–104, and *Ali Samatar*, *supra* note 14, paras 55–59.

[154] The US Secretary of State Condoleezza Rice observed in her declaration of 16 December 2008 before the Security Council: 'the international community already has sufficient legal authority and available mechanisms to apprehend and prosecute pirates, but sometimes the political will and the coordination have not been there to do so'; see UN Doc. S/PV.6046, *supra* note 10, at 10.

[155] Consequently, on 17 November 2010, a vessel of the European force *Atalanta*, after capturing pirates and seizing their weapons freed the pirates because the evidence collected was not deemed sufficient for prosecution, see Lang Report, *supra* note 2.

implications when exercising jurisdiction; and the possibility of pirates applying for asylum.[156]

An early, and not isolated,[157] case highlights these difficulties. On 17 September 2008, the Danish Navy ship *Absalon* captured 10 pirates in the waters off Somalia. After six days of detention and confiscation of their weapons, including ladders and other tools used to board ships, the Danish government decided to free the pirates by putting them ashore on a Somali beach. The Danish authorities had come to the conclusion that the pirates risked torture and the death penalty if surrendered to any of the Somali authorities. This was unacceptable as Danish law prohibits extraditing criminals when they may face death penalty. Moreover, they were not ready to submit them to put them on trial in Denmark as it would be difficult, in light of the possible abuses these pirates would risk, to deport them back to Somalia after their sentences were served.[158] It is clear that human rights considerations, or perhaps reasons of expediency presented as human rights concerns, prevailed over considerations concerning the fight against piracy. In the same vein, the British Foreign Office reportedly warned the Royal Navy against detaining pirates since this might violate their human rights and could lead to asylum claims in the United Kingdom.[159] Similarly, in 2010, Russia, having captured the pirates who had hijacked the Russian tanker *Russian University*, released them on the very skiff they had used to board the tanker, alleging that 'in the absence of the necessary legal agreements, it was impossible to bring these pirates to justice'.[160]

[156] A vivid description of the problems encountered by a state whose vessel has captured pirates was made by Katherine Shepherd, of the UK Foreign and Commonwealth office, Shepherd, 'Remarks by Katharine Shepherd', 103 *American Society of International Law, Proceedings of the 103rd Annual Meeting* (2009) 95. See also Dutton, 'Pirates and Impunity: Is the Threat of Asylum Claims a Reason to Allow Pirates to Escape Justice?', 34 *Fordham Law Review* (2011) 236. According to Neuhold, *supra* note 2, at 1254, note 48, one of the five pirates that was sentenced to five years' imprisonment by the District Court of Rotterdam (see the *'Cygnus'* Case, *supra* note 151) 'promptly applied for asylum'. See also Dinstein, *supra* note 2, at 1143 and Jacobsen, 'International Legal Cooperation to Combat Piracy in the Horn of Africa', in R. C. Beckman and J. A. Roach (eds), *Piracy and International Maritime Crimes in ASEAN, Prospects for Cooperation* (2012) 95, at 106–115.

[157] According to the Lang Report, *supra* note 2, para. 14, 'more than 90 per cent of the pirates apprehended by States patrolling the seas will be released without being prosecuted'. For further discussion, see Guilfoyle, 'Prosecuting Somali Pirates: A Critical Evaluation of the Options', 10 *Journal of International Criminal Justice* (2012) 767.

[158] See reports available online at http://www.iss-shipping.com/Attachments/WWTTS%20102408.doc (last accessed 23 July 2015); US Office of Naval Intelligence, Civil Maritime Analysis Department, 'Worldwide Threat to Shipping, Mariner Warning Information', 17 October 2008, at para. 10.

[159] See Rivkin Jr. and Casey, 'Pirates Exploit Confusion about International Law', *The Wall Street Journal* (19 November 2008).

[160] See Spilman, 'MV Moscow University—Why Anti-Piracy Efforts off Somalia Are Doomed to Fail', available online at http://www.oldsaltblog.com/2010/05/10/mv-moscow-university-why-anti-piracy-efforts-in-somalia-are-doomed-to-fail (last accessed 23 July 2015), and Spilman, 'Russian Special Forces Capture Oil Tanker Moscow University', available online at http://www.oldsaltblog.com/2010/05/06/russian-special-forces-capture-oil-tanker-moscow-university (last accessed 23 July 2015). Neuhold, *supra* note 2, at 1253, note 46, qualifies the Russian solution as 'brutal' because, according to this information, the pirates were released without food and navigation devices 'so that they were in all probability sent to their deaths'.

G. The Role of the SUA Convention in Prosecuting Pirates

The reluctance of the seizing states to prosecute and try pirates is implicitly taken into account in a paragraph repeated in various resolutions of the Security Council.[161] The latest version reads as follows:

> Calls *upon* all States, and in particular flag, port, and coastal States, States of the nationality of victims and perpetrators of piracy and armed robbery, and other States with relevant jurisdiction under international law and national legislation, to cooperate in determining jurisdiction and in the investigation and prosecution of all persons responsible for acts of piracy and armed robbery off the coast of Somalia, including key figures of criminal networks involved in piracy who plan, organize, facilitate, or illicitly finance or profit from such attack, consistent with applicable international law including international human rights law, to ensure that all pirates handed over to judicial authorities are subject to a judicial process, and to render assistance by, among other actions, providing disposition and logistics assistance with respect to persons under their jurisdiction and control, such as victims, witnesses, and persons detained as a result of operations conducted under this resolution[.][162]

This language is merely hortatory. However, most states involved as flag states of the ships that are victims of piracy or of the ships patrolling the waters off Somalia, or as neighbouring coastal states such as Djibouti, Kenya and Yemen, but not Somalia, are bound by the precise obligations contained in the Rome Convention for the Suppression of Unlawful Acts against the Safety of Maritime Navigation of 10 March 1988 (the SUA Convention).[163] This Convention—adopted in the wake of the *Achille Lauro* affair—provides that states parties shall establish a number of criminal offences, most of which correspond in whole or in part with actions committed by pirates or armed robbers including 'seiz[ing] or exercis[ing] control over a ship by force or threat thereof or any other form of intimidation'.[164] Notably, it does not require the presence of two ships and does not distinguish between maritime areas. In particular, it makes it compulsory to 'take such measures as may be necessary to establish jurisdiction' over such offences for the flag state of the ship against or on board of which the crime is committed, for the

[161] SC Res. 1816, *supra* note 9, para. 11; SC Res. 1846, *supra* note 11, para. 14; SC Res. 2125, *supra* note 11, para. 16.

[162] SC Res. 2184, *supra* note 5, para. 17.

[163] Convention for the Suppression of Unlawful Acts against the Safety of Maritime Navigation 1988, 1678 UNTS 221. Under Art. 4(1), the 'Convention applies if the ship is navigating or is scheduled to navigate into, through or from waters beyond the outer limit of the territorial sea of a single State, or the lateral limits of its territorial sea with adjacent States'. This means that only ships navigating between ports of the same state (cabotage) are excluded from the scope of the Convention. Even in this case, under Art. 4(2) the Convention applies if 'the offender or alleged offender is found in the territory of a State party other than the State referred to in para. 1'. On the SUA Convention see, with further references, Treves, 'The Rome Convention for the Suppression of Unlawful Acts against the Safety of Maritime Navigation', in N. Ronzitti (ed.), *Maritime Terrorism and International Law* (1990) 69, and Treves, 'The Convention for the Suppression of Unlawful Acts Against the Safety of Maritime Navigation', 2 *Singapore Journal of International and Comparative Law* (1998) 541.

[164] Convention for the Suppression of Unlawful Acts against the Safety of Maritime Navigation, *supra* note 163, Art. 3.

state in whose territory, including the territorial sea, the crime has been committed, and for the state whose national has committed the offence. It further authorizes other states to establish jurisdiction in additional cases, including when the national state of a person seized, threatened, injured or killed and the state, in which the offence was committed, attempts to compel to do or abstain from doing any act. In all cases, to establish jurisdiction is compulsory for the state in whose territory the alleged offender is present, unless it has extradited such offender to one of the states having established jurisdiction.[165]

While the SUA Convention is not mentioned in Resolution 1816, resolutions adopted in subsequent years, including the most recent one,[166] recall the obligations contained in it and urge states parties 'to fully implement' these obligations.

H. Transfer of Captured Pirates to Neighbouring States

Reluctance by the seizing states is not the only cause of lack of efficiency in dealing with captured pirates and armed robbers. As said in a preambular paragraph of Security Council Resolution 1851: 'the lack of capacity, domestic legislation, and clarity about how to dispose of pirates after their capture has hindered more robust international action against the pirates off the coast of Somalia and in some cases led to the pirates being released without facing justice'.

A solution seen with great interest by capturing states consists of surrendering the captured pirates to a state near the place of capture. This solution, however, raises difficulties with regards to questions about the ability and willingness of such states to exercise jurisdiction and to administer detention that is in full respect of human rights.

In order to overcome these difficulties, bilateral agreements with Kenya have been concluded by the United Kingdom, the United States[167] and the EU,[168] as well as by the latter with the Seychelles,[169] Mauritius[170] and Tanzania.[171] These

[165] Ibid., Art. 6. [166] SC Res. 2125, *supra* note 11, para. 24.

[167] Meade, 'US to Sign Kenya Deal to Prosecute Somali Pirates', *Lloyd's List* (16 January 2009).

[168] Council Decision 2009/293/CFSP of 26 February 2009, OJ 2009 L 79/47; Exchange of Letters between the European Union and the Government of Kenya on the Conditions and Modalities for the Transfer of Persons Suspected of Having Committed Acts of Piracy and Detained by the European Union-led Naval Force (EUNAVFOR), and Seized Property in the Possession of EUNAVFOR, from EUNAVFOR to Kenya and for Their Treatment after such Transfer, OJ 2009 L 79/49.

[169] Council Decision 2009/877/CFSP of 23 October 2009, OJ 2009 L 315/35; Exchange of Letters between the European Union and the Republic of Seychelles on the Conditions and Modalities for the Transfer of Suspected Pirates and Armed Robbers from EUNAVFOR to the Republic of Seychelles and for their Treatment after such Transfer, OJ 2009 L 315/37.

[170] Council Decision 2011/640/CFSP of 12 July 2011, OJ 2011 L 254/1; Agreement between the European Union and the Republic of Mauritius on the Conditions of Transfer of Suspected Pirates and Associated Seized Property from the European Union-led Naval force to the Republic of Mauritius and on the conditions of Suspected Pirates after Transfer, OJ 2011 L 254/3.

[171] Council Decision 2014/198/CFSP of 10 March 2014, OJ 2014 L 108/1; Agreement between the European Union and the United Republic of Tanzania on the Conditions of Transfer of Suspected Pirates and Associated Seized Property from the European Union-led Naval Force to the United Republic of Tanzania, OJ 2014 L 108/3.

allow for the transfer of suspected pirates captured by a patrolling navy to the custody of a regional state for prosecution.

These agreements sometimes provide for 'shipriders' as stated and encouraged by Resolution 1851 and others, although such provisions are never used in practice. 'Shiprider' arrangements consist of agreements between the states whose ships are patrolling the waters off the coast of Somalia and 'countries willing to take custody of pirates' for embarking on these ships to enable law enforcement officers (the 'shipriders') 'from the latter countries, in particular countries of the region, to facilitate the investigation and prosecution of persons detained'.[172] These arrangements require previous consent of the TFG 'for the exercise of third state jurisdiction by shipriders in Somali territorial waters', provided they 'do not prejudice the effective implementation of the Convention for the Suppression of Unlawful Acts'.

In practice, states appear to ground their jurisdiction over pirates on one of several bases. First and foremost is the assertion of universal jurisdiction, under national laws, by regional coastal states over suspects delivered to them by patrolling navies. Greater use of shipriders under the agreements discussed above also permits the jurisdiction of Kenya (or of other states whose officers are on board the seizing vessels) to be established on the fiction that it is a seizing state under Article 105 of UNCLOS. In other cases, the connecting factor is the nationality of the victim ship or of the victims. As a result, reportedly, Denmark agreed with the Netherlands to extradite five Somali pirates it had captured and who had attacked a Netherlands–Antilles cargo vessel in the Gulf of Aden.[173] The extradited pirates were tried and sentenced to five years' imprisonment by the Rotterdam Criminal Court in 2010.[174]

The European Union Joint Action 2008/851/CFSP,[175] which established Operation *Atalanta*, envisages the situation just considered. With a view to prosecuting persons arrested during the operation, it provides that if the competent authorities of the flag state of the ship 'which took them captive', 'cannot or does not wish to exercise its jurisdiction', they shall be transferred to a 'Member State or any third State which wishes to exercise its jurisdiction over the aforementioned persons'.[176] This provision does not exclude the practice of 'shipriders', but adds a possible transferral to other EU member states or to other willing third states. It is to be noted that this agreement, though not excluding their involvement, does not mention 'shipriders', reinforcing the conclusion they are not greatly used in practice.

[172] SC Res. 1851, *supra* note 11, para. 3. 'Shipriders' are used in some bilateral agreements concluded by the US regarding drug trafficking, see, e.g., Guilfoyle, *Interdiction*, *supra* note 2, at 91–94; they are mentioned also as 'Embarked Officers' in the 2009 Code of Conduct for the West Indian Ocean and the Gulf of Aden, *supra* note 31, Art. 7.

[173] Meade, *supra* note 167.

[174] Greene, 'Pirates Get 5 Years in Prison in First Trial in Europe' (CNN, 17 June 2010), available online at http://edition.cnn.com/2010/WORLD/europe/06/17/netherlands.pirate.trial (last accessed 23 July 2015).

[175] European Union Joint Action 2008/851/CFSP, *supra* note 45.

[176] Ibid., Art. 12(1). This provision may be read as implying that in the view of the European Union Art. 105 UNCLOS does not rule out exercise of universal jurisdiction by a state different from that having seized the ship.

I. Transfer of Suspect Pirates: Addressing Human Rights Concerns

It is well known that states may encounter limits in transferring persons within their jurisdiction to third states. Apart from cases in which refoulement is forbidden by the 1951 Geneva Refugee Convention,[177] further constraints are imposed by human rights treaties. The jurisprudence of the ECtHR highlights that contracting states may incur responsibility for breach of the ECHR, when the removal of an individual exposes that person to a foreseeable violation of certain rights in the country of destination. In particular, Article 3 of the ECHR prevents removal where substantial grounds have been shown for believing that the person in question would face a real risk of torture or inhumane treatment in the destination country.[178] Similarly, responsibility can arise under Article 2 of the ECHR, where the person concerned faces a real risk of being liable to capital punishment in the receiving country,[179] under Article 5 of the ECHR, if there is a real risk of a flagrant breach of that Article,[180] and under Article 6 of the ECHR, if that person would be exposed to a real risk of being subjected to a flagrant denial of justice.[181]

The legal framework for combating piracy in the Gulf of Aden addresses these concerns. In general, the resolutions of the Security Council stress the need for cooperation to combat piracy to be consistent with international human rights law,[182] and specifically request states to facilitate the transfer of suspects or convicted pirates in accordance with international human rights law.[183] Even more explicit is the legal framework governing the EU Operation *Atalanta*, which contains a general provision, stating:

> No persons . . . may be transferred to a third State unless the conditions for the transfer have been agreed with that third State in a manner consistent with relevant international law, notably international law on human rights, in order to guarantee in particular that no one shall be subjected to the death penalty, to torture or to any cruel, inhuman or degrading treatment.[184]

177 Art. 31, Convention Relating to the Status of Refugees 1951, 189 UNTS 150. Guilfoyle, *supra* note 40, at 153, argues that this provision is of little relevance, since pirates returned to Puntland would have no reasons to fear persecutions.

178 See, among many authorities, *Hirsi*, *supra* note 65, para. 113 ff; ECtHR, *Saadi v. Italy*, Appl. no. 37201/06, Judgment of 28 February 2008, para. 128; ECtHR, *Mamatkulov and Askarov v. Turkey*, Appl. nos. 46827/99 and 46951/99, Judgment of 4 February 2005, paras 90–91.

179 *Al-Saadoon and Mufdhi*, *supra* note 61, para. 123; and ECtHR, *Kaboulov v. Ukraine*, Appl. no. 41015/04, Judgment of 19 November 2009, para. 99.

180 ECtHR, *Othman (Abu Qatada) v. the United Kingdom*, Appl. no. 8139/09, Judgment of 17 January 2012, paras 233 and 285, and ECtHR, *El-Masri v. the 'Former Yugoslav Republic of Macedonia'*, Appl. no. 39630/09, Judgment of 13 December 2012, paras 212–214 and 239.

181 *Othman (Abu Qatada)*, *supra* note 180, paras 261 and 285.

182 Apart from references in the preambular para., references may be found in the dispositive part of the resolutions, see SC Res. 1816, *supra* note 9, para. 11; SC Res. 1846, *supra* note 11 para. 14; SC Res. 1851, *supra* note 11, paras 6–7; SC Res. 1897, *supra* note 11, paras 11–12; SC Res. 1918, *supra* note 11, para. 2; SC Res. 1950, *supra* note 11, paras 11–13; SC Res. 1976, *supra* note 11, paras 14 and 16; SC Res. 2015, *supra* note 11, paras 5 and 9; SC Res. 2020, *supra* note 11, paras 13–15; SC Res. 2077, *supra* note 11, paras 16–18; SC Res. 2125, *supra* note 11, paras 7, 16, 17 and 19; and SC Res. 2184, *supra* note 5, paras 7 and 17–19.

183 See SC Res. 1976, *supra* note 11, para. 20.

184 Joint Action 2008/851/CFSP, *supra* note 45, Art. 12(2).

Additional and detailed provisions for the protection of human rights of pirates captured by the EUNAVFOR and transferred to third states are included in the Transfer Agreements with Kenya,[185] Mauritius[186] and the Seychelles.[187] These provisions have two discrete effects. Firstly, they aim at securing international standards of treatment of prisoners and a fair trial, as well as additional obligations against the death penalty, which are to be respected in the receiving states that undertake international obligations. Secondly, they make clear that neither the EU nor its member states are relieved from their international human rights obligations in the transfer proceedings.

Looking at the problem from the perspective of obligations under the ECHR, two sets of considerations are in order.

In the first place, one should consider whether the assurances obtained by the EU through the transfer agreement are sufficient to exclude member states' responsibility under the ECHR. This was of particular concern with regards to transfers to Kenya, where, according to available sources, the condition of detention, the malfunctioning of the judicial system and the prevailing political situation casted doubt over the effective respect of relevant human rights.[188]

The position of the ECtHR as to the relevance of diplomatic assurances is far from settled. In principle, their importance is relative and they only constitute one of the elements to be taken into account when assessing the existence, as a matter of fact, of a real risk to the applicant. In fact, the ECtHR has made clear that the existence of legal guarantees in the receiving state, either deriving from purely domestic provisions at the constitutional or legislative level, or from the participation in relevant international human rights regimes, is not sufficient. Equally, in the leading case *Saadi v. Italy* the Grand Chamber stated that '[t]he weight to be given to assurances from the receiving State depends, in each case, on the circumstances prevailing at the material time'.[189] In this respect certain features of the assurances given, such as the binding nature of the instrument embodying them[190] and the provision of procedural mechanisms to monitor their actual respect,[191] are considered. However, case-law shows that, at least in certain cases, the assessment by

[185] See Arts 2(c), 3, 4 and 7 EU-Kenya Transfer Agreement, *supra* note 169 ('Nothing in this Exchange of Letters is intended to derogate, or may be construed as derogating, from any rights that a transferred person may have under applicable domestic or international law').

[186] See Arts 3(5), 4 and 5 Agreement between the European Union and the Republic of Mauritius, *supra* note 170.

[187] See EU–Seychelles Transfer Agreement *supra* note 170, para. 6(7) and Declaration by the EU, para. 1 ('The European Union (EU) notes that nothing in the Exchange of letters between the European Union and the Republic of Seychelles on the conditions and modalities for the transfer of suspected pirates and armed robbers is intended to derogate, or may be construed as derogating, from any rights that a transferred person may have under applicable domestic or international law').

[188] See, in this respect, the findings in *Re 'MV Courier'* (Oberverwaltungsgericht Münster), *supra* note 120.

[189] *Saadi, supra* note 178, para. 148.

[190] ECtHR, *Al-Moayad v. Germany*, Appl. no. 35865/03, Decision on Admissibility of 20 February 2007.

[191] ECtHR, *Soldatenko v. Ukraine*, Appl. no. 2440/07, Judgment of 23 October 2008, para. 73; ECtHR, *Shamayev and Others v. Georgia and Russia*, Appl. no. 36378/02, Judgment of 12 April 2005, para. 134.

the ECtHR tends to show a certain deference, especially when the country of destination is a contracting party.

In this framework, it seems that the detailed human rights provisions in transfer agreements, coupled with cooperative efforts to enhance the capacity of receiving states to improve the conditions of detention as well as the functioning of the judicial system, constitute a strong element of proof that the real risk of relevant human rights violations in the country of destination is, if any, offset. However, this does not seem to relieve states from a case-by-case evaluation, by assessing the peculiar position of each individual and the situation prevailing in the third state concerned and does not shield them from a similar analysis by the ECtHR to make a finding on their responsibility under the ECHR.

This brings us to the second set of considerations related to the procedural guarantees that are to be provided to captured suspects when their transfer is envisaged.

Firstly, according to well-established case-law of the ECtHR, effective protection against removal in breach of the ECHR requires, under Article 13 of the ECHR, that potential victims have the chance to submit their complaint to the 'close scrutiny' of a national authority.[192] Therefore, a remedy with *de jure* or de facto automatic suspensive effect shall be provided, which extends to those persons that come within the extraterritorial jurisdiction of contracting states.[193] On this basis, the mere possibility of challenging the transfer only after its execution, as was the case in *MV Courier*, would not comply with the standard required by the ECHR.

Secondly, it is disputed whether Article 5(3) of the ECHR allows for prompt judicial control over detention by judges of a state other than the arresting state. This issue was considered by the Administrative Court of Cologne in the *MV Courier* case, in which the suspects had been transferred to Kenya and were given the chance to appear before the judges of the latter state. The German Court found that the right to be brought promptly before a judge is respected if the judge of the third country satisfies the standard of independence, impartiality and competence required by Article 5(3) of the ECHR. However, it is doubtful whether the judge of the third state may have the competence to effectively scrutinize the legality of a sovereign act of another state's organs and hand down a finding that there was a violation as a basis for release of the defendant.[194]

J. The Search for New Solutions Beyond Transfer Agreements to Obtain the Trial of Pirates

Transfer agreements, although attractive for capturing states, cannot be the only solution to the problem of what do with captured pirates. Notwithstanding

[192] *Shamayev*, *supra* note 191, para. 448.

[193] *Hirsi*, *supra* note 65, paras 197–200.

[194] See, for this argument, Petrig, *supra* note 146, at 164–167, who also envisages different solutions which would avoid a black hole in protection, through control over detention by the judicial authorities of the arresting state, without jeopardizing the efficiency of counter-piracy operations.

substantial expenditure, especially by the EU and the United States, to strengthen the judicial and penitentiary systems of the states accepting to receive captured pirates, the capacity of these states is rather limited. In 2010, Kenya withdrew from the arrangements that it had entered into with Canada, China, Denmark, the EU, the United Kingdom and the United States for the transfer of piracy suspects, while indicating its readiness to consider transfers on an ad hoc basis.[195] Even though Kenya has subsequently received some new piracy cases for trial, the very announcement is an indication of unease and shows that other solutions must be sought.

Probably owing to the new Kenyan attitude, in the following months the Security Council focused on the link between prosecution of captured pirates and the efficacy in fighting against piracy. In Resolution 1918, passed on 27 April 2010, the Security Council affirmed 'that the failure to prosecute persons responsible for acts of piracy and armed robbery at sea off the coast of Somalia undermines anti-piracy efforts of the international community'.[196] On 25 August 2010, the President of the Security Council stated that '[t]he Security Council strongly believes that persons responsible for acts of piracy and armed robbery at sea off the coast of Somalia, including those who incite or intentionally facilitate such acts, should be brought to justice, and considers in this regard that the effective prosecution of suspected pirates and their supporters may deter future pirate attacks'.[197] In Resolution 1976 from 2011, the Security Council expressed its concern 'over a large number of persons suspected of piracy having to be released without facing justice' and reaffirmed 'that the failure to prosecute persons responsible for acts of piracy and armed robbery at sea off the coast of Somalia undermines anti-piracy efforts of the international community'.[198]

Acting on the basis of these resolutions, the UN Secretary General presented a report on 26 July 2010 about possible options for prosecuting captured pirates, in which seven such options were indicated.[199] On 26 August 2010, the UN Secretary General appointed the French former Minister Jack Lang as the Special Advisor on Legal Issues Related to Piracy. In light of the drawbacks of some of the seven options indicated by the Secretary General, Jack Lang's broad-ranging report favours the establishment of a court system comprising of specialized courts in Puntland and Somaliland and a specialized extraterritorial Somali court that could be located in Arusha, United Republic of Tanzania.[200]

[195] See UN Doc. S/2011/360, *supra* note 2, Annex V, para. 3 and the statements by Kenya's Attorney General Amos Wako of 30 March 2010 in 'AG Queried over Kenya's Role on Piracy Cases', *The Nation (Kenya)* (30 March 2010), available online at http://www.nation.co.ke/News/AG+queried+over+Kenya+role+in+piracy+cases/-/1056/889516/-/l25eie/-/index.html (last accessed 23 July 2015); and further indications in Roach, *supra* note 2, 404 note 36 and in Lang Report, *supra* note 2, para. 72.

[196] SC Res. 1918, *supra* note 11, para. 1.

[197] Statement by the President of the Security Council, UN Doc. S/PRST/2010/16, 25 August 2010. See the discussion in Security Council, 65th Year, 6374th Meeting, UN Doc. SC/PV/6374, 25 August 2010.

[198] SC Res. 1976, *supra* note 11, 15th preambular para. The same language is in SC Res. 2125, *supra* note 11, 7th preambular para.

[199] UN Doc. S/2010/394, *supra* note 2. For further analysis see Guilfoyle, *supra* note 157, at 767.

[200] The Lang Report, *supra* note 2, paras 116–41 deals with the indicated 'jurisdictional component' of the proposals set out in it.

In its resolutions adopted at the end of 2011, the Security Council seemed to orient itself in favour of at least some of these proposals. In Resolution 2015 it decided 'to continue its consideration, as a matter of urgency, without prejudice to any further steps to ensure that pirates are held accountable, of the establishment of specialized anti-piracy courts in Somalia and other states in the region with substantial international participation and/or support'.[201] This decision, reiterated in Resolutions 2020 and 2125, included also a request that the Secretary General undergo further consultations with Somalia and report within 90 days.

It is necessary to underscore, however, that the establishment of a Somali extraterritorial court to be located out of Somalia is not explicitly mentioned, although it might be read as implied in the expression 'specialized anti-piracy courts in Somalia *and other States in the region with substantial international participation and/or support*'.[202] As a matter of fact, the idea of establishing an extraterritorial Somali court outside Somalia had been unequivocally opposed during consultations held by representatives of the Secretary General, as well as by the TFG and the regional governments of Puntland and Galmadug.[203]

Therefore, the centrepiece of Jack Lang's proposals to the Security Council, the establishment of an extraterritorial Somali court with international involvement, has met with grave political difficulties. Not surprisingly, all references to this possibility have disappeared from the text of Resolution 2184, leaving only the reference to the establishment of regional Somali specialized courts in Somalia with international assistance.[204] This can hardly be seen as sufficient. Probably, the strengthening of the current mix of trials of pirates in Somalia, in the neighbouring states and in the captors' courts will remain the only option. While it is true that the number of pirates and armed robbers submitted to trial and often sentenced in courts of about 20 states is slowly growing,[205] this does not go very far towards making the operation of criminal justice a serious disincentive to the activity of pirates and armed robbers in the waters off the coast of Somalia.

[201] SC Res. 2015, *supra* note 11. [202] Ibid.
[203] UN Doc. S/2011/360, *supra* note 2, paras 52–55.
[204] SC Res. 2184, *supra* note 5, para. 18.
[205] UN Doc. S/2011/360, *supra* note 2, Annex I, para. 4; Report of the Secretary-General on the Situation with Respect to Piracy and Armed Robbery at Sea off the Coast of Somalia, UN Doc. S/2013/623, 21 October 2013, paras 45–46; and Report of the Secretary-General on the Situation with Respect to Piracy and Armed Robbery at Sea off the Coast of Somalia, UN Doc. S/2014/740, 16 October 2014, para. 35.

Dilemmas in Promoting Global Economic Justice through Human Rights Law

*Ralph Wilde**

1. Introduction

What is the value of ideas of international human rights in the struggle against global poverty and economic inequality? This question is not new, but recently a new aspect to it has emerged: what contribution might international human rights law make, on the basis of an 'extraterritorial' orientation, as far as state obligations are concerned? Such an enquiry has been foregrounded by a major international initiative by experts and activists: the 2011 'Maastricht Principles on the Extraterritorial Obligations of States in the area of Economic, Social and Cultural Rights' (the 'Principles').[1]

* The work on this chapter was funded by the European Research Council. My warm thanks to Dr Karen da Costa for excellent research assistance, and to the organizers who gave me the opportunity to present some of the ideas herein at the American Society of International Law Annual Meeting, European University Institute Human Rights Group, University of Memphis Law School, Mississippi College School of Law, Third World Approaches to International Law Conference at the American University in Cairo, Universidade Federal da Paraíba, the Fundação Getulio Vargas, Rio de Janeiro, and the ICON-S conference at New York University. I am grateful for the valuable feedback I received, notably from Dr Ebrahim Afsah, Professor Anthony Anghie, Professora Danielle da Costa Leite Borges, Professor Michael Freitas Mohallem, Emmanuel De Groof, Professor John Haskell, Professor Sarah Joseph, Professor Boris Mamlyuk, Professor Ernst-Ulrich Petersman, Professor Martin Scheinin, Dimitri Van Den Meerssche and Tleuzhan Zhunussova. Warm thanks also to Professor Nehal Bhuta and Anny Bremner at the EUI for their valuable feedback and support in the editorial process.

[1] Various authors, Maastricht Principles on Extraterritorial Obligations of States in the area of Economic, Social and Cultural Rights, adopted 28 September 2011, available at multiple places online including http://www.maastrichtuniversity.nl/web/Institutes/MaastrichtCentreForHumanRights/MaastrichtETOPrinciples.htm (last accessed 23 July 2015) (hereinafter 'Principles'). The official commentary to the Principles is De Schutter, Eide, Khalfan, Orellana, Salomon and Seiderman, 'Commentary to the Maastricht Principles on Extraterritorial Obligations of States in the Area of Economic, Social and Cultural Rights', 34 *Human Rights Quarterly* (2012) 1084 (hereinafter 'Commentary'). For other academic writing on the Principles, see F. Coomans and R. Künnemann, *Cases and Concepts on Extraterritorial Obligations in the Area of Economic, Social and Cultural Rights* (2012) (hereinafter 'Coomans and Künnemann'); M. Langford *et al.* (eds), *Global Justice, State Duties: The Extraterritorial Scope of Economic, Social, and Cultural Rights in International Law* (2013) (hereinafter 'Langford *et al.*'); De Schutter, 'Foreword', in F. Coomans and R. Künnemann (eds), *Cases and Concepts on Extraterritorial Obligations in the Area of Economic, Social and Cultural Rights* (2012) v (hereinafter

The present chapter offers a critical evaluation of this enquiry, by considering a set of dilemmas or tensions that are implicated in the topic, and exploring how they play out in how the substantive contours of the law are understood, and more broadly illuminate the potential and the limitations of the law in this area. It does so by using the Principles, the Commentary, and what has been said about this topic by some of the signatories to the Principles, as a case study, given that the Principles and the Commentary aspire to be an authoritative and detailed codification of the law in this area and, more broadly, illustrate how the value of this normative framework is viewed by many in the field of international public policy.

Section 2 establishes the context for the present study—'extraterritorial' human rights obligations, and the history of the treatment of issues of international economic justice in international law. It then explains the method adopted in this chapter for evaluating the tensions and dilemmas involved in efforts seeking to use international human rights law to address such issues. The subsequent two sections identify and explore related sets of tensions: in Section 3, the tensions between hope and reality, and in Section 4, the tensions between a statist and a global focus. Attention then turns to the normative regime of international human rights law, as set out in the Principles and the Commentary, analysing the potential and limitations of this regime informed by an appreciation of the dilemmas and tensions identified earlier. This begins in Section 5 with an explanation of the general contours of the legal framework, and the broader issues at stake when its merit is to be assessed. Subsequent sections then explore how this framework addresses two central issues implicated in the topic. Firstly, Section 6, 'power', considers how the projection of power is framed extraterritorially so as to conceive particular triggers for applicability. Secondly, Section 7, 'cooperation', considers how the idea of the economically advantaged being required to engage in resource and technology transfer to the economically less advantaged is approached.

'De Schutter: Foreword'); Coomans and Künnemann, 'General Introduction', in ibid., 1 (hereinafter 'Coomans and Künnemann: General Introduction'); Langford *et al.*, 'Introduction: An Emerging Field', in Langford *et al.* (eds), *Global Justice, State Duties: The Extraterritorial Scope of Economic, Social, and Cultural Rights in International Law* (2013) 3 (hereinafter 'Langford *et al.*: Introduction'); Gibney, 'On Terminology: Extraterritorial Obligations', in ibid. 32 (hereinafter 'Gibney'); Langford and Darrow, 'Moral Theory, International Law and Global Justice', in ibid. 419 (hereinafter 'Langford and Darrow'); Vandenhole, 'Beyond Territoriality: The Maastricht Principles on Extra-Territorial Obligations in the Area of Economic, Social and Cultural Rights', 29 *Netherlands Quarterly of Human Rights* (2011) 429 (hereinafter 'Vandenhole 2011'); Salomon and Seiderman, 'Human Rights Norms for a Globalized World: The Maastricht Principles on the Extraterritorial Obligations of States in the Area of Economic, Social and Cultural Rights', 3 *Global Policy* (2012) 458 (hereinafter 'Salomon and Seiderman'); Vandenhole, 'Emerging Normative Frameworks on Transnational Obligations', EUI Working Paper RSCAS 2012/17 (2012), available online at http://cadmus.eui.eu/handle/1814/21874 (last accessed 23 July 2015) (hereinafter 'Vandenhole 2012'); Salomon, 'The Maastricht Principles on Extraterritorial Obligations in the Area of Economic, Social and Cultural Rights: An Overview of Positive "Obligations to Fulfil"', *EJIL: Talk!* (16 November 2012), available online at http://www.ejiltalk.org/author/msalomon/(last accessed 23 July 2015) (hereinafter 'Salomon 2012'); Coomans, 'Situating the Maastricht Principles on Extraterritorial Obligations of States in the Area of Economic, Social and Cultural Rights', *Maastricht Faculty of Law Working Paper* (2013), available online at http://ssrn.com/abstract=2256836 (last accessed 23 July 2015) (hereinafter 'Coomans 2013').

2. Context and Method

The 'extraterritorial' dimension of state obligations in international human rights law concerns the question of norms addressing the relationship between people located in one part of the world, and people located in other parts of the world, when these differences are conceived in terms of territorial title. The 'extraterritorial' approach classifies people and their rights, and states and their obligations, according to the legal status of the territory within which the people reside, and the nature of the connection between that status and the legal identity of the state concerned. Human rights are 'territorial' when opposable to the state in whose territory the individuals reside. They are 'extraterritorial' when opposable to a foreign state lacking sovereignty-as-title over the territory where the individuals reside.

Attempting to address global poverty and economic inequality through this approach involves challenging an exclusively 'territorial' conception of state obligations in human rights law, so as to include 'extraterritorial' obligations, especially where the territorial and the extraterritorial distinction map on to, respectively, places in the world where people are relatively economically advantaged, and places in the world where people are relatively economically disadvantaged. In other words, put more crudely, seeking to make economically advantaged states obliged to address the economic position not only of people within their territory, but also of poor people extraterritorially.

International law has for some time been a site of efforts to challenge global poverty and economic inequality, notably in the period during the main wave of post-Second World War decolonization, where newly independent, former colonial and relatively economically disadvantaged states sought to promote a 'New International Economic Order' (NIEO). This period saw the promotion of a 'right to development' which would oblige economically advantaged states to enable, including through resource and technology transfer, economic development in economically disadvantaged states. Such efforts were hampered by general resistance by wealthier states, with articulation and codification efforts residing largely in General Assembly resolutions at the UN, vulnerable to the challenge that such 'soft law' is insufficient by itself, absent the necessary developments in treaty and/or customary law, to be normative.

By contrast, international human rights law, also being established at this time, met the standard test for normativity, being articulated not only in the Universal Declaration of Human Rights (UDHR), but also in a range of treaties and other instruments. Although many of these instruments address economic rights and contain provisions that speak to issues of international economic justice, the main focus of attention with respect to understandings and interpretations of all human rights instruments began as territorial, being concerned predominantly with the relationship between individuals and the state within which they are located.[2]

[2] See e.g. Coomans and Künnemann, 'General Introduction', *supra* note 1, at 1.

Internationally, efforts to promote international economic justice were dominated by initiatives outside international human rights treaty-based mechanisms, building on the earlier NIEO-focus in the UN political organs. The Bretton Woods institutions (BWIs), the World Bank and the International Monetary Fund (IMF), became the leading multilateral bodies concerned with 'development', cohabiting with *sui generis* political initiatives such as the 0.7 per cent of GNP target for the provision of development assistance (which came out of the 'right to development' initiatives), campaigns for debt relief and the elimination of tariffs and subsidies, and the adoption of the 'Millennium Development Goals' (MDGs). The World Bank, the IMF and later the World Trade Organization (WTO) became sites of resistance for social movements seeking different, more radical and transformatory approaches to global poverty and economic inequality.

Later into the lifespan of post-World War II international human rights law, however, it is possible to identify greater receptiveness to addressing extraterritorial situations when human rights treaties are discussed, interpreted and applied by expert bodies, courts and tribunals, states, non-governmental organizations (NGOs) and independent experts. The earliest and most prominent trend in this regard is contained in the jurisprudence relating to the European Convention on Human Rights (ECHR) (notably in decisions about the Turkish presence in Northern Cyprus), and subsequent decisions relating to the International Covenant on Civil and Political Rights (ICCPR) and other regional and global human rights instruments. This development was heightened by a greater critical focus in the international public consciousness with respect to the impact on human rights of US-led extraterritorial activities associated with/occurring during and continuing after the 'War on Terror'. Courts and expert bodies being called upon by petitioners to bring these activities within the regulation of human rights treaties have considered this through the aforementioned device of 'extraterritoriality': conceiving the spatial reach of human rights obligations as being either 'territorial' or 'extraterritorial', and setting out tests for when the latter form of obligations would be triggered.[3]

The push towards the affirmation and delineation of extraterritorial human rights treaty obligations can be seen perhaps to have been most prominent and developed in the field of civil and political rights when this set of rights is compared with economic, social and cultural rights. The relative difference can be explained in part due to the aforementioned prominence given to certain concerns relating to rights in the former category in the period after the attacks on the United States on 11 September 2001, both territorial and extraterritorial. Equally, it is partly explicable because of the greater opportunity for and significance of international expert review regarding civil and political rights resulting from the more long-standing existence and state acceptance of jurisdiction of bodies engaged in such review exclusively, notably the European Commission and Court of Human Rights and the UN Human Rights Committee. Also, of the only three

[3] On the case law relating to civil and political rights, see e.g. the discussion and sources cited in Wilde, 'The Extraterritorial Application of International Human Rights Law on Civil and Political Rights', in N. Rodley and S. Sheeran (eds), *Routledge Handbook on Human Rights* (2013) 635.

bodies that operate as courts and issue binding judgments with respect to complaints, the two applying instruments that cover economic, social and cultural rights—the Inter-American Court of Human Rights and the African Court on Human and Peoples' Rights—have had less opportunity to contribute to case-law compared to the European Court of Human Rights, and although the International Court of Justice, as part of its general move into human rights law, has made important pronouncements on the extraterritorial application of human rights law, including certain instruments covering economic, social and cultural rights, this has happened only recently, and in only a few instances, with significance more in the arena of norm-clarification than norm-enforcement.[4]

Whatever the cause, it is clear that when the extraterritorial application of human rights law has been addressed, whether before international interpretation bodies as in the jurisprudence mentioned above, or in popular discourse, or in academic literature, there had been until relatively recently a tendency for civil and political rights to be given greater and sometimes even exclusive focus when compared with economic, social and cultural rights. Writing in 2007, Alan Boyle and Christine Chinkin observed that 'despite human rights reports setting out the adverse impact of neo-liberal economic ideology and globalization on the human rights of the poor, of women and of other vulnerable peoples, there has been little real attempt to address these issues within the framework of international law'.[5]

There is now an effort to alter the balance of the agenda of extraterritoriality within international human rights law in favour of economic, social and cultural rights, building on important but sparse developments in this field, from certain statements made by international expert bodies and important early academic interventions. This is being spearheaded by a group of experts and activists (as will be discussed further below, not, of course, categories that are mutually exclusive), including members of international human rights expert bodies, NGO staffers and university professors. They are backed up by a broader expert/activist network including many NGOs working in the field of human rights generally and rights in the area of international economic justice and equality in particular, called the 'Extraterritorial Obligations Consortium', or 'ETO Consortium' for short.[6]

In 2011, 40 members of this movement adopted the 'Maastricht Principles on the Extraterritorial Obligations of States in the area of Economic, Social and Cultural Rights', hereinafter referred to as the 'Principles'.[7] This was followed a year later by a detailed and lengthy legal 'Commentary' by the six members of the

[4] See e.g. the discussion and sources cited in Wilde, 'Human Rights Beyond Borders at the World Court: The Significance of the International Court of Justice's Jurisprudence on the Extraterritorial Application of International Human Rights Law Treaties', 12 *Chinese Journal of International Law* (2013) 639.

[5] A. Boyle and C. Chinkin, *The Making of International Law* (2007), at 18.

[6] Information available online at http://www.etoconsortium.org (last accessed 23 July 2015). I am an academic member of the Consortium, which I joined after the Maastricht Principles had been adopted (an overview over the academic members is available online at http://www.etoconsortium.org/en/about-us/academic-members (last accessed 23 July 2015)). I played no role, formal or informal, in the process that led to their adoption.

[7] Principles, *supra* note 1.

drafting committee of the Principles, issued as an authoritative explanation for what was meant in each of the Principles.[8]

Backed up by this Commentary, the Principles stand alone as an effort to codify comprehensively in a series of treaty-like provisions the main contours of an international human rights law regime with respect to the actors and subject matter in its title. This is a landmark development in international law. It reflects an initiative that seeks to give efforts to promote international economic justice across borders in human rights law a boost when compared to similar efforts in the field of civil and political rights. Also, it seeks to set out authoritatively the substantive contours of a normative regime on this topic that may well prove highly influential in how the law in this area is understood.[9]

Such an initiative is worthy of close attention and detailed critical scrutiny, from a range of perspectives. The present chapter aims to make one contribution in this respect. However, the focus herein is tangential to the enterprise of appraising the Principles and Commentary. It will provide an appraisal of certain aspects, but as a by-product, not the main focus of attention. The aim is to consider more broadly the dilemmas that exist when seeking to use the obligations of states in international human rights law to pursue an agenda to promote international economic justice and equality, using the Principles and the Commentary as a case study of such an effort. What might these instruments indicate about such dilemmas, in what they say about the significance and content of the law? I will suggest that they are as significant for what they illuminate on this broader question as they are when it comes to being assessed on their own terms.

This chapter is not, therefore, a general assessment of the Principles on their own terms, for example providing a comprehensive appraisal of the merit of their substantive doctrinal position on what the extraterritorial application of international human rights law obligations of states in the field of economic justice is (though such an appraisal will be made in certain areas). Apart from any other consideration, there is already a significant body of scholarship on both the broader doctrinal topic in general and the Principles in particular, much of it (e.g. the Commentary) written by those involved in drafting the Principles, others who merely signed them, and yet others who are broader members of the Consortium.[10] What is considered instead are the background policy preferences embedded in the legal framework as it is described in these instruments, and, in the light of this, the potential and limitations of seeking to use international human rights law in this way to change the international economic system for the better. This is done through an analysis of the Principles, the Commentary, and a consideration of what has been said about them and/or the law they encapsulate more broadly in separately published work by some of the individuals who drafted and/or signed the Principles.[11]

[8] Commentary, *supra* note 1. On the connection between the members of the drafting committee and the authors of the Commentary, see ibid., at 1084, footnote (unnumbered).

[9] On this, see Salomon and Seiderman, *supra* note 1, at 459 and Vandenhole 2012, *supra* note 1, at 9.

[10] See the sources cited Salomon and Seiderman, *supra* note 1.

[11] See ibid.

When it comes to the question of the relationship between the obligations of states in international human rights law and the quest for global economic justice, there is only one generalized activist initiative currently on the international policy agenda: the Principles. This initiative has been conceived to be, and is now being forcefully advocated as, the best way of thinking about the role of state obligations in international human rights law in the field of international economic justice. Those involved in their adoption, and the ETO Consortium, have been and are involved in advocacy for the affirmation, adoption and citation of the Principles by states, IGOs, NGOs, courts, tribunals and expert bodies, as authoritative benchmarks against which the role of all states in efforts to combat global poverty and economic inequality should be judged.[12]

Why are such efforts being made? For some commentators, it is simply a matter of filling a normative gap between what is happening as a matter of fact, and what human rights law if understood exclusively territorially would cover. Since human rights law has usually been concerned predominantly or even exclusively with the territorial state, yet globalization is indicating the role of other states also being determinative of human rights, the regime needs to be expanded out to take in the latter actors.[13] According to Wouter Vandenhole, the fact that the territorial state may not be an adequate exclusive focus when it comes to promoting international economic justice poses:

> fundamental challenges to human rights law. In *practice*, human rights law may not be able to properly address these . . . situations, and therefore runs a risk of marginalization in endeavours to bring about social justice . . . [n]ew duty bearers such as foreign States . . . can be integrated into the human rights legal regime.[14]

For Vandenhole, '[h]uman rights law . . . needs to be re-thought, so as to make it responsive to realities on the ground . . . Economic globalisation has so far not been paralleled by a "globalisation of human rights law". But it should.'[15] One reading of these statements is that human rights law must apply extraterritorially simply for the sake of human rights law itself—to avoid the law becoming marginal.

But behind such statements are assumptions about the substantive merit of human rights law as a regime for regulating economic globalization. This is presumably held on the basis that its merit in the domestic economic context is similarly assumed, and that a transfer to the extraterritorial context will necessarily bring with it the same or equivalent benefits to those which operate domestically. So human rights law should not be marginalized, not for its own sake but because of the important positive difference that will be lost.

The current campaign for the acceptance and implementation of the contents of the Principles is based on the proposition that international human rights law has an important, perhaps even pre-eminent, positive role in combatting global poverty

[12] On this, see Coomans 2013, *supra* note 1, at 4 and 20; Coomans and Künnemann, 'General Introduction', *supra* note 1, at 4; Vandenhole 2011, *supra* note 1, at 433.

[13] See, e.g. Vandenhole 2012, *supra* note 1, at 2.

[14] Vandenhole 2011, *supra* note 1, at 430. See also Vandenhole 2012, *supra* note 1, at 1–2.

[15] Vandenhole 2012, *supra* note 1, at 1–2 (footnote omitted).

and economic inequality, and/or in somehow having a beneficial effect in regulating economic globalization. This forms part of a broader discourse about the purported benefits of international law generally, in providing global solutions to global problems. For Alan Boyle and Christine Chinkin, 'international law . . . is fundamental to a globalised world: the movement of people, goods and capital across state borders demand international standards'.[16]

Such ideas can be identified in statements by those who signed the Principles, and the broader ETO Consortium. The webpage of the latter asserts that:

> ETOs [extraterritorial obligations] are a missing link: Without ETOs, human rights could not assume their proper role as the legal bases for regulating globalization. With ETOs, an enabling environment for ESCRs [economic, social and cultural rights] can be generated, the primacy of human rights can be implemented, climate [change] and eco-destruction can be stopped, the dominance of big money broken, TNCs [transnational corporations] regulated, and IGOs [intergovernmental organizations] made accountable.[17]

A similar claim is made by Fons Coomans and Rolf Künnemann.[18] Reflecting a commonplace assumption within international human rights law policy, the suggestion is that the operation of human rights law extraterritorially will have substantive, even transformatory beneficial effects. This is why the 'proper role' of this normative system is 'regulating globalization'.[19]

As the above statement from the ETO website, with its claim that extraterritorial human rights obligations will 'end the dominance of big money', indicates, for some, there is the claim that human rights law is somehow anti-capitalist, and so in the context of economic globalization its extraterritorial application is going to assist in efforts to challenge the liberal international economic order.[20] Thus the Principles can be invoked as response to Alan Boyle and Christine Chinkin's aforementioned 2007 criticism about the scant efforts within international law to address issues of the 'adverse impact of neo-liberal economic ideology and globalization'.[21]

For others this positive benefit of human rights law extraterritorially is associated with ideas of legitimacy. Olivier De Schutter twins the benefit to human rights of its extraterritorial application with the benefits to that which it would apply, in terms of the conferral of legitimacy, thus:

> [t]he Maastricht Principles . . . contribute to . . . [the] renewal of human rights: they invite us to see human rights as global public goods, and a guide for the reshaping of the international legal order. As these norms and procedures develop, human rights gradually can turn into . . . a 'global public standard' to assess the normative legitimacy of global governance institutions—i.e., the 'right to rule' of these institutions, which cannot ensure compliance

[16] Boyle and Chinkin, *supra* note 5, at 19.
[17] Quote from the ETOs webpage, *supra* note 6.
[18] See Coomans and Künnemann, 'General Introduction', *supra* note 1, at 2–3.
[19] On this, see also ibid., at 1, 6 and 14, and Vandenhole 2011, *supra* note 1, at 2.
[20] See e.g. Coomans and Künnemann, 'General Introduction', *supra* note 1, at 14.
[21] Boyle and Chinkin, *supra* note 5, at 18.

with their decisions unless they are perceived as legitimate by those, including States, whom such decisions are addressed to.[22]

A related perspective on the potential beneficial effect of extending the applicability of human rights law is to understand it as introducing 'accountability' to the arena of economic globalization that is currently lacking in this regard. Olivier De Schutter asserts that 'if we accept to build on the extraterritorial obligations of States, the accountability gap that economic globalization has created can be closed'.[23] But do 'we accept' to do this, and on what basis—and who is the 'we'? The potential for this positive difference cannot be assumed. The merits of human rights law even in the domestic economic context are contested. Moreover, even if a case can be made in this context, it cannot be assumed that whatever benefits are considered to operate there will automatically be transferred to the very different extraterritorial context. The question, then, is whether an effort to avoid human rights law being relegated to the 'margins' when it comes to regulating economic globalization will itself make a significant, or marginal, positive difference in substantive economic rights. The case for making this effort depends in large part on the case on the latter question of the substantive difference. Without the latter case being proven, efforts such as these are vulnerable to the charge that they are a time-consuming distraction away from activities that might face a better chance of making a real difference, promising much but delivering something more limited. The stakes are high, and capacities for activism not unlimited. Does an effort such as the present one deserve a place on the agenda, and an allocation of time and resources, in the movements for global economic justice—and, if so, on what basis?

It is important to ask, therefore, what is at stake in all of this. What vision or visions for the economic future of the world are implicated and mediated, whether explicitly or implicitly—promoted, supported, affirmed, resisted, hampered, concealed—by the campaign to apply human rights law extraterritorially to combat economic injustice? What might the choices made as to how to frame the normative regime in the Principles and elaborate on their meaning in the Commentary indicate about the potential, limitations, compromises and anxieties that go into a legal project of this kind? Olivier De Schutter sees human rights law as having the potential to serve as a benchmark of 'legitimacy' against which global economic governance can be assessed, enabling the introduction of 'accountability' to economic globalization. But what of the substantive nature and merits of this benchmark? Who would win, and who would lose, in its operation? Standards of legitimacy and accountability can be used, of course, to 'legitimate' that which is objectionable, to make more difficult, not easier, more transformatory beneficial changes, and/or, at their least worst, to serve as very thin substantive benchmarks with only marginal positive benefits. One cannot assess the worth of such an enterprise without moving beyond formal notions of legitimacy and accountability to look at the substance.

22 De Schutter, 'Foreword', *supra* note 1, at viii.

23 Ibid., at v. See also Salomon and Seiderman, *supra* note 1, at 458, and Coomans 2013, *supra* note 1, at 2.

In the introduction to their edited volume on the 'extraterritorial scope of economic, social and cultural rights in international law', with the main title 'Global Justice, State Duties' (encapsulating a cosmopolitan/statist duality that will be considered further in due course), Malcolm Langford, Wouter Vandenhole, Martin Scheinin and Willem van Genugten state that they are not aiming to 'articulate a moral or normative basis for extraterritorial obligations' nor do they have an 'express reformist agenda which seeks to articulate how existing treaties or mechanisms could be improved or supplemented. Rather, this book seeks principally to interpret existing law.'[24] Implicit in this statement is that considerations of a 'moral' or 'normative' nature are exclusively relevant to questions of the existence, improvement and supplementing of obligations in this field. Since the authors are only concerned with mapping out the law as it is, such considerations are not to be addressed. But this assumes that the law *as it is* has merit. Otherwise, why bother with efforts to describe it? Yet such an assumption cannot be made and, moreover, 'moral' or 'normative' approaches are needed in order to appraise substantive merit.

Actually, the authors do address briefly some normative approaches to the topic. Here, they invoke and describe Martti Koskenniemi's critique of international human rights law thus: transforming human rights into law risks dissipating its moral power, with that power 'placed in the hands of bureaucrats and lawyers to depoliticize the rights and interpret them technically, cautiously and conservatively'.[25] The authors observe that:

> [t]hese critiques should be taken seriously, but they arguably underestimate the potential of human rights as legal norms. International human rights law, jurisprudence and procedures have shown the potential to partly adapt to the new scenario of enhanced extraterritorial power. Moreover, the language of human rights law is found increasingly at the forefront of civil society demands for global justice.[26]

Setting aside whether this description of Koskenniemi's ideas is actually authentic, it does offer a rebuttal to an absolutist assumption that law will always lead to a depoliticized, technical, cautious and conservative approach: in substance, there has been potential for 'adaptation' demonstrated, and the significance of the continued invocation of human rights law by civil society activists has to be acknowledged and reckoned with. But this is surely only the start of the analysis. One then has to turn to the substance: is human rights law up to delivering that which it promises, the existence of such promises being the reason why civil society turns to it? The language of the law having 'partly adapted' is, of course, redolent of the kind of caution and conservatism that the authors' description of Koskenniemi's criticism raised, yet is invoked as somehow a rebuttal to this criticism. What is the merit of this partial adaptation? Readers, including those civil society activists whose continued reliance on human rights law, something we are reminded of by the authors,

[24] Langford *et al.*, 'Introduction', *supra* note 1, at 9–10.

[25] Ibid., at 29, citing Koskenniemi, 'Human Rights Mainstreaming as a Strategy for Institutional Power', 1 *Humanity* (2010) 47.

[26] Langford *et al.*, 'Introduction', *supra* note 1, at 29.

is at stake, are not told. With no further consideration of this matter in the piece, we are left to take this crucial matter on trust. So, it seems, we are not to assume that human rights law applied extraterritorially will lead to outcomes that are depoliticized, technical, cautious and conservative, but on no evidence beyond a statement that ironically uses language actually suggestive of outcomes of this type. The making of one set of assumptions is being rebutted with the making of another.

In the final main chapter in the book, chapter 14, placed tellingly under an overall banner of an 'afterword', Malcolm Langford and Mac Darrow explore 'Moral Theory, International Law and Global Justice' as they relate to the topic. It is possible, then, for the introduction and 13 chapters to engage in a detailed mapping exercise of the law before any treatment is given to the broader normative questions that need to be addressed in considering whether and to what extent that which is mapped is of substantive merit. Moreover, even this treatment avoids the substance. The authors focus on the entry level question of whether human rights legal obligations should exist without an evaluation of the substance of that which would operate were the obligations to be in play. This approach is determined by the limits of the range of approaches they review, which runs between 'skeptical, modestly supportive, and strongly supportive of global justice obligations'.[27] So the 'skeptical' approaches include, as one would expect, ideas of communitarianism situated within a debate about whether states should have moral and political commitments outside their own bounded communities. What is missing from all this, which would involve moving beyond 'skepticism' to more radical 'critique', demonstrated by the description of Koskenniemi's ideas earlier, is an enquiry into the substance of that which would apply were human rights to be applicable.

The present chapter seeks to address some of the issues of substance that the approaches reviewed earlier seem determined to avoid. It does so by way of 'immanent critique', considering these important texts in terms of the broader policy ideas embedded in, and left out, of them, as an impressive and authoritative codification of the state of international human rights law in this area.[28] Such ideas can be identified, and are implicated, whether or not this was intended by the individual drafters and signatories. The present chapter is about the ideas suggested, or excluded, by the text, as a description of the law, regardless of whether the drafters and signatories intended such suggestions and exclusions, and/or supported (or rejected) that which is so suggested (or excluded). Indeed, in any collective drafting effort such as the one under evaluation, the resultant text is not only more than the sum of its individual contributor-parts. Also, because of the compromises needed to

[27] Langford and Darrow, *supra* note 1, at 421.

[28] This approach is inspired by 'ideology critique' developed from certain ideas of Marx by social theorists such as John Thompson, Terry Eagleton and Slavoj Žižek, and further explicated and applied in the context of international legal discourse by Susan Marks. See J. B. Thompson, *Ideology and Modern Culture: Critical Social Theory in the Era of Mass Communication* (1990); T. Eagleton, *Ideology—An Introduction* (1991); S. Žižek (ed.), *Mapping Ideology* (1994); S. Marks, *The Riddle of All Constitutions: International Law, Democracy and the Critique of Ideology* (2000), in particular Chapter 1; S. Marks, 'Big Brother is Bleeping Us—With the Message that Ideology Doesn't Matter', 12 *European Journal of International Law (EJIL)* (2001) 109.

achieve consensus, it is invariably divergent, to greater or lesser extent, from the personal views of each individual contributor to it.[29] Moreover, the Principles and the Commentary now have a life of their own, as texts requiring analysis in their own right because of the prominence they have had and will have as canonical documents, quite separately from the individuals with whom they were originally associated. These texts aspire to address comprehensively and in detail all the main areas of public international law relevant to the topic, notably international human rights law, the law of the UN Charter, customary international law and general norms of state responsibility. A consideration of them is, therefore, a means of addressing more generally the potential and limitations of international human rights law when it comes to the global quest to combat poverty and economic inequality.

This is an activist project that aims to deploy the existing mechanisms and structures of global governance to a particular end, promoting economic equality and combatting global poverty. In what follows, it will be argued that a series of tensions are embedded within any project for global governance of this kind. Such tensions are revealed by an evaluation of this particular project, just as the dilemmas of the project are in turn illuminated by a consideration of these tensions.

3. Tension 1: Hope versus Reality

A. Introduction: Apology versus Utopia

The Principles and the movement behind them aim to work pragmatically to deploy international legal and political structures to counter global poverty and economic inequality. This project implicates the tension that Martti Koskenniemi has identified in international legal thought, between elements of 'apology' and 'utopia', in seeking to both work within, and transcend, the status quo.[30]

The present section considers two sets of related tensions that reflect this broader apology/utopia dialectic, and which also raise further distinct challenges of their own: firstly, the tension between being an 'expert' and being an 'activist'; and secondly, the tension between elitism, imperialism and patriarchy, on the one hand, and representativeness in its many forms, on the other.

As mentioned earlier, the present study is not about the personal views of people who drafted and signed the Principles and commented on them but, rather, the ideas contained in these documents and by association the state of international human rights law. That said, what the documents say about the identity of authors, and how this corresponds to other evidence in this regard, and implicates broader ideas, is significant because it speaks to important questions about the nature and legitimacy of an initiative of this kind. Two particular aspects of this identity will be considered: firstly, what is said, and not said, about the professional

[29] See Vandenhole 2011, *supra* note 1, at 432.

[30] M. Koskenniemi, *From Apology to Utopia: The Structure of International Legal Argument* (reissue, 2005); Koskenniemi, 'The Politics of International Law', 1 *EJIL* (1990) 4.

orientation of the signatories to the Principles; secondly, what is said, and not said, but clearly evident, about the national origin/base and gender of the signatories to the Principles and the authors of the Commentary.

B. Experts/Activists

The Preamble states that the Principles were adopted 'at a gathering convened by Maastricht University and the International Commission of Jurists'[31] by 'a group of experts in international law and human rights . . . who came from universities and organizations . . . and include current and former members of international human rights treaty bodies, regional human rights bodies, and former and current Special Rapporteurs of the United Nations Human Rights Council'.[32] Thus the signatories are described as 'experts' only.[33] The text indicates that the gathering was convened by a university and an entity, the International Commission of Jurists, with a professional-sounding name. When it provides detail on the bodies to which the signatories are affiliated, these are described as expert bodies, the UN or vaguely-titled 'organizations'. Sometimes when the identities of the signatories are described by those writing about the Principles, it is with reference to the 'expert' members only.[34]

Significantly, in the Principles document, the signatories are not also described as 'activists'. The role of the aforementioned activist ETO Consortium is not mentioned.[35] The identity of some of the 'organizations' that some of the signatories work for as civil society/campaigning NGOs is left off, even though relatively more detail is provided when it comes to expert bodies and the UN.[36] Someone unfamiliar with the International Commission of Jurists might not, on simply reading its title, think that it is not only a professional body but also a campaigning organization.[37]

The categories 'expert' and 'activist', 'professional' and 'campaigning', are, of course, not mutually exclusive. Moreover, if one looks at the list of signatories at the end of Principles, the NGO-affiliation of some is clearly indicated. Equally, one might not assume that the International Commission of Jurists does not have an activist orientation and would find out that it does have such an orientation from a brief investigation.[38] The earlier discussion of what some of those who signed the Principles say about the supposed normative benefits of the Principles, in terms of regulating globalization generally, and in particular introducing much-needed benchmarks of legitimacy and accountability, clearly indicates that for such people—including Olivier De Schutter, who at the time when he signed the Principles

[31] Principles, *supra* note 1, Preamble. [32] Ibid.

[33] See also De Schutter, 'Foreword', *supra* note 1, at v; and Coomans and Künnemann, 'General Introduction', *supra* note 1, at 3.

[34] See e.g. Coomans 2013, *supra* note 1, at 3 and 20; Salomon and Seiderman, *supra* note 1, at 458.

[35] On the Consortium, see *supra* note 6.

[36] For this information on their affiliations, see Principles, *supra* note 1, Annex.

[37] See the Commission's website, available online at http://www.icj.org/about/(last accessed 23 July 2015).

[38] For example by looking at the website, referred to in the last footnote.

and when his works reviewed above were published was the UN Special Rapporteur on the Right to Food, i.e. an 'expert'—there is a normative agenda being advanced.[39] The initiative is, as described at the start of this chapter, an expert-activist one, in terms of both the formal matter of professional affiliations (signatories include members of treaty bodies and NGO staffers), and substantive abilities and views (all signatories could be understood to be both legal experts and people in possession of normative positions on the merits of the enterprise).

Nonetheless, the language of the Preamble has the effect of downplaying, even concealing, and certainly not expressly acknowledging, the activist side of things. The Preamble could have been more comprehensive and revealing in framing the professional orientation (activists as well as experts) and describing the professional affiliations (NGOs, not just 'organizations', as well as expert bodies and the UN). The reference only to expertise suggests a claim to authority on the subject matter; without anything further, however, there is potentially the suggestion of an unwillingness to declare the operation of an agenda when this expertise is deployed. So, for example, when Fons Coomans discusses the identity of the signatories and the significance of this in terms of expertise and activism, only the former is mentioned, and this is combined with a reference to 'authority': 'among the participants who adopted and endorsed the Principles were key human rights scholars and experts. This gives authority to the document.'[40] Continuing this theme, Coomans states:

> The experts which [sic] finally adopted and endorsed the Maastricht Principles did not do so on behalf of the ETO Consortium, but in their personal capacity. Among the 40 participants were 12 experts who had not been involved in the work of the ETO Consortium, among them former and present members of UN Treaty bodies, former and present UN Special Rapporteurs. The text is a legal expert opinion and not a Consortium document.[41]

Of course, just as the endorsement of the Principles by the 'experts' may not, we are told, have been on behalf of the ETO Consortium, presumably also, given the existence of obligations of independence and impartiality that they owed to the bodies they worked for, this endorsement was not formally 'on behalf of' these bodies either. Such a statement invokes 'personal capacity' only in the context of it somehow being a shield protecting from the (presumed) taint of activism implied by acting on behalf of the Consortium, failing to acknowledge that this capacity also prevents any formal connection being made between the signatories and the expert bodies they worked for. When such an omission is taken together with the omission of any mention of the affiliation of the other signatories, some of whom working for NGOs, and a discussion of the capacity in which these people signed the document, it is difficult not to wonder whether there is not a deliberate effort to foreground the expertise elements and downplay the activist elements.

[39] Olivier De Schutter was UN Special Rapporteur on the Right to Food from 2008 to 2014. Information available online at http://www.ohchr.org/EN/Issues/Food/Pages/FoodIndex.aspx (last accessed 23 July 2015). As one of the drafters, he signed the Principles in 2011 and co-authored the Commentary in 2012; the piece by him quoted herein was published in 2012.

[40] Coomans 2013, *supra* note 1, at 20.

[41] Ibid., at 3.

Why does this matter? Such a way of describing expertise—not acknowledged to be also allied to activism—has the potential to suggest a claim to be impartial and neutral. The point is not that such impartiality and neutrality is, in the final analysis, sustainable, but, rather, that the language used seems to suggest so. This has substantive significance, because it creates the potential for an impression that the content of the Principles is somehow to be understood outside a particular agenda for what the law is and should be, and more fundamentally, outside an agenda concerned with the value of the law itself. If activism is not even properly acknowledged, there is no place for an explanation and defence of the particular agenda being advanced in preference to potential alternative agendas, whether this agenda is to promote law alongside and even prioritize law in relation to other strategies, or to promote this particular view of the law in preference to alternative views. On the latter question, it can be taken even as a suggestion that there is only one 'legal' approach to be adopted, which can be identified and described neutrally through a scientific process of expert analysis.

Actually, of course, there are multiple choices to be made in any project seeking to describe what the law is and should be, and more broadly the value of focusing on, and advocating for, the acceptance and enforcement of the law. Broader ideas that map onto the intellectual palette of and therefore overlap with the substantive work of the 'activist' are clearly implicated in the choices made here, whether or not acknowledged, either fully or at all, by those involved. This is demonstrated by the bold normative claims made about the Principles by some of the 'experts' as discussed earlier. But as that earlier discussion revealed, the claims made have tended to be made by way of assumption only, without a treatment of their foundation. An emphasis on neutral, apolitical 'expertise' is certainly compatible with such an approach and, indeed, a shift towards the activist, normative side of things reveals, as discussed above, that much is missing from the current analysis.

The selective emphasis on expertise shorn of activism is also clearly potentially helpful in the objective of seeking the affirmation and adoption of the legal standards contained in the Principles by those to whom they would apply: states. A tone can be struck that emphasizes neutrality and impartiality in what is a field of hugely contested issues. Moreover, it is significant that, as reviewed above, those behind the Principles view extraterritorial human rights obligations as having the potential to introduce constraints—'accountability'—on the behaviour of states in economically privileged positions that are new. It can be speculated that there is deemed to be pragmatic utility in making the case for such constraints from the standpoint of neutral expertise rather than partisan activism.

The exclusive or predominant focus on the 'expert' side of the ledger is not the only account, however. It cohabits with other explanations, sometimes by the same people, which place more, even sometimes exclusive, emphasis on the 'activist' side, stressing the role of the ETO Consortium, and describing the identity of those involved exclusively as NGO staffers and scholars, not also IGO 'experts'.[42]

[42] See Salomon and Seiderman, *supra* note 1, at 458; Coomans 2013, *supra* note 1, at 2–3; Vandenhole 2012, *supra* note 1, at 3–4.

As will be explored more in due course, the combination of expertise and activism embedded in the Principles is at once a tension that runs through the initiative, and also, when emphasis is, as reviewed above, placed selectively on one more than, or even to the complete exclusion of, the other, the source of a productive device for addressing different audiences and deploying different arguments that are, taken together, broader in range than would be possible otherwise.

C. Elitism, Orientalism and Patriarchy

> ...are there obligations to ensure strangers are not hungry, poor, without access to the necessities of healthcare and education?
>
> Margot Salomon and Ian Seiderman[43]

The second important aspect of the way in which the identity of the signatories to the Principles and the Commentary is described, or not, is in terms of national origin or base and also in terms of gender. Beginning with national origin or base, as already mentioned, the Preamble to the Principles states that the signatories 'came from universities and organizations located in all regions of the world and include current and former members of international human rights treaty bodies, regional human rights bodies, and former and current Special Rapporteurs of the United Nations Human Rights Council'.[44]

Like the earlier reference to 'experts', here language is deployed to create an impression about the identity of the signatories in terms of where they are from. The bodies they are affiliated with are from 'all regions of the world' and include entities with an international and regional orientation. It is hard not to escape the conclusion that this language is being used to have normative import, implying a claim to be globally representative. Why mention the global reach of the signatories' affiliations if it does not matter? And if it does matter, how, exactly?

The notion of being globally representative in connection with an initiative relating to international human rights law implicates long-standing debates about universalism and cultural relativism in connection with this area of law. More broadly, it foregrounds the significance of ideas that have been developed in the context of anti-colonialism, the legacy of colonialism, and neo-colonialism: 'post-colonial studies'.[45] Elements of ideas from this body of work have been invoked and applied to international law, including international human rights law: 'third world approaches to international law' (TWAIL).[46] What is the relevance of these ideas to the question of the extraterritorial application of international human rights law?

[43] Salomon and Seiderman, *supra* note 1, at 459.

[44] Principles, *supra* note 1, Preamble.

[45] See the sources cited in R. Wilde, *International Territorial Administration: How Trusteeship and the Civilizing Mission Never Went Away* (2008), List of Sources, Section 5.3.3.

[46] See the sources cited in the following: http://waynemorsecenter.uoregon.edu/conferences-symposia/twail/twail-primer (last accessed 23 July 2015); Gathii, 'TWAIL: A Brief History of its Origins, its Decentralized Network, and a Tentative Bibliography', 3 *Trade Law and Development* (2011) 26; Wilde, *supra* note 45, List of Sources, Section 5.3.4.

Adopting the territorial/extraterritorial axis that is the frame of reference for the present study, the dominant strand of focus of the universalism/cultural relativism debate in international human rights law has been an exclusively territorial one. The main point of the debate has concerned whether the supposed 'universal' standards of international human rights law are actually of universal purchase in each national situation to which they purport to apply, when that national system is understood in terms of the relationship between the state and the people in its territory exclusively. The question is whether the same standards are legitimate in each national situation, or whether these standards are in some way better understood to be of more particular relevance in some national contexts than others, *viz.* those states in the global North/the West/Europe, and are therefore culturally relative and of questionable legitimacy when it comes to their operation globally, notably in the global south. For cultural relativists, one aspect of this debate concerns the way in which ideas of universalism are deployed to mask particularism.

These issues cut differently when the extraterritorial context is considered. The question is not whether universal standards are of common legitimate purchase in every country as far as the internal operation of each national system is concerned. Rather, it is whether universal standards on the relationship *between* national or territorially-based systems further an agenda that is of interest to all people in the world in a just and equal fashion. Who wins, and who loses, across the globe, in the normative regime of the extraterritorial application of economic, social and cultural rights, and to what extent do the winners and the losers map onto broader distinctions that are foregrounded by post-colonial analysis: the global north and global south; European states and former colonial states, for example? Indeed, this question of the legitimacy of the standards that operate extraterritorially might be seen as more acute and complex than in the exclusively territorial context, because unlike that context it implicates broader questions about how the global economy should be structured, how states should relate to each other, how historical and contemporary causal relationships across boundaries should be understood and addressed, etc.

This general question is of particular significance to the topic of the extraterritorial application of *economic* rights, because of the economic dimensions of post-Renaissance European colonialism, and the way in which distinctions in economic grounds, which would form the basis for extraterritorial obligations (e.g. the more economically privileged bearing obligations with respect to the economically disadvantaged) often map onto the global north/global south divide that in many ways finds its origins in the earlier colonial divisions of the world. Indeed, as will be discussed further, one particular ethical basis for extraterritorial obligations in the economic sphere, beyond ideas concerned with combatting inequality, is the notion of reparation for earlier colonial domination, exploitation and abuse.

Furthermore, post-colonial ideas remind us that contemporary initiatives of advocacy for norms to promote economic justice across borders, from the rich to the poor, can be traced directly to colonial-era ideas of trusteeship over people and the civilizing mission. They invite us to consider how the humanitarians of today are engaged in a project that bears important connections back to the humanitarianism of a century and more ago. Post-colonial thought, including the history of colonialism, reveals a long tradition of those in economically privileged parts of the world seeking to articulate what is in the best interests of others in less economically privileged parts of the world, and seeking to further this through the notion of obligations, including international legal obligations, borne by their own states to save/assist/develop the 'other'. In the colonial era, this was furthered by some through the advocacy of trusteeship: the idea of taking over direct control of people deemed incapable of running their own affairs, ostensibly in their own interest.[47] When this idea of trusteeship over people was supposedly repudiated by the post-Second World War turn against colonialism and in favour of self-determination for colonial peoples, such ideas morphed, into, for example, the projects for international economic governance and 'development' in the aforementioned BWIs and into ideas relating to the provision of development aid/assistance. So, then, post-colonial thought is relevant to the present project because of the link between the nature of the contemporary enterprise, and the ideological ideas and legal norms associated with colonial trusteeship.

Earlier it was observed that the language of exclusive 'expertise' used in the Principles risked concealing the activist agenda being promoted by this initiative. When such an agenda is acknowledged, the next step is, of course, to ask important critical questions about it. Such questions are foregrounded when post-colonial ideas are brought into the frame. It might be said that this activist effort is in sync with a post-colonial critique of international law, because it is concerned with the economic obligations of the global rich to the global poor. At the very least, it can be seen, as mentioned earlier, to follow from earlier trends within international law where former colonial states sought to promote the NIEO.

But to stop at this superficial treatment would not do justice to the more challenging questions raised by post-colonial ideas, some of which, indeed, placing the legitimacy of the NIEO efforts into question and potentially leading to an opposing conclusion from that arrived at when viewing things more superficially. Such ideas require a consideration of more profound questions concerning the structure of the world into sovereign states, and the substantive agenda being furthered, beyond a general idea of extraterritorial economic obligations. Which obligations of what kind? What difference will they make? Is international human rights law a legitimate and important means through which global economic inequality and poverty can be addressed? According to whom?

Of course, just as narratives of exclusive 'expertise' could be deployed, as discussed earlier, in efforts to bring states on board, here an emphasis on them could be effective in closing down such questions, by deploying ideas of neutral impartiality to underscore assumptions that the substantive content of project, as objectively discernible by anyone with the necessary 'expertise,' is of universal purchase. Thus in one sense claims to exclusive expertise can be deployed to resist claims by both states and civil society.

[47] See e.g. Wilde, *supra* note 45, ch. 8, and sources cited therein.

But if one is to take seriously what post-colonial scholars have observed about how universalism has often worked to conceal particularism, one has to look behind the formal invocation of universalism and face up to the importance of the question of who decides and who describes what the agenda is and should be. The claim to universalism has to be considered in the context of the existence of social movements across the world, many of whom being engaged in issues that implicate extraterritoriality, human rights and economic justice, involving individuals with expertise in international human rights law, and located in places where the economic situation is such that the stakes are high. The term 'globalization', invoked by some of the proponents of the Principles as reviewed above, has of course been used to describe the interconnected nature of the global economy and the international structures of law and institutions, such as the WTO and the BWIs that enable it to operate: the broader context in which the extraterritorial obligations in human rights law that are the subject of the present study would operate. In this context these movements of resistance and advocacy for international economic justice have sometimes been termed 'globalization from below'.[48]

As mentioned earlier, despite the exclusive language of 'expertise' used in the Preamble to the Principles, actually a significant number of the signatories come from activist NGOs working on human rights and issues of global poverty and economic justice. In this sense, the narrative of exclusive expertise conceals an aspect of the project that is relevant, in a potentially positive manner, to its claims of legitimacy when considered through the lens of post-colonial thought. Here, then, is demonstrated the significance of the alternative accounts that foreground the role that NGOs played in the adoption of the Principles. Just as, earlier, the emphasis on neutral 'expertise' potentially does work in the context of bringing states on board, here, by contrast, foregrounding 'activism' and in particular the role of civil society is significant when it comes to the legitimacy of the project as far as the needs of those who are supposedly its primary beneficiaries, people in the world at the sharp end of economic globalization, especially the very poor.

This element of the enterprise feeds into broader arguments that are invoked to imply the normative value of the substantive content of human rights law. It will be recalled that when reviewing the significance of critical approaches to human rights law to the extraterritoriality project, Langford, Vandenhole, Scheinin and van Genugten caution against the view that human rights law will always lead to depoliticized, conservative and cautious approaches, because 'the language of human rights law is found increasingly at the forefront of civil society demands for global justice'.[49] The claim is that activity of civil society organizations in invoking human rights law legitimates the substantive merit of the law. Such a claim about human rights law generally then feeds into moves that foreground the role of NGOs in this particular initiative concerning its extraterritorial applicability.

[48] On the international law aspects of 'globalization from below' see e.g. B. Rajagopal, *International Law from Below: Development, Social Movements and Third World Resistance* (2003).

[49] Langford *et al.*, 'Introduction', *supra* note 1, at 29.

Such involvement can be deployed as means of resisting post-colonial critiques: the present initiative is, in part, a manifestation of 'globalization from below'.

Here it is instructive to situate the claims to global diversity made in the Preamble, and the 'activist'-emphasized accounts of the provenance of the Principles, in the light of further aspects of the identities of the signatories. Internet searches of the individuals who signed the Principles indicate the following about where the people were from originally and, if different, were based at the time of signature. In most cases, this information was subsequently verified through direct enquiries with the individuals involved. Of the 40 signatories, 26 have European/US/Canadian/Australian/New Zealand nationality.[50] Of the 14 signatories who have nationality from outside the aforementioned parts of the world at the time the Principles were adopted, 7 (i.e. half) were based in western countries, not their countries of origin or nationality;[51] of the other half, 2 were based in South Africa, and 1 was based in each of the following countries, namely the Philippines, India, Uganda, Argentina (and Switzerland) and the Republic of Korea.[52] Of these seven, three were university academics, one was a UN official, two were members of UN treaty bodies, and one was a member of a global network of civil society organizations.[53] Of the six drafters of the Principles and co-authors

[50] Catarina de Albuquerque (Portugal), Theo van Boven (Netherlands), Fons Coomans (Netherlands), Olivier De Schutter (Belgium), Julia Duchrow (Germany), Asbjørn Eide (Norway), Cees Flinterman (Netherlands), Mark Gibney (USA), Thorsten Göbel (Germany), Paul Hunt (United Kingdom/New Zealand), Rolf Künnemann (Germany), Malcolm Langford (Australia), Nicholas Lusiani (USA (not verified with signatory)), Claire Mahon (Australia and New Zealand), Maija Mustaniemi-Laakso (Finland), Gorik Ooms (Belgium), Sandra Ratjen (France), Aisling Reidy (Ireland), Margot Salomon (Canada (not verified with signatory)), Martin Scheinin (Finland), Ian Seiderman (USA), Sigrun Skogly (Norway), Philippe Texier (France), Wouter Vandenhole (Belgium), Duncan Wilson (UK) and Michael Windfuhr (Germany).

[51] Meghna Abraham (country of origin India, at the time of signature based in the UK), Maria Virginia Bras Gomes (country of origin India, at the time of signature based in Portugal), Ashfaq Khalfan (country of origin Kenya, at the time of signature based in the UK), Marcos Orellana (country of origin Chile, at the time of signature based in the USA/Switzerland (not verified with signatory)), Magdalena Sepúlveda (country of origin Chile, at the time of signature based in Switzerland), Ana María Suárez Franco (country of origin Colombia—but has also German nationality, at the time of signature based in Switzerland), Sisay Yeshanew (country of origin Ethiopia, at the time of signature based in Finland).

[52] Lilian Chenwi (country of origin Cameroon, at the time of signature based in South Africa), Danwood Chirwa (country of origin Malawi, at the time of signature based in South Africa), Virginia Dandan (Philippines is country of origin and base at the time of signature), Miloon Kothari (India is country of origin and base at the time of signature), Christopher Mbazira (Uganda is country of origin and base at the time of signature), Fabián Salvioli (country of origin Argentina, at the time of signature based in Argentina/Switzerland (not verified with signatory)) and Heisoo Shin (country of origin the Republic of Korea, at the time of signature based in the Republic of Korea).

[53] Lilian Chenwi (was working at the University of Witwatersrand/Johannesburg), Danwood Chirwa (was working at the University of Cape Town), Christopher Mbazira (was working at the Makerere University, Kampala), Virginia Dandan (was serving as UN Independent Expert on Human Rights and International Solidarity), Fabián Salvioli (was serving as a member of the UN Human Rights Committee), Heisoo Shin (was serving as a member of the UN Committee on Economic, Social and Cultural Rights), Miloon Kothari (was working as coordinator of the South Asian Regional Programme of the Habitat International Coalition's (HIC) Housing and Land Rights Network, a global network of civil society initiatives for rights related to habitat).

of the Commentary, all are based in the West, four having western nationality originally.[54]

Obviously these figures suggest that as a group the signatories were dominated by people from the global north (more than half) and people based in that part of the world (more than three quarters). People for whom, as the above quotation from Margot Salomon and Ian Seiderman (two of the drafters) indicates, the supposed beneficiaries of the Principles are 'strangers'. As far as where people were based is concerned, the entire continent of Africa was represented by three people (two based in South Africa and one based in Uganda); Central and South America/Latin America was represented by one person who was based partly in Argentina and partly in Switzerland. There was no one from China, nor was an area stretching from central Europe through to central Asia represented either by nationality or base. By contrast, within a much larger European grouping there were three people based in each of Belgium and the Netherlands and four people based in Germany.[55] Although, as mentioned, there was significant NGO representation in the group, actually as far as people based outside the West who worked for civil society organizations were concerned, there was a single representative (although many of the other organizations for which the other officials work do operate outside the West). Six of the seven people based outside the West were either university professors or UN officials.

These characteristics of elitism and global imbalance of course map onto some of the distinctions highlighted earlier, between richer states and poorer states and between states that had colonies and states formed of territories that were colonies. As mentioned earlier, there is no suggestion in the Principles that the states which would be bound by these obligations had a formal role in their formulation or adoption. That said, certainly as far as the states in relation to whom the obligations would potentially have the most significance in terms of requirements to change behaviour, *viz.* relatively economically advantaged states (which are, for example, in a position to transfer some of their wealth to the global poor), they are disproportionally represented (with the glaring exceptions of Brazil, Russia and China—one might see this as a G7 rather than G20 view of the world's more economically advantaged countries) as far as the countries where the signatories are based is concerned. These characteristics of elitism reflect a broader feature of international law-making, as discussed by Alan Boyle and Christine Chinkin, that whereas non-state actors are involved in the process of identifying fundamental norms, especially those associated with a notion of an 'international community' (a cosmopolitanist

[54] Olivier De Schutter (Belgium), Asbjørn Eide (Norway), Ashfaq Khalfan (country of origin Kenya, at the time the principles were signed based in the UK), Marcos Orellana (country of origin Chile, at the time the principles were signed was based in the USA/Switzerland (not verified with signatory)), Margot Salomon (country of origin Canada, at the time the Principles were signed based in the UK (not verified with signatory)), Ian Seiderman (country of origin USA, at the time the Principles were signed, was based in Switzerland).

[55] At the time of signature, based in Belgium: Olivier De Schutter, Gorik Ooms and Wouter Vandenhole. At the time of signature, based in the Netherlands: Theo van Boven, Fons Coomans and Cees Flinterman. At the time of signature, based in Germany: Julia Duchrow, Thorsten Göbel, Rolf Künnemann and Michael Windfuhr.

idea that will be addressed further below), 'international law-making remains unrepresentative as participants are largely drawn from elite groups within and across societies. The input of those who remain stranded at the peripheries... remains minimal.'[56]

Why does this matter? Might these all be well-meaning people capable of stepping outside their personal circumstances and national identities or bases to articulate an agenda that is universally legitimate? One way into this question is to consider two separate but related ideas from the canon of post-colonial thought: Edward Said's 'orientalism' and Gayatri Chakravorty Spivak's work on the 'subaltern'. Said defined 'orientalism' as 'the corporate institution for dealing with the Orient—dealing with it by making statements about it, authorizing views of it, describing it, by teaching it, settling it, ruling over it'.[57]

Said argued that the nature of the perspective of the commentator—rooted in an identity 'other' than the identity of those whose experience is being described—creates the danger that representations will be mediated by a desire on the part of the commentator to understand him or herself through their conception of an alienated, oriental 'other'. As Said revealed, narratives of the colonial encounter in Western literature are replete with representations of the colonial 'other' that reveal much more about the self-image of those crafting the representation than the reality of those being represented.[58] These insights require us to question whether efforts by the predominantly globally privileged to articulate an agenda for the globally underprivileged might similarly be faulty as far as their claim to legitimately articulate what is in the interests of the underprivileged is concerned. They remind us that such efforts might be illuminating as to the self-image of those who would wish their own states, or at least the states in which they are based, to do more to end global poverty, and have an idea of what it would be appropriate for those states to do, from the perspective of the states taking action. But Said requires us to speculate whether the agenda being pursued might have been different had the voices of those whose interests these efforts are supposed to serve—articulated, as mentioned, in social movements throughout the world—had been more prominent. I will return to the significance of this in due course, when certain aspects of the substantive content of the law is reviewed.

There is, moreover, a further problem with the representational imbalance manifest in the drafters of and signatories to the Principles, and more generally the elite grouping that the signatories are drawn from. Even if the legitimacy and accuracy of the agenda being furthered by the Principles is somehow not considered to have been compromised because of the self-realizing nature of the act of representing the interests of 'other', nonetheless the representational act itself is problematic because it necessarily involves, in the words of Said, 'dominating,

[56] Boyle and Chinkin, *supra* note 5, at 17.
[57] E. W. Said, *Orientalism: Western Conceptions of the Orient* (1995 edn), at 3.
[58] Ibid.

restructuring and having authority over' that which is represented.[59] As theorists such as Gayatri Chakravorty Spivak suggest, in such circumstances, the story of those subject to domination is told through a process that is itself a form of intellectual domination, in that it is crafted mostly by those in a privileged position coming from outside the community being represented, and/or elites within that community.[60] Regardless of whether such representations can somehow be considered to be 'accurate', they are problematic because of the nature of domination involved in having one's story told by someone else or in telling someone else's story. Any international effort that seeks to articulate the needs of those who it does not involve in a significant manner is vulnerable to the charge that it is compounding the economic and physical domination it seeks to combat, with intellectual domination of its own.

Critiques of domination are also of course central to certain feminist approaches to ideas, and, indeed, a further significant feature of the identity of the individual signatories to the Principles and authors of the Commentary is gender. Although, as mentioned, reference is made to both the professional orientation ('experts') and geographical reach ('all regions of the world') of the signatories to the Principles, there is no express statement about gender balance. In one respect, this is perhaps as well, because just as the signatories are, despite their suggestions, not only experts but also activists, and not geographically representative, they do not include an equal number of women and men. Out of 40 signatories to the Principles, 15 are women and 25 are men, constituting a 37.5/62.5 percentage split. Women constitute over half the world's population, but are represented in only just over one third of the signatories to the Principles. The imbalance in the drafters, and the authors of the commentary, is even more acute; of its six authors, five are men and one is a woman—Margot Salomon, the co-author of the quotation at the start of this section. It is striking that whereas the Principles at least acknowledge the significance of being geographically representative, albeit in a manner that appears hollow if one moves from the formal language used to consider the substantive demographics of the personnel involved, the notion of gender balance is not even mentioned, let alone substantively realized.

These statistics map onto the gender imbalance in international law and institutions, in terms of the demographic features of the elites who run the international system.[61] Chakravorty Spivak's point about intellectual domination is equally valid here: a project seeking to vindicate the economic rights of women as well as men has not been crafted with their equal involvement. Problematic in its own terms, it also raises a question as to the legitimacy of the normative regime in terms of economic rights of women in particular. Indeed, feminist work on international law/development and poverty has foregrounded how global poverty disadvantages

[59] Ibid.

[60] G. Chakravorty Spivak, *A Critique of Postcolonial Reason: Toward a History of the Vanishing Present* (1999).

[61] On feminist approaches to international law and institutions, see e.g. H. Charlesworth and C. Chinkin, *The Boundaries of International Law: A Feminist Analysis* (2000), *passim*, and sources cited therein.

women more than men, because of a range of factors ranging from unequal pay to the disproportionate representation of women in low-paid and unremunerated work, the reduced access women have to assets such as property, land and credit, and the way in which liberal economic policies of reducing welfare, food subsidies, social provision and state services disproportionately affect women because of their greater involvement in childcare, domestic economics, and the public employment sector.[62] Whereas efforts to bring about international economic justice are in the interests of all, the stakes are higher for women, who are disproportionately represented amongst the world's poor.[63] Moreover, there is a documented track record of development assistance being provided in a manner that discriminates against women, for example, as Hilary Charlesworth and Christine Chinkin point out, targeting 'household heads, usually assumed to be men', or providing 'aid to sectors from which women are excluded'.[64] The significance of this will be revisited in due course.

4. Tension 2: 'Global Justice, State Duties'

A. Introduction

As previously mentioned, a book was published after the Principles were adopted, which was edited by, and includes contributions from, many of those involved in the process of drafting, adopting and commenting on the Principles, and is entitled 'Global Justice, State Duties'.[65]

The global/state distinction and combination illuminates two important aspects of the present topic, which will be addressed in turn.[66] In the first place, it foregrounds how the topic of the extraterritorial obligations of states operates on the basis of, but also seeks to transcend, territorial boundaries. In the second place, it implicates broader ideas concerned with statism/sovereignty, on the one hand, and cosmopolitanism/globalism, on the other, which are embedded in the topic.

B. Retaining and Crossing Boundaries

The title 'Global Justice, State Duties' epitomizes the two different spatial orientations implicated in an approach to promoting global economic justice through state obligations in international human rights law. On the one hand, the aspiration to economic freedom is global in reach, for all people, everywhere in the world, regardless of territorial boundaries. On the other hand, the actors who are the exclusive focus of attention when it comes to realizing this aspiration, i.e. 'states',

[62] Ibid., at 6–7. [63] On this, see, e.g. ibid. at 8, and sources cited therein.
[64] Ibid., at 7. [65] Langford *et al.*, *supra* note 1.
[66] A further aspect, not addressed here, is the way in which a project concerned with transnational activities is concerned exclusively with the duties of states, not addressing also non-state actors such as corporations and international organizations.

are defined on the basis of a division of the world, via territorial boundaries, into mutually exclusive sovereign states. This approach is commonly associated (not without dissenters) by theorists and historians with the Treaty of Westphalia and is therefore sometimes referred to in shorthand as a 'Westphalian' approach to the world.

The latter, sovereign-state-focused approach is, of course, inevitable when the starting point is international human rights treaty law, the stuff exclusively of states as concerns the identity of both those who are parties to the treaties, and, according to the orthodox position (adopted in the Principles and the Commentary), those who are subject to obligations under them. But whereas, on the one hand, the global boundaries between sovereign states are adopted and affirmed as an essential component of working through public international law, on the other hand the substantive features of this particular area of law at issue disrupt these boundaries, being concerned exclusively with extraterritoriality, the focus of which is the direct opposite of a world-view of entirely mutually exclusive sovereign units. As will be illustrated in the following sections, an appreciation of this enterprise informed by its combination of statism and globalism is illuminating as far as the nature, potential and limitations of the enterprise are concerned.

C. Statism versus Cosmopolitanism

The question of the role of international legal rights and obligations in efforts to combat global poverty and economic inequality implicates broader ideas about the dialectic between narrow state interest and a global cosmopolitan public interest. On the one hand, a certain set of ideas places emphasis on the notion of states and their governments being concerned with and responsible to their own people and 'interests', often classified in terms of 'sovereignty' and associated with realist thought, whether Thomas Hobbes in the Enlightenment era or Hans Morgenthau in the 20th century. On the other hand, cosmopolitan ideas reference an 'international community' of shared values that include concerns relating to the welfare of all people everywhere, associated with Immanuel Kant and Hugo Grotius in the Enlightenment era and David Held and Mary Kaldor in the late 20th century. In international law, this dialectic is implicated in the positivist/natural law distinction; Martti Koskenniemi's critique of the apology/utopia tension in international legal thought is, in a sense, a critique of a fundamental tension within Enlightenment ideas as they have been brought to bear on the 'international' by what from the 20th century has been called the discipline of 'International Relations'.

In international law, norms conceived in a manner that enshrines a cosmopolitan ethic can be identified in several different areas, including the concept of 'community obligations' and obligations operating *erga omnes*—where all states have a legitimate interest to see them complied with everywhere—and debates about so-called 'humanitarian intervention' and the 'responsibility to protect'—both concerned with the question of the legitimacy of states taking action with respect to individuals who are not their own (cf. Nicholas Wheeler's description of the former as 'saving strangers').[67] This said, that these norms are conceived to be exceptional suggests a default position locating interests more exclusively at the individual state level, and even in their relatively narrow field of operation the norms themselves are often highly contested and their content uncertain, further reinforcing the predominantly sovereign-state-centric dimension to international law.

The dialectic between statism and cosmopolitanism is of central significance to the present topic; the question of whether and to what extent states owe obligations concerned with the economic position of people outside their own territories is by definition a statist/cosmopolitanist *problématique.* Thus, as will be addressed further later in this chapter, the Commentary invokes the idea that 'the preservations of human rights is in the interests of all states', and the concept of *erga omnes*, to undergird its assertions about extraterritorial applicability.[68] The more things are tilted in favour of such obligations, the more 'cosmopolitanist' the enterprise; equally, a tilt in the opposite direction brings things more closely to a 'statist' focus on the state's relationship to the people in its own territory. More fundamentally, the aforementioned dialectical enterprise of seeking to work on the basis of a division of the world between sovereign states, and focusing on the obligations of states not also those of non-state actors, on the one hand, but also seeking to disrupt territorial boundaries by advocating 'extraterritorial' obligations, on the other hand, reflects a paradoxical attempt to combine statism with cosmopolitanism. Equally, as in the previously mentioned link to Koskenniemi's apology/utopia dialectic, the two elements can be identified in the expert/activist tension: experts, in this context, being of the world of states (cf. the detail given on membership of state-appointed treaty bodies), and activist international NGOs being the world of transnational cosmopolitan non-state civil society actors. Similarly, the elitist tenor to the list of signatories enables certain claims to authority that resonate with the state elites, whose support is needed to ensure the norms are accepted by those to whom they apply but, equally, the claims to be internationally representative are important in efforts to resist the charge that the agenda being furthered is not cross-culturally legitimate.

One general tension relevant to the present topic flows from the statism/cosmopolitan dialectic: debates in rights discourse about how the relationship between the individual and the state is conceived so as to form the basis for a normative regime of rights and obligations between the two. The statist orientation places emphasis on a relationship bounded by the state's borders, delineating the limits of the state itself and so, for present purposes, the primary focus in terms of individual human welfare. Political ideas, whether liberal social contractarian ideas or international legal concepts of self-determination, root the legitimacy of the state in terms of its purpose of serving the interests of the people within its territory. An extreme and simplistic application of such ideas would necessarily rule out any extraterritorial obligations, whether in the sphere of economic justice or any other

[67] On *erga omnes* see *Barcelona Traction, Light and Power Company, Limited (Belgium v. Spain)*, Judgment, 24 July 1964, ICJ Reports (1970) 3, para. 79. For 'saving strangers', see N. Wheeler, *Saving Strangers: Humanitarian Intervention in International Society* (2000).

[68] Commentary, *supra* note 1, at 1103.

issue, apart from, perhaps, situations where a state's own nationals are outside its territory. Put differently, extraterritorial obligations require an alternative political conception of the individual and the state, operating in a radically different fashion from that which operates within a state's own territory. Moreover, present efforts seek to include obligations operating in this different way within the existing arrangements, co-habiting with 'territorial' obligations operating on the basis of the orthodox statist approach.

'Extraterritoriality' is not the displacement of statism with cosmopolitanism, then, but, rather, an effort to combine the two. Significantly, this is not a matter of the two elements operating in mutually exclusive contexts but, rather, an issue of their interplay in overlapping contexts where the reach of one is bound up in the extent of the other. Because, as previously discussed, these efforts simultaneously operate on the basis of and seek to transcend a world divided by state boundaries, so the substantive outcomes they aspire to bring about are determined by a multi-faceted matrix of statist/communitarian dialectics. This is indicated in the quote from Salomon and Seiderman above, which asks about extraterritorial obligations concerning poverty and hunger—a cosmopolitan enquiry—using a statist conception of the individual beneficiaries of such obligations, as 'strangers' (echoing the language used by Wheeler in relation to 'humanitarian intervention').

These general tensions are illustrated in key passages from the Principles and the Commentary. On the one hand, the Preamble to the Principles asserts that '[s]tates have recognized that everyone is entitled to a social and international order in which human rights can be fully realized and have undertaken to pursue joint and separate action to achieve universal respect for, and observance of, human rights for all'.[69] This affirms a cosmopolitan orientation when it comes to the substantive obligation (notably combined with an express reference to a statist form of authority ('states have recognized'), a quintessential *apology-utopia* formulation). On the other hand, the Commentary pulls things back from absolute cosmopolitanism, stating that '[t]he obligation to comply with internationally recognized human rights . . . should not be understood as implying that each state is responsible for ensuring the human rights of every person in the world'.[70]

In Principle 4, the statist and cosmopolitan elements are combined and differentiated from each other: 'Each State has the obligation to realize economic, social and cultural rights, for all persons within its territory, to the maximum of its ability. All States also have extraterritorial obligations to respect, protect and fulfil economic, social and cultural rights as set forth in the following Principles.'[71]

The oblique language in the second sentence reflects the *lingua franca* of international human rights law—the tripartite conception of 'respect, protect, fulfil'—when placed in the context of the first sentence, with its relatively clear language of an obligation to realize within the territory, is to be understood as a reference to the extraterritorial context (of course, the tripartite concept of obligations would also apply in the territorial context). In this way, then, both the

[69] Principles, *supra* note 1, Preamble. [70] Commentary, *supra* note 1, at 1090.
[71] Principles, *supra* note 1, Principle 4.

territorial and the extraterritorial contexts are referenced, but the nature of the obligation in each is conceived using different language—to realize rights, and to respect, protect and fulfil rights, respectively. There is a movement out to cosmopolitanism while retaining statism and, moreover, establishing important (although vaguely articulated) differences in the nature and scope of substantive obligations as between the two arenas of normativity.

These differences, on the one hand, and the aforementioned interplay between statism-cosmpolitanism-statism in the way the cosmopolitan obligations of one state to the people of another state are mediated by the statist obligations of the latter state to the same people, on the other hand, are illustrated by the proviso in the Commentary that 'the existence of extraterritorial obligations of other states to contribute to the realization of human rights throughout the territory of one state in no way detracts from the latter state's obligation to ensure economic, social, and cultural rights within its territory to the maximum of its ability'.[72]

Similarly, the Commentary reinforces the distinction between the substantive requirements in the territorial and the extraterritorial contexts articulated in the above extract from Principle 4:

> [e]xtraterritorial obligations differ from territorial obligations, however, in that such obligations can be shared with other states. A state does not bear extraterritorial obligations to individually realize the economic, social, and cultural rights of all people everywhere; rather it is bound by obligations to people outside its borders under the conditions, and in the circumstances set out in these principles.[73]

One might read the first sentence as a *non-sequitur*: clearly, the other side of the coin from the existence of *extraterritorial obligations* resulting in human rights obligations being 'shared' by the territorial and the extraterritorial state is that, for the territorial state, its *territorial obligations* co-exist with the extraterritorial obligations of the extraterritorial state, a mirror situation of 'shared' obligations. The agenda of extraterritorial human rights obligations necessarily creates the possibility of 'shared' obligations in all contexts. The conception of difference makes sense, however, with an appreciation of the different statist/cosmopolitan concepts of rights that inform the aforementioned difference in the way territorial obligations are articulated when compared to extraterritorial obligations. All things being equal, these two sets of obligations are being conceived to be profoundly different; where they overlap, then, it is not a simpler matter of even-handed 'shared' obligations. Thus, although in any given situation, in a more general sense human rights obligations are being 'shared', because territorial obligations are being conceived to be substantively different from extraterritorial obligations, and in any given place the former only (usually) reside in one state whereas the

[72] Commentary, *supra* note 1, at 1096. In the particular context of the obligation to 'fulfil', which includes for foreign states the provision of development assistance, the Commentary stresses that 'the duty of all states to contribute to the fulfilment of economic, social, and cultural rights in other states should not be interpreted as limiting the scope of the obligation of any state to discharge its obligations towards all individuals located on its territory'. Ibid., at 1146.

[73] Ibid., at 1097.

latter can potentially reside in a number of states, when obligations are disaggregated between the territorial and the extraterritorial, only the latter are 'shared'.

As will be demonstrated in due course, elements of the dialectic between the two different political conceptions of the relationship between the individual and the state play out as discrete elements of the normative regime for extraterritorial obligations, and an appreciation of them can illuminate the challenges jurists have in seeking to conceive such obligations.

5. Law: What It Is and What Is at Stake

A. Introduction

As reflected in the Principles and the Commentary, and the broader ETO Consortium activist network promoting the Principles and other writing about this initiative, it is suggested by some that international human rights law sets out a substantive normative framework that speaks in a valuable way to the position of states as far as the realization of economic, social and cultural rights outside their territories is concerned, and more broadly in efforts to combat global poverty and economic inequality. Thus the law is invoked to intervene in a highly contested area of public policy, where a broad range of very different preferences could be adopted and promoted, and/or avoided and ignored, and/or undermined, through and by it. It is important, then, to ask: which polices are given preference over the alternatives by international human rights law? What is possible, what is prevented, what is included, what is excluded, in the wide range of ways that might exist to order the world so as to better combat global poverty and economic inequality?

The following sections address this question by considering the two main features of the substantive policy framework enshrined in the law, using the Principles and the Commentary as a resource on how the law is understood. Before turning to the substantive features, the present section paves the way for a consideration of them by setting out briefly the general conceptions of areas of obligation in this field, and sketching out some of the main policy issues at stake in an enquiry as to the value of this legal framework.

B. The Legal Framework—Power and Cooperation

Principle 8 defines extraterritorial obligations thus:

> a) obligations relating to the acts and omissions of a State, within or beyond its territory, that have effects on the enjoyment of human rights outside of that State's territory; and
> b) obligations of a global character that are set out in the Charter of the United Nations and human rights instruments to take action, separately, and jointly through international cooperation, to realize human rights universally.[74]

[74] Principles, *supra* note 1, Principle 8.

The obligations in paragraph (a) can be understood as conceptualizing a trigger for the operation of legal regulation if and when a particular type of power relationship operates between a state and people outside its territory. Only if this power relationship is present are the obligations triggered. According to this approach, the very existence of obligations operates on the basis of a default position of exclusively territorial significance (in terms of the location of the rights-holders) which is departed from if a particular power relationship is considered to exist extraterritorially. In what follows the notion of a 'power' conception of extraterritorial obligations will be used as shorthand for this feature of the normative framework.

The obligations in paragraph (b) arise not only and as a consequence of the existence of a power relationship extraterritorially but, rather, in any event. They are concerned not with regulating exceptional power relationships if and when they arise, but, rather, addressing the 'normal' situation of economic interdependence between states understood as a permanent state of affairs, seeking to graft onto this certain requirements on the part of states in position to do so to improve economic rights outside their territories, described as being about 'cooperation'. Thus there is no trigger that needs to be present in order for the obligations to be in operation; they operate all the time. In what follows, the notion of obligations concerned with 'cooperation' will be used as shorthand for this feature of the normative framework.

C. What Is at Stake

Clearly there are many and varied ways in which the structures of the global economy and international economic relations could be changed in order to combat poverty and economic inequality, and a range of different rationales for these changes. The choice between these options is contested, implicating different conceptions of economic and political theory, and historical record, involving varying degrees of difference, from modest reform to radical transformation of the *status quo*, and a matter on which a wide range of stakeholders, from grassroots civil society activists to the elites of the international economic system, are and will be engaged. Bearing all of this in mind, how might what international human rights law is said to offer implicate these broader debates? Whose agenda does it further, and whose does it undermine?

The point of this enquiry is not to adopt a particular substantive approach to, and/or the interests of a particular stakeholder about, how the global economy might be ordered better. Rather, it is to ask how the law might mediate the choices made about, and the fortunes of particular stakeholders in relation to, these contests, bearing in mind the particular policy preferences embedded in legal norms. Whereas it is for broader debates and processes to contest and determine the merit of these preferences, it is important to know what they are, so as to know what particular agenda is being furthered by advocacy of the law in this field.

In the foregoing analysis, the following considerations will be borne in mind. In the first place, in a situation of complex economic independence, a multitude of different causal and power relationships and linkages operate in all sorts of ways and at all sorts of levels to determine the economic position of most people in the world. Economies are intertwined, and operate on the basis of many varied and dynamic power and control hierarchies. How does international human rights law understand and seek to mediate these relationships? In the second place, how does the way the law is conceived relate to rationales that underpin options for realizing international economic equality and the range of possible options themselves? The following two sections analyse the potential and limitations of the two key features of the substantive legal regime.

6. Law: Power

It will be recalled that the 'power' basis for extraterritorial human rights obligations is concerned with defining a set of circumstances extraterritorially (sometimes with a territorial origin) that have to be met before, and in order that, obligations are triggered. These circumstances are conceived in Principle 8 thus: 'the acts and omissions of a State, within or beyond its territory, that have effects on the enjoyment of human rights outside of that State's territory'.[75]

A plain reading of this provision, in isolation from the rest of the Principles, suggests an idea that is potentially very broad in what it takes in by way of economic interdependence, because of the inclusion of omissions as well as acts, the idea of all 'effects', defined simply as such, as a basis for obligation, and how it covers acts and omissions existing not only extraterritorially but also territorially. However, this expansive potential is lessened considerably by Principle 9, which states that:

> A State has obligations to respect, protect and fulfil economic, social and cultural rights in any of the following:
> a) situations over which it exercises authority or effective control . . . ;
> b) situations over which State acts or omissions bring about foreseeable effects on the enjoyment of economic, social and cultural rights, whether within or outside its territory;
> c) situations in which the State . . . is in a position to exercise decisive influence . . . to realize economic, social and cultural rights extraterritorially.[76]

Also relevant is Principle 13, which states:

> States must desist from acts and omissions that create a real risk of nullifying or impairing the enjoyment of economic, social and cultural rights extraterritorially. The responsibility of States is engaged where such nullification or impairment is a foreseeable result of their conduct.[77]

The import of these provisions is to set up a more qualified and varied approach to conceiving power so as to trigger obligations relating to the enjoyment of human rights extraterritorially. On the one hand, if the state is present on the ground extraterritorially, exercising 'authority or effective control', then it has a broad obligation to 'respect, protect and fulfil' economic, social and cultural rights there (Principle 9a). This retains the breadth of the original articulation in Principle 8,

[75] Ibid., *supra* note 1, Principle 8. [76] Ibid., Principle 9. [77] Ibid., Principle 11.

but is limited to unusual situations where states are present in this kind of direct way outside their territories. It is reminiscent of how the ECHR and the ICCPR have been understood to apply extraterritorially, via a definition of the term 'jurisdiction' in these treaties to include the exercise of effective control extraterritorially.[78] The term 'jurisdiction' is used in the heading for Principle 9, and was invoked by the ICJ, without authority, to have this meaning in the context of the extraterritorial application of the ICESCR in the *Wall* Advisory Opinion, although actually the term is not used in that treaty.[79]

On the other hand, the more commonplace projection of power extraterritorially that falls short of direct extraterritorial presence is covered only if, on the one hand, states are in a position to exercise 'decisive influence' to 'realize' economic, social and cultural rights (Principle 9c), or, on the other hand, in the context of 'acts and omissions' that have 'foreseeable effects on the enjoyment of economic, social and cultural rights' (Principle 9b) or if it is 'foreseeable' that they create a 'real risk of nullifying or impairing' such enjoyment (Principle 13).

Setting aside the narrow circumstances of direct extraterritorial presence on the ground, the language used to address all other forms of economic interaction is either limited to a high threshold of 'direct influence', or, otherwise, seems to be concerned with power relationships that are in some way deemed to be harmful (cf. 'nullifying or impairing'). The suggestion that this is about harm is supported in the Commentary, which explains the general distinction between the 'power' and 'cooperation' bases for obligations in Principle 8 paragraphs a) and b), the former being the present focus of attention, thus:

> ... the obligation to provide assistance to other states in order to strengthen respect for human rights in those states, in the absence of any particular link between a state and the denial of human rights in those states, arises only by virtue of the obligation of a global character as described in Principle 8 (b).[80]

Here, then, is the idea that the 'power' conception for obligations can be understood holistically as being about a 'particular link between a state and the denial of human rights'. Furthermore, the language suggests that of the two types of extraterritorial obligations, only 'power' is concerned with responsibility arising out of harm; 'cooperation' (in Principle 8b) is described in language suggesting a different rationale and objective (the word 'cooperation' itself, and the way the substantive action required of a state here is to 'provide assistance'—hardly the language of reparation for harm). This notion of 'harm-' or 'fault-' based responsibility reflects the ideas discussed earlier that invoke the introduction of 'accountability' into the arena of economic globalization as a rationale for the present project.

The language used also suggests that the nature of harm is to be limited from the full extent of possible options available—only a 'particular link' which has to be

[78] On this, see e.g. Wilde, *supra* note 4, Section 3.3.

[79] *Legal Consequences of the Construction of a Wall in the Occupied Palestinian Territories*, Advisory Opinion, 9 July 2004, ICJ Reports (2004) 136, at para. 112.

[80] Commentary, *supra* note 1, at 1101–1102.

foreseeable and involving a 'real risk'. The relatively limited definition of causation is underscored by the Commentary, which states:

> Principle 9 (b) acknowledges that the obligations of a state under international human rights law may effectively be triggered when its responsible authorities know or should have known the conduct of the state will bring about substantial human rights effects in another territory. Because this element of foreseeability must be present, a state will not necessarily be held liable for all the consequences that result from its conduct where the proximity between that conduct and the consequences is remote.[81]

In the same way, the Commentary to Principle 13 states that '[f]oreseeability serves an important limiting function by ensuring that a state shall not be surprised with claims of responsibility for unforeseeable risks that are only remotely connected to its conduct'.[82]

Clearly discussion and disagreement can be had regarding work in related areas of law such as the law of state responsibility drawn upon in considering, how these key terms can and should be defined legally, from the notion of 'particular' types of harm that are 'proximate' and 'foreseeable' not 'remote' to the idea of a 'real risk' with effects that are 'substantial'. But whichever approach is taken in the range of options for the scope of liability here, from narrow to broad, more fundamentally the range itself only covers a sub-set of the wide linkages that exist globally between national economies, given how they are intertwined in an acute, complex and constant fashion. This is a limited notion of international economic relations in not taking in the full potential for causal relationships that can mediate the state of economic rights.

Moreover, recalling the earlier discussion of statism and cosmopolitanism, it is clear also that in the 'power' area of extraterritorial obligations, the rationale is not some cosmopolitan idea of the worth of human beings globally shorn of nationality, but a narrower fault-based idea that seems to reserve broader conceptions of duties in the economic sphere exclusively to the territorial domain. Under this paradigm, obligations are owed extraterritorially not because of a cosmopolitan commitment to human welfare generally, but because of a narrower notion of a particular conception of fault connecting the state to an extraterritorial human rights situation.

7. Law: Cooperation

> ... governments may feel bound to act, but that feeling of obligation may simply come from their own sense of altruism rather than a belief that human rights bind all governments to help if the government most directly responsible fails to fulfil its duties...
>
> Andrew Heard, quoted by M. Langford, *et al*[83]

[81] Ibid., at 1109. [82] Ibid., at 1113.

[83] Heard, 'Human Rights: Chimeras in Sheep's Clothing?', *Simon Fraser University Online* (1997), available online at http://www.sfu.ca/~aheard/intro.html (last accessed 23 July 2015), cited in Langford *et al.*, *supra* note 1, 8.

A. Introduction

The second area of obligations, those relating to 'cooperation' in the realization of economic, social and cultural rights extraterritorially, would suggest that the idea of 'help' is, indeed, derived not simply from altruism but also legal obligation. But what is the scope of this 'help' and, indeed, what does conceiving it as 'help', and associating it with the idea of 'altruism', indicate about its nature and potential?

As previously indicated, the 'cooperation' obligations are not conceived to be triggered by the existence of a particular power relationship between a state and an extraterritorial human rights situation. Rather, they operate generally. As such, they have the potential to be of much wider relevance to international economic relations, and so to be much more important to efforts to combat global poverty and economic inequality, than the first set of obligations. They are also, given what has been said earlier about the fault-based nature of the 'power' obligations, the main option within this regime for conceptualizing a 'cosmopolitan' idea of rights rooted simply in humanity, regardless of global location.

It will be recalled that Principle 8 defines the 'cooperation' category of extraterritorial obligations as being 'of a global character... to take action, separately, and jointly through international cooperation, to realize human rights universally'.[84] The main human rights instrument enshrining the obligation to cooperate in this way is the ICESCR, in Article 2.[85] Principle 9 states:

> A State has obligations to respect, protect and fulfil economic, social and cultural rights in... c) situations in which the State, acting separately or jointly, whether through its executive, legislative or judicial branches, is in a position... to take measures to realize economic, social and cultural rights extraterritorially.[86]

This law on 'cooperation' includes, arguably as its most important norm, and falling within the particular obligation to 'fulfil' in this area, an obligation 'to provide assistance,' in Principle 33.[87] The obligation to provide assistance to enable the realization of socio-economic rights extraterritorially is the only area of this legal regime that speaks to the fundamental issue of financial, technological and resource transfer across borders from the economically privileged to the economically disadvantaged in order to combat poverty and reduce economic inequality, not simply, as in the 'power' area of law, to make amends for certain forms of foreseeable and non-historical harm. It is the area within which the 'right to development', economic redistribution, and development assistance and aid, including the setting of targets for such aid must fit, if they fit at all, as far as the contours of international human rights law are concerned.

[84] Principles, *supra* note 1, Principle 8.

[85] International Covenant on Economic, Social and Cultural Rights 1966, 993 UNTS 3 (ICESCR).

[86] Principles, *supra* note 1, Principle 9.

[87] Ibid., Principle 33.

B. Assistance

The Commentary asserts that '[d]espite its provision in binding international instruments, disagreement persists as to the legally binding nature of the obligation of international cooperation as expressed in' the ICESCR.[88] This is a significant observation when situated within the law of human rights extraterritorially in general, and, more broadly, international human rights law in particular and international law as a whole. Actually, 'disagreement' exists across the board in many areas of international law, and, notably, about many aspects of the law of the extraterritorial application of human rights. However, this is the only rule on extraterritoriality where the 86-page Commentary invokes the existence of 'disagreement'.[89] Given the wider context of disagreement in international law, one has to ask why a particular rule is being singled out as the only one in relation which disagreement exists, especially when, as the statement acknowledges, the rule is expressly articulated in a treaty. Moreover, this approach is in marked contrast to the way, as mentioned, the Principles seem to adopt the 'jurisdiction' basis for triggering obligations in this sphere, and the effective control basis on which that term has been defined in case-law, as operative in relation to economic, social and cultural rights, even though the term is not contained in the ICESCR and the case-law defining it in this way is derived, as mentioned with one exception in a dictum from the ICJ, from the other human rights treaties that do use it and are limited to civil and political rights.

The transposition of the standard from the law on civil and political rights is also significant in two further respects. In the first place, actually, even in that area of law extraterritorial applicability is disputed; there is 'disagreement'.[90] In the second place, the area of applicability that the standard is being transposed to—economic rights in situations where control and authority is exercised 'on the ground' extraterritorially—addresses activities by states which are, as mentioned, although significant when they happen, unusual when situated within the broader projection of power by states extraterritorially and the effects of this on the economic position of people worldwide. Given the limited conception of the 'power' test for applicability as reviewed above, much of the broader picture is only going to be addressed by the law through the alternative 'cooperation' conception of responsibilities. Yet here, it seems, the very existence of a binding obligation is in question. The consequence of all this is that there is a bold affirmation of normativity, where such normativity is actually disputed, to unusual situations, and a questioning of normativity, despite the existence of binding treaty provisions on the issue, to a much broader area of international economic relations.

In this context, is hard not to view the questioning of the binding nature of the obligation to cooperate internationally as over-compensation. It seems that in this

[88] Commentary, *supra* note 1, at 1094.

[89] In a footnote it is also acknowledged that there are disagreements about the 'Lotus presumption'. Ibid., at 1138 no.136.

[90] See e.g. the discussion and sources cited in Wilde, *supra* note 3.

area it is deemed prudent to play it safe in terms of the extent to which economically privileged states will have to act and international economic relations altered. So safe, actually, that challenges to the binding nature of express provisions of a treaty will be acknowledged.

It can hardly be a surprise, then, that what follows from this is very limited. The Commentary concludes that on the question of the provision of assistance, it is probably only possible to say that states should coordinate with each other, including on the allocation of responsibilities, and have foreign assistance programmes.[91] Within this, on the crucial question of how much resources are to be allocated to such programmes, the Commentary adopts the standard 'progressive' approach adopted in relation to positive obligations to fulfil economic, social and cultural rights generally, that states have to assist to the maximum of their available resources.[92]

The progressive test requiring best efforts ('in a position to do so') to be made in the area of fulfilling economic, social and cultural rights is, of course, a challenging idea even if just applied to the domestic context (given that, for example, the level of available resources is not fixed, being determined, rather, by prior matters involving contested choices between fundamentally different economic and political systems). But when it is being applied to extraterritorial assistance, it has to reckon with a new complicating factor: how are resources to be divided up as between welfare 'at home' and welfare 'abroad', assuming a zero sum equation? This is, of course, a crucial matter that goes to the heart of a regime that purports to conceive extraterritorial norms in the area of economic rights. It operates at one axis of the statist/cosmopolitanist dialectic. Here, again, we see that the law is not somehow replacing the former with the latter, but engaged in a process that involves both and, in this case, implicates an idea that requires a balance to be struck between them. The 'best efforts' test by itself is insufficient, because it is also necessary to know, within its operation, whether and to what extent states can privilege the economic welfare of their own nationals or, put differently, the extent to which states should be required to put the welfare of foreigners ahead of that of their own nationals.

There is, actually, an international standard of some pedigree that speaks to the crucial quantum question. As the Commentary acknowledges, the aforementioned target of 0.7 per cent of GNP to be allocated to overseas development assistance by wealthier countries has been affirmed in a range of instruments.[93] This is the closest international law has come to a benchmark for economic redistribution through

[91] Principles 30 and 33. See also Principles 28–29, 31–32, 34–35 and the relevant sections of the Commentary, *supra* note 1.

[92] Principles, *supra* note 1, Principle 33. See also, on coordination, Principle 30, and capacity and resources, Principle 32, and the relevant sections of the Commentary, *supra* note 1. On the 'progressive' standard, see ICESCR, *supra* note 85, Art. 2.

[93] Resolution adopted by the General Assembly 2626 (XXV)—International Development Strategy for the Second United Nations Development Decade, UN Doc. A/RES/25/2626, 24 October 1970, para. 43; Preparatory Committee for the International Conference on Financing for Development Fourth Session, UN Doc. A/AC.257/32, 7 December 2001, para. 42; Resolution adopted by the General Assembly on 24 December 2008—Doha Declaration on Financing for Development: Outcome Document of the Follow-up International Conference on Financing for Development to

aid, thereby speaking to the crucial issue of where the balance is to be struck between welfare at home and welfare extraterritorially. It feeds into Goal 8 of the aforementioned MDGs, on a 'Global Partnership for Development', Target 13 of which, concerned with 'Least Developed Countries', involves a pledge for 'more generous official development assistance for countries committed to poverty reduction' and includes as indicators levels of development assistance provision.[94]

The Principles were adopted 11 years after the MDGs, when the period set for the targets they enshrined, which implicate realization of the 0.7 per cent standard, had four more years to run, and when the 'post-MDG' normative regime, which might be expected to have some relevance to this matter, was being discussed and formulated. The Principles were, thus, introduced at an important moment in the broader normative development of an issue of fundamental relevance to the issues they seek to address.

However, the Commentary only invokes the MDGs as a generalized indication lending 'strength to the legal commitment to internationalized responsibility... in this area'—i.e., a responsibility to cooperate.[95] Significantly, the Commentary discusses the 0.7 per cent target in its main text only because of its relevance to the discrete, ultimately less important question of the relevance of joint, in addition to individual, state action in the context of cooperation.[96] The more fundamental matter of whether or not this target is, or might become, legally obligatory is not itself addressed.[97] Obviously, a discussion can be had as to whether the target has attained normativity, whether generally or at least for certain states. But what is striking about the coverage in the Commentary is that the possibility of this discussion, and the potential of the standard concerning aid allocation to be or become binding, is not even directly addressed.

The closest things get to addressing normativity is in the discussion of Principle 30, which obliges states to coordinate, including in the allocation of responsibilities in this regard. The Commentary states that '[i]nternational law recognizes a principle of common but differentiated responsibilities among states and there are several examples of negotiated systems of burden-sharing established to address challenges or duties of a global character'.[98] This sentence ends with a footnote that includes a citation to the arrangements dealing with the 0.7 per cent target, as one of the 'examples', alongside others that are similarly concerned with burden-sharing in different fields, e.g. the Kyoto Protocol. Oddly, then, something which actually directly relates to the subject at hand, being concerned with levels of development assistance, is relegated to the margins of a footnote, and within this only invoked as an example, amongst others, of the idea of burden-sharing in the general field of international law. Moreover, the main text continues from the earlier quotation to

Review the Implementation of the Monterrey Consensus, UN Doc. A/RES/63/239, 19 March 2009, para. 43.

[94] See http://www.unmillenniumproject.org/goals/gti.htm#goal1 (last accessed 23 July 2015), Goal 8, Target at 13, and indicators at 33–37.

[95] Commentary, *supra* note 1, at 1095.

[96] Ibid., at 1151–1152.

[97] Ibid., at 1152.

[98] Ibid., at 1149–1150 (mid-sentence footnote omitted).

qualify the significance of all this as being relevant not to substantive obligations directly (the question of how much aid must be given), but only to the idea of a second-order procedural obligation to devise the substantive obligations (the question of agreeing how much aid should be given).[99]

Just as, earlier, the 0.7 per cent target was invoked for its side-relevance to the matter of states acting not only individually but also jointly, here, it is picked up (in a footnote) only because of what it indicates about a second-order norm requiring states to agree on burden-sharing. Whereas it might indeed have significance in indicating such a procedural norm, it also, first and foremost, might have something to say on the substance of what it covers. Yet the passage above suggests that on the substance, things are only 'being developed'. At a stroke, a standard that has been invoked and affirmed since 1970 is still, it would seem, in a stage of crystallization when it comes to being binding. As mentioned, perhaps this is actually the case; the point is that the Commentary assumes it without offering any analysis or authority whatsoever.

Earlier it was observed that narratives of the identity of the personnel who signed the principles that foreground 'expertise' and marginalize NGO 'activism' might have been deemed helpful in reassuring and obtaining the support of those who would be obligation-bearers in this system: states. This hypothetical explanation for the stylistic move may also lie behind the substantive move of affirming a very modest position accepting of the notion that the obligation of cooperation is of questionable normativity. Although not mentioned in the Commentary, some of those involved in the initiative raise in their separate writings on the Principles the resistance of wealthier states to the notion that there is a legal obligation to cooperate in general and an obligation to provide particular levels of assistance in particular.[100] This may be, then, a pragmatic decision made to accept, not challenge, the resistance of such states to accepting obligation in this area, in order, presumably, to ensure that they come on board on the regime more generally, which, in order for this logic to work, has to be worth the price paid in jettisoning some of the core aspects of the obligation to cooperate. But the merits of this position are not self-evident, requiring a considered cost-benefit analysis that is reasoned and persuasive. We are not given this (although, as will be addressed in due course, there is one statement by some of the signatories writing separately that seems to speak to the issue).

C. Welfare, Assistance, Statism, Cosmopolitanism and Nationality Discrimination

Earlier it was explained how 'extraterritoriality' is not the displacement of statism with cosmopolitanism, but, rather, an effort to combine the two in overlapping contexts where the reach of one is bound up in the extent of the other. Thus

[99] Commentary, *supra* note 1, at 1150. See also Salomon and Seiderman *supra* note 1, at 460.

[100] See Salomon 2012, *supra* note 1; Coomans 2013, *supra* note 1, at 6; Langford *et al.*, *supra* note 1, at 26.

distinctions between home and abroad and so, necessarily, between a state's own nationals and everyone else in the world, are accepted and affirmed. This is not, then, an absolutist cosmopolitan project seeking to transcend nationality completely and, as the Commentary indicates, obliging 'each state' to be 'responsible for ensuring the human rights of every person in the world' on an equal basis.[101] Rather, it involves a complex series of dialectical moves and, ultimately, a balance struck between, statism and cosmopolitanism. This is illustrated in how the law addresses the question of whether and to what extent states must provide development assistance/aid to other countries. Initially, there is cosmopolitan shift of focus from the home (the territorial state) to the world (other states) as far as the potential aid provider is concerned. But then in determining on how duties to those at home versus those at abroad are to be calibrated, there is a flip back to a statist consideration as far as the other (assisting) states are concerned (their relationship to their own people). Moreover, in requiring a consideration of how the contribution by other states is to be balanced against the welfare role of the state whose people the aid would be targeted to, there is a further flip back to statism, in this case addressing the relationship between the recipient state and its people. The vagueness as to the normativity and substantive content of the obligation to provide assistance internationally suggests that the outcome of this dialectic is ultimately to leave things in an overwhelmingly statist orientation. How this is brought about can be illuminated further in how the Principles and the Commentary invoke nationality discrimination.

The Principles and the Commentary articulate a seemingly 'utopian', cosmopolitan absolutist prohibition of nationality discrimination at odds with the very modest statist 'reality' of the position adopted on cooperation. The Commentary provides the following definition of 'discrimination' in general:

> In human rights law, discrimination constitutes any distinction, exclusion, restriction or preference, or other differential treatment based on any ground, such as race, color,... national or social origin... birth, or other status... which has the purpose or effect of nullifying or impairing the recognition, enjoyment, or exercise by all persons, on an equal footing, of all rights and freedoms.[102]

Clearly, approaches taken by a state which privilege people in its own territory, most of whom are its own nationals, over people elsewhere, most of whom are non-nationals, as far as the enjoyment of rights are concerned, can be understood as discrimination as defined here. For example, a decision by a state to allocate more of its resources to combat poverty at home, especially in relation to its own citizens, than to combat poverty in the rest of the world, in circumstances where in material terms those abroad are in equal or greater need, necessarily involves a departure, via distinction based on 'national or social origin', from the notion that all individuals enjoy a right to be free from poverty 'on an equal footing'. Direct discrimination on grounds of nationality is inherent in such an approach; indirect discrimination on grounds of race, colour and birth might also be understood to be implicated in it.

[101] Commentary, *supra* note 1, at 1090.

[102] Ibid., at 1088.

Indeed, one might even say a distinction grounded in nationality is, ultimately, the fundamental rationale for the distinction between territorial and extraterritorial obligations that is adopted as a central feature of this normative regime, in ultimately providing greater protections in the former context than the latter context, even when all other things are equal. It is a notion of a profoundly more important connection between a state and its own nationals compared to the relationship between that state and people in the rest of the world that leads to a different conception of territorial and extraterritorial human rights obligations.

An appreciation of the project in terms of its statist/cosmopolitan dialectic, and in the light of the scope of the norm of 'cooperation' it is willing to accept, suggests that the significance of nationality discrimination to it is more subtle and complicated than an absolute articulation of the principle might suggest. Extraterritorial obligations seek to mediate distinctions a state might wish to make between the welfare of its own nationals (and non-nationals) at home, and the welfare of foreigners (and some nationals) in the rest of the world. Such obligations as articulated in this project accept and enable such distinctions, but insofar as they push things further towards the welfare of foreigners abroad than a state might otherwise accept, they necessarily reduce the state's ability to place its own nationals first (assuming a zero sum scenario in terms of available resources), an outcome that can be understood in terms of reducing that state's ability to discriminate in favour of its own nationals.

Even so, Principle 2 articulates the obligation of non-discrimination on grounds of nationality in general terms, 'at all times'.[103] If non-nationality-discrimination were articulated only in and relating to a particular extraterritorial context where the state's involvement in that context is a pre-existing given, such as the unusual scenario of plenary direct effective territorial control addressed earlier as one of the categories of 'power'-based extraterritorial applicability, then it would leave outside its scope distinctions between the territorial and extraterritorial context that might indeed be rooted in nationality. The absolute articulation, by contrast, suggests the operation of a principle in all circumstances, territorially and extraterritorially. If this were taken literally, and one were to apply it, for example, to the needs-based 'best efforts' standard of social provision, the conclusion would be that all but the very core welfare provisions that wealthier states currently focus on people in their own territories would need to be transferred to assisting the much poorer people in other parts of the world.

Of course, actually this is far from what the law requires, as far as the description of it in the Principles and the Commentary is concerned. Moreover, the foregoing analysis on the questionable nature of the binding status of the obligation to 'assist' and the specific matter of allocating certain levels of GNP to overseas aid suggests that international human rights law does not rule out a more transformatory conception of extraterritorial obligations in the sphere of economic rights through an express acknowledgement and acceptance of nationality discrimination, something which would bring this key statist operating principle to the surface. Rather,

[103] Principles, *supra* note 1, Principle 2. See also ibid., Principle 32, and Commentary, *supra* note 1, at 1156.

it rules it out by omission in the way the obligation to assist is conceived: by simply requiring an active programme of extraterritorial assistance, and not also addressing how much assistance this should involve, it leaves the quantum to the discretion of states, thereby enabling them to devote most resources to welfare at home, while still being compliant with the legal regime.

How, then, can the inclusion of an absolutist affirmation of anti-discrimination in these instruments be understood? Recalling the earlier discussion of hope versus reality, we see the 'utopian' element of anti-nationality-discrimination, with its cosmopolitanist significance, being invoked without an acknowledgement of how it is mediated by the 'apologetic' elements in the rest of the project, with their statist acceptance and reinforcement of the ability of states to put their own people first. As with the earlier problems caused by the misleading presentation of exclusive 'expertise' without also acknowledging 'activist' tendencies, here there is a reverse problem: the way the project is concerned with a compromise between a state's duties to the welfare of its own people, and its duties to the welfare of people around the world ('reality'), is concealed by an absolute articulation of anti-nationality-discrimination ('hope'). Just as being less than candid about one's activism gets one off the hook in terms of defending the particular agenda being furthered in preference to the alternatives, here concealing the existence of a compromise enables the compromise itself to be shielded from critical scrutiny.

D. Charity, Which Begins (Largely) at Home

What, then, of the substantive nature of the compromise, in terms of where it has been struck? The very existence of an obligation to assist is called into question, and no proper consideration is given to the crucial question of how resources are to be allocated by more economically advantaged states as between welfare at home and welfare internationally, let alone the matter of whether the 0.7 per cent target of GNP, which would in any event be remarkably modest, is/might be binding. More fundamentally, the language of 'assistance' and 'cooperation' indicates very limited notions of action. It suggests a pre-existing reality taken as a given and, moreover, in relation to which locates responsibility for realizing socio-economic rights exclusively in the territorial state, as in the quotation from Andrew Heard at the start of this section, cited by Langford, Vandenhole, Scheinin and van Genugten, with its reference to the provision of 'help if the government most directly responsible fails to fulfil its duties'. Other states then 'assist' that government in this, although not by any clear level in terms of resources. Broader, more fundamental approaches, including of redistribution, that would involve a more radical transformation of the world economy, are not considered.

This is a model that takes the existing structures of the global economy as a given, grafting onto them relatively minor modifications which do not in any significant way challenge things to bring about a significant change in levels of poverty and economic inequality across borders. There is no place here for the kind of radical restructuring of the world economy that would be of much more significance to the global poor, the call for which of course being associated with social movements in the global south and in certain ideas from post-colonial and approaches to international law and politics. One cannot help wondering whether such a limited horizon of options would have been articulated, and then set up, as discussed above, as an urgent priority for global activism, had more activists from the global south been formally involved as determinative actors, via inclusion as drafters and/or signatories, in this initiative.

Equally, one cannot help wondering whether a greater involvement of this kind by women might have led to a different substantive outcome. It will be recalled that feminist ideas have foregrounded how in various ways women are disproportionately negatively affected by global poverty. It might have been thought that an initiative such as this one would seek to integrate a consideration of that fundamental insight into the way it conceives the substantive regime. Unfortunately, there are only very few, and all tokenistic, references to sex, gender and women in the Principles and Commentary. Gender equality is included in the general affirmation of 'non-discrimination' in Principle 2.[104] However, the relevant section of the Commentary makes no reference to the special position of women, as discussed above, as being disproportionately negatively affected by global poverty.[105] This suggests a thin, formal notion of equality that does not address structural differences in the position of women and men.

A related approach is to invoke a more radical idea of equality, but only in the context of a relatively marginal aspect of the substance being covered. Principle 7 concerns the right of people to 'informed participation in decisions which affect their human rights'.[106] The Commentary observes that 'human rights standards require a high degree of participation from communities, civil society, minorities, women, young people, indigenous peoples, and other identified groups that in general are weakly represented in normal decision-making processes'.[107] This does seek to address structural inequalities ('weakly represented') and suggests approaches to address them that go beyond formal equality to prioritize the involvement of hitherto underrepresented groups ('high degree of participation'). It is an irony that, as discussed above, this approach was not adopted in the process that led to the drafting and signature of the Principles, as concerns the personnel formally involved in this process. Moreover, the approach is only articulated in relation to substantive norms in the context of what is ultimately, on this topic, a second-order issue of 'participation'. Actually it is relevant across the board, significant also to more fundamental matters such as the nature and scope of the core 'power' and 'cooperation' obligations reviewed above. One wonders whether, had it in its 'participation' manifestation been much more seriously followed in the process of formulating the Principles, at the formal level of drafters and/or signatories, the role of the voices included might have led to this broader significance being appreciated.

Other references to sex and women are similarly limited. There is a sideways reference to Article 55 of the UN Charter, which concerns the promotion of respect for human rights without distinction, including as to sex, in the context of the

[104] Principles, *supra* note 1, Principle 2.
[105] Commentary, *supra* note 1, at 1087–1090.
[106] Principles, *supra* note 1, Principle 7.
[107] Commentary, *supra* note 1, at 1100.

obligation to respect human rights articulated in Principle 19. This seems to have been included not on the discrimination issue as such but because of its link to Article 56 of the UN Charter, with its reference to the taking of 'joint and separate action', which the Commentary argues is the conceptual basis for an extraterritorial understanding of the obligation to promote human rights as articulated in Principle 19.[108] Similarly, the Commentary cites Guideline 20 from the precursor to the Maastricht Principles, the Maastricht Guidelines on Violations of Economic, Social and Cultural Rights, in the context of stating that references in the Principles to 'persons' are to 'include individuals and groups'.[109] The Guideline, which is extracted in the Commentary, states that 'both individuals and groups can be victims of violations of economic, social, and cultural rights. Certain groups suffer disproportionate harm in this respect such as . . . women'.[110] However, the Commentary does nothing with this idea of disproportionate harm in the way it goes on to conceive the substantive obligations.

When in 2000 Hilary Charlesworth and Christine Chinkin reviewed the Declaration on the Right to Development and associated ideas and instruments, their criticism included the fact that the declaration 'does not specify discrimination against women as a major obstacle to development, nor to the fair distribution of its benefits' and that UN deliberations that have referred to the gender implications of development have tended to present concerns as 'discrete, soluble by the application of special protective measures, rather than as central to development'.[111] A further criticism was that the right to development 'does not regard systemic discrimination on the basis of sex as a barrier to development, despite the global evidence of the disparity between the economic position of women and men'.[112] These criticisms could equally be made of the Principles and the Commentary, which, then, would seem to mark a continuation of, not a break from, earlier, problematic approaches.

E. Historical Responsibilities/Responsibilities Because of Historical Legacies

Post-colonial, NIEO and TWAIL approaches to the international economic system form the basis for an agenda that seeks to address global economic inequality as a present injustice that should be resisted, but that is not their only impact. These approaches have also been the site of arguments to the effect that international economic relations should be reconceived because of historical injustices, notably those associated with colonialism and imperialism. The two strands of argumentation are related insofar as current economic inequalities can in part be linked back to colonial and imperial structures of the past. One link would be in how industrialization in the West, with its ongoing legacy in terms of economic inequality and environmental destruction, was bound up in and enabled by slavery, the imposition

[108] Commentary, *supra* note 1, at 1127. [109] Commentary, *supra* note 1, at 1128.
[110] Ibid. [111] Charlesworth and Chinkin, *supra* note 61, at 241. [112] Ibid., at 243.

of unequal trade relations, and the exploitation of people and the plunder of natural resources in colonial territories. Another link would be the colonial legacy of externally imposed arbitrary boundaries which formed the contours of the borders of post-colonial states. This meant that many newly independent states began as entities facing considerable challenges in forming cohesive and functioning political communities, placing them at a disadvantage in this regard compared to many western states.[113] At the same time, historical questions of responsibilities for the abuses and exploitation of the colonial era, and associated calls for redress and reparation, are not limited to matters which, directly or indirectly, feed into contemporary global inequalities: they are also significant in their own right.

Taken together, these strands of related argumentation suggest that the present topic cannot be appreciated simply by taking the unequal world as it is now, without an appreciation of the historical context which both contributed to this inequality and also suggests a series of unresolved injustices.

As highlighted earlier, the way the Commentary describes the relationship between the 'power' and 'cooperation' conceptions of extraterritorial responsibilities indicates that as far as duties arising in some way as a result of fault, harm, etc., are to be addressed only by obligations in the former category (given the use of the language referring to the 'denial of human rights') and not also the latter category (given the non-compensatory/restitutionary language of 'assistance'—in the words of Andrew Heard, to 'help' the government 'most directly responsible'). It is also clear from the language used in relation to obligations in the former category that they have a temporal orientation limited to situations that arise only after they come into operation, not also those of a historical character.

This legal regime does not, then, address ideas of extraterritorial responsibilities arising out historical considerations, whether the historical origins of contemporary global economic inequalities or the question of redress for historic economic exploitation and abuse across borders. These broader matters are only addressed once in the Commentary, when addressing the description in Principle 31 of 'capacity and resources' as, 'inter alia', the benchmark against which a state must take action to fulfil economic, social and cultural rights extraterritorially. The Commentary explains:

> Principle 31 indicates by the use of the term 'inter alia' that capacity and resources do not exhaust the basis for assigning obligations of international assistance and cooperation. It leaves open the possibility of assigning obligations on the grounds of other bases, for example, historical responsibility or causation, which take a compensatory approach based on some determination of liability for contributing to a problem that undermines the fulfilment of economic, social, and cultural rights extraterritorially.[114]

A footnote after the text above states:

> Capacity offers both a specific and a general requirement: specific in that it is one of the bases that points to the requisite duty-bearers, e.g. 'those in a position to assist,' and general

[113] See Mutua, 'Why Redraw the Map of Africa: A Legal and Moral Inquiry', 16 *Michigan Journal of International Law* (1995) 1113.

[114] Commentary, *supra* note 1, at 1153.

in that it is a prerequisite to discharging any obligation. Thus, even if it were argued for example that historical responsibility should form a basis for assigning international obligations, but capacity would still be a necessary element in order to see that obligation fulfilled even when the basis is determined on some other ground.[115]

It would seem, then, that historical bases for responsibilities are only a possibility that is open in that they are not ruled out by the law as it stands. Implicit in this is that they do not yet form part of the law. Moreover, how this might come about, and what the contours of the substantive norms might be, are not given any consideration other than that the 'capacity' test would operate as a general prerequisite for discharging any obligation that might come to be adopted in this area. As with the accepted area of cooperation/assistance, of course, the operation of the 'capacity' test would require the fundamental matter, not addressed here, of the division of resources as between welfare at home and providing redress for historical matters.

8. Conclusions

The Principles and the Commentary are, as Margot Salomon (co-drafter of the former and co-author of the latter) indicates, a 'giant step' when it comes to the codification effort of mapping out the substantive contours of the extraterritorial application of human rights law in the field of socio-economic rights.[116] But what is the substantive merit of that which has been put forward? How 'responsive', in substance, is international human rights law to global deprivation? Will the giant step in doctrine bring about a giant reduction in global poverty levels? And even if its potential is much more limited, should the current legal settlement serve as the departure point, from which to go further, making refinements? Is it the right place to start?

The foregoing analysis suggests, as mentioned, that the current legal regime takes the fundamental structures of global economic relations largely as is, grafting onto them relatively discrete areas of liability, concerned either with certain forms of power relations and harm understood in terms of direct or foreseeable causation, or vague notions of 'cooperation' that do not extend to particular levels of financial and resource transfer.

At the start of this chapter, it was observed that some of the proponents of the Principles invoke them in the context of economic globalization, as being a much-needed introduction of accountability into this area. A further feature of this invocation of economic globalization, which indicates the nature and the limitations of that which is being advocated, is a description of it as in some sense a 'new' phenomenon. The Preamble to the Principles contextualizes the contemporary need for that which it contains as the 'advent' of economic globalization.[117]

[115] Ibid., at 1153 no. 179. [116] Salomon 2012, *supra* note 1, at 3.
[117] Principles, *supra* note 1, Preamble.

An account of economic globalization, its problems, and the consequent need of human rights law to regulate it, as 'new' or 'recent' runs through much of the writing in this area.[118]

Such an approach to economic globalization ignores the way in which international economic relations have been globalized for centuries. Why does this matter for the project at hand? Conceptualizing economic globalization as novel or at least of relatively recent pedigree perhaps explains why the approach for addressing its problems advocated by this initiative fails to address the way such problems are partly structural and historically rooted. Rich countries and their populations are operating on a blank slate in terms of the historical past and their inheritance from previous generations. No investigation is to be made into how the economic inequalities of today are in part rooted in such inequalities in the past. Thus any matters of global economic reconstruction and redistribution can be understood exclusively in terms of debates around communitarianism and charity—resulting in very modest economic consequences—not unfair, inherited privilege based on past inequality and exploitation—which might require more profound, transformatory change.

It would seem, then, that some of the grand claims made for the potential of international human rights law in the context of global poverty and economic inequality reviewed at the start of this chapter do not stand up to scrutiny. It has to be asked, then, whether a campaign to put human rights obligations at the centre of activism in this field is a valuable use of the limited time and resources of those involved. And, in consequence, the concern must also be that the modest nature of the substantive law creates a danger that it will merely serve to bolster the continuation of the *status quo* which can now be further legitimated by states through claims to be 'human rights compliant'.

But could not a more modest position be adopted, that certain limited improvements might be effected at the margins, and that more radical efforts seeking transformatory changes can be, and indeed perhaps should be, left to broader struggles taking place outside the structures of international human rights law? Such broader struggles could, as human rights by definition cannot, involve ideas that offer more fundamental challenges to the structural aspects of global economic life, from the division of the world into sovereign states itself to the substantive models of economics that form the basis for the world economy. Modesty in the expectations made of the law can also be used to limit the legitimating power the law holds when it comes to undergirding the status quo: if activists were not making grand claims about the value of the law, states would be undermined in their efforts to use the law to legitimate business as usual.

Part of the problem with this approach is that it substitutes an overblown account of the law's emancipatory potential with an alternative narrative that obscures how the law enables particular substantive policies to be furthered.

[118] See Vandenhole 2011, *supra* note 1, at 430; Coomans and Künnemann, 'General Introduction', *supra* note 1, at 1; Langford *et al.*, *supra* note 1, at 29; Vandenhole 2012, *supra* note 1, abstract and 2.

A model of extraterritorial obligations in the economic sphere that is limited to narrow conceptions of direct or foreseeable harm, direct territorial control, or vague notions of cooperation, maps onto a liberal economic model of laissez faire, with a modicum of light-touch regulation and modest social provision in exceptional areas, outside unusual situations where direct territorial control is exercised by a foreign state. International economic inequality is accepted as a given, bar narrow areas where there is more direct transboundary harm (only in the present), and the possibility of 'assistance' which is unquantified and thereby left largely in the realm of charity and discretion. This model not only lacks more substantial socialist or solidarist elements; for its proponents, of course, it would be conceived to be an alternative to a model with these elements. For an economist, international human rights law would appear to have come down on one side in the hugely contested debate about the operation of the global economy.

One way this approach is enabled is by touching upon issues that clearly imply substantive economic ideas, doing so just enough to dismiss more solidarist approaches in sweeping terms, but not long enough to acknowledge the substantive significance of, let alone engage in a discussion of, the economic ideas in play. Langford, Vandenhole, Scheinin and van Genugten argue that an 'inordinate amount of time' has been taken up with debates over the provision of development assistance and fiscal resource transfers.[119] This is 'unfortunate' because of the emergence of middle-income countries where the poor are located, where 'international development assistance is rapidly becoming less relevant'.[120] Moreover, '[e]ven many low-income countries have set themselves a goal of graduation from development assistance. Thus the approach of reducing global poverty through fiscal transfer to poorer States has an increasingly limited scope.'[121] Also, it is 'unfortunate' because 'extraterritorial obligations may be even more relevant and effective in other areas. This might include the structure of the world economy.'[122] What is cast as a purely empirical treatment of key facts of course implies a series of economic preferences, such as the idea that fiscal transfers are only relevant if somehow local capacities are deficient, ignoring more structural links across borders determinative of 'local' capacities and denying the validity of alternative rationales for transfers such as redress for historical injustices. And when we bear in mind the substantively limited nature of extraterritorial obligations in 'other areas' as reviewed above, which hardly seem capable of transforming the global economy, the notion of jettisoning efforts for the adoption of solidaristic norms involving resource transfer as a waste of time only makes sense if the neo-liberal model of economic relations that is left is to be preferred.

A more typical approach, which is illustrated in some of the statements from proponents of the Principles reviewed, is to insist that human rights law is in some sense anti-capitalist. Olivier De Schutter, for example, posits the 'neoliberal agenda' as somehow 'other' than human rights law, and its 'imposition' something which has led to the pledges in that area of law being forgotten.[123] But, as has been

[119] Langford *et al.*, *supra* note 1, at 30. [120] Ibid., at 30. [121] Ibid., at 31.
[122] Ibid., at 31. [123] De Schutter, 'Foreword', *supra* note 1, at vi.

suggested, the nature of the substantive legal framework in the field of extraterritoriality would seem to approximate most to a liberal view of the global economy. It could also be said that this forms part of the broader way in which international law is compatible with, and indeed often the enabler of, liberal economic governance, most obviously in investment and trade law, and that, as a result, international lawyers have to understood their relationship to neo-liberal economics, not as something 'other' than international law which has been 'imposed,' but, rather, as an agenda that the law has played a role in fostering. If De Schutter wishes to resist the neo-liberal agenda, then, it may not even be 'merely' about ensuring compliance with human rights law. Such compliance might be part of the problem.

If this is correct, then it is not possible simply to assume that the law offers a modest, neutral foundation on which all manner of developments, including progressive, transformatory and solidarist ones, might be possible. The foundation might determine that which is possible. It sets the trajectory that would, therefore, have to be altered, not followed, if different conceptions of international economic relations were to be attempted. This is equally true on the earlier, ahistorical conception of economic globalization and its seeming connection to an absence of responsibilities for historical injustices. Although there has been for some time a vibrant field of 'transitional justice' seeking to address, *inter alia*, questions of responsibility for historical human rights abuses, an internal statist focus has predominated, with transnational issues dealt with relatively occasionally and mostly those of more recent provenance (transitional justice has also tended to focus more on civil and political rights than socio-economic rights). There remains a huge absence of, and resistance to, a reckoning for historical transnational human rights abuses, especially in the context of the colonial era and the actions of victorious belligerents. In recent years, certain efforts have had some success in challenging this, for example the litigation brought against the British concerning the displacement of the Chagos Islanders and the atrocities perpetrated during the *Mau Mau* rebellion in Kenya. In this context, the present initiative, in failing to address the idea of historic inequalities and abuses as a factor in understanding how the normative regime should operate, in its omission intervenes in a debate on the side of those who would deny the significance of this factor.

Finally, as a project of international human rights law, this initiative, although coming out of the work of non-state experts/activists, and in its subject matter seeking to disrupt state boundaries, ends up legitimating the state-based international system that might be one of the structural causes of international economic inequality (cf. TWAIL critiques). Moreover, on its own terms, this system privileges states in the area of norm-generation and transformation. The modest nature of the current regime for extraterritoriality could be built upon not only, as its proponents intend, by those who aspire to progressive development; it could also be captured by powerful states, and for different ends. Indeed, in language that could have been lifted from Koskenniemi's *Apology to Utopia*, Olivier De Schutter suggests the potential for the development of the normative system to be determined by states:

. . . they [the Principles] are *relatively incomplete*. They are sufficiently precise to provide a focal point for deliberations as to how to build international regimes . . . yet . . . vague enough not to pre-empt the result of these deliberations. They thus allow true ownership by the actors, primarily States, who contribute to the establishment of international regimes.[124]

124 Ibid., at viii (emphasis in original).

A Human Rights Approach to Extraterritorial Environmental Protection?

An Assessment

*Jorge E. Viñuales**

1. Introductory Remarks

One important question that arises in connection with the extraterritorial scope of human rights obligations concerns its implications for other areas of international law. This question cannot be answered in the abstract. It requires a particular context that makes its reformulation possible in terms that can lead to a meaningful answer. In turn, such reformulation requires a basic understanding of what is meant by the extraterritorial scope of human rights obligations.

The understanding that I will assume here is that states may be held responsible for human rights violations taking place beyond their territory but within an extended conception of their 'jurisdiction'. State jurisdiction may be extended by virtue of specific circumstances such as de facto powers over the victim (e.g. military occupation, secret detention facilities in foreign countries, or the overriding power of a military aircraft over a civil aircraft) or, potentially, over the means to cause, cease or prevent a violation (e.g. international sanctions, or power over vital resources). It is important to note that the use of the term 'extraterritoriality' in this regard can be misleading because the link necessary to consider that a situation is taking place within a state's extended 'jurisdiction' detaches that same situation from the place where it actually occurs. This is not a purely academic point. It introduces, in fact, an important nuance as to how questions of 'extraterritoriality' arise in the human rights context, which significantly differs from the way in which they arise in other contexts. In the human rights context a state is made responsible for what happens abroad, whereas in most other contexts a state claims the power to regulate what happens abroad. I will come back to this distinction later in the chapter.

As for the particular context with respect to which the implications of such understanding will be spelt out, I will focus on the prevention of environmental

* I am grateful to Nehal Bhuta for valuable comments on an earlier version of this chapter. I would also like to thank Jessica Allemann and Maria de la Colina for excellent research assistance in preparing this chapter.

threats and harm. I chose this context on the basis of three considerations. Firstly, a detailed analysis of the extraterritorial scope of human rights obligations is provided in the other chapters included in this volume. Secondly, the implications of this question for environmental protection have received scant attention so far.[1] Thirdly, extraterritorial environmental protection is likely to gain increasing importance in the future as a result of a lack of general agreement among states on how to address global environmental issues through multilateral treaties or, and relatedly, of the broad manner in which such treaties may have to be formulated to accommodate markedly different positions.

Combining this specific context with the above understanding, the question addressed in this chapter can be formulated as follows: what are the implications of the extraterritorial scope of human rights obligations for the power or duty of states to prevent harm to the environment of other states or areas beyond national jurisdiction? It is necessary to note two important considerations when exploring this question. First of all, I will not discuss the more traditional issue of unilateral state action to protect itself from transboundary environmental injury.[2] Despite its practical importance, the relevance of the extraterritorial scope of human rights obligations for this form of environmental regulation is limited. The second consideration concerns the need to take into account a wide array of norms, treaties and legally linked systems of treaties normally organized under different 'branches' of international law. The pedagogical but artificial distinctions among different 'branches' of international law must be overcome if one is to understand how different norms and treaties apply together to a given question.[3] Let us then become 'colour-blind', oblivious to whether a norm or a treaty is traditionally classified under one or another 'branch' of international law, in order to understand how norms derived from different areas come together to address the above question.

In line with this approach, the analysis is organized from the perspective of a state which adopts measures to prevent environmental harm beyond its territory. It is, in fact, a human rights approach to extraterritorial environmental protection. From a policy perspective, such an approach is most appropriately characterized as a tactic. Referring to human rights in a variety of difficult environmental debates, such as biodiversity loss or climate change, may be a useful tactic for three main reasons:[4] (i) the holders of human rights are numerous and can be specifically identified as individuals, whereas the protection of the environment does not allow a clear 'right-holder' to be identified;[5] (ii) such numerous and specifically identifiable right-holders

[1] Alan Boyle is correct when he notes that commentators have so far overlooked this important question. See Boyle, 'Human Rights and the Environment: Where Next?', 23 *European Journal of International Law (EJIL)* (2012) 613, at 637.

[2] See Bilder, 'The Role of Unilateral State Action in Preventing International Environmental Injury', 14 *Vanderbilt Journal of Transnational Law* (1981) 51.

[3] See Viñuales, 'Cartographies imaginaires: Observations sur la portée juridique du concept de "régime spécial" en droit international', 140 *Journal du droit international (Clunet)* (2013) 405.

[4] See P.-M. Dupuy and J. E. Viñuales, *International Environmental Law* (2015), ch. 10.

[5] This is why the Institut de Droit International has proposed the creation of a 'High Commissioner for the Environment' who would act for the 'international community' in the context of responsibility and liability claims. See Art. 28, 'Responsibility and Liability under International Law for Environmental Damage', *Annuaire de l'Institut de droit international* (1997) (Session of Strasbourg).

can bring a claim before a growing number of adjudicatory and quasi-adjudicatory bodies, including, *inter alia*, regional courts and committees, which are more sophisticated than those available in international environmental law;[6] and (iii) human rights are perceived, at least for now, as having a higher value and, as a result, having a stronger social and political pull than pure environmental considerations.[7]

In what follows, I first look at the scope for a human rights approach to extraterritorial environmental protection. In this regard, in Section 2, I draw a distinction between 'principal' (inter-state and multilateral) and 'ancillary' (unilateral and extraterritorial) regulatory approaches and clarify the type of unilateral environmental measures that are most directly concerned by the extraterritorial scope of human rights. The legal analysis proper is undertaken in Section 3, which aims to identify different ways in which such extraterritorial environmental action can be justified in international law, with specific reference to the extraterritorial scope of human rights obligations. I then turn to a number of specific illustrations in order to assess the operation of extraterritorial human rights in a variety of contexts in Section 4. Finally, these steps provide the basis for my overall assessment of a potential human rights approach to extraterritorial environmental protection in Section 5.

2. Scope for a Human Rights Approach to Extraterritorial Environmental Protection

A. Principal versus Ancillary Regulatory Approaches

The principal means for addressing global environmental problems is admittedly international cooperation aimed at developing a multilateral negotiated regime. This is by now almost an article of faith. My intention here is not to break away from it, but simply to clarify the room left for a human rights approach to extraterritorial environmental protection.

From a theoretical standpoint, a multilateral cooperative approach is preferable because it avoids a sub-optimal scenario (e.g. the 2/2 'Nash equilibrium' in the prisoner's dilemma) and allows for an optimal one (e.g. a 3/3 equilibrium achieved through cooperation in repeated games). How and under what conditions cooperation can achieve a better result has been studied at length in the political science literature, and the arguments are sufficiently known among social scientists and lawyers not to call for further comment here.[8]

[6] See A. Boyle and M. Anderson (eds), *Human Rights Approaches to Environmental Protection* (1996).

[7] See Shelton, 'Substantive Rights', in M. Fitzmaurice, D. Ong and P. Merkouris (eds), *Research Handbook on International Environmental Law* (2010) 265, particularly at 265–266.

[8] See among many others: R. Axelrod, *The Evolution of Cooperation* (1984) (explaining how in a repeated prisoner's dilemma game—which may provide a good approximation to the situation in which states negotiate some environmental treaties—the best strategy is 'tit-for-tat', namely to start by cooperating in the first round and then do what the other did in the previous round); U. Luterbacher and D. Sprinz (eds), *International Relations and Climate Change* (2001) (applying game theoretical

From a legal perspective, the preference given to inter-state cooperative approaches is pervasive in declarations, treaties and decisions from courts and tribunals, even before the Stockholm Conference on the Human Environment in 1972, which placed environmental concerns within the remit of the United Nations (UN).[9] More specifically, there is a legal obligation to cooperate in good faith and such obligation is fully applicable to environmental problems.[10] An early statement of this general obligation appears in the decision of the International Court of Justice (ICJ) in the *North Sea Continental Shelf* cases:

> [T]he parties are under an obligation to enter into negotiations with a view to arriving at an agreement, and not merely to go through a formal process of negotiation as a sort of prior condition for the automatic application of a certain method of delimitation in the absence of agreement; they are under an obligation so to conduct themselves that the negotiations are meaningful, which will not be the case when either of them insists upon its own position without contemplating any modification of it.[11]

The roots of this obligation are deep and can be traced back not only to the Charter of the United Nations, particularly Article 33, but also to the practice of the Permanent Court of International Justice (PCIJ), the ICJ's predecessor.[12] In a specifically environmental context, references to an inter-state obligation to cooperate appear in several cases, including some cases that were decided prior to 1972. For example, in the *Lake Lanoux* case, the arbitral tribunal rejected Spain's argument that France was under an obligation not to alter the water flow of the River Carol and added:

> States are today perfectly conscious of the importance of the conflicting interests brought into play by the industrial use of international rivers, and of the necessity to reconcile them by mutual concessions. The only way to arrive at such compromises of interests is to conclude agreements on an increasingly comprehensive basis.[13]

More recently, the obligation of cooperation has been reaffirmed by the ICJ in the *Pulp Mills* case concerning the River Uruguay. In this case, the Court derived a

approaches to modelize climate change negotiations); E. Ostrom, *Governing the Commons: The Evolution of Institutions for Collective Action* (1990) (surveying and analysing an array of cooperation techniques used in practice to manage common resources).

[9] On this conference see Kiss and Sicault, 'La Conférence des Nations Unies sur l'environnement (Stockholm, 5–16 June 1972)', 18 *Annuaire français de droit international* (1972) 603; Kennet, 'The Stockholm Conference on the Human Environment', 48 *International Affairs* (1972) 33.

[10] On the duty to cooperate on environmental matters in a transboundary context see Francioni and Neuhold, 'International Cooperation for the Protection of the Environment: The Procedural Dimension', in W. Lang, H. Neuhold and K. Zemanek (eds), *Environmental Protection and International Law* (1991) 203; Boisson de Chazournes and Sangbana, 'Principle 19: Notification and Consultation on Activities with Transboundary Impact', in J. E. Viñuales (ed.), *The Rio Declaration on Environment and Development. A Commentary* (2015) 493.

[11] *North Sea Continental Shelf Case*, Judgment, 20 February 1969, ICJ Reports (1969) 3, at para. 85.

[12] See ibid. at paras 86–87 (examining, *inter alia*, several precedents in the jurisprudence of the Permanent Court of International Justice).

[13] *Lake Lanoux Arbitration (Spain v. France)*, Award, 16 November 1957, XII *Reports of International Arbitral Awards* (2006) 281, at para. 13.

specific consequence from this broad obligation, namely that 'as long as the procedural mechanism for cooperation between the parties to prevent significant damage to one of them is taking its course, the State initiating the planned activity is obliged not to authorize such work and, *a fortiori*, not to carry it out'.[14]

However, in all these cases, what is at stake is not specifically the duty to cooperate multilaterally to address a global problem but simply an obligation to cooperate, which is sometimes narrowed down to starting negotiations in good faith, in a transboundary context. When one moves from such a transboundary narrow context to broader regional or global environmental problems, the legal grounds of the duty to cooperate become less clear.

This is not to say that international law does not favour multilateral cooperative solutions to global environmental problems but only that the legal foundations for such a policy preference are for the time being less solid. One potential basis in this regard is provided by the first sentence of Principle 7 of the Rio Declaration, according to which '[s]tates shall cooperate in a spirit of global partnership to conserve, protect and restore the health and integrity of the Earth's ecosystem'.[15] Principle 12 also states a clear preference for multilateral approaches in the specific context of trade: 'Unilateral actions to deal with environmental challenges outside the jurisdiction of the importing country should be avoided. Environmental measures addressing transboundary or global environmental problems should, as far as possible, be based on an international consensus.'[16] Principle 27 is perhaps the most general exhortation to pursue a multilateral approach: 'States and people shall cooperate in good faith and in a spirit of partnership in the fulfilment of the principles embodied in this Declaration and in the further development of international law in the field of sustainable development.'[17]

Interestingly, this principle is not confined to inter-state cooperation and also encompasses cooperation involving 'people'. The legal grounds for such a duty of cooperation is not entirely clear. One possibility would be to link it to the 'public trust doctrine', as suggested by Peter Sand.[18] Another possibility would be to link it to a number of programmatic principles or concepts, such as those of 'common concern of mankind', 'common heritage of mankind', 'common but differentiated responsibilities' of states or, more generally, the 'differential treatment' that may be accorded to states on the basis of their particular situation.[19] Some judicial decisions have also made reference, either implicitly or explicitly, to a preference

[14] *Pulp Mills on the River Uruguay (Argentina v. Uruguay)*, Judgment, 20 April 2010, ICJ Reports (2010) 14, at para. 144.

[15] Rio Declaration on Environment and Development, UN Doc. A/CONF.151/26.Rev.1, 13 June 1992.

[16] On this principle see Young, 'Principle 12: The Environment and Trade', in Viñuales, *supra* note 10, 325.

[17] On this principle see Sand, 'Principle 27: Cooperation in a Spirit of Global Partnership', in Viñuales, *supra* note 10, 617.

[18] Ibid.

[19] Commission on Sustainable Development, Report of the Expert Group Meeting on Identification of Principles of International Law for Sustainable Development, Geneva, Switzerland, 26–28 September 1995, at paras 75–102.

for multilateral inter-state cooperation. In a pending dispute between Costa Rica and Nicaragua, the ICJ encouraged the parties to cooperate through the Secretariat of the Ramsar Convention,[20] a multilateral environmental agreement, in order to prevent harm to a wetland of international importance.[21] Although this is an example of bilateral cooperation on a transboundary issue, the fact that the Court expects the parties to articulate their cooperation through the Ramsar Convention's Secretariat suggests a preference for bringing the multilateral approach to bear on the issue. A clearer expression of a preference for inter-state multilateral solutions can be found in the case-law of the World Trade Organization (WTO) dispute settlement body. In the well-known *Shrimp-Turtle* case, the WTO Appellate Body viewed the lack of serious attempts by the United States to address the environmental problem at hand through diplomacy, rather than unilateral action, as an indication that the measure was a discriminatory and unjustifiable restriction to international trade.[22]

These and other decisions lend some support to a legal preference for inter-state multilateral approaches to environmental problems, but one should not overestimate the scope of such preference. A state is not legally bound to develop or participate in a multilateral environmental agreement or to refrain generally from taking unilateral action. Multilateral approaches are favoured because they establish a level playing field and set ex ante parameters for state action in pursuance of a set of agreed goals and, as the case may be, through a set of agreed means. Yet, unilateral action remains not only frequent in practice but also important to achieve environmental protection goals. Commentators have referred to several goals potentially pursued by unilateral action, ranging from responding to a domestic political constituency, to creating momentum for the development of a multilateral regime, to strengthening such a regime's operation.[23] These and other goals may be pursued separately or jointly by unilateral action. However, from an analytical standpoint, it is important to clarify what type of 'unilateral action' is at stake.

B. Types of Unilateral Environmental Action

Several classifications of unilateral environmental regulation have been advanced in the literature. Here, I review only those that I find useful for present purposes.

One taxonomy is provided by Richard Bilder, who identifies five forms of unilateral environmental action:[24] (i) action primarily intended to address domestic environmental problems; (ii) action primarily intended to protect the territory of

[20] Convention on Wetlands of International Importance especially as Waterfowl Habitat 1971, 996 UNTS 245, 2 February 1971.

[21] *Certain Activities Carried Out by Nicaragua in the Border Area (Costa Rica v. Nicaragua)*, Order, 8 March 2011, ICJ Reports 2011 6, at paras 80 and 86(2).

[22] WTO, *United States—Import Prohibition of Certain Shrimp and Shrimp Products*, Report of the Appellate Body (12 October 1998) WT/DS58/AB/R, paras 167–169.

[23] See Bodansky, 'What's So Bad About Unilateral Action to Protect the Environment', 11 *EJIL* (2000) 339; Boisson de Chazournes, 'Unilateralism and Environmental Protection: Issues of Perception and Reality of Issues', 11 *EJIL* (2000) 315.

[24] Bilder, *supra* note 2, at 59 ff.

other states, or individuals based therein, from environmental threats arising from the regulating state; (iii) action primarily intended to protect common areas, including international air space or the high seas, from environmental threats arising from the regulating state; (iv) action primarily intended to protect the territory and population of the regulating state from environmental threats arising from abroad; and (v) action primarily intended to protect other states or common areas from threats arising from abroad. According to Bilder, these hypotheses differ because in the first three cases the environmental threat arises in the regulating state, whereas in the latter two it arises from the activities conducted abroad. Bilder concludes that, to the extent that only the latter two types of unilateral action target entities and activities based beyond the territory of the regulating state, these raise the most difficult questions. He therefore focuses on these two forms of unilateral action. It is important to note, however, that these two forms of unilateral action by the regulating state are not directly influenced by the extraterritorial scope of human rights norms. In the context of Bilder's taxonomy, the extension of human rights norms is mostly important for categories (ii) and (iii). Indeed, it is the regulating state's potential responsibility for the effects of the environmental threats arising from its territory that could justify an expansion of the concept of 'jurisdiction' to attribute to it the ensuing human rights violations. As noted in the introduction, we must look at the extent to which a state can be made responsible for what happens abroad, which is different from the extent of the state's power to regulate what happens abroad. Of course, if a state has a duty arising from human rights to regulate what happens abroad, it may also claim a power to do so based on this duty. However, this distinction remains important from an analytical standpoint because depending on the focus the type of unilateral action at stake will not be the same and, more fundamentally, because there is a clear distinction between obligation and mere authorization to act.

Another taxonomy advanced by Daniel Bodansky seeks to capture the extent to which action, or inaction, can be considered 'unilateral' or 'multilateral'. He distinguishes four degrees:[25] (i) measures that are unilateral in their basis and their objective (presumably this means that there is neither an international norm requiring or authorizing the measure, nor one identifying the goal pursued by the measure as one pursued by the international community); (ii) measures that are unilateral in their basis but not in their objective; (iii) measures to enforce an international environmental norm that does not specify the means of its implementation; and (iv) measures to enforce an international environmental norm which specifies its means of enforcement. This taxonomy is perhaps less waterproof from an analytical perspective but it has the merit of highlighting the need to clarify the relationship between international environmental norms and domestic environmental measures. Like Bilder, Bodansky has in mind a situation quite different from the one targeted by the discussions regarding the extraterritorial scope of human rights obligations. The international norms he refers to are primarily inter-state environmental obligations. He is not concerned with the duty of states to prevent

[25] See Bodansky, *supra* note 23, at 342 ff.

human rights violations abroad arising from the environmental threats under their control.

Still another classification, this time specifically focusing on human rights-related issues, has been provided by Jennifer Zerk in a report on extraterritorial jurisdiction prepared to inform the work of the UN Special Representative on Business and Human Rights.[26] Aside from the traditional categories of 'prescriptive', 'adjudicative' and 'enforcement' jurisdiction, which she incorporates into her analysis, Zerk makes a useful distinction between 'direct extraterritorial jurisdiction' and 'domestic measures with extraterritorial implications'. The latter category seeks to highlight the extraterritorial dimension of domestic regulatory action adopted by a major market, such as the United States or the European Union. Such action may condition access to a major market upon the satisfaction of certain requirements. Although purely domestic in appearance, the importance of operating in such a market may lead companies to comply with the foreign regulation. In some controversial cases, such incentive may even place a foreign company in a dilemma between, on the one hand, complying with the market's regulation and, on the other hand, respecting the laws of the country where it is based. Another hypothesis covered by this category concerns domestic regulation that targets a locally incorporated parent company and requires it to apply the same standards to its foreign subsidiaries or even its subcontractors. This is particularly important in the context of extraterritorial human rights obligations as the 'jurisdiction' of the regulating state could arguably be extended by virtue of its legal powers over parent companies, which would, in turn, have significant influence over the activities of their subsidiaries and subcontractors. Yet, again, there may be controversial cases where the home country requirements collide with the host country requirements.

The insights derived from these three taxonomies can be combined to further specify the measures analysed in this chapter. I will focus on categories (ii) and (iii) of Bilder's analysis as well as on his category (i) when such measures have extraterritorial implications as characterized by Zerk. These three types of measures will be considered only when they are sufficiently unilateral, namely under Bodansky's first three degrees, but to the exclusion of cases where the measure is multilaterally defined in both the objective and the means of implementation. Summing up, my analysis of implications of the extraterritorial scope of human rights on environmental protection will focus on: (a) domestic environmental measures with extraterritorial implications; (b) measures primarily intended to protect the territory of other states, or individuals based therein, from environmental threats under the control of the regulating state; and (c) measures primarily intended to protect common areas from environmental threats under the control of the regulating state. These are, in my view, the measures most directly influenced by the recognition of the extraterritorial scope of human rights.

[26] See Zerk, 'Extraterritorial Jurisdiction: Lessons for the Business and Human Rights Sphere from Six Regulatory Areas', *Corporate Social Responsibility Initiative Working Paper No. 59* (2009), at 14 ff.

3. Legal Foundations of a Human Rights Approach to Extraterritorial Environmental Protection

A. Extraterritorial Action Between Principle and Exception

The normative space in which the analysis of human rights approaches to extraterritorial environmental protection must be conducted is provided by general international law. The question of extraterritorial jurisdiction in this broader context has been approached in two main ways, which basically differ on whether extraterritorial jurisdiction is seen as the principle (only limited by certain exceptions) or the exception (requiring some identifiable legal basis).

The traditional approach, deeply embedded in classic international law, was expounded by the PCIJ in the famous *Lotus* case:

> Far from laying down a general prohibition to the effect that States may not extend the application of their laws and the jurisdiction of their courts to persons, property and acts outside their territory, it [international law] leaves them in this respect a wide measure of discretion which is only limited in certain cases by prohibitive rules.[27]

The statement of the Court is limited in several respects. Firstly, read in its context, the reference to 'outside their territory' means an extension to cover an event occurring in the high seas, an area beyond national jurisdiction. Secondly, the Court refers to the application of laws (prescriptive jurisdiction) or the jurisdiction of courts (which encompasses prescriptive jurisdiction extending the power of a court to hear cases with extraterritorial components and court proceedings in the regulating state). Acts of enforcement abroad are therefore not covered. An exercise of public authority in the territory of another country would clearly be a violation of territorial sovereignty. The main question that remains open concerns the possibility for a state to exercise public authority, namely enforcement acts, in a common area and, more specifically, whether such acts could be performed as a matter of principle or as a matter of exception requiring a specific basis.

In the view of many commentators, including judges of the ICJ, the *Lotus* approach must be confined to its specific factual configuration and should not be taken as a reflection of the current state of general international law on extraterritorial jurisdiction. The question was discussed in several dissenting or separate opinions appended to the ICJ's *Advisory Opinion on the Legality of the Threat or the Use of Nuclear Weapons*.[28] Several judges questioned the contemporary relevance of the *Lotus* decision. President Bedjaoui noted in his own vote that:

> The resolutely positivist, voluntarist approach of international law still current at the beginning of the century—and which the Permanent Court did not fail to endorse in the aforementioned Judgment [in the *Lotus* case]—has been replaced by an objective

[27] *SS Lotus (France v. Turkey)*, 1927 PCIJ Series A, No. 10, at 18–19.

[28] *Legality of the Threat or Use of Nuclear Weapons*, Advisory Opinion, 8 July 1996, ICJ Reports (1996) 226.

conception of international law, a law more readily seeking to reflect a collective juridical conscience and respond to the social necessities of States organized as a community.[29]

Judge Weeramantry discussed this question in some detail. Although his main point was to contextualize the *Lotus* decision and distinguish it from the nuclear weapons question, particularly in connection with the application of international humanitarian law, parts of his dissenting opinion are apposite for the analysis of our own question. According to Judge Weeramantry:

> It is to be noted also that just four years earlier [than the *Lotus* decision], the Permanent Court, in dealing with the question of State sovereignty, had observed in *Nationality Decrees Issued in Tunis and Morocco* that the sovereignty of States would be proportionately diminished and restricted as international law developed... In the half century that has elapsed since the '*Lotus*' case, it is quite evident that international law—and the law relating to humanitarian conduct in war—have developed considerably, imposing additional restrictions on State sovereignty over and above those that existed at the time of the '*Lotus*' case. This Court's own jurisprudence in the *Corfu Channel* case sees customary international law as imposing a duty on all States so to conduct their affairs as not to injure others, even though there was no prohibition *ipsissimis verbis* of the particular act which constituted a violation of the complaining nation's rights. This Court cannot in 1996 construe '*Lotus*' so narrowly as to take the law backward in time even beyond the Martens Clause.[30]

Six years later, in a joint separate opinion appended to the judgment of the ICJ in the *Arrest Warrant* case, Judges Higgins, Kooijmans and Buergenthal took the position with respect to the aforementioned *dictum* made in the *Lotus* case that '[t]he application of this celebrated dictum would have clear attendant dangers in some fields of international law... the dictum represents the high water mark of laissez-faire in international relations, and an era that has been significantly overtaken by other tendencies'.[31]

There is little point in multiplying the references expressing doubt as to the contemporary relevance of the *Lotus* approach to extraterritorial jurisdiction. In fact, whether one considers that extraterritorial jurisdiction is the principle or the exception in general international law, it seems clear that a human rights violation cannot be deemed to occur under the extended 'jurisdiction' of a state unless there is a link justifying such extension. From a legal standpoint, the question then becomes: what could be the basis for linking an environmental threat arising from a state and the human rights violations it causes abroad? The 'link' or 'connecting factor' bringing environmental harm on individuals located abroad under the 'jurisdiction' of the state in which the environmental threat originates is of a composite nature: it targets specific factual configurations that may be covered by one or more norms at the same time. There are two types of international norms that can perform this function: either inter-state obligations generally relating to the idea of prevention

[29] Ibid., Declaration of President Bedjaoui, at para. 13.

[30] Ibid., Dissenting Opinion of Judge Weeramantry, at 495–496.

[31] See *Arrest Warrant of 11 April 2000 (Democratic Republic of the Congo v. Belgium)*, Judgment, 14 February 2002, ICJ Reports (2002) 3, Joint Separate Opinion of Judges Higgins, Kooijmams and Buergenthal, at paras 50–51.

of environmental harm, or human rights obligations with environmental components. In what follows, after some conceptual clarifications on the relations between these two types of norms, I analyse the prospects for the recognition of a 'link' capable of bringing under a state's jurisdiction human rights violations occurring abroad as a result of pollution originating in said state. Finally, I explore the potential and limitations arising from the recognition of this link to the development of human rights approaches to extraterritorial environmental protection.

B. Prevention Obligations and Environmental Rights: Two Faces of the Same Coin?

The analysis of the connection between inter-state prevention obligations and human rights norms with environmental components is not only conceptually useful to understand how the two can strengthen each other, it is also tactically important.

Despite the considerable number of inter-state environmental obligations, mostly based on treaty law with some based on customary law, these are often perceived as lacking traction or, at least, as having less traction than human rights provisions. I have already mentioned the main reasons explaining the appeal of human rights approaches to environmental protection. They are related to agency (human rights have specific—and most often specifically affected—right-holders), institution availability (human rights have better mechanisms for their enforcement) and perception (human rights can add a sense of urgency to environmental protection). This is also true when two norms, such as an inter-state environmental obligation and a human right provision, require fundamentally similar conduct from a state. Thus, in analysing the synergies in content of environmental norms and human rights norms, my main purpose is to add traction to the former by spelling out the impact of the latter. I should include one additional nuance, namely that, from a strictly legal perspective, it matters little whether a given norm is classified under 'human rights law' or 'environmental law' as a branch of law. What matters is the scope of application and the ensuing legal effects. Let me discuss this point in more detail.

To reiterate, the starting point of the analysis is the type of action under consideration in this chapter: (i) domestic environmental measures with extraterritorial implications; (ii) measures primarily intended to protect the territory of other states, or individuals based therein, from environmental threats under the control of the regulating state; and (iii) measures primarily intended to protect common areas from environmental threats under the control of the regulating state. States can and do refer to inter-state environmental obligations to justify the legality of their extraterritorial environmental action. Most often, they do so to justify the protection of their own environment from external threats,[32] but they

[32] Such were the measures adopted by the EC (a moratorium on the commercialisation of GMOs) and some European countries (adopting sanitary and phytosanitary measures) in WTO, *European*

also refer to inter-state environmental obligations to justify action preventing harm to the environment abroad.[33] The latter hypothesis is the one that must retain our attention. The most representative norm requiring prevention of environmental harm abroad is the prevention principle stated in Principle 21 of the Stockholm Declaration on the Human Environment[34] and Principle 2 of the Rio Declaration on Environment and Development.[35] The customary basis of this principle was recognized by the ICJ in its *Advisory Opinion on the Legality of Nuclear Weapons*, where the Court stated that states have a general obligation 'to ensure that activities within their jurisdiction and control respect the environment of other States or of areas beyond national control is now part of the corpus of international law relating to the environment'.[36] The ICJ further referred to this principle in the *Gabčíkovo-Nagymaros* case, according to which:

> [I]n the field of environmental protection, vigilance and prevention are required on account of the often irreversible character of damage to the environment and of the limitations inherent in the very mechanism of reparation of this type of damage.[37]

More recently, in the *Pulp Mills* case, the ICJ further confirmed this principle and spelt out its origins in the 'no harm' principle.[38] Accordingly, there is no doubt that states have an inter-state (horizontal) obligation to take measures in order to prevent harm to the environment abroad arising from the activities conducted under their control. The more difficult question is: what is the extent of this obligation? This question can be approached from two perspectives.

The first is the perspective currently adopted by most tribunals, policy instruments and commentators, and it consists in looking only at inter-state norms defining the level of 'due diligence' required from a state. This perspective is epitomized by the International Law Commission's 2001 draft articles on the Prevention of Transboundary Harm from Hazardous Activities,[39] which neglect the role of human rights in environmental protection. In the *Pulp Mills* case, the ICJ followed a similar perspective in clarifying the level of due diligence expected from states. Although the Court's analysis relates to the provisions of the Statute of the River Uruguay, its reasoning suggests that the prevention principle requires

Communities—Measures Affecting the Approval and Marketing of Biotech Products, Panel Report (29 September 2006) WT/DS291/R, WT/DS292/R, WT/DS293/R.

33 See e.g. WTO, *Shrimp–Turtle* case, *supra* note 22 (where the US referred to the CITES to justify measures to protect turtles located beyond their territory); Case C-366/10, *Air Transport Association of America and Others v. Secretary of State for Energy and Climate Change*, [2011] ECR I-13755 (ECLI: EU:C:2011:864) (where the EU referred to several inter-state norms to justify the extension of the Emissions Trading Directive to the aviation sector).

34 Declaration of the United Nations Conference on the Human Environment, UN Doc. A/CONF 48/14/Rev.1, 16 June 1972 (Stockholm Declaration).

35 Rio Declaration, *supra* note 15.

36 *Legality of Nuclear Weapons*, *supra* note 28, para. 29.

37 *Gabčíkovo-Nagymaros Project (Hungary/Slovakia)*, Judgment, 25 September 1997, ICJ Reports (1997) 7, at para. 140.

38 *Pulp Mills*, *supra* note 14, paras 101 and 185.

39 Draft Articles on the Prevention of Transboundary Harm from Hazardous Activities, UN Doc. A/56/10 (2001).

(i) an obligation of conduct and, more specifically, of cooperation for the implementation and application of appropriate measures for the preservation of the environment[40] and (ii) the obligation to conduct an environmental impact assessment where the proposed activity is likely to have a significant adverse impact in a transboundary context, especially with respect to a shared resource.[41] The measures required by the prevention principle are, mostly, of a purely domestic nature. They seek to regulate potential sources of environmental harm within the territory or under the control of the regulating state. It is only insofar as they do so to avoid causing harm to the environment abroad that they may be said to have an extraterritorial dimension. However, their extraterritorial dimension becomes clearer—and closer to the extended 'jurisdiction' that counts as extraterritoriality in the human rights context—in connection with activities in common areas but under the control of the regulating state. This broader dimension of the prevention principle with respect to the environment in common areas had already been recognized in the *Advisory Opinion on the Legality of Nuclear Weapons.* Despite this, the level of due diligence required in this respect was only clarified from an inter-state perspective in 2010 in the Advisory Opinion of the Seabed Chamber of the International Tribunal on the Law of the Sea (ITLOS) on the *Responsibilities and Obligations of States Sponsoring Persons and Entities with Respect to Activities in the Area.*[42] The Seabed Chamber specifically refers to paragraph 187 of the *Pulp Mills* decision in order to characterize the obligation 'to ensure' arising from Article 139(1) of UN Convention on the Law of the Sea (UNCLOS)[43] as an obligation 'of conduct' or 'due diligence'.[44] According to the Seabed Chamber, the 'due diligence' obligation encompasses: (i) the obligation of states to adopt appropriate measures and ensure that they are reasonably enforced;[45] (ii) the obligation (based both on the UNCLOS and customary international law) to conduct an environmental impact assessment;[46] and (iii) the obligation to apply the precautionary approach not only as a requirement of the applicable regulations of the Seabed Authority but also as a component of the 'due diligence' obligation and, possibly, of customary international law.[47] Although more clearly extraterritorial, as states are deemed to be potentially responsible for the activities of their sponsored entities operating in the global commons, human rights are not brought into the picture.

Let me now turn to the second perspective concerning the extent of the prevention obligation. Two reminders are necessary in order to grasp its contours.

[40] *Pulp Mills, supra* note 14, paras 102, 181–189. [41] Ibid., para. 204.

[42] *Responsibilities and Obligations of States Sponsoring Persons and Entities with Respect to Activities in the Area*, Advisory Opinion of 1 February 2011, ITLOS Reports (2011) 10.

[43] United Nations Convention on the Law of the Sea 1982, 1833 UNTS 397.

[44] *Advisory Opinion on the Area, supra* note 42, paras 110–111.

[45] Ibid., at para. 115 (referring to the interpretation of the obligation of 'due diligence' provided by the ICJ in the *Pulp Mills* case), para. 116 (referring to the ILC Project on Prevention) and paras 117–120 (referring in para. 120 to the more detailed answer given by the Chamber in response to the third question put to it).

[46] Ibid., at para. 145. [47] Ibid., at paras 125–135, particularly at paras 131 and 135.

One is simply that we should not pay attention to the 'branch' under which a given norm may traditionally be classified. The other is the additional traction that human rights approaches can add to the goals pursued by inter-state environmental obligations. With these two reminders in mind, one may ask what norms of international law, irrespective of their origin, may oblige a state to prevent activities under its control from causing environmental harm abroad. Inter-state environmental obligations would still feature as part of the answer but, in addition, the duty of states not to allow activities under their control to cause violations of human rights under their extended jurisdiction would also come into play.

One potential objection that must be addressed before proceeding further is the exclusion of human rights norms on the grounds that inter-state environmental norms would apply as *lex specialis*. This objection, anticipated—and discarded—by Alan Boyle in his illuminating account of the relations between human rights and environmental law,[48] has a thin legal basis. Firstly, while the debtor of the obligation is the same, the right-holder is not (in the inter-state norm it is the other state, whereas in human rights it is the individual). Secondly, it is unlikely that environmental norms would in all events trump human rights. The latter would likely prevail on the basis of the principle of *lex superior*. Thirdly, even if the environmental norm does apply as *lex specialis*, this is not to say that human rights norms would be excluded *ipso facto*. The principle of *lex specialis* does not necessarily displace *in toto* the more general norm.[49] It is rather a question of how the two norms capture the different aspects of a situation considered as a unit for analytical purposes. Fourthly, at the very least, human rights should be taken into account to interpret the environmental norms, much as the latter are taken into account when interpreting the former in the practice of human rights courts. Fifthly, environmental norms tend to be regarded as ancillary norms for the regulation of different types of activities, including international trade, foreign investment, or the conduct of hostilities. This would be difficult to conciliate with an approach whereby, suddenly, environmental norms are considered specific and exclusive, particularly in connection with harm caused to individuals. Sixthly, in reality these types of conflicts would arise before human rights courts and not in—yet to be developed—environmental courts. The use of human rights mechanisms is a key reason why human rights approaches to environmental protection are pursued, and it is highly unlikely that a human rights body would conclude that an inter-state environmental norm excludes the application of a human rights norm. Thus, the *lex specialis* objection has a thin legal, and common sense, basis. The question is not which norm, but which *norms* apply and how they come into play to govern a given factual configuration.

In their contemporary understanding, human rights entail three types of correlative obligations from states, namely to respect, to protect from deprivation (by

[48] Boyle, *supra* note 1, at 634.

[49] *Conclusions of the Work of the Study Group on the Fragmentation of International Law: Difficulties Arising from the Diversification and Expansion of International Law*, UN Doc. A/61/10 (2006), available online at http://daccess-dds-ny.un.org/doc/UNDOC/GEN/G06/636/20/PDF/G0663620.pdf?OpenElement (last accessed 23 July 2015), para. 251.

third parties) and to fulfil.[50] The obligations to respect and protect from deprivation have been elaborated in some detail by human rights bodies, including in an environmental context.[51] The extraterritorial scope of human rights obligations has mostly been recognized in connection with state obligations to respect the human rights of individuals who, despite being located abroad, are deemed to be under the state's extended jurisdiction. However, there is no obstacle, as a matter of principle, for such extension to operate for other types of obligation, in particular to protect from deprivation resulting from the act of third parties, such as polluters based in the regulating state's territory.

For those sensitive to this second perspective the question of what would be the contours of a combined assessment of a state's duty to prevent environmental harm abroad can now be concisely answered. It would have the three dimensions of the prevention principle: (i) the right for a state to exploit its natural resources, conditioned on the obligation to ensure that activities under its jurisdiction or control respect (ii) the environment of other states, and (iii) the environment beyond national jurisdiction. But it would be strengthened because the exercise of due diligence by the state would apply (iv) to the respect of the environment abroad for the additional reason that this may be necessary to comply with the extraterritorial human rights obligations owed to individuals abroad.

The latter point is the main implication of the extraterritorial scope of human rights obligations for environmental protection. Of course, such an assemblage of norms can only operate under certain conditions, in particular that the state must be bound by both norms and that the power over the source of environmental harm must be considered as sufficient to extend the jurisdiction of the state under human rights instruments. Although the latter link has not been recognized yet, its recognition would heavily depend upon the environmental scope of the rights granted. Such scope can, in turn, be expanded either through law-making processes or through systemic interpretation techniques, such as referring to environmental norms, in accordance with Article 31(3)(c) of the Vienna Convention on the Law of Treaties.[52] In the next section, I analyse the prospects for the recognition of a 'link' capable of extending the jurisdiction of a state for violations of environmental rights abroad.

[50] On this influential conceptualisation see: H. Shue, *Basic Rights: Subsistence, Affluence and U.S. Foreign Policy* (1980); Report on the Right to Adequate Food as a Human Right. Final Report Presented by the Special Rapporteur Asbjørn Eide, UN Doc. E/CN.4/Sub.2/1987/23, 7 July 1987, paras 66–69; Committee on Economic, Social and Cultural Rights, General Comment No. 12: The Right to Adequate Food (Art. 11), UN Doc. E/C.12/1999/5, 12 May 1999, para. 15; Human Rights Committee (HRC), General Comment No. 6: Art. 6 (Right to Life), UN Doc. HRI/GEN/1/Rev.9 (Vol. I), 30 April 1982, paras 3–5; Koch, 'Dichotomies, Trichotomies or Waves of Duties?', 5 *Human Rights Law Review* (2005) 81.

[51] See, e.g. African Commission on Human and Peoples' Rights, *Social and Economic Rights Action Center (SERAC) and Others v. Nigeria*, Comm. no. 155/96, 27 October 2001 (*Ogoni* case), paras 44–47 (structuring this set of obligations as four duties). The African Commissions Communications are available online at http://www.achpr.org/communications (last accessed 23 July 2015).

[52] Vienna Convention on the Law of Treaties 1969, 1155 UNTS 331.

C. The 'Link' Between Human Rights and Extraterritorial Environmental Degradation

1. Two Meanings of the 'Link' Requirement

For environmental degradation to amount to a violation of a human right, adjudicatory and quasi-adjudicatory bodies require the existence of a link between these two terms. More specifically, a link must be established between an act or an omission of a state, environmental degradation, and serious and direct harm to an individual. Such is the conventional understanding of the 'link' requirement in the relations between human rights and environmental protection.[53] However, in the context of the extraterritorial extension of human rights obligations, the 'link' requirement has a different meaning. It seeks to establish a sufficient connection, or a connecting factor, between the acts or omissions of a state and environment-related harm suffered by individuals located abroad. In the domestic context the link refers principally, albeit not exclusively,[54] to a matter of causality, whereas in the extraterritorial context one has to also accommodate the existence of human rights obligations of the foreign state where the harm occurs.

The following hypothetical example will help circumscribe the situation: if the activities under the control of state A cause environmental harm to the population of state B, does state A have (extraterritorial) jurisdiction and therefore responsibility for breaching human rights, or is it the responsibility of state B to protect its population from deprivation by the acts or omissions of state A or the entities located in it? In order to understand the extent to which state A may be responsible for the protection of the environment affecting human rights in state B, it is necessary to conduct two distinct inquiries: (i) is there a direct link between state A's action or inaction, environmental degradation abroad, and a violation of a human right, and (ii) does the situation fall under the extended jurisdiction of state A?

2. First Inquiry: Causality

The first inquiry concerns a traditional question in the analysis of human rights approaches to environmental protection in a domestic context. I will therefore deal with it briefly in order simply to recall the conditions under which environmental harm, irrespective of where it takes place, may amount to a human rights violation.

The scope for environmental protection in all existing human rights, as interpreted by their respective adjudicatory bodies, is conditioned upon the establishment of a 'link' between environmental degradation and the impairment of a protected right. Depending on the legal context, this link is narrowly or more broadly understood. Although the expression 'legal context' should normally refer

[53] For a contemporary study of this link see R. Pavoni, *Interesse pubblico e diritti individuali nella giurisprudenza ambientale della Corte europea dei diritti umani* (2013).

[54] Human rights treaties are not strict liability regimes. The responsibility of the state is based on a breach, which in turn requires failure to meet the standards of diligence imposed by human rights norms.

here to the treaty in question (e.g. the European, American or African Conventions), a more detailed analytical grid is required to capture the limitations arising from the 'link' requirement. Indeed, the adjudicatory bodies of each 'treaty context' have taken different stances depending on the particular 'human right' at stake (e.g. Articles 6 or 8 of the European Convention on Human Rights (ECHR)) as well as the 'circumstances' of the case. For this reason, it is difficult to set a level sufficiently detailed to capture the nuances of the case-law while at the same time broad enough to draw general conclusions. In what follows, we set a rather broad level in order to highlight the pervasive need for a 'link'. More detail can be found in the specialized literature.[55]

The aforementioned regional human rights adjudicatory systems have recognized the need for a link with more or less precision depending on the context. By way of illustration, the European Court of Human Rights (ECtHR) noted in *Kyrtatos v. Greece*, with regard to Article 8 ECHR, that '[n]either Article 8 nor any of the other Articles of the Convention are specifically designed to provide general protection of the environment as such; to that effect, other international instruments and domestic legislation are more pertinent'.[56] The same point was made in the context of Article 6 ECHR in *Athanassoglou v. Switzerland*: 'The applicants in their pleadings . . . were alleging not so much a specific and imminent danger in their personal regard as a general danger in relation to all nuclear power plants; and many of the grounds they relied on related to safety, environmental and technical features inherent in the use of nuclear energy.'[57]

In the American context, the Inter-American Commission on Human Rights (IACommHR) made a similar point in connection with a petition against the construction of a road running through a natural reserve in Panama:

> The Commission . . . holds the present complaint to be inadmissible since it concerns abstract victims represented in an actio popularis rather than specifically identified and defined individuals. The Commission does recognize that given the nature of the complaint, the petition could hardly pinpoint a group of victims with particularity since all the citizens of Panama are described as property owners of the Metropolitan Nature Reserve. The petition is inadmissible, further, because the environmental, civic, and scientific groups considered most harmed by the alleged violations are legal entities and not natural persons, as the Convention stipulates. The Commission therefore rules that it has not the requisite

[55] See among others: Francioni, 'International Human Rights in the Environmental Horizon', 21 *EJIL* (2010) 41; Loucaides, 'Environmental Protection through the Jurisprudence of the European Convention on Human Rights', 75 *British Yearbook of International Law* (2004) 249; Schall, 'Public Interest Litigation Concerning Environmental Matters before the Human Rights Courts: A Promising Future Concept?', 20 *Journal of Environmental Law* (2008) 417; Inter-American Commission on Human Rights (IACommHR), *Indigenous and Tribal Peoples' Rights over Their Ancestral Lands and Natural Resources: Norms and Jurisprudence of the Inter-American Human Rights System*, (2009); Pasqualucci, 'The Inter-American Human Rights System: Progress Made and Still to Be Made', 52 *German Yearbook of International Law* (2009) 181; Sironi, 'La tutela della persona in conseguenza di danni all'ambiente nella giurisprudenza della Corte europea dei diritti umani', 5 *Diritti umani e diritto internazionale* (2011) 5; Pavoni, *supra* note 53.

[56] ECtHR, *Kyrtatos v. Greece*, Appl. no. 41666/98, Judgment of 22 May 2003, at para. 52.

[57] ECtHR, *Athanassoglou and others v. Switzerland*, Appl. no. 27644/95, Judgment of 6 April 2000, at para. 52.

competence ratione personae to adjudicate the present matter in accordance with jurisprudence establishing the standard of interpretation for Article 44 of the Convention as applied in the aforementioned cases.[58]

Even the more open jurisprudence of the Inter-American Court of Human Rights (IACtHR) with respect to the rights of indigenous and tribal peoples maintains the need for a link without which environmental protection would not be required. In *Saramaka People v. Suriname*, the Court clarified the reason why the environment is to be protected under Article 21 of the Convention (right to property) as follows:

> The aim and purpose of the special measures required on behalf of the members of indigenous and tribal communities is to guarantee that they may continue living their traditional way of life, and that their distinct cultural identity, social structure, economic system, customs, beliefs and traditions are respected, guaranteed and protected by States.[59]

As for the African Commission, despite the explicit recognition of a peoples' right to a generally satisfactory environment in Article 24 of the African Charter,[60] pure environmental degradation does not (so far) appear sufficient to conclude that there has been an impairment of a human or a people's right. Indeed, in the *Ogoni* case,[61] the African Commission interpreted Article 24 in the light of Article 16 (right to health) and spoke of a 'right to a healthy environment'. Although it characterized the obligations arising from Article 24 in a general manner,[62] it grounded its conclusion that the Charter had been violated upon the effects of the activities in question on the Ogoni community and its members:

> Undoubtedly and admittedly, the Government of Nigeria, through NNPC has the right to produce oil, the income from which will be used to fulfil the economic and social rights of Nigerians. But the care that should have been taken as outlined in the preceding paragraph and which would have protected the rights of the victims of the violations complained of was not taken. To exacerbate the situation, the security forces of the government engaged in conduct in violation of the rights of the Ogonis by attacking, burning and destroying several Ogoni villages and homes.[63]

The expansion of the spatial scope of human rights obligations may either leave unchanged the causality requirement or, most likely, strain it even more. In other words, such spatial expansion may potentially come at the price of a contraction of the scope for environmental protection per se.

[58] IACommHR, *Metropolitan Nature Reserve v. Panama*, Case 11.533, Report No. 88/03, 22 October 2003, at para. 34.

[59] IACtHR, *Saramaka People v. Suriname*, Judgment, 28 November 2007, at para 121.

[60] African Charter on Human and Peoples' Rights 1981, (1982) 21 ILM58.

[61] *Ogoni case, supra* note 51.

[62] According to the Commission, this right requires the state 'to take reasonable and other measures to prevent pollution and ecological degradation, to promote conservation, and to secure an ecologically sustainable development and use of natural resources', ibid. at para. 52.

[63] Ibid., para. 54.

3. *Second Inquiry: Sufficient Basis for Responsibility*

The second inquiry can take as a starting point a much-discussed observation of the ECtHR in the *Bankovic* case:

> The Court considers that the applicants' submission is tantamount to arguing that anyone adversely affected by an act imputable to a Contracting State, wherever in the world that act may have been committed or its consequences felt, is thereby brought within the jurisdiction of that State for the purpose of Article 1 of the Convention . . . The Court is inclined to agree with the Government's submission that the text of Article 1 does not accommodate such an approach to 'jurisdiction'.[64]

Despite the criticism levelled against this stance, the ECtHR makes here an important point as to the meaning of the term 'jurisdiction'. Jurisdiction cannot be equated with 'causality' or 'attribution'. The fact that, in practice, the three terms are normally aligned, because states control (through their agents) the areas under their jurisdiction, does not mean that they are necessarily aligned. States may extend their jurisdiction (prescriptive and adjudicative) over areas already subject to other jurisdiction (the territory of another state) or non-capable of appropriation (e.g. the high seas), where they do not necessarily exercise control (i.e. they do not have the ability to enforce their jurisdiction). In addition, a state may exercise control without being entitled to exercise jurisdiction (e.g. secret activities of its agents in another country). It is in this context that the question of state responsibility for extraterritorial human rights violations arising from environmental harm must be addressed.

The most articulate answer to this question is, to my knowledge, the one given by Alan Boyle in his article 'Human Rights and the Environment: Where Next?'.[65] Boyle makes four arguments in support of the proposition that causing environmental harm abroad may amount to a breach of a state's (extraterritorial) human rights obligations. My purpose in the next paragraphs is to analyse these arguments, focusing on their strengths and weaknesses.

According to Boyle, such a case can be made in the context of transboundary environmental harm because: (i) human rights treaties, as interpreted by their relevant adjudicatory and quasi-adjudicatory bodies, extend the scope of human rights obligations beyond state territory to areas where they may be deemed to have 'jurisdiction', particularly as a result of military occupation or cross-border action by the state's agents, but also, arguably, in cases of transboundary environmental harm; (ii) the 'jurisdiction' of states for environmental harm caused beyond their territory is regularly recognized in transnational environmental tort litigation, civil liability treaties and environmental treaties such as the Aarhus Convention on Access to Information, Public Participation in Decision-making and Access to Justice in Environmental Matters;[66] (iii) it would be a violation of the prohibition

[64] ECtHR, *Bankovic and Others v. Belgium and Others*, Appl. no. 52207/99, Decision on Admissibility of 12 December 2001, para. 75.

[65] Boyle, *supra* note 1, at 638 ff.

[66] Aarhus Convention on Access to Information, Public Participation in Decision-making and Access to Justice in Environmental Matters 1998, 2161 UNTS 447 (Aarhus Convention).

of discrimination enshrined in several human rights and other instruments to treat individuals differently in different states; and (iv) it would be inconsistent to recognize (ii)–(iii) without allowing for the potential enforcement of its results before human rights bodies in cases where state authorities would refrain from implementing (ii)–(iii). This is a powerful case for recognizing state responsibility for environmental harm caused to individuals abroad. It is also not purely academic, to the extent that, as Boyle suggests in his article, this case was in fact made before the ICJ in a now settled dispute between Ecuador and Colombia.[67]

The *first argument* made by Boyle is that, despite the rather restrictive approach initially followed by the ECtHR in connection with human rights extraterritorial jurisdiction (with reference to the *Bankovic* case), the Court has subsequently loosened its approach. This is, in fact, consistent with the more receptive approach taken by the IACommHR. Although none of the relevant cases involve environmental dimensions, an analogy can be made between the type of threats found to expand 'jurisdiction' in those cases and environmental degradation as an extraterritorial problem. To assess this argument one must start by reviewing two sets of human rights instruments, namely those that refer to the 'territory' or the 'jurisdiction' of states to define the spatial scope of application of human rights obligations,[68] and those that contain no explicit clause in this regard.[69] I will leave the latter category aside for the moment and focus on decisions relating to the interpretation of the first category of instruments. These decisions have considered that a state has 'jurisdiction' when it exercises effective control.[70] Whether it is the ICJ,[71] the Human Rights Committee (HRC),[72] the ECtHR[73] or the

[67] *Aerial Herbicide Spraying (Ecuador v Colombia)*, Order of 13 September 2013, ICJ Reports (2013) 278 (removing the case from the docket).

[68] Art. 2(1), International Covenant on Civil and Political Rights 1966, 999 UNTS 171 (ICCPR) ('territory and subject to its jurisdiction'); Art. 1, Convention for the Protection of Human Rights and Fundamental Freedoms 1950, 213 UNTS 221 ('everyone within their jurisdiction'); Art. 1(1), American Convention on Human Rights 1969, 1144 UNTS 123 (ACHR or American Convention) ('persons subject to their jurisdiction').

[69] International Covenant on Economic, Social and Cultural Rights 1966, 993 UNTS 3 (ICESCR); African Charter, *supra* note 60; American Declaration of the Rights and Duties of the Man 1948.

[70] See L. Doswald-Beck, *Human Rights in Armed Conflict* (2011), at 9–29.

[71] *Legal Consequences of the Construction of a Wall in the Occupied Palestinian Territory*, Advisory Opinion, 9 July 2004, ICJ Reports (2004) 136, at paras 108–112; and *Application of the International Convention on the Elimination of All Forms of Racial Discrimination (Georgia v. Russian Federation)*, Provisional Measures, Order, 15 October 2008, ICJ Reports (2008) 353, at 386, para. 109.

[72] HRC, *Delia Saldias de Lopez v. Uruguay*, Comm. no. 52/1979, 29 July 1981, paras 12.1 and 12.3; General Comment No. 31, Nature of the General Legal Obligation Imposed on States Parties to the Covenant, CCPR/C/21/Rev.1/Add.13, 26 May 2004, para. 10.

[73] ECtHR, *Al Skeini and others v. United Kingdom*, Appl. no. 55721/07, Judgment of 7 July 2011, paras 130–140 (particularly 136); *Öcalan v. Turkey*, Appl. no. 46221/99, Judgment of 12 March 2003, para. 91; *Ilascu and others v. Moldova and Russia*, Appl. no. 48787/99, Judgment of 8 July 2004, paras 310–319, 376–394; *Issa and Others v. Turkey*, Appl. no. 31821/96, Judgment of 16 November 2004, para. 71; *Cyprus v. Turkey*, Appl. no. 25781/94, Judgment of 10 May 2001, para. 78; *Mansur Pad and others v. Turkey*, Appl. no. 60167/00, Admissibility Decision of 28 June 2007, paras 54–55.

IACommHR,[74] the extension of the spatial scope of human rights obligations requires control, and not the mere existence of 'prescriptive' or 'adjudicative' jurisdiction. Boyle's analysis acknowledges this point when he writes that '[t]he ratio of these and other similar cases is that where a state exercises control over territory or persons abroad, human rights obligations will follow'.[75] A question that arises at this stage is whether such control must concern the victim or the instrument through which human rights are violated. In the cases referred to so far the focus is on control over the victim. As noted by the ECtHR, '[w]hat is decisive in such cases is the exercise of physical power and control over the person in question'.[76] Normally, effective control over one of these terms implies some form of control over the other. This is the case even under the broadest theories of extraterritorial jurisdiction, such as the so-called 'state agent authority' approach, which justifies the extension of jurisdiction on the basis of the factual power of a state agent over a given situation.[77] Yet, there is no necessary relationship between control over the instrument and control over the victim.

The distinction is important because in cases involving environmental harm, the state of origin (state A in my example above) has control over the source of environmental harm but not over the victims, who are under the effective control of the affected state (state B). Such difference calls for three additional observations. The first is that the normal understanding of effective control applied in other cases would sustain the conclusion that it is state B, not state A, that has effective control. Thus, extending the jurisdiction of state A through a constructive notion of effective control would come at the price of ignoring the content of this same notion with respect to state B and, thereby, to potentially disrupt the principles arising from the body of case-law following this more conventional understanding of effective control. The second observation is implicit in the first. The idea of effective control introduces a significant difference between the operation of inter-state and human rights norms. Whereas the environmental harm caused by state A may breach an inter-state obligation owed to state B, in order to breach a human rights obligation owed to the individuals under the effective control of state B it is necessary to take into account the human rights obligations of state B, particularly to protect from deprivation. Thus, whereas inter-state obligations involve one responsible state, human rights obligations involve, in an extraterritorial context, two potentially responsible states. The third observation concerns the proper legal understanding of the responsibility of state B. One view could be that state B's human rights obligations interrupt the causality link between the acts or omissions

[74] IACommHR, *Alejandre and Others v. Cuba*, (1999), Case 11.589, Report no. 86/99, paras 23–25; IACommHR, *Ecuador v. Colombia*, (2010), Inter-State Petition IP-02, Report no. 112/10, para. 91.

[75] Boyle, *supra* note 1, at 637.

[76] *Al-Skeini v. United Kingdom*, *supra* note 73, at para. 136.

[77] See M. Milanovic, *Extraterritorial Application of Human Rights Treaties* (2011), at 173 ff. See also *Issa and others v. Turkey*, *supra* note 73, para. 71, 74–82 (asserting theoretically the possibility of extending jurisdiction if sufficient control was exercised but rejecting this argument on the facts of the case).

of state A and the harm caused to individuals in state B. That would take us back to square one and to a pure causality analysis. In my opinion a more accurate view would be that state B's obligations may or may not interrupt causality. Indeed, state B's obligations in this context are not absolute. They consist of a duty of due diligence or, in other terms, of a pro-active and positive obligation to take steps to protect individuals from deprivation by third parties, including other states or polluters based therein. Such duty can be fully satisfied even if state B is unable to effectively eliminate the consequences of the external environmental threat. Thus, three scenarios are possible: state B may be solely responsible, which is the traditional territorial approach to human rights obligations; state A may be solely responsible if state B has fully discharged its human rights duties; both state A and state B may be responsible because different elements of the factual configuration that amounts to a human rights violation are in the hands of each state.[78] For present purposes, it is the factual element underlying the second and third hypotheses that must retain our attention.

The *second argument* advanced by Boyle is that 'while it is less plausible to say that the polluting state "controls" the territory of the state affected by pollution, it is entirely plausible to conclude that the victims of transboundary pollution fall within the "jurisdiction" of the polluting state—in the most straightforward sense of legal jurisdiction'.[79] This is a subtle argument but it has some difficulties. As noted in the preceding paragraph, the basis for the extraterritorial responsibility of state A for human rights violations in state B is not 'any' type of 'jurisdiction' but a specific understanding of jurisdiction as effective control. The 'most straightforward sense of legal jurisdiction' mentioned by Boyle refers to 'prescriptive' or 'adjudicative' jurisdiction and not effective control. The allocation of such legal jurisdiction in private international law follows a different logic than the one underpinning human rights. In private international law, overlapping 'adjudicative' jurisdiction is admitted and even encouraged in order to enhance, rather than restrict, access to the courts. Unlike international law, where a specific jurisdictional basis is required for an international court to hear a case, in domestic law—including in private law situations with international components—the existence of a competent court is the rule and not the exception. Most often, this form of domestic adjudicative jurisdiction is distributed in an orderly fashion, assigning principal and secondary jurisdiction to different *fora*. As for 'prescriptive' or 'adjudicative' jurisdiction over tort claims, the primary aim is to ensure compensation to the victims as much as possible.[80] By contrast, 'jurisdiction' for human

[78] See den Heijer, 'Issues of Shared Responsibility before the European Court of Human Rights', *SHARES Research Paper 06* (2012); *Ilascu v. Moldova and Russia, supra* note 73, paras 352, 385, 393 (responsibility for distinct and separate action or inaction respectively by Moldova and Russia); *Al-Skeini v. United Kingdom, supra* note 73, para. 137.

[79] Boyle, *supra* note 1, at 638.

[80] See McLachlan, 'Transnational Tort Litigation: An Overview', in C. McLachlan and P. Nygh (eds), *Transnational Tort Litigation: Jurisdictional Principles* (1996) 1, at 11; P. Mayer and V. Heuzé, *Droit international privé* (2010), at 203; B. Audit, *Droit international privé* (2006), at 288; D. Mcclean and K. Beevers, *The Conflict of Laws* (2009), at 395–396.

rights purposes must be allocated to the state that has de facto power over the victim because this state is in a better position to prevent or cease violations of human rights, while awarding compensation in this context is secondary. This is why the human rights obligations of state B in the above example cannot be simply ignored, because it is state B that exercises effective control over the individuals in its territory. Of course, the arguments that can be made by reference to the underpinning logics of different sets of norms are largely of a policy or, at best, an interpretive nature. Perhaps more important from a strictly legal perspective is the effective control requirement that translates the logic underpinning human rights law. This requirement targets a factual configuration, the power over the situation or at least over some aspects of it. It is the effective control over the source of pollution by state A that may trigger certain legal effects under human rights law, irrespective of the legal effects attached by other norms, including domestic tort law, private international law rules or civil liability treaties to the same situation. In fact, even when there is no basis to establish the 'legal jurisdiction' referred to in Boyle's analysis, it may be considered under some human rights instruments that factual power over the source of harm entails some measure of responsibility for the resulting human rights violations.

The UN Committee on Economic, Social and Cultural Rights specifically addressed this hypothesis in its General Comment 8, in connection to international sanctions, stating:

> Although the Committee has no role to play in relation to decisions to impose or not to impose sanctions, it does, however, have a responsibility to monitor compliance by all States parties with the Covenant. When measures are taken which inhibit the ability of a State party to meet its obligations under the Covenant, the terms of sanctions and the manner in which they are implemented become appropriate matters for concern for the Committee... The Committee believes that two sets of obligations flow from these considerations. The first set relates to the affected State... The second set of obligations relates to the party or parties responsible for the imposition, maintenance or implementation of the sanctions, whether it be the international community, an international or regional organization, or a State or group of States. In this respect, the Committee considers that there are three conclusions which follow logically from the recognition of economic, social and cultural human rights... First, these rights must be taken fully into account when designing an appropriate sanctions regime... Second, effective monitoring, which is always required under the terms of the Covenant, should be undertaken throughout the period that sanctions are in force. *When an external party takes upon itself even partial responsibility for the situation within a country (whether under Chapter VII of the Charter of otherwise), it also unavoidably assumes a responsibility to do all within its power to protect the economic, social and cultural rights of the affected population*... Third, the external entity has an obligation 'to take steps, individually and through international assistance and cooperation, especially economic and technical' in order to respond to any disproportionate suffering experienced by vulnerable groups within the targeted country.[81]

[81] Committee on Economic, Social and Cultural Rights, *General Comment 8: The Relationship between Economic Sanctions and Respect for Economic, Social and Cultural Rights*, UN Doc. E/C.12/1997/8, 12 December 1997, paras 9–14 (emphasis added).

The African Commission also addressed this issue in the context of a specific application of sanctions by a group of African countries against Burundi:

> The critical question and one which may affect the legitimacy of the action is whether such action as has been determined is excessive and disproportionate, is indiscriminate and seeks to achieve ends beyond the legitimate purpose. Sanctions therefore cannot be open-ended, the effects thereof must be carefully monitored, measures must be adopted to meet the basic needs of the most vulnerable populations or they must be targeted at the main perpetrators or authors of the nuisance complained of. The Human Rights Committee has adopted a General Comment in this regard precisely in order to create boundaries and limits to the imposition of sanctions.[82]

In these two statements, the control of the state(s) over the source of harm, or the sanction, is assumed to be sufficient for the purpose of extending the spatial scope of its/their human rights obligations, irrespective of any legal jurisdiction other than the one arising from the relevant human rights instrument. A similar argument can be made with respect to Article 3(9) of the Aarhus Convention, referred to by Boyle. The relevant environmental information and decision-making processes, as well as the judicial control over their proper administration, are all manifestations of state A's control over the source of pollution. This question has arisen in two recent communications brought before the Aarhus Compliance Committee. The first communication, brought by a group of German citizens against the Czech Republic,[83] claims that the Czech government violated Article 3 (9) of the Aarhus Convention because it did not allow foreign citizens to participate in the decision-making procedure of a nuclear power project to the same extent as local citizens. In the second case, a German citizen claims that the United Kingdom breached Article 6 of the Convention because it failed to provide adequate participation to the German public in the environmental impact assessment procedure of two nuclear reactor projects.[84] In both cases, the spatial extension of the scope of the procedural rights provided in the Convention is based on the control over the source of (potential) harm, i.e. a project with transboundary implications.

The *third argument* made by Boyle refers to the application of the non-discrimination principle enshrined in a variety of instruments, including human rights treaties and the Aarhus Convention. It is essential to make the same caveat mentioned in the preceding paragraph in relation to this argument. There cannot be any doubt that treating two individuals differently in the same situation would be contrary to the prohibition of discrimination. However, to what extent would an individual under the effective control of state A and suffering from pollution originating in state A be in a similar situation as an individual suffering from this

[82] African Commission on Human and Peoples' Rights, *Association pour la sauvegarde de la paix au Burundi v. Tanzania, Kenya, Uganda, Rwanda, Zaire and Zambia*, Comm. no. 157/96, 29 May 2003, para. 75.

[83] See ACCC/C/2012/71, submitted in 2012.

[84] See ACCC/C/2013/91, submitted in June 2013.

same source of pollution but under the effective control of state B for all other purposes? It would be 'unconscionable', as noted by the HRC, 'to so interpret the responsibility under article 2 of the Covenant as to permit a State to perpetrate violations of the Covenant on the territory of another State, which violations it could not perpetrate on its own territory'.[85] But this is because the state in question has effective control over the victim situated in the other state. The HRC stated in its General Comment No. 31 on the Nature of the General Legal Obligation Imposed on States Parties to the Covenant:

> The enjoyment of Covenant rights is not limited to citizens of States Parties but must also be available to all individuals, regardless of nationality or statelessness, such as asylum seekers, refugees, migrant workers and other persons, who may find themselves in the territory or subject to the jurisdiction of the State Party. *This principle also applies to those within the power or effective control of the forces of a State Party acting outside its territory, regardless of the circumstances in which such power or effective control was obtained, such as forces constituting a national contingent of a State Party assigned to an international peace-keeping or peace-enforcement operation.*[86]

Whereas two individuals based in different countries may be in a similar position for some purposes (e.g. they may both have access to a court in state A), this is not to say their position is similar for all purposes. Specifically, the fact that two individuals are under the effective control of two different states places them in a different position for the purpose of assigning responsibility for human rights violations, even if the individual under the effective control of state B falls under the 'prescriptive' or 'adjudicative' jurisdiction of state A. If such were not the case, then the purely 'prescriptive' or 'adjudicative' jurisdiction of state B over a territory that it no longer controls, as a result of state A's occupation, would be sufficient to assign state B responsibility for human rights violations. In other words, mere legal jurisdiction over an individual is not the same as effective control over the individual for the purpose of assessing human rights responsibility. It is a factual element—the similar exposure of two individuals to environmental harm irrespective of where they are based—that may, if at all, provide a sufficient basis for extending the spatial scope of state A's human rights obligations.

The *fourth argument* advanced by Boyle concerns the overall consistency of personal injury-based systems of protection. As noted by Boyle:

> There is little point in requiring that national remedies be made available to transboundary claimants if they cannot also resort to international or regional human rights law when necessary to compel the polluting state to enforce its own court orders or laws or to assess and take adequate account of the harmful effects of activities which it authorizes and regulates. That is exactly how domestic claimants have successfully used human rights law in environmental cases.[87]

This is, again, a subtle argument but one of a policy nature. One can only agree with the proposition that a refusal of a state to stop harming an individual under

[85] *Lopez v. Uruguay*, *supra* note 72, at para. 12.3.
[86] HRC, General Comment No. 31, *supra* note 72, para. 10 (emphasis added).
[87] Boyle, *supra* note 1, at 639.

its effective control must be subject to review by human rights courts, as in the abundant case-law before the ECtHR (on Article 8 ECHR), the IACtHR (on Article 21 of the American Convention on Human Rights (ACHR)) or the African Commission (on Articles 16, 21 and 24 of the African Charter). But, in extending this proposition to extraterritorial situations, one must introduce three caveats.

Firstly, the aforementioned body of cases concerns situations where the responsible state had effective control over the source of the injury *and* the victim.

Secondly, access to human rights courts in this case may in fact be granted for a different purpose, i.e. to redress the failure of state A to enforce a remedy sought within state A. Such failure—if at all in violation of state A's human rights obligations—takes place within state A. By way of illustration, if a foreign national comes to the courts of state A to claim compensation for transboundary environmental harm and the claimant is discriminated against or otherwise mistreated, the claimant may resort to human rights courts against state A for such mistreatment, which has taken place in the territory, and under the effective control, of state A. Such a claim will most likely be related to non-discrimination or breach of due process rather than to environmental harm suffered extraterritorially. Different 'torts' or 'injuries' are thus channelled through different remedies. The environmental tort is channelled through international tort litigation. The discrimination suffered by the international litigant is channelled through human rights litigation before an international court.

The third caveat concerns a remaining scenario: would it be possible for the applicant to argue that state A violated the applicant's human rights because it caused transboundary harm and it then did not compensate the applicant, even in the absence of any impropriety in the tort proceedings before state A's courts? It may be possible, but it seems far more difficult because the applicant would face again the question of whether or not state A had effective control. In other words, the policy argument advanced by Boyle can be made but it cannot be used, as a matter of law, to get around the issue of effective control.

Taken as a whole, a legal case (as distinguished from the policy case, which will be discussed below) for a human rights approach to extraterritorial environmental protection can be made for the reasons advanced by Boyle with the caveats introduced here. The main legal challenge, i.e. moving beyond mere causality to the level of responsibility based on the control over the source of pollution, could be overcome by analogy to the limitations imposed on international sanctions as a result of their extraterritorial effects on human rights. Although difficult, the extraterritorial dimension of human rights obligations could thus be mobilized to require states to take measures to tackle pollution abroad. Two questions arise at this stage: what type of measures could be adopted in this regard and to what extent would they be consistent or inconsistent with other obligations arising for states under international law? In the next section, after a brief overview of these questions, I will analyse them in the light of some illustrations.

4. Specific Illustrations

A. Protecting the Environment Abroad: Overview

I have already referred to three types of measures as the object of the legal analysis in this chapter: (a) domestic environmental measures with extraterritorial implications, (b) measures primarily intended to protect the territory of other states, or individuals based therein, from environmental threats under the control of the regulating state, and (c) measures primarily intended to protect common areas from environmental threats under the control of the regulating state. This is, of course, an abstract or condensed characterization of such measures. To make it more real, one could zoom in and gain a better understanding of the parcels of reality potentially encompassed by such characterization. The purpose of the following paragraphs is to provide some concrete examples in order to assess the operation of the legal principles discussed in the previous sections and, when relevant, their interactions with other potentially applicable norms of international law.

Significantly, the ability of states to adopt the types of measures under consideration does not take place in an international legal vacuum. On the contrary, even measures that are clearly linked to the protection of the human rights of individuals living in the territory of a state, such as the regulation of extractive industries and utilities or redress processes, may be challenged as breaches of other norms of international law, such as international investment agreements (IIAs).[88] *A fortiori*, when the adverse impact of such activities takes place, either partly or entirely, outside the territory of the regulating state, the grounds for challenging such measures may gain in persuasiveness. Similarly, the regulation of activities conducted abroad, whether directly (through a clear extraterritorial extension of prescriptive jurisdiction) or indirectly (domestic measures with effects abroad), can conflict with norms regulating international trade transactions.

As I will discuss in three specific contexts, different types of norms may come into play simultaneously depending on the factual configuration, some as legal justifications of a given measure and others as an obstacle to its international legality.

[88] For some examples relating to utilities (gas and water) see: *CMS Gas Transmission Company v. Argentine Republic*—Award, 12 May 2005, ICSID Case no. ARB/01/08 (this decision was subsequently annulled but on a different point); *LG&E v. Argentine Republic*—Decision on Liability, 13 October 2006, ICSID Case no. ARB/02/1; *Suez, Sociedad General de Aguas de Barcelona, S.A. and Vivendi Universal, S.A. v. The Argentine Republic*—Decision on Liability, 31 July 2010, ICSID Case no. ARB/03/19 (Suez v. Argentina—03/19); *Suez, Sociedad General de Aguas de Barcelona S.A. and InterAguas Servicios Integrales del Agua S.A. v. The Argentine Republic*—Decision on Liability, 31 July 2010, ICSID Case no. ARB/03/17 (Suez v. Argentina—03/17). For some examples relating to extractive industries (gold and oil) see: *Glamis Gold Ltd. v. The United States of America*, NAFTA (UNCITRAL Rules), Award, 16 May 2009; *Chevron Corporation and Texaco Petroleum Company v. Ecuador*—First Partial Award on Track I, 17 September 2013, PCA Case no. 2009–23.

B. Extraterritorial Aspects of the Right to Water

1. Overview

The right to water is recognized,[89] to varying degrees, in a number of international instruments,[90] and it is also seen as a condition for the fulfilment of other 'general' human rights.[91] Approaching the extraterritorial protection of freshwater resources from a human rights perspective would have the advantages generally associated with human rights approaches to environmental protection, namely more specific right-holders, better enforcement mechanisms and a stronger sense of urgency. Yet, recognizing an extraterritorial dimension to the right to water would also be politically difficult because it would add a powerful reason for states to be required to share their own water resources with the populations of other states.

As a result, the types of measures that could be called for to satisfy a right to water claimed by individuals based in a foreign state (state B, to continue with our example above) may include not only the protection of the water resources flowing from state A to state B but also the sharing and transfer to state B (or other states) of resources entirely located in state A. In order to understand the interactions between inter-state norms and human rights norms in this context, some additional clarifications on the rules potentially applicable seem warranted.

I will proceed in two steps. Firstly, I will discuss the extraterritorial dimensions of the right to water and its links to the traditional inter-state rules on shared water resources. Secondly, I will analyse the interactions between this combined set of norms and other applicable norms regulating activities within state A and water transfers from state A to state B.

[89] *See* generally Dupuy, 'Le droit à l'eau: droit de l'homme ou droit des Etats?', in M. G. Kohen (ed.), *Promoting Justice, Human Rights and Conflict Resolution Through International Law/La promotion de la justice, des droits de l'homme et du règlement des conflits par le droit international: Liber Amicorum Lucius Caflisch* (2007) 701; Fitzmaurice, 'The Human Right to Water', 18 *Fordham Environmental Law Review* (2007) 537; P. Thielboerger, *The Human Right(s) to Water* (PhD thesis on file at the European University Institute, Florence); I. T. Winkler, *The Human Right to Water* (2012); M.-C. Petersmann, *Les sources du droit à l'eau en droit international* (2013); Boisson de Chazournes, 'Le droit à l'eau et la satisfaction des besoins humains: Notions de justice', in D. Alland et al. (eds), *Unity and Diversity of International Law: Essays in Honour of Professor Pierre-Marie Dupuy* (2014) 967.

[90] See e.g. Art. 14.2(h), Convention on the Elimination of All Forms of Discrimination Against Women 1979, 1249 UNTS 13; Art. 24.2(c), Convention on the Rights of the Child 1989, 1577 UNTS 3; Arts 5(m) and 9(1)(b), Protocol on Water and Health to the 1992 Convention on the Protection and Use of Transboundary Watercourses and International Lakes 1999, 2331 UNTS 202; Arts 20, 26, 29 and 46, Geneva Convention Relative to the Treatment of Prisoners of War 1949, 75 UNTS 31; Arts 85, 89 and 127, Geneva Convention Relative to the Treatment of Civilian Persons in Time of War 1949, 75 UNTS 287; Arts 54 and 55, Protocol Additional to the Geneva Conventions of 12 August 1949, and Relating to the Protection of Victims of International Armed Conflicts 1977, 1125 UNTS 3; Arts 5 and 14, Protocol Additional to the Geneva Conventions of 12 August 1949, and Relating to the Protection of Victims of Non-International Armed Conflicts 1977, 1125 UNTS 609.

[91] See e.g. Arts 1(2), 6(1), ICCPR, *supra* note 68; Arts 11 and 12, ICESCR, *supra* note 69, read in the light of Committee on Economic, Social and Cultural Rights, General Comment No. 15, The Right to Water (Arts 11 and 12 of the International Covenant on Economic, Social and Cultural Rights), UN ESCOR Doc. E/C.12/2002/11, 26 November 2002 (GC 15).

2. *The Human Right to Water and Inter-State Norms*

The right to water, as it is increasingly recognized at the international level, has substantive and procedural dimensions. Perhaps the most representative account of the content of the right to water appears in General Comment No. 15 of the Committee on Economic, Social and Cultural Rights (GC 15). The Committee read into the International Covenant on Economic, Social and Cultural Rights (ICESCR) the existence of a right to water implied in Articles 11(1) (right to an adequate standard of living) and 12(2)(b) (right to health), with the following content: 'The human right to water entitles everyone to sufficient, safe, acceptable, physically accessible and affordable water for personal and domestic uses.'[92] In this regard, four main points must be noted.

The first is that, despite the relative diversity of angles and scopes of the instruments concerning the right to water, they all share a focus on personal uses of water. The right to water for other uses, either large-scale irrigation or industrial processes, is not covered by these instruments.

The second point concerns the express recognition of a procedural dimension of the right to water. Paragraph 12(c)(iv) of the GC 15 mentions, as one of the four components of access to water, 'the right to seek, receive and impart information concerning water issues'. Moreover, where water services are operated or controlled by third parties, the GC 15 requires states to establish an 'effective regulatory system' including, *inter alia*, 'genuine public participation'.[93] Paragraph 48 of the GC 15 further adds that '[t]he right of individuals and groups to participate in decision-making processes that may affect their exercise of the right to water must be an integral part of any policy, programme or strategy concerning water'.[94] More generally, participation is also required by the Aarhus Convention,[95] which, as discussed earlier, prohibits discrimination against individuals based in the state of origin of the threat as compared to those based in the affected state.

The third point is that, within the protected use, the GC 15 makes a distinction between 'core obligations' with 'immediate effect'[96] and other obligations, which can be progressively fulfilled. Paragraph 38 emphasizes, in connection with core obligations, that 'it is particularly incumbent on States parties, and other actors in a position to assist, to provide "international assistance and cooperation, especially economic and technical" which enables developing countries to fulfil their core obligations'.

[92] GC 15, *supra* note 91, at para. 2. [93] Ibid., para. 24.

[94] See also Arts 4, 18, 20 and 30, International Law Association, *Berlin Rules on Water Resources*, 21 August 2004.

[95] See *supra* note 66.

[96] GC 15, *supra* note 91, at para. 37. The concept of 'core obligations' was introduced by the Committee on Economic, Social and Cultural Rights in its General Comment No. 3, The Nature of States Parties' Obligations (Art. 2, para. 1), UN Doc. E/1991/23, 14 December 1990, at para. 19.

The fourth, and arguably most important, point for present purposes is that the Committee expressly refers to the extraterritorial dimension of the right to water in a series of paragraphs that, given their relevance, must be quoted *in extenso*:

> 31. To comply with their international obligations in relation to the right to water, States parties have to respect the enjoyment of the right in other countries. International cooperation requires States parties to refrain from actions that interfere, directly or indirectly, with the enjoyment of the right to water in other countries. *Any activities undertaken within the State party's jurisdiction should not deprive another country of the ability to realize the right to water for persons in its jurisdiction.*
>
> 32. States parties should refrain at all times from imposing embargoes or similar measures, that prevent the supply of water, as well as goods and services essential for securing the right to water. Water should never be used as an instrument of political and economic pressure. In this regard, the Committee recalls its position, stated in its General Comment No. 8 (1997), on the relationship between economic sanctions and respect for economic, social and cultural rights.
>
> 33. Steps should be taken by States parties to prevent their own citizens and companies from violating the right to water of individuals and communities in other countries. Where States parties can take steps to influence other third parties to respect the right, through legal or political means, such steps should be taken in accordance with the Charter of the United Nations Charter and applicable international law.
>
> 34. Depending on the availability of resources, States should facilitate realization of the right to water in other countries, for example through provision of water resources, financial and technical assistance, and provide the necessary aid when required. In disaster relief and emergency assistance, including assistance to refugees and displaced persons, priority should be given to Covenant rights, including the provision of adequate water. International assistance should be provided in a manner that is consistent with the Covenant and other human rights standards, and sustainable and culturally appropriate. The economically developed States parties have a special responsibility and interest to assist the poorer developing States in this regard.
>
> 35. States parties should ensure that the right to water is given due attention in international agreements and, to that end, should consider the development of further legal instruments. With regard to the conclusion and implementation of other international and regional agreements, States parties should take steps to ensure that these instruments do not adversely impact upon the right to water. *Agreements concerning trade liberalization should not curtail or inhibit a country's capacity to ensure the full realization of the right to water.*[97]

In these paragraphs, the extraterritorial dimension of the right to water is largely qualified by the use of the conditional mode, except in paragraph 31, and the reference to international cooperation or, in other words, to inter-state norms. In a footnote to paragraph 31, the Committee seeks to buttress the extraterritorial obligations arising from the right to water by reference to basic inter-state obligations applicable to shared watercourses, such as reasonable utilization (by the upstream state) and no harm (to the downstream state), reflected in the (now in force) UN Convention on the Non-Navigational Uses of International

[97] GC 15, *supra* note 91 (emphasis added).

Watercourses.[98] Thus, human rights and inter-state norms are read together in order to define the appropriate conduct to be adopted by state A in connection with the satisfaction of the right to water abroad.

Importantly, paragraphs 31 and 32 of the GC 15 expressly capture the responsibilities of a state arising from its control over the (potential) source of harm, in this case the power over water resources. Such power alone is deemed to create obligations with respect to individuals abroad, although the use of the conditional ('should not deprive' and 'should refrain') suggests that, at the time the GC 15 was adopted, such statements were more exhortations than binding obligations. Power or effective control over water resources is envisaged from two perspectives: (i) the potential pollution of water affecting the downstream state and its population; and (ii) the power of the upstream state (or, more generally, of water rich states) over the availability of water in the downstream state (or other states where water is scarce). Paragraphs 31 *in fine* and 33 target primarily the first form of power and they state, in this connection, the obligations to respect and protect from deprivation. Paragraphs 32 and 34 target instead the second form of power, and they qualify the extraterritorial obligations in two ways. For restrictions arising from sanctions, the qualifications are identified by reference to abovementioned General Comment No. 8. As for the sharing of water resources, this obligation is conditioned upon 'the availability of resources'. Thus, the legal implications that these human rights norms attach to control over the source of harm differ to some extent.

A similar distinction can be found in the Maastricht Principles on Extraterritorial Obligations of States in the area of Economic, Social and Cultural Rights (known as the 'Maastricht Principles').[99] This is a private codification effort developed under the aegis of the International Commission of Jurists, a non-governmental organization (NGO) based in Geneva. The Principles are structured around the obligations to respect, protect and fulfil. Water pollution by the upstream state is captured under these three types of obligations. Principles 13 (obligation to avoid causing harm) and 14 (impact assessment and prevention) provide the context in which the obligation to respect stated in Principle 20 (direct interference) must be assessed for present purposes. Similarly, Principle 25(a) clarifies the scope of the obligation to protect from deprivation of economic, social and cultural rights in other countries making specific reference to situations 'where the harm or threat of harm occurs on [the upstream state's] territory'. As for the obligation to fulfil, Principle 29 (obligation to create an international enabling environment) refers to duties of cooperation to achieve, *inter alia*, environmental protection. By contrast, the power over the availability of water in the other state is addressed with qualifications similar to those used by the GC 15. Principle 22 (sanctions and equivalent measures) formulates a duty to respect in the following terms:

[98] United Nations Convention on the Law of the Non-Navigational Uses of International Watercourses 1997, (1997) 36 ILM 700.

[99] Maastricht Principles on Extraterritorial Obligations of States in the Area of Economic, Social and Cultural Rights, adopted on 18 September 2011, available online at http://www.globalhealthrights.org/wp-content/uploads/2013/10/Maastricht-Principles-on-Extraterritorial-Obligations-of-States-in-the-area-of-Economic-Social-and-Cultural-Rights.pdf (last accessed 23 July 2015).

States must refrain from adopting measures, such as embargoes or other economic sanctions, which would result in nullifying or impairing the enjoyment of economic, social and cultural rights. Where sanctions are undertaken to fulfil other international legal obligations, States must ensure that human rights obligations are fully respected in the design, implementation and termination of any sanctions regime. *States must refrain in all circumstances from embargoes and equivalent measures on goods and services essential to meet core obligations.*[100]

Whether water is envisaged as a good or service, there can be no doubt that it falls plainly within the scope of the last sentence. As for the sharing of water resources, Principle 31 introduces a qualification similar to paragraph 34 of the GC 15, based on, *inter alia*, 'available resources':

A State has the obligation to fulfil economic, social and cultural rights in its territory to the maximum of its ability. Each State must separately and, where necessary, jointly contribute to the fulfilment of economic, social and cultural rights extraterritorially, commensurate with, inter alia, its economic, technical and technological capacities, available resources, and influence in international decision-making processes. States must cooperate to mobilize the maximum of available resources for the universal fulfilment of economic, social and cultural rights.

Thus, a combined reading of the GC 15 and the Maastricht Principles suggests a more nuanced understanding of the legal effects that may arise from the factual powers of a state over its water resources. The analysis of the extraterritorial dimensions of the right to water is therefore relevant not only to assess the potential of human rights approaches to extraterritorial environmental protection in this particular context but also to make a more general point: from a legal perspective, the factual power over the source of harm may have different implications depending on the specific legal context (here the right to water). What distinguishes the right to water as a legal context from other legal contexts (e.g. other human rights or other environmental problems) is the importance of water for life and the absence of any known substitute. The clearest manifestation of this feature is the specific regime contemplated in Paragraph 32 of the GC 15 and Principle 22 of the Maastricht Principles in connection with international sanctions.

3. *Interactions with Investment and Trade Regulation*

The second analytical step identified at the beginning of this section concerns the interactions between the right to water as a requirement for extraterritorial action and other norms of international law applicable to the relevant activities. The starting point is, as before, the types of measures that an upstream state (state A) could take to respect, protect or fulfil the extraterritorial dimensions of the right to water. Assuming the state has a policy interest to do so, which is not obvious in connection with the sharing of water resources, such measures would involve (i) the prevention of transboundary pollution of water resources through the regulation

[100] Ibid. (emphasis added).

of domestic activities, and (ii) the sharing of water resources through a variety of avenues, including through the regulation of the water sector.

The first hypothesis focuses on the traditional province of domestic environmental regulation, with the caveat that the pollution of water would have extraterritorial effects (in addition to domestic effects). The human rights obligations to respect and protect (the individuals in other states) from deprivation (by the polluters in the regulating state) would apply in addition to any relevant inter-state obligation concerning the protection of the environment domestically or abroad. The legal basis provided by these norms could, however, collide with the international norms protecting the economic operators potentially affected by such regulation, particularly foreign investment disciplines. I have analysed such potential collisions in some detail elsewhere.[101] For present purposes, it will suffice to make three observations. Firstly, the majority of the investment disputes raising the potential application of the right to water have concerned the privatization of water distribution services and, in this context, the right to water has been analysed in a purely territorial context.[102] Secondly, the right to water has so far not been seen as a sufficient basis to justify the actions of the regulating state, although some tribunals have acknowledged that this right has to be taken into account in the interpretation of investment agreements.[103] Thirdly, there is only one investment dispute touching upon the extraterritorial dimension of water regulation, *Bayview v. Mexico*,[104] which was dismissed at the jurisdictional level. A short reference to this case is useful nevertheless because it provides an example of the second hypothesis.

A group of Texan irrigation districts brought a claim under Chapter 11 of the NAFTA.[105] They argued that Mexico had expropriated their right to a certain amount of water from the Rio Grande, allegedly conferred by inter-state norms (i.e. a 1944 treaty between the United States and Mexico),[106] as a result of the development of a system of dams and reservoirs affecting the flow of the tributaries of the Rio Grande. This argument supposed that such water rights could constitute a protected investment under the NAFTA despite the fact that the claimants were based in the territory of the United States. As noted above, the tribunal declined to hear the case on the grounds that such water rights were not a protected investment under the NAFTA. In other words, they were not under Mexico's jurisdiction,

[101] See J. E. Viñuales, *Foreign Investment and the Environment in International Law* (2012), ch. 7.

[102] See e.g. *Aguas del Tunari S.A. v. Republic of Bolivia*—Decision on Respondent's Objections to Jurisdiction, 21 October 2005, ICSID Case no. ARB/02/3; *Azurix Corp v. Argentine Republic*—Award, 14 July 2006, ICSID Case no. ARB/01/12; *Biwater Gauff (Tanz.) Ltd. v. United Republic of Tanzania*—Award, 24 July 2008, ICSID Case no. ARB/05/22; *Suez v. Argentina—03/19 supra* note 88; *Suez v. Argentina—03/17, supra* note 88. Although technically distinct, the two tribunals have the same composition.

[103] See e.g. *Suez v. Argentina—03/19, supra* note 88, at para. 262 (italics in original); *Suez v. Argentina—03/17, supra* note 88, at para. 240.

[104] *Bayview Irrigation District et al v. United Mexican States*—Award, 19 June 2007, ICSID Case no. ARB(AF)/05/1.

[105] North American Free Trade Agreement 1992 (1993) 32 ILM 296.

[106] Treaty between the United States of America and Mexico Relating to the Utilization of the Waters of the Colorado and Tijuana Rivers and of the Rio Grande 1944, 3 UNTS 314.

which the claimant had sought to extend. The reasoning of the tribunal was based on the idea that, in order to be protected, an investment must have a 'legally significant connection' with the state adopting the measures challenged.[107] For present purposes, this case is interesting because, on the one hand, it illustrates how measures aimed at restricting the share of water reaching other states could be brought before an investment tribunal. On the other hand, it suggests that investment protection and extraterritorial human rights protection could potentially be aligned, limiting the ability of states to restrict water transfers to other states. The latter point can be further illustrated by the notice of claim filed in 1999 by an American investor, Sun Belt Water Inc., against Canada to challenge a measure adopted by British Columbia limiting and later suspending the licence of the claimant to operate bulk water transfers.[108] The claim was not pursued further but, judging on other analogous non-water-related cases,[109] the main legal issue would not be whether the scheme constitutes an investment (as in the Bayview case) but rather the extent to which a trade restriction may amount to a breach of trade and investment rules.

Concerns that international trade and investment norms may constrain the ability of states to retain their water resources were expressed in the early 1990s in connection with the negotiation of the NAFTA. Such fears were assuaged by the adoption of a joint statement by the three states parties to the NAFTA, according to which '[t]he NAFTA creates no rights to the natural water resources of any Party to the Agreement'. The statement further notes:

> Unless water, in any form, has entered into commerce and become a good or product, it is not covered by the provisions of any trade agreement, including the NAFTA. And nothing in the NAFTA would oblige any NAFTA Party to either exploit its water for commercial use, or to begin exporting water in any form. Water in its natural state in lakes, rivers, reservoirs, aquifers, water basins and the like is not a good or product, is not traded, and therefore is not and has never been subject to the terms of any trade agreement . . . International rights and obligations respecting water in its natural state are contained in separate treaties and agreements negotiated for that purpose.[110]

At the same time, the statement recognized that water could be treated as a tradable good. This was further confirmed in the broader context of multilateral trade law by the inclusion of water in the tariff headings used to identify products

[107] *Bayview v. Mexico, supra* note 104, at para. 101.

[108] NAFTA, *Sun Belt Water Inc. v. Her Majesty the Queen (Canada)*—Notice of Claim and Demand for Arbitration, 12 October 1999.

[109] NAFTA (UNCITRAL), *S.D. Myers, Inc. v. Government of Canada*—Partial Award, 13 November 2000 (case involving an export restriction of hazardous waste); NAFTA (UNCITRAL), *Pope & Talbot v. Government of Canada*, Interim Award on Merits I, 26 June 2000, Interim Award on Merits II, 10 April 2001 (case involving export restrictions of softwood lumber); NAFTA (UNCITRAL), *Merrill & Ring Forestry L.P. v. Government of Canada*, Award, 31 March 2010 (case involving export restrictions of logs).

[110] See Statement by the Governments of Canada, Mexico, and the United States, 2 December 1993, available online at http://dsp-psd.pwgsc.gc.ca/Collection-R/LoPBdP/EB/prb995-e.htm#(11) (last accessed 23 July 2015).

covered by the GATT.[111] One may ask what is the relationship between these two dimensions of water. In this regard, Canada took the position that the inclusion of 'natural waters' as a tariff heading 'does not tell us if and when water is a good; it only tells us that when water is classified as a good, it falls under a particular tariff heading'.[112]

4. *Concluding Observations*

All in all, the analysis of the extraterritorial dimension of the right to water suggests three main conclusions.

Firstly, there is a quite detailed elaboration of the legal foundations of action to prevent violations of the right to water abroad. The main sources are the GC 15 and the Maastricht Principles read in the light of other UN General Comments (particularly GC 8) and the broader body of case-law from human rights courts and bodies. The importance of water for life makes restrictions to the availability of water abroad, such as sanctions or embargoes, potentially illegal under human rights law.

Secondly, domestic measures preventing pollution of waterbodies with transboundary effects could collide with states' obligations, particularly those arising from investment agreements.

Thirdly, and significantly, trade and investment disciplines could also be aligned with the extraterritorial requirements of the right to water when it comes to sharing water resources. Thus, taking into account trade and investment norms tends to confirm the distinction made by human rights instruments between the differing legal implications of two forms of factual power over the source of harm, such as transboundary water pollution and availability of water abroad.

C. Collective Subjects and Extraterritorial Environmental Protection

1. *The Aerial Spraying Case as a Starting Point*

The arguments advanced by Boyle in connection with the scope for environmental protection within the context of the extraterritorial application of human rights obligations were of particular relevance to a dispute, now settled, between Ecuador and Colombia. The dispute concerned the aerial herbicide spraying by the Colombian forces of parts of Ecuador's territory. The facts of this dispute provide a potential illustration of how the actions of a state (Colombia's aerial spraying),

[111] See Brown Weiss, 'The Evolution of International Water Law', 331 *Recueil des Cours* (2009) 163, at 364, referring to Headings 22.01 ('waters, including natural or artificial mineral and aerated waters, not containing added sugar or other sweetening matter nor flavoured; ice and snow'), 22.02 ('waters, including mineral waters and aerated waters, containing added sugar or other sweetening matter or flavoured and other non-alcoholic beverages, not including fruit or vegetable juices of Heading 2009') and 25.01 ('salt (including table salt and denatured salt) . . . ; sea water').

[112] Cited in ibid., at 365.

leading to the transboundary pollution of the environment of another state (Ecuador), could as a result violate the human rights obligations (under the ACHR) of Colombia owed to individuals in Ecuador. An additional component of this dispute is the issue of minority rights. Indeed, the aerial spraying of the Ecuadorian border affected the health and property of the indigenous peoples living in the area.[113]

The reason why this additional component calls for further scrutiny lies in the special relations between indigenous peoples and their environment, or more specifically their traditional land, as recognized by the IACommHR and the IACtHR as well as by the African Commission. In the context of the extraterritorial application of human rights obligations, this relationship can be important to identify the holder of the affected rights, which can be a collective rather than an individual subject, and to assess the scope for environmental protection. The environment of a collective subject (protected by human rights norms) is closer conceptually to the environment of another state (protected by inter-state norms) than the environment relevant for an individual subject could ever be. In addition, a claim by an indigenous people as a collective subject would be closer conceptually to a collective or mass claim than piecemeal individual litigation and, as such, it could provide more room for environmental protection.

In what follows, I briefly discuss the recognition of collective human rights subjects in the Inter-American and African contexts and then elaborate on its relevance for a human rights approach to extraterritorial environmental protection. I do not discuss the interactions between these bases for extraterritorial environmental protection, and other norms of international law such as investment and trade disciplines, because they do not raise any major legal issues in addition to those already addressed in the previous section.[114]

2. *The Recognition of Collective Human Rights Subjects*

In a series of cases starting in 2001, the IACtHR has progressively expanded the scope of Article 21 (the right to property) to protect the relationship between indigenous and tribal peoples or communities and their traditional lands.[115] This amounts not only to giving a voice to such entities as a distinct subject of human

[113] Boyle refers in this connection to two reports prepared under the aegis of the UN Human Rights Council: Report of the Special Rapporteur on the Situation of Human Rights and Fundamental Freedoms of Indigenous People (Rodolfo Stavenhagen): Mission to Ecuador, 25 April–4 May 2006, UN Doc. A/HRC/4/32/Add.2, 28 December 2006; Report of the Special Rapporteur on the Right of Everyone to the Enjoyment of the Highest Attainable Standard of Physical and Mental Health (Paul Hunt): Preliminary Note on Mission to Ecuador and Colombia, Addendum, UN Doc. A/HRC/7/11/Add.3, 4 March 2007. See Boyle, *supra* note 1, at 636.

[114] For a detailed discussion of the interactions between the protection of minorities and foreign investment law see Viñuales, *supra* note 101, ch. 8.

[115] The leading case on this point is IACtHR, *Mayagna (Sumo) Awas Tingni Community v. Nicaragua*, Judgment, 31 August 2001, particularly at paras 145–155. For a retrospective of the relevant case-law see Judgment (merits and compensation), IACtHR, *Indigenous People Kichwa of Sarayaku v. Ecuador*, Judgment, 27 June 2012, at paras 145–147 (right to property) and paras 159–168 (participatory rights).

rights but also extends the scope of environmental protection to the entire area potentially affecting such peoples, which in all likelihood is far broader than the one affecting a specific individual. Moreover, the centre of gravity of the protection offered is not human health and integrity, broadly conceived, but the general state of the environment, at least to the extent that such environment must be preserved to ensure the traditional way of life of indigenous and tribal peoples.

The rights protected are not merely those of a particular individual but those of a collective subject. As noted by the IACtHR in *Sarayaku v. Ecuador*:

> On previous occasions, in cases concerning indigenous and tribal communities or peoples, the Court has declared violations to the detriment of members of indigenous or tribal communities and peoples. However, international legislation concerning indigenous or tribal communities and peoples recognizes their rights as collective subjects of International Law and not only as individuals [reference to the UN Declaration on the Rights of Indigenous Peoples, ILO Convention 169 and the African Charter]. Given that indigenous or tribal communities and peoples, united by their particular ways of life and identity, exercise certain rights recognized by the Convention on a collective basis, the Court points out that the legal considerations expressed or issued in this Judgment should be understood from that collective perspective.[116]

And these collective subjects are in a better position than any individual to speak for the environment and to claim general environmental redress because they are more broadly concerned with the state of the environment than any particular person or family living in a specific location. As noted in the UN Declaration on the Rights of Indigenous Peoples: 'Indigenous peoples have the right to the conservation and protection of the environment and the productive capacity of their lands or territories and resources.'[117] In addition, the ability to bring environment-related collective claims is further strengthened by the existence of a procedural basis in Article 44 of the ACHR, according to which any 'group of persons, or any nongovernmental entity legally recognized in one or more member states of the Organization [the OAS], may lodge petitions with the Commission [IACommHR] containing denunciations or complaints of violation of this Convention by a State Party'. Thus, in the American context, the environment benefits from a collective voice both at the substantive and procedural level.

With respect to the African context, the need for jurisprudential elaboration of collective claims is less acute because the African Charter explicitly provides for collective rights and representation. An example is provided by the *Ogoni* case,[118] which was brought before the African Commission by two European NGOs and concerned individual (e.g. Article 16) and collective (e.g. Articles 21 and 24) rights.

Environment-related collective claims are therefore possible because there are criteria to identify a class (cultural criteria defining indigenous and tribal peoples) with a special link to its environment, there is a class representative (the authorities

[116] *Sarayaku v. Ecuador, supra* note 115, at para. 231.

[117] United Nations Declaration on the Rights of Indigenous Peoples, UN Doc. A/RES/61/295, 13 September 2007, at para. 29(1).

[118] *Ogoni* case, *supra* note 51.

of the indigenous or tribal people or an entity acting on its behalf), and all these elements are recognized by the human rights bodies in the Inter-American and African contexts.

3. Implications for a Human Rights Approach to Extraterritorial Environmental Protection

The reason why collective personality may be relevant in the context of a human rights approach to extraterritorial environmental protection can be concisely stated.

Conceptually, a state's environmental protection obligations arising, on the one hand, from the extraterritorial application of human rights and, on the other hand, from traditional inter-state environmental norms, are more closely aligned to the context of collective subjects than to individual subjects. The recognition of collective personality allows for a more direct argument to be made, according to which a state harming the environment of another state in breach of an inter-state prevention obligation would also breach the rights of indigenous or tribal peoples living in the affected area. To use the terminology identified in the third section of this chapter (under letter C), whereas the 'responsibility' inquiry would remain intact, the 'causality' inquiry would be facilitated by virtue of the special relation between the collective subject and its environment.

This answer remains hypothetical for now as there is no case, to my knowledge, addressing this specific issue. As I will discuss next, the IACommHR did not address the merits of a petition brought by the Inuit people against the United States,[119] which raised questions of extraterritorial environmental harm affecting an indigenous people and a potential breach of human rights obligations enshrined in the American Declaration.

D. Climate Change Redress

1. Climate Change and Human Rights

At present, the possibility of using human rights approaches to tackle environmental questions such as climate change or its effects, particularly through the so-called 'slow onset events', which are very difficult to capture legally, is being explored.[120] Climate change is especially challenging to accommodate under the 'link' requirement discussed earlier in this chapter (see Section 3.C.2) because the applicant must establish that acts or omissions of the state have resulted in interference with the

[119] See *infra* note 122.

[120] See S. Humphreys (ed.), *Human Rights and Climate Change* (2009); the special number of the *Harvard Environmental Law Review* (vol. 33, no. 2, 2009) devoted to the relations between human rights and climate change; Limon, 'Human Rights Obligations and Accountability in the Face of Climate Change', 38 *Georgia Journal of International and Comparative Law* (2010) 543; OHCHR, Report of the Office of the United Nations for Human Rights on the Relationship between Climate Change and Human Rights, UN Doc. A/HRC/10/61, 15 January 2009.

climate system such that it has triggered a specific extreme, or slow onset, weather event, which has affected the rights of individuals.

This complex configuration normally takes place in a global context, which human rights law can only address through the assertion of human rights obligations with an extraterritorial spatial scope, despite the lack of effective control over individuals abroad. Conceptually, the 'responsibility' inquiry identified above is at present less pressing, although not less important, than the 'causality' inquiry. This is because causality is a precondition for responsibility and, for the extraterritorial dimension of human rights to come into play in a climate change context, one must start by satisfying our current legal frontier, i.e. the causality inquiry.

2. *Causality in the Climate Change Context*

Establishing causality in the context of a climate change-related human rights claim would require three steps: (i) the state through its acts or omissions interferes with the climate system; (ii) such interference causes an extreme weather event (e.g. a drought, a heat wave, a hurricane, etc.) or a slow onset event (e.g. melting of polar icecaps or rise of the sea level); and (iii) this extreme or slow onset event results in a specific and sufficiently severe impairment of a human right.

The practice of human rights courts has only addressed some parts of this complex configuration. Instead of extreme or slow onset environmental phenomena, the practice so far looks at more localized environmental threats or degradation. The causality inquiry has two main components in this more localized context: linking state action or inaction to such threats or degradation (first link) and linking the latter to an individual impairment of a human right (second link). Although the proof of these connections may be challenging, it is far from impossible in the territorial context where environmental cases have arisen, as suggested by the many decisions where human rights courts have found violations to their respective treaties.

However, in the context of climate change, these two links are far more complex to prove. Whereas it is now well established that emissions of greenhouse gases are the main driver of climate change since the twentieth century (first link),[121] the attribution of a specific weather event to climate change is still too difficult to establish. This difficulty interrupts the causality flow. It is widely known that climate change causes an increase in the frequency of extreme weather events and sets in motion slow onset events. It is even possible to identify which types of events (e.g. heat waves, droughts, hurricanes, ice-melting, sea level rise, redistribution of some diseases, etc.) can be triggered by climate change. What is missing is the link

[121] See Intergovernmental Panel for Climate Change (IPCC), *Climate Change 2013: The Physical Science Basis, Summary for Policymakers*, available online at http://www.climatechange2013.org (last accessed 23 July 2015) Section B, at 2, and Section D.3, at 15 stating that 'Warming of the climate system is unequivocal, and since the 1950s, many of the observed changes are unprecedented over decades to millennia [...] It is *extremely likely* that human influence has been the dominant cause of the observed warming since the mid-20th century' (the term 'extremely likely' indicates, in the language of the IPCC, a probability of no less than 95%).

with a specific event affecting a specific area on a specific date. That is precisely what the second link seeks to establish. As discussed next, such difficulties can be illustrated by reference to the Inuit Petition before the IACommHR.[122]

3. *The Inuit Petition Before the IACommHR*

The petition was brought by the Inuit Circumpolar Conference on behalf of 63 named individuals and the Inuit people against the United States for breach of the American Declaration on Human Rights. According to the petition, through its acts and omissions, the United States, as the then world's major emitter of greenhouse gases, had contributed to climate change with the end result that the Arctic environment, where the Inuit live, had been severely modified in a way so as to violate the human rights of the petitioners. The petition faced major obstacles in its attempt to establish the two causal links mentioned above.

With respect to the first link, the petition referred to the correlation between the United States estimated historical emissions, resulting from its lack of regulatory action, and 30 per cent of the observed increase in temperature of approximately 0.6 celsius degrees in the period from 1850 and 2000.[123] The petitioners acknowledged, however, that 'the actual correlation between cumulated emissions and temperature increase is subject to some uncertainty'.[124] And even if it were not, correlation is not a substitute for causation.

Regarding the second causal link, the petition identified in its Section C several effects on the Arctic environment attributable to climate change, including changes in ice and snow conditions, thawing permafrost, species redistribution and increasingly unpredictable weather conditions. But no specific link between climate change, a specific weather event and a specific impairment of a human right could be established, let alone between an instance of regulatory deficiency and these other steps.

As already noted, the IACommHR did not take position on the merits of the Inuit Petition.[125] It, therefore, remains unclear whether the scientific evidence currently available on the impact of global warming on the Arctic environment would be sufficient for litigation purposes before an international human rights body. That said, the approach followed by the petition to formulate its claim

[122] See Inuit Circumpolar Conference, *Petition to the Inter American Commission on Human Rights Seeking Relief from Violations Resulting from Global Warming Caused by Acts and Omissions of the United States* (2005), available online at http://www.inuitcircumpolar.com/uploads/3/0/5/4/30542564/finalpetitionicc.pdf (last accessed 23 July 2015). On this case see Shelton, 'Human Rights Violations and Climate Change: The Last Days of the Inuit People', 37 *Rutgers Law Record* (2010) 182.

[123] Inuit Petition, *supra* note 122, sections IV.D and V.D, at 68–69.

[124] Ibid., at 69.

[125] Revkin, 'Inuit Climate Change Petition Rejected', *New York Times* (New York, 16 December 2006) available online at http://www.nytimes.com/2006/12/16/world/americas/16briefs-inuitcomplaint.html (last accessed 10 October 2014). But see UN Human Rights Council Resolution 10/4, *Human Rights and Climate Change*, UN Doc. A/HRC/RES/10/4, 31 March 2009 (adopting a position on the issue); Human Rights Council Resolution 7/23, *Human Rights and Climate Change*, UN Doc. A/HRC/RES/7/23, 28 March 2008 (deciding to study the issue).

provides a good illustration of the types of challenges faced in international human rights litigation in connection with climate change. Of note is the fact that whereas the first causal link could be addressed scientifically, albeit through 'correlation', the second link seemed far more difficult to bridge in this way.

4. *Overcoming the Causality Obstacle in the Climate Change Context*

There are different ways to overcome the causality obstacle. The first way is of a scientific nature. Instead of changing the legal requirements, the approach would be to wait until it is scientifically possible to attribute a specific weather event to climate change. The Inter-Governmental Panel on Climate Change (IPCC) has tried to gather scientific evidence in the last several years to develop precisely this type of specific attribution.[126] However, whereas this link may eventually become well established for some high-profile weather events, it would be much more difficult to establish it for any extreme weather event that may arise in litigation. Some current research suggests that, following probabilistic methodologies, it would be possible to assess the likelihood of lower-profile weather events, particularly heat waves and droughts, in the presence (or absence) of climate change.[127] Until such methodologies are sufficiently developed, if they indeed reach such a point, it may be necessary to explore alternative courses of action.

The second way would be to establish a compensation fund based on the contributions of states and companies that emit large amounts of greenhouse gases. This solution consists, in fact, in overcoming the aforementioned obstacle in a legal manner by setting up a system that treats the emission of greenhouse gases on the same footing as a hazardous but economically beneficial activity. For example, this is the case with nuclear energy production or oil pollution damage. Such an approach could potentially fall under the remit of the 'loss and damage' negotiations conducted under the UN Framework Convention on Climate Change, although developed countries have strongly opposed attempts at framing this negotiation from a 'compensation' perspective.[128]

A third possibility would be to overcome this obstacle legally by recognizing a right to an 'ecologically balanced' or 'generally satisfactory' environment with the understanding that significant interference with the climate system (the first causal

126 Special Report of the Intergovernmental Panel on Climate Change, Managing the Risks of Extreme Weather Events and Disasters to Advance Climate Change Adaptation 2011 (so-called 'SREX'), available online at http://www.ipcc.ch/pdf/special-reports/srex/SREX_Full_Report.pdf (last accessed 23 July 2015).

127 See Allen, 'Liability for Climate Change', 421 *Nature* (2003) 891; Lewis and Karoly, 'Anthropogenic Contributions to Australia's Record Summer Temperatures of 2013', 40/14 *Geophysical Research Letters* (2013) 3705; Fischer and Knutti, 'Anthropogenic Contribution to Global Occurrence of Heavy-precipitation and High-temperature Extremes', *Nature Climate Change* (2015), available online at http://dx.doi.org/10.1038/nclimate2617 (last accessed 23 July 2015).

128 See UN Framework Convention on Climate Change, Report of the Conference of the Parties on its Nineteenth Session, Held in Warsaw from 11 to 23 November 2013, Decisions Adopted by the Conference of the Parties, Warsaw International Mechanism for Loss and Damage Associated with Climate Change (Decision 2/CP.19), FCCC/CP/2013/10/Add.1, 31 January 2014, at 6.

link) may amount to a breach of such a right. This possibility has not been explored yet, and it may well remain unexplored until the implications of choosing the appropriate 'adjective' to characterize the right to an environment of a certain quality are better understood. Whereas such an approach would still pose several causality difficulties (e.g. What would amount to 'significant' interference with the climate? What is the meaning of 'ecologically balanced' or 'generally satisfactory' as a qualification?), they would arise at the level of the first causal link, which is currently more manageable than the second one. Moreover, granting this right to a collective human rights subject, such as an indigenous or tribal people, another minority or perhaps even an entire population, would facilitate the proof that the environment is not 'generally satisfactory' for a group that has traditionally lived in a now-melting area, such as the Inuit,[129] or in a low-lying island that may disappear as a result of sea level rise.[130] In the context of the present assessment of human rights approaches to extraterritorial environmental protection, this solution would consist not only of expanding the spatial scope of human rights obligations, but also the substantive content of a specific human right.

5. Human Rights Approaches to Extraterritorial Environmental Protection: An Assessment

The storyline, on which this assessment is based, began by reference to two international legal trends: the significant expansion of human rights obligations so as to cover situations arising in the territory of other states and in common areas, and the need to consider alternatives, even purely tactical, to multilateral environmental negotiations. It is against this broad background that the potential of a human rights approach to extraterritorial environmental protection must be assessed.

From a strictly legal perspective, the main question to be answered is whether the extraterritorial scope of human rights obligations could (further) require, or even justify, measures aimed primarily or incidentally at protecting the environment abroad. From a policy perspective, the main question is the extent to which the advantages of human rights approaches to environmental protection available in a territorial context could be extended to an extraterritorial one. The answers to these questions are closely connected.

Regarding the *legal question*, it can be answered from (i) a general or (ii) a case-specific perspective. Generally, the extent to which a state can be held responsible for violating the human rights of individuals abroad depends on the factual

[129] Inuit Petition, *supra* note 122, at 70.

[130] See e.g. Seneviratne, 'Tuvalu Steps Up Threat to Sue Australia, US' (Pacific Islands Reports, 8 September 2002) available online at http://www.tuvaluislands.com/news/archived/2002/2002-09-10.htm (last accessed 123 July 2015) (Describing the efforts of Tuvalu to initiate a lawsuit against the United States and Australia. In this case, the lawsuit envisioned was of an inter-state nature, but the population of Tuvalu could be considered as a collective subject in a human rights context). The Maldives have also been very active in linking climate change to human rights. See Knox, 'Linking Human Rights and Climate Change at the United Nations', 33 *Harvard Environmental Law Review* (2009) 477.

configuration. Normally, such extension can only take place when the relevant state exercises effective control over the victim. But in the environmental protection context, such requirement will most likely not be met. Is it nevertheless possible to hold the state responsible for the pollution it causes abroad? Although the question has not yet been addressed in the case-law, a possible extension of state responsibility could arise from its effective control over the source of the harm, as noted by some human rights bodies in connection with international sanctions. Two inquiries would have to be conducted. One concerning causality (the link between, firstly, state action or inaction and environmental degradation and, secondly, between such degradation and an impairment of human rights abroad) and the other one concerning responsibility (in order to factor in the responsibility, or lack thereof, of the state exercising effective control over the victim).

Moving to the case-specific perspective, depending on the circumstances of the case, a variety of norms may come into play, some supporting the extension of responsibility (typically inter-state environmental norms) and others constraining the room for such extension (e.g. investment disciplines). In some cases, the specific features of the object targeted by the measures may strengthen the case for extraterritorial protection, as in the case of international sanctions affecting access to water or, potentially, the recognition of collective human rights subjects. In others, on the other hand, such as in climate change redress, it may pose formidable challenges.

Regarding the *policy question*, focusing on the purely territorial horizon, there are three main advantages sought through a human rights approach to environmental protection abroad: (i) a better identification of the right-holders or 'voices' who would be speaking for the environment; (ii) the use of the more sophisticated institutional mechanisms developed at the international level to protect human rights; and (iii) the sense of urgency that human rights discourse can add in the political sphere to the regulation of environmental questions. The extent to which these advantages would extend to extraterritorial environmental protection varies from one advantage to the other as well as for different types of environmental threats.

Concerning the first advantage, the spatial extension of human rights obligations may indeed have implications for the identification of the right-holders. The individuals under the effective control of a foreign state which is not a party to a regional or a global human rights treaty may, nevertheless, be brought under the jurisdiction of a state party to such treaty, as a result of the latter's control over the source of pollution. What is being extended in this case is, potentially, the right to bring a complaint but only in connection with the individual harm for which that state is 'responsible' as a result of its factual control over the source of harm. The number of entities that can potentially speak for the environment abroad consequently grows. In addition to the affected state (under inter-state norms), individuals and collective subjects (indigenous and tribal peoples, and perhaps other minorities) would also be able to bring a claim relating to the protection of the environment abroad. Of course, the link requirement would limit the scope for environmental protection available to such right-holders, which would be substantively more limited than the one that the affected state could claim. The main advantages would be to 'personalize' harm to the environment, which may increase the incentives to act, to diversify the entities with a right to bring a claim (when the affected state is unwilling or unable to do so) and, perhaps most importantly, to open new procedural avenues to complain about environmental degradation. However, the latter advantage, which is critical for the operation of the two others, depends upon the receptivity of human rights courts and bodies to such claims.

Can such institutional mechanisms be used to bring a human rights claim for environmental degradation abroad? This is, of course, a legal matter. As discussed in response to the first question mentioned in these concluding remarks, there is a fair legal case to be made for a human rights approach to extraterritorial environmental protection in general, particularly by analogy to the responsibility of states in the context of international sanctions, but any assessment of the actual legal grounds must be made at a case-specific level. These more specific assessments will likely depend on the object of environmental protection. In some cases the legal basis for action will be stronger (e.g. water and the relation between a collective human rights subject and its environment) than in others (e.g. protection of species abroad or of the operation of the climate system). And even in those areas where there seems to be a strong legal basis, the actual case has not been admitted yet. Does this mean that a human rights approach to extraterritorial environmental protection is, at least for now, of limited practical relevance?

I do not think so. Even if the extraterritorial scope of human rights were not applied to situations of environmental degradation abroad for years to come, the mere fact that there is an increasingly articulate case for its use is a useful advocacy tool. Human rights discourse is politically powerful because it gives a sense of urgency and it connects public policy with visible problems. Such discourse can be mobilized in contexts as diverse as the protection of forests and biodiversity, the fight against desertification, the protection of water bodies, the control of hazardous substances and activities, or even the fight against climate change. Depending on the environmental problem at stake or the specific dimensions within the same problem, human rights discourse may have a significant impact on policy-making. By way of illustration, the Analytical Study of the Office of the High Commissioner for Human Rights on the *Relationship between Human Rights and the Environment*[131] devotes an entire chapter to the extraterritorial dimension of human rights, and it highlights transboundary pollution, climate change and pollution arising from the operations of multinational companies abroad as areas, where this dimension should be further explored. The latter area has been significantly developed under the aegis of the UN Special Rapporteur on Business and Human Rights, which prompted the elaboration of several studies[132] and position

[131] Office of the High Commissioner on Human Rights, Analytical Study on the Relationship between Human Rights and the Environment, UN Doc. A//HRC/19/34, 16 December 2011, at paras 64–73.

[132] See e.g. Zerk, *supra* note 26; Ascencio, 'Extra-territoriality as an Instrument', Contribution to the work of the UN Secretary-General's Special Representative on Human Rights and Transnational Corporations and Other Businesses (September 2010) available online at http://business-humanrights.

papers[133] concerning extraterritorial jurisdiction. Within the *UN Guiding Principles on Business and Human Rights*, one of the two 'foundational principles' expressing a state's obligation to protect human rights (from deprivation by business companies) provides: 'States should set out clearly the expectation that all business enterprises domiciled in their territory and/or jurisdiction respect human rights throughout their operations.'[134] The commentary recognizes that '[a]t present States are not generally required under international human rights law to regulate the extraterritorial activities of businesses domiciled in their territory and/or jurisdiction' but it adds '[n]or are they generally prohibited from doing so, provided there is a jurisdictional basis'. On these grounds, it reasons that '[w]ithin these parameters some human rights treaty bodies recommend that home States take steps to prevent abuse abroad by business enterprises within their jurisdiction' and, among the factors that may justify such action, one is 'whether they are grounded in multilateral agreement'. This is but one example of frank and open advocacy, recognizing the limits of the current law but also its potential. And potential there is. There is a significant number of multilateral environmental treaties (inter-state norms), the implementation of which could be rendered more direct and urgent by mobilizing human rights discourse through the type of advocacy displayed by UN Special Rapporteurs, human rights treaty bodies and, perhaps, in the near future, a lucid and progressive court.

Keeping this possibility open is a sufficient reason, in my view, to pursue the analysis and refinement of a human rights approach to extraterritorial environmental protection.

org/sites/default/files/media/documents/ruggie/extraterritoriality-as-instrument-ascensio-for-ruggie-dec-2010.pdf (last accessed 23 July 2015).

133 Letter from IOE, ICC & BIAC transmitting 'The Role of Business in Weak Governance Zones' Paper to John Ruggie, 21 December 2006, available online at http://business-humanrights.org/sites/default/files/media/bhr/files/Role-of-Business-in-Weak-Governance-Zones-Dec-2006.pdf (last accessed 23 July 2015).

134 Report of the Special Representative of the Secretary-General on the Issue of Human Rights and Transnational Corporations and Other Business Enterprises, Guiding Principles on Business and Human Rights: Implementing the United Nations 'Protect, Respect and Remedy' Framework, UN Doc. A/HRC/17/31, 21 March 2011, at 7.

Index

The manufacturer's authorised representative in the EU for product safety is Oxford University Press España S.A. of el Parque Empresarial San Fernando de Henares, Avenida de Castilla, 2 – 28830 Madrid (www.oup.es/en or product.safety@oup.com). OUP España S.A. also acts as importer into Spain of products made by the manufacturer.

www.ingramcontent.com/pod-product-compliance
Lightning Source LLC
LaVergne TN
LVHW011756200926
848484LV00003B/719

* 9 7 8 0 1 9 8 7 6 9 2 7 9 *